MEDIATING
EXTRACTIVE CONFLICTS

A Practitioner's Handbook for
Company-Community Disputes.

THOMAS GAULTIER

For permission requests, contact:

Thomas Gaultier

www.thomasgaultier.com

ISBN: 978-989-36770-0-1

DISCLAIMER

This handbook is intended for educational and informational purposes only.

The information, strategies, and guidance contained in this publication do not constitute legal advice, medical advice, psychological counseling, or any other form of professional consultation. Readers should not rely on the content of this handbook as a substitute for professional legal counsel, medical treatment, or therapeutic support.

The views, techniques, and recommendations expressed herein reflect solely the opinions, interpretations, and personal experiences of the author. They do not represent the official position of any organization, institution, or professional body.

Every mediation situation is unique, and the application of principles discussed in this handbook must be adapted to the specific circumstances, cultural context, and legal framework of each case. The author makes no representations or warranties regarding the accuracy, completeness, or suitability of the information provided for any particular purpose.

Readers are strongly encouraged to:

- Seek independent legal advice when dealing with matters that have legal implications
- Consult qualified medical and mental health professionals when addressing trauma, psychological distress, or health-related concerns
- Engage local experts familiar with the applicable laws, customs, and regulations in their jurisdiction

The author and publisher disclaim any liability for damages, losses, or adverse outcomes arising from the use or misuse of the information contained in this handbook. By using this material, readers acknowledge that they do so at their own risk and accept full responsibility for any decisions made based on its content.

CONTENTS

1.

INTRODUCTION

1.1 Purpose of This Handbook

This handbook guides professional mediators, NGO workers, company representatives, and community leaders engaged in mediation between companies and local communities. Whether the dispute concerns mining operations, oil and gas projects, infrastructure development, or energy projects affecting neighboring populations, this manual offers the principles, skills, and practical tools needed to facilitate constructive dialogue and reach mutually beneficial agreements.

The need for such guidance is urgent. Around the world, communities and companies find themselves in conflict over issues ranging from environmental impacts and land use to employment opportunities and benefit sharing. These disputes can escalate into costly legal battles, violent confrontations, operational disruptions, and lasting damage to relationships. Yet destructive escalation is not inevitable.

Mediation offers an alternative to adversarial processes such as litigation, protests, or prolonged standoffs. When conducted skillfully, it transforms conflict into collaboration, turning opponents into problem-solving partners. The mediator serves as a neutral facilitator, helping parties communicate effectively, understand each other's perspectives, and develop solutions that address their underlying interests.

This handbook is grounded in mediation theory and international best practice while remaining practical and action-oriented. Drawing on fifteen years of experience as a mediator and mediation trainer, this handbook integrates direct field knowledge with insights and exchanges shared by participants in training programs for practitioners in social performance and conflict resolution. The content reflects field experience across diverse contexts: mining communities in Africa, Asia and South America, renewables projects in Europe and oil and gas disputes in East Africa. The principles presented are universal, though their application must be adapted to local contexts. This collective expertise ensures that the guidance offered is both theoretically sound and tested in the complex realities of real-world dispute resolution.

> **Key Concept:**
> Mediation is fundamentally different from arbitration or adjudication. In mediation, the parties themselves create the solution with the mediator's help. No decision is imposed from outside. This party-driven approach leads to higher satisfaction, better compliance, and more durable outcomes.

1.2 Who Should Use This Handbook

This guide is designed for multiple audiences, each playing a crucial role in resolving company-community disputes:

Professional Mediators: Those facilitating disputes between companies and communities will find detailed guidance on process design, communication techniques, and handling complex dynamics, including power imbalances and trauma. Whether you are an experienced mediator expanding into this specialized field or a newcomer developing your practice, this handbook provides frameworks and tools you can apply immediately.

Your priority pathway:

1. Chapter 8 (When Mediation Should NOT Proceed) establishes the ethical boundaries you must recognize before accepting any case.
2. Chapter 6 (Designing Mediation Processes) provides the step-by-step framework from preparation to agreement.

3. Chapter 12 (Managing Power Asymmetries) addresses the distinctive challenge of company-community power imbalances.
4. Chapter 11 (Mediator Health) supports sustainable practice in demanding contexts.
5. Chapter 14 (Resistance Scenarios) prepares you for common challenges, including walkouts, intimidation, and bad faith.

Then expand to include: Chapters 3 and 4 for foundational principles and communication skills; Chapter 5 for conflict dynamics; Chapter 10 for trauma-informed approaches; Chapter 13 for impasse navigation; and Chapter 15 to learn from common mediator mistakes.

NGO Workers and Advocates: Staff supporting communities in dialogue with companies will use this handbook to understand mediation principles, help communities prepare, and ensure processes are fair. You serve as advisors to community participants, observers ensuring process integrity, or conveners bringing parties to the table.

Your priority pathway:

- Chapter 3 (Core Principles and Ethics) helps you evaluate whether proposed processes are genuine mediation.
- Chapter 12 (Managing Power Asymmetries) equips you to support community participation in unequal contexts.
- Chapter 8 (When Mediation Should NOT Proceed) helps identify situations where you should advise communities against participating.
- Chapter 10 (Trauma-Informed Approaches) ensures you can support traumatized community members appropriately.
- Chapter 17 (Case Studies) shows how mediation has worked, and failed, in comparable situations.

Then expand to: Chapter 6 for understanding process design; Chapter 14 for anticipating resistance scenarios; and Chapter 18 for simulation exercises to practice support skills.

Company Representatives: Corporate social responsibility managers, community relations officers, and grievance mechanism staff will gain insight into how mediation works and how to participate constructively. Understanding mediation principles helps you engage authentically, make credible commitments, and rebuild trust with affected communities.

Your priority pathway:

- Chapter 3 (Core Principles and Ethics) establishes expectations for genuine good-faith participation.
- Chapter 12 (Managing Power Asymmetries and Restoring Trust) helps you understand how power dynamics affect community engagement.
- Chapter 5 (Understanding Conflict Dynamics) explains how disputes escalate and what early intervention can accomplish.
- Chapter 17 (Case Studies) demonstrates outcomes when companies engage authentically versus when they do not.
- Chapter 6 (Designing Mediation Processes) helps you understand process expectations and prepare effective participation.

Then expand to: Chapter 4 for communication skills applicable to community engagement; Chapter 10 for trauma-informed approaches when communities have experienced harm; and Chapter 8 to understand why mediators sometimes decline.

> **Caution: For Company Representatives**
>
> Companies that approach mediation as a form of reputation management or as a delay tactic undermine both the process and their own long-term interests. Mediators are trained to recognize bad faith, and the community will certainly recognize it, as well. Authentic engagement, including willingness to make real commitments, typically produces better outcomes for all parties than adversarial approaches.

Community Leaders: Local leaders and representatives can learn what to expect from mediation, how to articulate community interests effectively, and how to evaluate whether proposed processes are fair.

Your priority pathway:

- Chapter 3 (Core Principles and Ethics) helps you understand your rights in the process and recognize genuine versus false mediation.
- Chapter 8 (When Mediation Should NOT Proceed) helps you identify situations where participation may not serve your community's interests.
- Chapter 12 (Managing Power Asymmetries) explains how mediators address imbalances and what protections parties should expect.
- Chapter 6 (Designing Mediation Processes) shows what a fair process looks like so you can evaluate proposals.
- Chapter 17 (Case Studies) provides examples of how other communities have navigated similar situations.

Then expand to: Chapter 4 for communication techniques you can use in dialogue; Chapter 14 for understanding how to respond if things go wrong; and Chapter 10 to understand how trauma affects participation.

Government Officials and Policymakers: Those overseeing or facilitating company-community relations will find frameworks for designing effective dispute resolution mechanisms.

Your priority pathway:

- Chapter 3 (Core Principles and Ethics) provides the standards any legitimate mediation process must meet.
- Chapter 6 (Designing Mediation Processes) offers frameworks for institutionalizing effective dispute resolution.
- Chapter 17 (Case Studies) shows outcomes across different contexts and regulatory environments.
- Chapter 8 (When Mediation Should NOT Proceed) helps identify situations requiring formal legal intervention rather than mediation.
- Chapter 12 (Managing Power Asymmetries) addresses how policy can support more balanced engagement.

Then expand to: Chapter 5 for understanding conflict dynamics in your jurisdiction; Chapter 9 for mediator competencies to include in training requirements; and Chapter 16 for digital mediation considerations.

Practical Tip: This Handbook as a Tool

Regardless of your role, approach this handbook as both a reference and a learning tool. Read it through once to understand the overall framework, then return to specific chapters as different situations arise. The simulation exercises in Chapter 18 are valuable for any audience, as practicing mediation skills builds confidence and competence.

1.3 How to Use This Handbook

This handbook is organized into nineteen chapters that build progressively, but each chapter can also stand alone as a reference on its topic. The structure reflects the natural flow of a mediation process, from foundational principles through preparation, process, and resolution, while also addressing real-world challenges, specialized contexts, and learning opportunities that experienced practitioners encounter.

Chapters 3 and 4 establish foundational principles and core communication skills that mediators need. Chapter 3 covers voluntariness, self-determination, neutrality, confidentiality, informed consent, safety, honesty, and the do-no-harm principle. Chapter 4 develops active listening, empathy, effective questioning, reframing, summarizing, and facilitation techniques. Chapters 3 and 4 provide the conceptual foundation for everything that follows.

Chapter 5 helps you understand conflict dynamics and recognize escalation patterns. It examines the three dimensions of conflict (substantive, emotional, and process), root causes of company-community conflicts, psychological dynamics, Friedrich Glasl's nine-stage escalation model, early warning signs, de-escalation strategies, and conflict assessment methods. Before you can resolve a conflict, you must understand how it developed and where it stands.

Chapter 6 provides a step-by-step guide to designing and conducting mediation processes. From Phase 0 (preparation and pre-mediation) through Phase 6 (reaching agreement), this chapter walks you through each stage with practical guidance, sample language, and a comprehensive process design checklist.

Chapter 7 addresses post-agreement implementation, examining why implementation matters, how to design agreements for success, monitoring and oversight systems, communication infrastructure for accountability, early warning systems, compliance mechanisms, managing implementation challenges, re-engagement strategies when agreements break down, and sustaining long-term success.

Chapter 8 addresses a fundamental question: When should mediation not proceed? This chapter examines genocide and crimes against humanity, ongoing violence, severe power asymmetry combined with bad faith, mediator capture, and hidden decision-makers. Knowing when to decline matters as much as knowing how to proceed.

Chapter 9 details the analytical tools and personal competencies in a mediator's toolbox. It covers conflict mapping, stakeholder analysis, BATNA/WATNA analysis, timeline construction, caucusing, shuttle diplomacy, joint fact-finding, visual aids, emotional intelligence, patience, cultural competence, impartiality in practice, creativity, credibility, documentation, and pathways for developing your competencies.

Chapter 10 addresses trauma-informed and culturally sensitive approaches. Many company-community disputes involve genuine harm and cultural dimensions requiring special care. This chapter provides guidance on recognizing trauma responses, creating psychological safety, practical trauma-informed techniques, cultural sensitivity, and understanding psychological dynamics in conflict.

Chapter 11 focuses on mediator health. Working with conflict and suffering takes a toll on mediators themselves. This chapter examines the psychological demands of company-community mediation, vicarious trauma, secondary trauma from working with specific populations, burnout, the ethical obligation to step back when depleted, building sustainable resilience, organizational responsibilities, and treatment and recovery. Sustainable practices are essential for long-term effectiveness and ethical conduct.

Chapter 12 addresses managing power asymmetries and restoring trust. The imbalance between corporate resources and community capacity is a defining feature of these disputes. This chapter explores practical strategies for mediators working with unequal parties. Topics include identifying power asymmetries, empowering weaker parties, and implementing procedural safeguards. The chapter also covers active mediator intervention, trust-building principles, recognition and apology for wrongdoing, and early confidence-building measures. Structural safeguards for trust and positioning the mediator as a trust bridge complete the toolkit.

Chapter 13 offers strategies for navigating impasses and rebuilding cooperation. When negotiations stall, these techniques can restart momentum and guide parties toward resolution. The chapter covers recognizing impasses, understanding their causes (miscommunication, lack of trust, face-saving, unrealistic expectations, external pressures, emotional barriers, and power dynamics), strategies to break impasses, what to do when impasses persist, rebuilding cooperation, preventing future impasses, and case examples.

Chapter 14 addresses resistance scenarios that mediators commonly encounter in the field. From silent participants and intimidation tactics to walkouts, internal community divisions, confidentiality breaches, government interference, and bad faith reversals, this chapter provides practical strategies for managing challenging behaviors that can derail the mediation process.

Chapter 15 examines common mediator mistakes and how to avoid them. Drawing on field experience and reflective practice, this chapter explores the "hero mediator" trap, false balance fallacy, cultural erasure, burnout blindness, co-optation risk, premature closure, and additional traps. These include confirmation bias, process rigidity, emotional contagion, documentation failures, scope creep, confidentiality breaches, power blindness, and solution fixation.

Chapter 16 introduces digital mediation. Topics include virtual session protocols, hybrid mediation approaches, digital tools for enhanced mediation, and managing confidentiality in virtual spaces. The chapter examines when virtual mediation saves the process versus when it undermines it, addresses technology access and the digital divide, and covers participant preparation and ethical considerations in digital contexts.

Chapter 17 presents real-world case studies from Africa and Europe, including the Kintinian community and Siguiri gold mine dispute in Guinea and the Stuttgart 21 infrastructure conflict in Germany. These examples illustrate principles in action and offer lessons from actual mediations, demonstrating both what works and what can go wrong.

Chapter 18 provides simulation exercises and role-play scenarios for training. Practice is essential for developing mediation skills. This chapter includes foundational communication drills, multi-party mediation simulations (the Alpha Mining Co. dispute, Beta Mining Co. new development dispute, and landowner-company negotiation), specialized exercises for challenging situations, and facilitation guidance for trainers.

The Conclusion synthesizes the handbook's themes and offers a personal note to practitioners entering this demanding but rewarding field.

The Resources Section includes comprehensive templates for every mediation stage. Pre-mediation tools include conflict assessment forms, stakeholder mapping templates, and readiness checklists. Session resources feature agreement-to-mediate templates, ground rules reference cards, and communication quick references. Interest exploration and problem-solving tools include interest mapping worksheets and BATNA/WATNA analysis. Post-session and agreement resources include settlement agreement templates, implementation monitoring checklists, session debrief forms, cultural sensitivity guides, and trauma-informed practice references.

The Glossary defines terms used throughout the handbook.

The Index offers an alphabetical listing of concepts, techniques, and topics covered across all chapters, making it easy to find specific subjects.

The Curated Bibliography offers selected texts organized by topic, covering mediation theory, mining and community relations, conflict resolution, trauma and psychology, power and gender, digital mediation, social performance and impact assessment, and institutional reports and frameworks.

Throughout the handbook, you will find special text boxes that highlight key information, including:

Key Concept: Important Principle or Definition

Key Concept boxes highlight fundamental principles and definitions for understanding mediation. These concepts form the theoretical foundation for effective practice.

Practical Tip: Takeaways

Practical Tip boxes offer actionable guidance for real-world application. These suggestions come from experienced mediators and can be implemented immediately in your practice.

Caution: Warnings for Practitioners

Caution boxes highlight common pitfalls and sensitive areas that require care. Heeding these warnings can help you avoid mistakes that could undermine the mediation process or harm participants.

Sample dialogues throughout the handbook illustrate how mediators can phrase questions, reframe statements, and guide discussions in practice. These examples show what skilled mediation sounds like, not as scripts to follow rigidly, but as models of effective communication.

1.4 The Value of Voluntary Mediation

Why choose mediation over other approaches to company-community disputes? Among the available options, which include litigation, arbitration, protests, political pressure, and simply enduring an unsatisfactory status quo, voluntary mediation offers several distinct advantages, including:

Party Control and Self-Determination: Unlike litigation or arbitration, where a third party imposes a decision, mediation keeps decision-making in the hands of those directly affected. Solutions reflect the parties' own priorities and creativity, not the limited remedies available under law. A community's concerns about cultural heritage, future generations, or relationships with the land cannot be adequately captured in legal claims, but they can be fully explored in mediation. Similarly, a company's interests in operational flexibility, reputation, and long-term community relationships can be incorporated into mediated solutions in ways that court orders cannot achieve.

Relationship Preservation and Repair: Mediation focuses on problem-solving rather than blame. This enables immediate dispute resolution while building or repairing relationships for ongoing coexistence. In most company-community situations, the parties will continue to live and work in proximity after the dispute is resolved. A litigation victory that destroys the relationship may prove pyrrhic, while a mediated agreement that rebuilds trust creates a foundation for future cooperation.

Flexibility and Customization: Mediation processes can be adapted to local contexts, cultural norms, and the specific needs of the parties. A mediation in a remote mining community may look very different from one involving an urban infrastructure project. The mediator can incorporate traditional dispute resolution practices, adjust timing to accommodate seasonal work patterns, use local languages, and design processes that feel legitimate to all participants.

Efficiency and Cost-Effectiveness: While complex disputes may require extended mediation, the process is typically faster and less costly than litigation. Court cases can drag on for years, consuming resources that could have been used to fund community development or company operations. Mediation can often achieve resolution in weeks or months. More importantly, mediated outcomes stick because all parties have bought into them.

Confidentiality and Privacy: Mediators keep mediation discussions private, allowing parties to speak candidly without fear that their words will be used against them publicly or in court. A company representative might acknowledge a mistake without creating legal liability. A community member might reveal what they truly need rather than posturing for public consumption.

Broad-Based Solutions: Mediation can address underlying interests, relationships, and emotions, not just legal rights. Agreements can include elements that address the full range of community concerns, from environmental monitoring and local employment to cultural preservation and acknowledgment of past harms. They can establish ongoing mechanisms for communication, joint decision-making, and dispute prevention.

Caution: Mediation Suitability

Mediation is not appropriate for every situation. It requires willing participants, good-faith engagement, and circumstances where negotiated solutions are possible. Where there are ongoing safety threats, active criminal conduct, or fundamental human rights violations that require legal accountability, mediation may not be suitable or may need to be combined with other interventions. Chapter 5 will help you assess when mediation is appropriate.

Case Example: The Power of Mediation

In Guinea, a gold mining operation faced years of conflict with a displaced community. Legal complaints had been filed, trust had collapsed, and operational disruptions were costly for both sides. Through a mediation process facilitated by the International Finance Corporation's (IFC) Compliance Advisor Ombudsman, the parties engaged in dialogue over several years, reaching interim agreements on water access, schooling, and healthcare before achieving a comprehensive final settlement. The agreement included individual compensation for affected families and established a Sustainable Development Fund for ongoing community projects. Both sides described the process as transformative, having moved from adversaries to partners in community development. This case, detailed in Chapter 17, illustrates how mediation can resolve even deeply entrenched disputes.

1.5 Guiding Philosophy

This handbook is built on several foundational beliefs that shape its approach to company-community mediation. These include:

Conflict is natural, but violence and prolonged hostility are not inevitable. Peacebuilding research (Lederach, 1997) confirms that conflicts can be transformed through structured dialogue when root causes are addressed rather than suppressed. Disagreements arise whenever people with different interests, values, or perspectives interact. This is especially true when commercial activities affect communities that did not choose to become neighbors with industrial operations. But while conflict is natural, its destructive escalation is not. With the right process and skills, most disputes can be resolved constructively. The goal is not to eliminate conflict but to channel it toward productive dialogue and mutually acceptable solutions.

All parties have legitimate interests. Companies need viable operations to fulfill their obligations to employees, shareholders, and other stakeholders. Communities need livelihoods, health, dignity, and the ability to shape their own futures. Neither set of interests is inherently more valid than the other. Good mediation does not ask which side is "right" but rather how both sets of legitimate interests can be honored.

Process matters as much as outcome. A fair, respectful process builds trust and acceptance, even when parties don't get everything they want. Conversely, a flawed process can poison even a reasonable outcome. People who feel unheard, disrespected, or railroaded will resist agreements and harbor grievances that resurface later. This handbook devotes substantial attention to process design (Chapter 6), communication skills (Chapter 4), and procedural fairness because how mediation is conducted determines whether its outcomes will hold.

Power imbalances must be actively addressed. Transformative mediation theory (Bush and Folger, 2005) emphasizes that addressing power imbalances through recognition and empowerment is not optional but central to ethical practice. Without deliberate attention, mediation can simply ratify the preferences of the more powerful party. A company with lawyers, technical experts, and deep pockets naturally has advantages over a rural community with limited education, resources, and experience with formal processes. Effective mediators recognize these imbalances and take steps to level the playing field. Chapter 12 addresses these challenges in depth.

Cultural context shapes everything. What works in one setting may not work in another. Communication styles, decision-making processes, concepts of time, attitudes toward authority, gender roles, and countless other cultural factors influence how mediation should be conducted. Mediators must approach each context with humility, curiosity, and a willingness to learn. Chapter 10 provides guidance on culturally sensitive practices.

Trauma is real and deserves honor and recognition. Many company-community conflicts involve genuine harm: displacement from ancestral lands, environmental contamination that affects locals' health, violence from security forces, loss of livelihoods, and destruction of sacred sites. These are not just negotiating positions but real injuries that have affected real people. Healing requires acknowledgment, not just negotiation. Mediators must be sensitive to trauma, create safe spaces for its expression, and avoid processes that retraumatize participants. Chapter 10 provides guidance on trauma-informed practice.

Key Concept: Principles that Guide the Process

These guiding principles are not just ideals but practical orientations that shape effective mediation. A mediator who believes conflict can be resolved will persist through setbacks. One who respects all parties' interests will work harder to understand positions that seem unreasonable at first. And one who is intentional about process will create experiences that build trust even before an agreement is reached. These beliefs become self-fulfilling when mediators consistently embody them.

1.6 How This Handbook Is Different

Many resources address mediation in general terms. This handbook is specifically designed for the unique challenges of company-community disputes, particularly in extractive industries and infrastructure development. It differs from generic mediation guidance in several important ways.

Grounded in Field Experience

The guidance here emerges from extensive real-world practice, including mediating thousands of claims at mining operations in Africa, navigating multi-year company-community mediations in West Africa, and working with contested infrastructure projects in Europe. Theory is valuable, but this handbook prioritizes what actually works, along with honest acknowledgment of what does not. Chapter 17's case studies and Chapter 15's examination of mediator mistakes reflect this commitment to learning from experience.

Emphasis on Voluntariness

Voluntariness is not merely a checkbox. This principle of party self-determination, central to interest-based negotiation (Fisher and Ury, 1981), ensures that outcomes reflect genuine agreement rather than imposed solutions. It is the foundation that distinguishes genuine mediation from coerced negotiation. Chapter 3 examines what voluntariness truly means in contexts of severe power asymmetry, Chapter 6 addresses how to assess whether parties can genuinely choose to participate, and Chapter 8 explains what to do when voluntariness is compromised.

Explicit Refusal Ethics

Most mediation handbooks assume the mediation will proceed. This one dedicates substantial attention (Chapter 8) to situations where mediation should not proceed, including genocide and crimes against humanity, ongoing violence, severe bad faith, mediator capture, and hidden decision-makers. Ethical mediation requires the capacity to say no.

Commitment to Do No Harm

The do-no-harm principle runs throughout this handbook as an active obligation, not a passive hope. This means assessing whether mediation might retraumatize participants (Chapter 10), worsen power imbalances (Chapter 12), or legitimize injustice (Chapter 8). In these cases, mediators must decide whether to modify or decline the process accordingly. Good intentions are insufficient; the mediator must consider actual impacts.

Attention to Mediator Health

Chapter 11 addresses an often-neglected topic: the psychological demands of company-community mediation and the mediator's obligation to maintain their own well-being. Generic self-care advice is inadequate for the specific challenges of this work, which can include exposure to trauma narratives, moral complexity, threats, and cumulative stress. Sustainable practice requires intentional attention to mediator resilience.

Honest About Limitations and Failures

Chapter 15 examines common mediator mistakes not to discourage practitioners but to help them learn from the field's collective experience. The "hero mediator" trap, the false balance fallacy, cultural erasure, and other patterns are discussed, along with practical guidance on recognition and correction. Acknowledging that mediators are fallible is what makes improvement possible.

Attention to Implementation

Many mediation resources focus on reaching an agreement but give little attention to what happens afterward. Chapter 7 comprehensively addresses post-agreement implementation, recognizing that an agreement is only as good as its execution. Monitoring systems, compliance mechanisms, and re-engagement strategies are essential components of successful mediation.

Practical Tools Throughout

Every chapter includes practical tools, sample language, checklists, or templates that practitioners can apply immediately. The Resources section consolidates these into ready-to-use formats. Chapter 18's simulation exercises help practitioners develop skills in realistic scenarios before encountering them in the field.

Practical Tip: Using This Handbook

This handbook can be read sequentially or consulted as a reference. The role-based pathways in Section 1.2 help you identify the most relevant chapters for your immediate needs. The Resources section provides templates and tools for practical application. Return to specific chapters as situations arise and use Chapter 18's simulations to build skills through practice.

2.

EXECUTIVE OVERVIEW

2.1 What Company-Community Mediation Is and Is Not

What Mediation Is

When a mining company and a farming community reach an impasse over water contamination, or when an energy project threatens ancestral lands, the consequences of failure extend far beyond the negotiating table. Livelihoods, ecosystems, and the social fabric of entire communities hang in the balance. Company-community mediation exists precisely for these high-stakes moments, offering a structured path toward resolution when other avenues have failed or proven inadequate.

Company-community mediation is a structured, voluntary process in which a neutral third party facilitates dialogue between companies (such as mining, infrastructure, or energy enterprises) and affected local communities. This definition aligns with the mediation process framework established by Moore (2014), which identifies the mediator as a neutral facilitator who assists parties in reaching mutually acceptable agreements through structured dialogue. The goal is to help parties understand each other's interests, explore options, and reach mutually acceptable agreements on disputes ranging from environmental concerns to benefit-sharing arrangements.

Unlike litigation or arbitration, where a judge or arbitrator imposes a decision, mediation empowers the parties themselves to craft their own solutions. Rather than judging who is right or wrong, the mediator creates conditions for genuine dialogue, ensuring all voices are heard and helping parties move from adversarial positions to shared understanding.

> **Key Concept: The Essence of Mediation**
>
> Mediation is a voluntary, confidential process where a neutral facilitator helps disputing parties communicate, understand each other's interests, and develop their own solutions. The mediator has no power to impose outcomes; all agreements are made by the parties themselves.

Effective company-community mediation typically involves:

- **Voluntary participation** by all parties, who choose to engage and can withdraw at any time
- **A neutral, impartial mediator** who does not take sides or have a stake in any particular outcome
- **Confidentiality** that creates a safe space for honest dialogue
- **Focus on interests rather than positions,** exploring underlying needs rather than rigid demands
- **Self-determination,** meaning parties retain complete control over whether and how to resolve their dispute
- **Respect for cultural context,** adapting processes to local customs, languages, and power structures

What Mediation Is Not

Understanding what mediation is not matters, particularly because the term is sometimes misused to describe processes that violate its core principles.

Several common misapplications corrupt the mediation concept and can cause significant harm. Mediation is not adjudication or arbitration, where a third party issues a binding ruling. Nor is it a public relations exercise in which companies use the language of dialogue to manage reputation rather than genuinely address grievances. When serious crimes have been committed, including human rights violations, mediation cannot substitute for legal accountability. Coerced negotiation, where overwhelming power forces a weaker party into unfavorable terms, violates the voluntariness that makes mediation legitimate. Mediation differs from therapy and counseling, though trauma-informed practice is integral to good mediation (see Chapter 10). Each of these misapplications can cause significant harm to participants who enter the process expecting something fundamentally different.

> **Caution: Recognizing False Mediation**
>
> Be alert to processes labeled "mediation" that lack core principles. Warning signs include: mandatory participation requirements, mediator bias toward one party, pressure to reach an agreement quickly, lack of confidentiality protections, or use of the process to delay rather than address legitimate grievances. These are not characteristics of mediation; they are features of its opposite.

Understanding what mediation is and is not provides the conceptual foundation. This raises a practical question: in what circumstances should a mediator agree to take on a case, and when must mediation be declined (see Chapter 8)?

2.2 When Mediation Is Appropriate and When It Must Be Refused

Conditions Favoring Mediation

Several conditions support effective mediation. Before agreeing to facilitate, mediators should assess whether these exist:

1. **Genuine willingness to engage:** All parties voluntarily choosing to participate and demonstrating at least minimal good faith supports effective mediation. This does not mean they must agree on anything initially, but they must be open to dialogue.
2. **Identifiable decision-makers:** Effective mediation benefits from participants who have authority to make commitments, or clear access

to those who do. Mediation fails when participants lack the actual power to make agreements.

3. **Absence of active violence:** While mediation can address conflicts with histories of violence, active ongoing violence prevents genuine dialogue and endangers participants.
4. **Manageable power asymmetries:** Power imbalances are common in company-community disputes, but process design can address them (see Chapter 12). When asymmetry is so severe that one party cannot meaningfully participate, mediation is inappropriate until conditions change.
5. **Issues suitable for negotiation:** The matters in dispute must be things the parties can actually negotiate, such as compensation, benefit-sharing, operational practices, or future commitments. Fundamental rights violations typically require formal legal remedies, not negotiated settlements.

   In extractive disputes, appropriateness requires additional scrutiny. Mediation must not substitute for enforcement of environmental regulations, mining license conditions, or indigenous peoples' right to free, prior, and informed consent. When legal protections exist but go unenforced, mediation risks legitimizing a process that should be addressed through regulatory or judicial channels. Dispute systems design research (Ury, Brett, and Goldberg, 1988) demonstrates that mediation is most effective when parties have ongoing relationships and when interests, rather than legal rights alone, are at stake.

6. **Retaliation-free participation is essential. This requires physical safety, freedom from intimidation, and protection from adverse consequences for speaking honestly.**

When Mediation Must Be Refused

Ethical practice sometimes means declining to mediate. There are situations in which mediation would cause harm, enable injustice, or violate the mediator's professional obligations. Chapter 8 addresses these situations in detail, but key categories include:

Genocide, war crimes, and crimes against humanity. These violations require formal accountability mechanisms. Mediation cannot substitute for criminal justice, and attempting to mediate such matters risks legitimizing perpetrators and denying victims appropriate remedies.

Ongoing violence or immediate safety threats. When active violence continues, or participants face imminent harm, the priority must be safety and security, not mediation. Dialogue can resume when conditions permit safe participation.

Severe bad faith combined with power asymmetry. When a powerful party uses mediation as a delay tactic, a reputation-laundering exercise, or a tool to extract concessions under duress, the mediator becomes complicit in harm by continuing to mediate. The key question is whether the weaker party can genuinely say no and walk away.

Mediator capture or manipulation. When the mediator realizes they are being used as a tool by one party to legitimize predetermined outcomes, they must withdraw. Continuing would betray the other party's trust and undermine the integrity of mediation itself.

Hidden decision-makers. When the real power holders refuse to participate or acknowledge their role, mediation becomes theater. Agreements reached without genuine authority are not binding and may actively harm the party who relied on them.

Practical Tip: The Refusal Conversation

When declining to mediate, be clear about the reasons without blaming either party. Focus on conditions rather than character: "The current situation does not support effective mediation because . . . " Offer guidance on what would need to change, and leave the door open for future engagement when conditions improve.

Once a mediator has determined that a case is appropriate for mediation, the question shifts from whether to engage to how to conduct oneself. The mediator's role carries both responsibilities and limits that shape every interaction.

2.3 The Mediator's Role, Limits, and Ethical Posture

The Mediator's Core Functions

Process facilitation, rather than decision-making, defines the mediator's role. Core functions include:

- **Creating a safe space** for honest dialogue by establishing ground rules, ensuring confidentiality, and managing the physical and emotional environment
- **Facilitating communication** through active listening, reframing, summarizing, and helping parties understand each other's perspectives
- **Managing the process** by designing appropriate structures, setting agendas, keeping discussions productive, and knowing when to call breaks or caucuses
- **Balancing power** by ensuring all parties can participate meaningfully, providing capacity support where needed, and preventing domination by stronger parties
- **Exploring interests** beneath positions, helping parties articulate what they truly need rather than what they initially demand
- **Generating options** by encouraging creative problem-solving and helping parties see possibilities they might not discover on their own
- **Reality testing** by helping parties evaluate whether proposed solutions are realistic, sustainable, and address core concerns

The Mediator's Limits

Equally important are the boundaries of mediator conduct:

- **Do not impose solutions.** The mediator may suggest options or reality-test proposals, but must never pressure parties into specific outcomes. Self-determination means parties decide.
- **Do not provide legal advice.** Even mediators trained in law benefit from recognizing when parties need independent legal counsel.
- **Do not serve as a therapist or counselor.** Effective mediators practice trauma-informed approaches and recognize when participants need professional mental health support, facilitating access to it.

- **Do not take sides.** Even when one party's position seems more sympathetic, impartiality remains important. The moment parties perceive bias, trust in the process collapses.
- **Do not guarantee outcomes.** The mediator can promise a fair process but cannot promise resolution. Making outcome promises creates unrealistic expectations and may pressure parties inappropriately.
- **Do not mediate beyond their competence.** Complex disputes may require technical expertise, cultural knowledge, or experience that the mediator lacks. Knowing when to bring in additional resources or decline the case is essential.

Ethical Posture

The mediator's ethical posture encompasses several interconnected commitments, including:

Neutrality and Impartiality

Neutrality and impartiality. The mediator must be neutral on the issues (having no stake in particular outcomes) and impartial toward the parties (showing no favoritism). Some practitioners prefer the term "multipartial," meaning they have an equal commitment to helping all parties, rather than "neutral," which may suggest detachment. Either framing requires treating all parties with equal respect and giving all voices equal consideration. Chapter 3 explores multipartiality and related ethical principles in greater depth.

Voluntariness and Informed Consent

Commitment to voluntariness. Continuous attention to ensuring that participation remains voluntary and that parties can withdraw without penalty proves important, especially when power asymmetries might make refusal appear costly. Mediators should periodically check in with the parties to assess their willingness to continue.

Do No Harm and Accountability

Do no harm. This principle requires ongoing vigilance. Will this process retraumatize participants? Will it legitimize injustice? Will it worsen power imbalances? Could it endanger anyone? These questions offer guidance for mediator decision-making, and honest answers may require modifying the process or withdrawing entirely.

In extractive-industry mediation, this vigilance is particularly acute. Mediation may involve communities that have experienced water contamination, land displacement, or loss of traditional livelihoods. Assessing whether a company's participation reflects genuine commitment to resolution, rather than a reputational exercise to maintain operations, is part of the do-no-harm obligation. These ethical commitments reflect the principles codified in the Model Standards of Conduct for Mediators (American Arbitration Association, American Bar Association, and Association for Conflict Resolution, 2005), which establish neutrality, informed consent, and self-determination as foundational mediator obligations.

Transparency about the process. Parties benefit from understanding what mediation involves, the mediator's role, what confidentiality means, and what happens if an agreement is not reached. Informed consent requires that participants understand the process they are entering.

Accountability for conduct. While mediators facilitate rather than decide, they remain responsible for how they conduct the process. This includes managing their own biases, maintaining professional boundaries, seeking supervision when needed, and acknowledging mistakes.

Key Concept: The Do No Harm Principle

Do no harm is not passive. It requires active assessment of potential consequences and willingness to modify or end processes that risk causing harm. This may mean refusing to mediate, pausing when safety is threatened, ensuring adequate support for traumatized participants, or withdrawing when the mediator realizes they are being used to legitimize injustice.

Self-Care as Professional Obligation

Self-care demands active engagement, not optional indulgence. Mediators working in company-community disputes regularly encounter trauma, power imbalances, and morally complex situations (see Chapter 11 for details). Vicarious trauma and burnout are occupational hazards that, if unaddressed, compromise the mediator's effectiveness and may harm participants.

Recognizing warning signs and seeking support when needed enables mediators to step back from cases when their well-being is compromised.

These three elements, the nature of mediation, the conditions for its appropriate use, and the ethical posture of the mediator, form an integrated framework. A mediator who understands what mediation is but misjudges when to use it risks causing harm. One who correctly identifies an appropriate case but lacks ethical grounding risks losing the trust that makes the process work. The chapters that follow build on this foundation, providing the practical skills, cultural awareness, and strategic tools needed to translate these principles into effective practice.

This framework of mediation principles, appropriateness criteria, and mediator ethics integrates three essential foundations. First, mediation is a structured yet flexible process where neutral facilitators enable voluntary dialogue and self-determined outcomes. Second, its effective use depends on assessing specific conditions, recognizing when mediation serves justice and when other mechanisms must take precedence. Third, the mediator's own ethical grounding, self-awareness, and commitment to doing no harm determine whether these principles translate into genuine practice. These three elements form an inseparable whole. A mediator who understands mediation but misjudges when to use it risks causing harm. One who correctly identifies an appropriate case but lacks ethical grounding risks losing the trust that makes the process work. The chapters that follow build on this foundation, providing the practical skills, cultural awareness, and strategic tools needed to implement these principles effectively in company-community disputes.

Key Takeaways

1. Mediation is a voluntary, structured process facilitated by a neutral third party, not a tool for corporate compliance or public relations.

2. The do-no-harm principle requires mediators to assess whether their involvement could legitimize injustice or deepen power imbalances.
3. Six conditions must be present for mediation to proceed: genuine willingness, identifiable issues, adequate representation, safety, basic power balance, and good faith.
4. Mediators have an ethical duty to refuse cases involving active human rights violations, ongoing violence, or attempts to use the process as a delay tactic.
5. Community mediation in extractive contexts requires sensitivity to the unique dynamics of land, livelihood, and long-term environmental impact.

Reflection Questions

1. Think of a dispute in your context. Do the six conditions for appropriate mediation apply? Which conditions are weakest?
2. How would you assess whether a company's request for mediation reflects genuine willingness or a strategy to manage opposition?
3. What is your personal threshold for declining a mediation? Have you ever accepted a case you should have refused?
4. How does the do-no-harm principle apply differently in extractive-industry disputes compared to other mediation contexts?

With these principles as our foundation, let us turn to the core principles and ethics that underpin effective mediation.

3.

CORE PRINCIPLES AND ETHICS OF MEDIATION

With the handbook's philosophical foundation and scope now established, we turn to the specific principles and ethical standards that must guide every mediation engagement. These ensure fairness, respect, and legitimacy in voluntary mediation between companies and communities. When mediators embody these values, they enable genuine dialogue and durable agreements.

Principles shape every decision, from room arrangement to handling emotional outbursts. A mediator who deeply understands these principles can navigate novel situations with confidence, knowing that principled responses generally lead to good outcomes.

This chapter covers core principles: voluntariness, impartiality, self-determination, confidentiality, and informed consent, explaining what each means, why it matters, and how it applies in practice. It also addresses four subsidiary principles, namely safety and respect, honesty and transparency, do no harm, and structured process with flexibility, that guide ethical practice in company-community contexts.

Figure 1 below provides a foundational framework for understanding how mediation functions across different contexts.

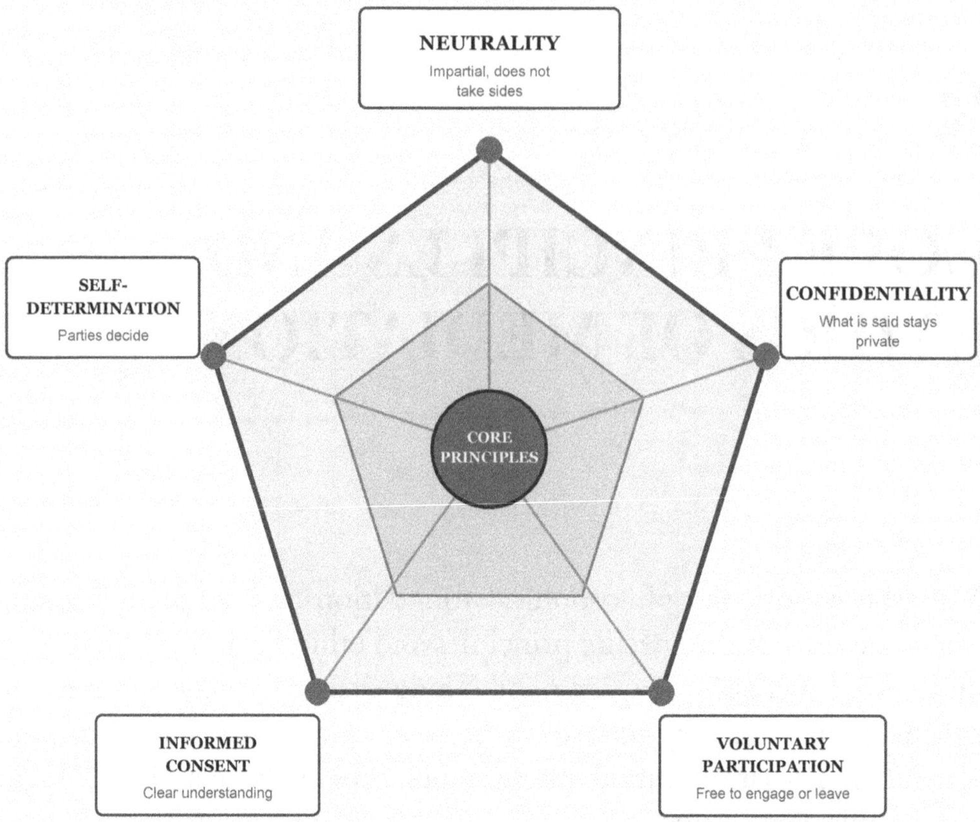

Figure 1: The five foundational principles of mediation: voluntariness, impartiality, self-determination, confidentiality, and informed consent.

These five principles form the foundation of everything that follows in this handbook, and understanding their interconnection will help you recognize when a mediation process is on track.

3.1 Voluntariness

Voluntariness means participation is entirely optional. No one is compelled to attend, forced to stay, or pressured into accepting an agreement. Each party enters and continues by free choice, from initial agreement through final resolution.

Voluntariness is mediation's foundation of legitimacy. When people participate freely, they engage genuinely, share real concerns, consider options seriously, and commit to agreements they helped shape.

Coerced participation breeds resentment. People forced into mediation may attend physically while withholding genuine engagement, providing misleading information, or abandoning agreements at the first opportunity. Additionally, agreements reached under coercion rarely hold because parties have not genuinely committed.

Voluntariness distinguishes mediation from arbitration or court proceedings. In mediation, parties retain ultimate control. They cannot be forced in, and they cannot be forced to accept any particular outcome.

Protecting voluntariness benefits from continuous attention. At the outset, clearly state that participation is optional and that parties can withdraw at any time without penalty. Ensure the parties truly understand their choices and the alternatives available.

Throughout the process, periodically confirm the continued willingness to participate, especially after difficult moments or when one party appears to be emotionally withdrawing. Avoiding pressure on uncomfortable proposals tends to produce more durable agreements.

Caution: Economic Coercion

When a community depends economically on a company (jobs, services, infrastructure), participation appears voluntary but involves hidden coercion. Watch for signs that community members fear economic retaliation for speaking honestly or withdrawing.

Be alert to external pressures coercing participation. A community may feel they "have to" participate because refusing would anger powerful actors. In such cases, address external pressures directly, help parties understand their genuine options, or decline to proceed if true voluntariness is impossible (see Chapter 8).

> **Practical Tip: Testing Voluntariness**
>
> Before each session, privately ask each party: "Do you feel any pressure to be here today?" and "Is there anything preventing you from speaking freely?" Genuine voluntariness requires ongoing verification, not just initial consent.

> **Sample Dialogue**
>
> *Mediator: "Before we begin, I want to emphasize that you're here by choice. You can leave at any time, and nothing will be decided without your agreement. Is there anything making you feel like you have to be here?"*
>
> *Community Representative: "The regional government told us that if we don't participate, they won't support our other complaints."*
>
> *Mediator: "Thank you for being honest. That kind of pressure concerns me. Let me explore this with you privately, and perhaps we can address the government's concerns while ensuring you have a genuine choice in the matter."*

Sample Dialogue

Mediator: "Before we begin, I want to emphasize that you're here by choice. You can leave at any time, and nothing will be decided without your agreement. Is there anything making you feel like you have to be here?"

Community Representative: "The regional government told us that if we don't participate, they won't support our other complaints."

Mediator: "Thank you for being honest. That kind of pressure concerns me. Let me explore this with you privately, and perhaps we can address the government's concerns while ensuring you have a genuine choice in the matter."

Signs of Involuntary Participation

- Participants who appear disengaged, making minimal eye contact or providing only brief responses
- Frequent references to what others expect ("The board told us to try mediation")

- Quick agreement to proposals without genuine consideration
- Expressions of hopelessness ("It doesn't matter what we want")

Practical Tip: Graceful Exit Options

Create multiple opportunities to exit without embarrassment. Rather than asking "Do you want to continue?" try "We've covered a lot. Let's take a break, and everyone can decide whether to continue tomorrow." This normalizes the option to withdraw.

3.2 Self-Determination

Self-determination means parties retain control over the outcome. The mediator facilitates but does not impose solutions. All decisions rest with the disputing parties themselves.

Self-determination respects the agency and dignity of all participants. Community members are active participants shaping their futures, not passive recipients of decisions. This respect is especially vital within communities that have historically been excluded from decisions affecting their lives. When power imbalances threaten genuine self-determination (see Chapter 12), mediators must modify process design to equalize power.

Self-determination also produces better outcomes. Parties understand their situations, priorities, and constraints better than any outsider. A mediator cannot know what it feels like to be displaced from ancestral land or what operational pressures the company faces. Solutions designed by parties are more likely to address real needs.

Key Concept: Informed Self-Determination

Self-determination requires not just the absence of pressure, but adequate information. A party cannot truly determine its outcome if it lacks understanding of technical issues, legal implications, or available options. Mediators support self-determination by ensuring information asymmetries are addressed.

Respecting self-determination means resisting the temptation to solve problems for parties. Even when a mediator sees an obvious solution, imposing it undermines ownership.

Ask questions rather than give advice. Compare "You should consider a development fund" with "What options do you see for addressing long-term benefit concerns?" Giving advice positions the mediator as an expert rather than a facilitator, while asking questions invites the parties to think through their options.

Sample Dialogue

Company Representative: "What do you think we should do? You've seen situations like this before."
Mediator: "I appreciate the question, but the best solution is one you and the community develop together. You understand your situation far better than I do. I can help you think through implications, but ultimately, you decide what works."

Key Concept: Facilitate, Don't Fix

The mediator's role is to facilitate, not fix. Help parties communicate, understand each other, and generate options. They decide what works. The moment a mediator begins imposing solutions, the process shifts from mediation to something else.

3.3 Neutrality and Impartiality

Neutrality means the mediator has no stake in the outcome. Impartiality means treating all parties fairly, without bias or favoritism. Together, these ensure the mediator serves the process rather than any particular interest.

Trust in the mediator matters. Suspected favoritism silences parties and invites withdrawal. A community that believes the mediator works for the company will not reveal its true concerns. Likewise, a company that believes the mediator sympathizes with the community will not share sensitive information.

Some practitioners prefer the term multipartiality, referring to a mediator who is fully supportive of all parties reaching a fair outcome. This captures the active quality: not passive neutrality, but active support for everyone.

Practical Tip: Perception Management

Perceived neutrality matters as much as actual neutrality. If community members see you chatting casually with company representatives during breaks, they may question your impartiality. Be intentional about distributing attention, body language, and informal interactions equally.

Give each party equal opportunity to speak, use balanced language when summarizing each party's views, and be intentional about distributing attention equally. For a detailed breakdown of impartiality in practice, including specific techniques for managing perceptions, checking biases, and ensuring process fairness, see Chapter 9: Tools and Competencies in the Mediator's Toolbox.

When one side uses emotionally charged language and the other uses clinical terms, find neutral phrasing that acknowledges both perspectives without endorsing either.

Caution: Structural Bias Awareness

Even well-intentioned mediators may harbor unconscious biases favoring more articulate, educated, or professionally presented parties. Regularly examine whether your process design inadvertently advantages one party, such as formal meeting rooms that feel natural to executives but intimidating to villagers.

Sample Dialogue

Community Member: "The company has never listened to us. They don't care about our problems."
Mediator: "It sounds like you've felt unheard, and that's been very frustrating." Turns to the company. "I'd like to hear the company's perspective as well. How do you see the history of communication?"

Practical Tip: Small Gestures Matter

Sit equidistant from both sides. Make eye contact equally. Use each party's name with equal respect. Avoid nodding more when one side speaks. Spend approximately equal time in caucus with each party. These subtle behaviors signal impartiality.

3.4 Confidentiality

Confidentiality means what is said in mediation stays in mediation. Discussions, documents, and proposals are not disclosed outside, except as agreed or required by law. This enables honest dialogue.

Figure 2 provides a structured approach to managing the boundaries of information sharing during the mediation process.

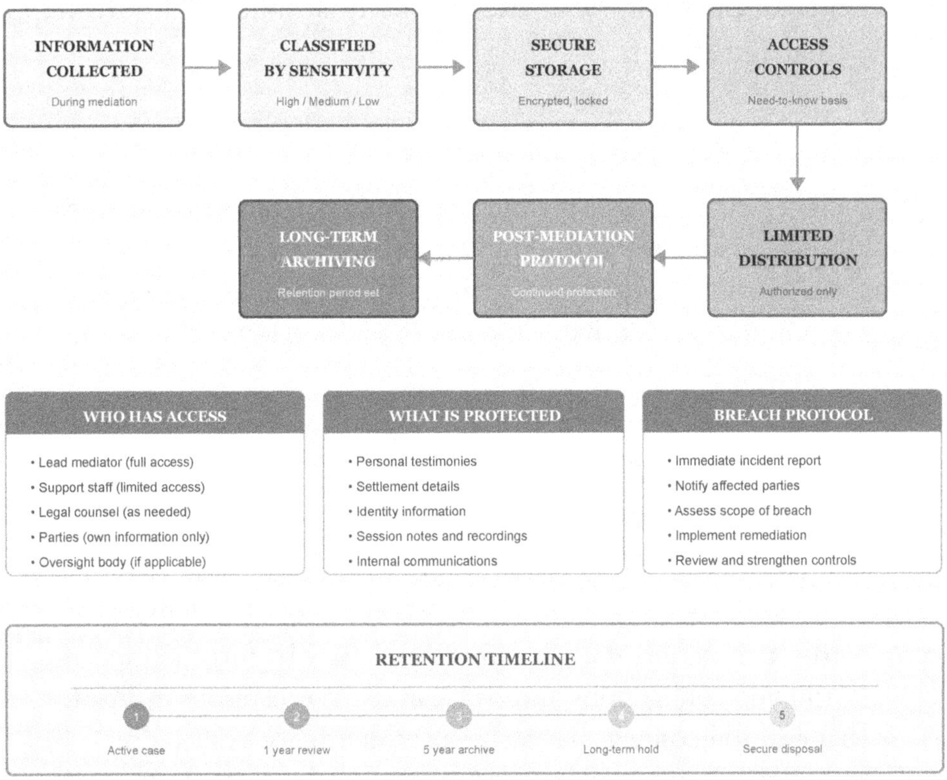

Figure 2: A framework for managing information sharing boundaries during mediation, clarifying what information can be disclosed and to whom.

Understanding these management approaches allows mediators to navigate the often-conflicting needs to protect confidentiality while also facilitating the trust-building exchanges that parties need.

When people know their words will not be quoted in the media, used in court, or reported to critics, they speak more freely. A company representative might acknowledge a mistake. A community member might reveal what they truly need rather than posturing. This candor enables finding real solutions.

Confidentiality also encourages creative problem-solving. Parties can float tentative ideas without fear that rejected proposals will be held against them. This exploratory conversation is often where breakthroughs happen.

Protecting confidentiality requires clear agreements, careful practices, and consistent behavior. Explain confidentiality rules at the outset: what will be kept confidential, what exceptions exist, and what will happen with any final agreement.

Practical Tip: Explaining Exceptions

Always clarify exceptions at the outset: mandatory reporting of threats, legal subpoenas, and any agreed public statements. Use concrete examples: "If someone discloses a plan to harm another person, I am legally required to report that. Otherwise, nothing leaves this room."

Key Concept: Confidentiality Limits

Confidentiality has limits. Mediators typically cannot promise confidentiality if someone discloses imminent harm, child abuse, or certain criminal matters. Legal requirements vary by jurisdiction. Understand your obligations and be clear about exceptions upfront. Note that cultural context may shape confidentiality expectations differently across communities (see Chapter 10).

Sample Dialogue

Mediator: "Everything we discuss here is confidential. None of us will share what's said with people outside this room, unless we all agree otherwise. There are exceptions: I cannot keep confidential any disclosure of imminent harm. Apart from those rare situations, what happens here stays here. Does everyone understand and accept this?"

3.5 Informed Consent

Informed consent means parties understand the mediation process and agree to participate with full knowledge of what it involves, including their rights, the mediator's role, and how any agreement might be used.

You cannot voluntarily consent to something you do not understand. Informed consent ensures participation is truly voluntary and prevents later disputes about whether people knew what they were agreeing to.

This is particularly important in cases of power or educational imbalances. A community unfamiliar with formal dispute resolution needs a clear explanation. Without it, their "agreement" may reflect confusion rather than genuine consent.

Key Concept: Layered Consent

Informed consent is not a one-time event but a continuous process. Obtain initial consent, then re-confirm at key junctures: before sensitive topics, before signing agreements, and before any information is shared externally.

Explain the process in clear, accessible language. Cover what mediation is and how it differs from court, the mediator's role as facilitator, not judge, the right to withdraw, confidentiality, the right to advisors, and how agreements would be formalized.

Practical Tip: Pre-Mediation Orientation

For communities unfamiliar with mediation, hold a separate orientation session beforehand. This gives community members time to discuss, ask questions, and make a genuine decision about participation without feeling rushed.

3.6 Safety and Respect

Safety means creating an environment where participants are physically secure and emotionally protected. Respect means treating all participants with dignity. Together, these create conditions for genuine dialogue.

People cannot engage constructively if they feel threatened or demeaned. Fear shuts down honest communication. Disrespect breeds resentment. A safe, respectful environment allows vulnerability, which enables honest dialogue that leads to real solutions.

Choose neutral locations away from sites associated with conflict. Meeting at the company headquarters may make community members feel unsafe. A neutral venue signals that no party controls the space.

Practical Tip: Pre-Session Safety Check

Arrive early to assess the space. Check for multiple exits, adequate lighting, comfortable seating, and the absence of intimidating elements. For high-conflict situations, consider a neutral observer and establish a discrete signal system for participants who feel unsafe.

Emotional safety requires ground rules against personal attacks, threats, and intimidation. Establish these at the outset and enforce consistently. When violations occur, intervene immediately.

Sample Dialogue

Company Representative: "The community is just trying to extort money. They're liars."

Mediator: "I need to pause. Our ground rules require addressing issues, not making personal characterizations. Let me reframe: you have concerns about some claims. Can you explain specifically what concerns you without characterizing motives?"

Caution: Emotional Safety

Safety is not just physical. Pushing trauma survivors to relive experiences, dismissing concerns, allowing one party to dominate, or creating time pressure that forces rushed decisions all violate safety. Be vigilant for these less visible threats.

3.7 Honesty and Transparency

Honesty means all participants, including the mediator, communicate truthfully. Transparency means being open about the process, intentions, and relevant information. These create the foundation for trust.

Mediation depends on trust, and trust requires honesty. If parties believe the other side is lying, they will not engage in good faith. Agreements based on false information do not hold because they do not address the real situation.

In company-community disputes, information asymmetries are common. The company typically has detailed information that the community lacks. If the company hides or distorts this information, the community cannot make informed decisions.

> **Caution: The Transparency Paradox**
>
> Complete transparency can sometimes harm the process. Revealing everything from private caucuses may destroy trust. Disclosing one party's vulnerabilities may enable exploitation. Balance transparency with discretion, being honest about what you cannot share and why.

> **Key Concept: Honest but Not Cruel**
>
> Honesty does not mean brutal frankness. Information can be shared constructively and sensitively. The goal is truthful communication that builds understanding, not harsh statements that destroy relationships.

3.8 Do No Harm

Do no harm means ensuring the process does not make things worse, particularly for vulnerable parties. Good intentions are not enough. An unskillful process can worsen power imbalances, force premature forgiveness, retraumatize survivors, or harm vulnerable parties through flawed agreements.

Assess whether mediation is appropriate before proceeding. Some situations require other interventions first. If ongoing safety threats exist, mediation may need to wait. If the power imbalance is so severe that fair mediation is impossible, different approaches may be warranted.

Do not force disclosures or emotional confrontations that people are not ready for. Trauma survivors should control what they share and when. The pace should be set by the parties' readiness, not the mediator's timeline.

For further discussion of this principle, see also Chapter 10, Trauma-Informed Approaches.

Key Concept: Secondary Harm

Harm extends beyond immediate participants. An agreement benefiting present parties may harm future generations, absent community members, or the environment. Ask: "Who is not at this table but will be affected by our decisions?"

Sample Dialogue

Mediator: "I'm noticing this topic is causing significant distress. Let's take a break." Then, in private, "I want to check in. This process should help, not hurt. If continuing is too painful, we can find other ways forward. Your well-being matters more than reaching an agreement today."

Caution: Working with Trauma Survivors

Mediating with trauma survivors requires particular care to avoid retraumatization. Do not probe for graphic details, pressure forgiveness, or suggest people "move on" from legitimate grievances. For comprehensive guidance on trauma-informed mediation practices, including recognizing trauma responses, grounding techniques, and creating safety for survivors, see Chapter 10: Trauma-Informed Approaches.

3.9 Structured Process with Flexibility

A structured process means mediation follows a clear framework. Flexibility means adapting that framework to specific needs, local culture, and circumstances. Effective mediation requires both sufficient structure for predictability and fairness, and sufficient flexibility to address the actual situation.

Structure provides predictability. When parties know what to expect, they feel more secure. It ensures all voices are heard and prevents one party from dominating.

But rigid adherence to a formula proves counterproductive. Different cultures have different communication and decision-making styles. What works for one mediation will not work for another.

Practical Tip: Transparent Agenda Flexibility

When departing from the planned structure, explain why. "I notice strong emotions around this issue. I'm going to suggest we take a break and return with a different approach." This maintains trust while allowing necessary adaptation.

Sample Dialogue

Mediator: "Typically, I'd suggest opening statements, then identifying issues, then working through them. But does that approach work for you? I understand important discussions in your community often begin with certain traditions. Should we incorporate those?"

Practical Tip: Ask About Cultural Practices

Asking "Is there a way discussions like this usually happen in your community?" "Are there traditions we should incorporate?" People appreciate the respect implicit in the question.

3.10 Putting Principles into Practice

These principles are practical guides for action. Every decision should reflect these values. When situations arise that are not covered by specific techniques, these principles provide guidance.

Self-Check Questions for Each Principle:

Principle	Questions to Ask Yourself
Voluntariness	Are parties here by genuine choice? Is anyone being coerced?
Self-Determination	Am I facilitating their decision or pushing my solution?
Neutrality	Am I giving equal respect to all parties? Could I be perceived as favoring one side?
Confidentiality	Have I protected what was shared? Are the rules clear and followed?
Informed Consent	Do parties truly understand the process? Have I checked, not assumed?
Safety/Respect	Does everyone feel safe? Is everyone treated with dignity?
Honesty	Am I being truthful? Is relevant information being shared?
Do No Harm	Is this process helping or hurting? Are there signs of harm?
Flexibility	Is my process serving the parties, or forcing them into my framework?

The framework presented in Figure 3 shows how mediators balance competing interests.

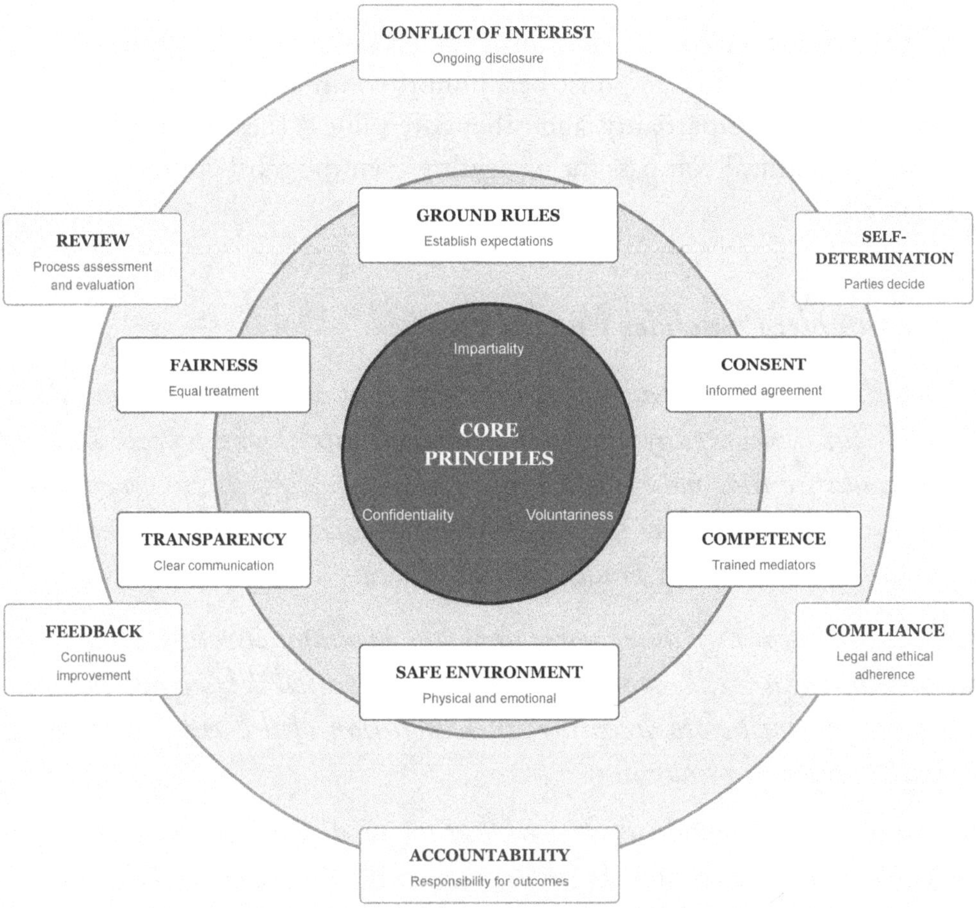

Figure 3: A practical framework for translating ethical principles into concrete procedural decisions throughout the mediation process.

By using this framework as a checklist, you can move from abstract ethical principles to concrete daily decisions that strengthen the integrity of your mediation practice.

By adhering to these core principles, mediators establish a foundation of trust and integrity that enables resolution. Parties who see the process as principled are more likely to engage genuinely, take risks, and commit to agreements.

Key Concept: Return to Principles

When in doubt, return to these principles. If unsure how to handle a situation, ask which response best honors voluntariness, self-determination, impartiality, and other core values. These principles provide an ethical compass for navigating even the most complex situations.

Case Example: Principles Under Pressure

In a mediation between a mining company and an affected community in West Africa, the company offered a settlement late in the process. The mediator could see that most stated concerns were addressed. However, several community representatives seemed hesitant, glancing at each other without responding. The company pressed for acceptance.

Rather than encourage quick agreement, the mediator invoked self-determination. During a break, community members revealed they needed to consult elders not present before accepting. In recognition of this cultural need, the mediator proposed adjourning.

The company was initially frustrated, but the mediator explained the importance of genuine consent for durable agreements. A week later, the community accepted a slightly modified package with full commitment. The agreement held because it reflected genuine self-determination.

The following chapters will build upon the foundational skills established here. As we move forward, we will look more deeply at specific skills, processes, and techniques. Understand each as an application of these principles, as they remain the foundation throughout.

4.

KEY COMMUNICATION AND FACILITATION SKILLS

Principles and ethics set the standard for what mediation should achieve. Realizing those standards requires specific communication and facilitation skills. In company-community disputes, the challenges are immense: emotions run high, mistrust pervades every exchange, and parties often have vastly different communication styles and cultural expectations.

This chapter covers the communication and facilitation skills that help mediators work through these challenges. These skills serve interconnected purposes: creating psychological safety, gathering accurate information, transforming accusations into problem-solving conversations, and modeling respectful communication that parties can adopt.

4.1 Active Listening

Active listening underpins mediation communication. It involves giving the speaker your full attention, understanding both the explicit content and the underlying emotions, and communicating that understanding in ways that make the speaker feel genuinely heard.

In extractive disputes, this dual attention is essential. A community member expressing frustration about water quality is not simply venting emotion; the concern reflects measurable contamination levels, changing water tables, or pipeline impacts on local water sources. Skilled mediators track both the technical substance of such claims and the emotional weight of living with environmental degradation.

When people feel unheard, they repeat themselves louder, become more entrenched, and disengage from problem-solving. When people feel genuinely heard, the dynamic shifts:

- Emotional intensity decreases. When someone has fully expressed their concern and seen it acknowledged, the pressure to keep pushing diminishes.
- Trust begins to build. Listening demonstrates respect and genuine care, enabling eventual trust-building between parties.
- Information flows more freely. People share more when they believe their words matter. A farmer initially states only that he wants compensation, but when truly listened to, reveals that his real concern is whether his grandchildren will have any future in the village.
- Modeling occurs naturally. Parties often mirror the mediator's listening behavior, transforming communication dynamics.
- Validation provides relief. For communities that have felt dismissed by powerful institutions, being heard validates that their concerns are legitimate.

Physical Presence

Your body communicates attention before you speak. Position yourself at the same physical level as speakers when possible. Maintain appropriate eye contact (while remaining sensitive to cultural norms). Face speakers directly with an open posture. Minimize fidgeting, phone-checking, and paper-shuffling. Use small nods and responsive facial expressions to show engagement.

> **Practical Tip: Centering Yourself Before a Session**
>
> Before each session, take a moment to settle yourself. Put away devices, take a breath, and consciously decide to be fully present. This mental preparation helps you show up with the focus required for active listening.

Mental Engagement

Physical presence isn't enough if your mind is elsewhere. Set aside thoughts about what to say next. Track both content (facts, claims, requests) and emotion (feelings, energy, passion). Notice hesitations, topic avoidance, and contradictions. Suspend judgment while listening; your job is to understand, not evaluate. Approach each speaker with genuine curiosity, as if they have something important to teach you.

Verbal Responses That Demonstrate Listening

- Brief encouragers: "Mm-hmm," "I see," "Go on," "Tell me more" signal you're following without interrupting.
- Paraphrasing: Restating the speaker's message in your own words confirms understanding. Begin with "So what I'm hearing is . . . " or "It sounds like . . . "
- Reflecting feelings: Naming emotions shows deep understanding. Saying, "It sounds like this has been incredibly frustrating," validates emotional experience without requiring explicit disclosure.
- Clarifying questions: When unclear, ask for elaboration: "Can you help me understand what you mean by . . . ?"
- Summarizing: Periodically pull together key points, especially before transitioning to new topics.

Paraphrasing in Practice

Paraphrasing most directly demonstrates understanding. When done well, it captures essence without parroting, maintains emotional weight without escalating language, and uses different words than the speaker. Always end with a check: "Did I get that right?"

Imagine this scenario. A community elder speaks harshly about the company's "theft," "lies," and "disrespect." Rather than repeating accusations, the mediator paraphrases: "So over the years, the community was given certain expectations about jobs, infrastructure, and environmental protection. When those weren't met, it felt like a betrayal, and now there's deep skepticism about whether any new promises will be kept." This captures the essence while making it easier for the company to hear without becoming defensive.

Reflecting Feelings

Reflecting feelings means naming the emotions you perceive behind someone's words. This validates emotional experience and demonstrates understanding at a deeper level than content alone.

When an elder describes ancestral lands being converted to mining operations, reflecting those feelings might sound like: 'You are grieving the loss of land your family has relied on for generations, and you are worried that remediation promises will not restore what has been lost.' This kind of reflection acknowledges both the cultural and the environmental dimensions of extractive-industry disputes.

Sample Dialogue

Community member: "Every time we try to meet with the company, they send someone who can't make decisions. We've had twelve meetings in three years and nothing has changed."
Mediator: "That sounds exhausting and demoralizing. You've invested significant time, sacrificing work your family depends on, and it feels like your commitment hasn't been matched. I imagine that's left you feeling frustrated and disrespected."

Key Concept: Reflecting vs. Endorsing

Reflecting feelings is not agreeing with someone's interpretation or endorsing their position. You can reflect that the community feels betrayed without accepting that the company actually betrayed them. You're acknowledging emotional reality, which exists regardless of who is factually correct.

Listening for What's Not Said

Skilled mediators listen to silences, gaps, and patterns as much as to words. Notice topics carefully avoided, hesitation before answering, contradictions between words and tone, who remains silent in group settings, and questions deflected rather than answered. If everyone discusses employment and water freely but changes the subject when land compensation arises, that avoidance signals sensitivity worth exploring.

Common Barriers to Active Listening

- Planning your response while the other person is still speaking. Trust that you'll find the right words when it's your turn.
- Judging or evaluating whether the speaker is being reasonable or honest. Judgment is appropriate later; during listening, focus only on understanding.
- Filtering for expectations. If you've mediated many mining disputes where water was central, you might miss that this community's primary concern is actually sacred sites.
- Jumping to solutions before fully understanding the problem. If you move too quickly, your solutions will miss the mark.
- Mind-reading or assuming you know what someone means. "Consultation" might mean very different things to the company and the community.

> **Caution: Listening Fatigue**
>
> Extended active listening is mentally exhausting. After several hours, your capacity to attend fully diminishes. Schedule breaks before fatigue compromises your listening ability. A tired mediator who appears inattentive can undo hours of rapport-building.

Cultural Variations in Listening

Listening norms vary significantly across cultures. Eye contact that shows respect in one context signals disrespect in another. Silence signals thoughtful reflection or uncomfortable disagreement. Frequent verbal feedback demonstrates engagement or feels like an interruption. When mediating across cultures, observe before acting. Watch how community members interact with each other, then adapt accordingly.

> **Practical Tip: Asking About Cultural Norms**
>
> When uncertain about cultural norms, ask directly: "I want to make sure I'm being respectful. Is there anything about how I'm conducting myself that I should adjust?" Most people appreciate the genuine effort to understand their culture.

4.2 Empathy and Emotional Intelligence

Listening captures what people say; empathy connects with what they feel. Empathy is the ability to understand and share another person's feelings, to imaginatively enter their experience. Emotional intelligence is the broader capacity to recognize, understand, and skillfully respond to emotions in yourself and others.

Why Empathy Matters

Conflict is inherently emotional. People feel angry about injustice, afraid for their futures, hurt by perceived betrayal, and humiliated when they feel ignored. These emotions are not obstacles to problem-solving; they reveal what matters most. Unaddressed emotions block productive engagement. In trauma contexts (see Chapter 10), emotional responses may be intensified or include triggers that mediators must recognize and manage with care.

- Emotions drive behavior. A community that feels disrespected rejects objectively fair offers because accepting would feel like capitulation.
- Feeling understood reduces defensiveness. When pain is recognized, the urgent need to convince diminishes, creating space for listening and problem-solving.
- Empathy builds trust. Demonstrating that you "get it" creates a connection. Community members who feel the mediator genuinely grasps their situation are more likely to trust the process.

- Modeling empathy teaches it. When the mediator consistently shows empathy to all parties, participants begin extending empathy across party lines.

Demonstrating Empathy

Acknowledge emotions directly: "This has clearly been devastating for your family." Validate that their response makes sense given everything that's happened. Show genuine interest in their experience, not just the facts: "What has been the hardest part for your family?" Be fully present during difficult moments without rushing to the next topic.

> **Sample Dialogue**
>
> *Company representative: "People don't understand the pressure we're under. If we don't meet production targets, the board will shut down this operation entirely. Then everyone loses their jobs."*
>
> *Mediator: "It sounds like you're carrying a heavy burden, trying to keep the entire operation viable while also addressing these community concerns. That's an incredibly difficult position. I imagine that's exhausting."*

> **Key Concept: Empathy vs. Agreement**
>
> Empathy does not require agreement. You can understand why a company representative feels unfairly blamed without endorsing their position. Saying "I can see why this feels frustrating from your perspective" validates emotion without taking sides on substance.

Emotional Intelligence Components

- Self-awareness: Recognizing your own emotional reactions and how they affect your thinking. Notice when you're feeling frustrated, when you're starting to favor one party, or when something has triggered your personal experiences.
- Self-regulation: Managing your emotions so they don't derail the process. Even when a party says something outrageous, maintain

composure. This means experiencing emotions without being controlled by them.

- Social awareness: Reading emotional states, including subtle cues. Notice when someone is becoming defensive, shutting down, or holding back. Understand group dynamics: who has influence, who others silence, and what tensions exist within each party.
- Relationship management: Using emotional awareness to guide interactions. Know when to take breaks, when to probe deeper, when to shift topics, and how to frame observations in ways people can hear.

Reading Emotional Cues

Beyond words, emotions are expressed through multiple channels: tone of voice (volume, pitch, speed), body language (posture, gestures, facial expressions), and word choice. Repeated themes reveal what matters most. Energy shifts, animation, or withdrawal on particular topics signal deeper concerns. Inconsistencies between verbal content and nonverbal expression warrant special attention. Trust behavior over words when they conflict.

Consider this scenario as an example. During a break, you notice that the community elder, who has been vocal during the session, is sitting alone while younger members cluster together, avoiding him. When the session resumes, he's quieter. These observations suggest possible tension within the community delegation, perhaps signaling a disagreement about strategy or authority. A skilled mediator might later create an opportunity for a private conversation.

Managing Your Own Reactions

- Notice your reactions: Develop the habit of internal monitoring. "I'm feeling irritated by this person's tone."
- Pause before acting: Create space between stimulus and response. Take a breath. A moment's pause lets you choose your response rather than simply react.

- Understand the source: Is your reaction about what's happening now, or is something from your own history being triggered?
- Use reactions as information: Your response may mirror what others feel. If you're frustrated by someone's style, others probably are too.
- Seek support afterward: Difficult mediations take an emotional toll. Debrief with colleagues and don't carry the weight alone.

> **Caution: Empathy Distribution**
>
> Unconsciously, mediators often show more empathy toward parties they personally relate to. Monitor your empathic responses. Are you acknowledging company representatives' stress as readily as community members' grief? Imbalanced empathy undermines perceived neutrality.

Responding to Strong Emotions

- Don't rush past them. Emotions that are bypassed go underground and resurface later, often more powerfully.
- Name what you observe. "I can see this is bringing up strong feelings." Naming creates acknowledgment without requiring explanation.
- Normalize the emotion. "It's completely understandable to feel angry about something like this." This helps people feel less alone.
- Allow space. Sometimes, respectful silence while someone collects themselves is the most appropriate response.
- Check in before continuing. "Are you okay to continue, or do you need more time?" This respects autonomy.

4.3 Effective Questioning

Questions are among the mediator's most versatile tools. The right question at the right moment can clarify confusion, uncover hidden interests, challenge assumptions, open new possibilities, and move parties toward collaboration.

Functions of Questions

- Information gathering: Learning what happened, what each party wants, what constraints exist, and what options might be available.
- Clarification: Ensuring everyone understands what's being said. Ambiguous terms cause serious misunderstandings.
- Exploration of interests: Moving beneath stated positions to underlying needs. Solutions that address interests are often easier to find than those that satisfy positions.
- Reality testing: Helping parties examine assumptions and consider consequences without the mediator having to argue or convince.
- Engagement: Drawing out quieter participants and ensuring all perspectives are heard.

> **Key Concept: Curiosity Over Judgement**
>
> Questions model curiosity rather than judgment. When a mediator asks genuine questions, it signals that understanding matters more than being right. This stance is contagious; parties often become more curious about each other.

Open-Ended Questions

Open-ended questions invite expansive responses and cannot be answered with yes or no. They typically begin with "what," "how," "tell me about," or "describe." Use them to:

- Begin exploration: "What concerns you most about the proposed expansion?" This lets speakers identify priorities rather than respond to your assumptions.
- Encourage storytelling: "Can you walk me through what happened?" Stories provide context, emotion, and detail that direct questions miss.
- Understand interests: "What would addressing this issue make possible for your community?" This seeks the "why" behind what they're asking for.

- Generate options: "What approaches might address both your needs and theirs?" This invites collaborative thinking.

Having a prepared repertoire of open-ended questions helps mediators respond flexibly in real time without having to think through question phrasing in the moment. The following figure provides a quick reference bank of tested open-ended questions organized by purpose.

Figure 4: A curated bank of open-ended questions organized by purpose, designed to help mediators explore issues, interests, and potential solutions.

Having this bank at your fingertips during preparation and early sessions helps you avoid the trap of relying on the same few questions and instead tailor your approach to each party's unique situation.

Transforming Closed Questions into Open Ones

Closed (Limited)	Open (Expansive)
Did the company consult you?	What has communication with the company been like over the years?
Is compensation the main issue?	What are the most important issues for you?
Are you willing to negotiate?	What would help you feel comfortable exploring options?
Do you trust the company?	What would the company need to do to build your confidence?

Caution: Question Overload

Rapid-fire questioning feels like interrogation. After asking a question, allow silence. Resist the urge to clarify, rephrase, or ask follow-ups immediately. Let speakers think and respond at their own pace.

The following figure illustrates how these different question types form a continuum, helping mediators choose the most appropriate approach depending on the stage of discussion and the kind of information they need to elicit.

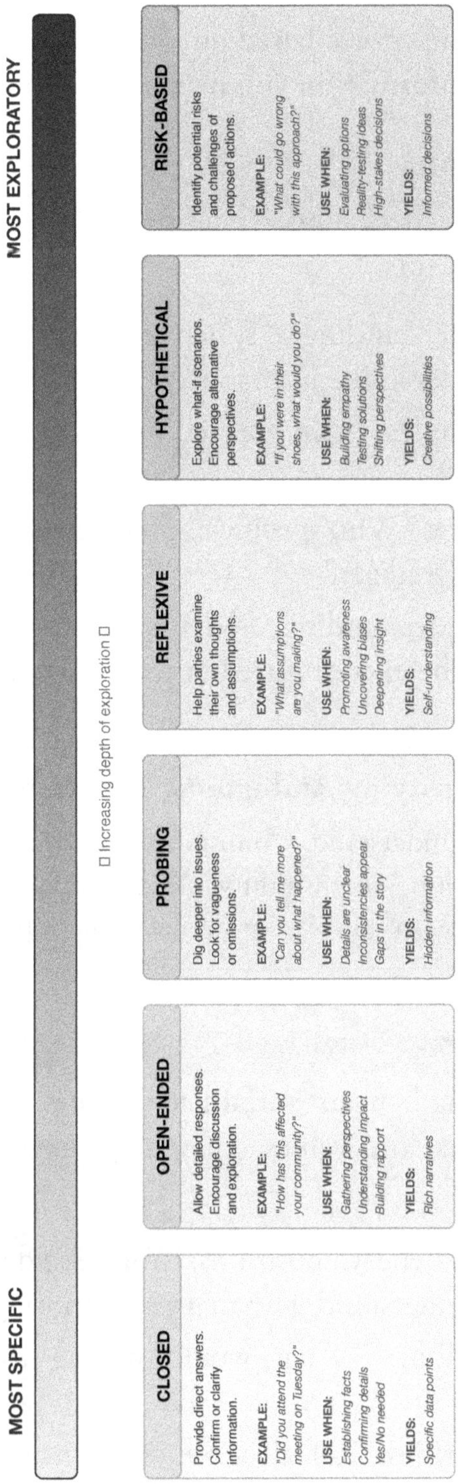

Figure 5: A visual representation of the continuum from open-ended to closed questions, showing when and how each type is most effective.

This continuum shows that there is no single right way to ask questions, but rather a deliberate choice based on where parties are in their understanding and what information you need at that moment.

Clarifying Questions

Clarifying questions check understanding, seek specificity, and resolve ambiguity. Use them to:

- Check your understanding: "When you say 'proper consultation,' what would that look like in practice?"
- Get specific examples: "Can you tell me about one specific example in detail?"
- Resolve ambiguity: "Who specifically was included in those meetings with community leaders?"
- Ensure shared understanding: "What specifically do each of you understand to have been committed in that 2019 meeting?"

> **Practical Tip: Clarifying Ambiguous Language**
>
> Never assume you understand. Common words can mean very different things: "compensation," "community," "consultation," "adequate," "reasonable," and "soon" all require clarification. When in doubt, ask.

Probing Questions

Probing questions dig beneath surface statements to explore underlying interests, motivations, and values. They help move conversations from positions to interests.

- Uncover interests beneath positions: "You've said you want the school built. Help me understand why that's so important."
- Explore motivations: "What would having that mean for your families?"
- Understand priorities: "Of all these concerns, which matters most right now?"
- Identify fears: "What are you most worried might happen?"

- Build cross-party understanding: "What do you think the company's main concerns are about your proposal?"

Sample Dialogue

Community: "We want $5 million in compensation."

Mediator: "Help me understand what that money would make possible for your community. What would you use it for?"

Community: "We need to rebuild the water system. Then, create a scholarship fund for children whose families lost their farms. And support for elders who can no longer work their land."

Notice how probing revealed specific interests (water infrastructure, education, elder care) that open possibilities beyond a fixed dollar amount.

Practical Tip: The Power of "What Else?"

After a party answers, simply ask "What else?" This open invitation often yields the most important information, which people may have been hesitant to volunteer initially.

Hypothetical and Future-Focused Questions

Hypothetical questions invite parties to consider possibilities without commitment. "Just hypothetically, if the company established a community development fund with local oversight rather than direct payments, what would you think?" This framing creates a sense of safety because parties aren't committing to anything.

Future-focused questions shift energy when parties are stuck in blame about the past. Ask: "What would a good relationship look like five years from now?" "If this conflict were resolved, what would be different in your daily life?" These questions tap into hopes rather than grievances, unlocking creativity and goodwill.

Reality-Testing Questions

Sometimes parties hold unrealistic expectations or fail to consider consequences. Reality-testing questions gently introduce pragmatism: "What happens if you can't reach an agreement here?" "How do you think the company would respond to that demand?" "What's the most likely outcome if this goes to court?" Private caucus sessions work best for this work. They allow parties to consider hard truths without losing face.

Closed Questions

Closed questions seek specific, often yes or no, answers. While overuse limits discussion, they have important applications:

- Confirming facts: "Was the agreement signed in March 2019?" When you need to verify specific information, closed questions get direct answers.
- Checking understanding: "So you're saying you were never formally notified about the expansion?" A closed check ensures you've understood correctly before proceeding.
- Getting commitment: "Are you willing to try this approach for a three-month trial period?" When moving toward agreement, closed questions clarify whether there is commitment.
- Narrowing options: "Would meeting on Tuesday or Thursday work better for you?" When decisions need to be made, closed questions help parties choose.
- Moving toward closure: "Can we agree that this point is now resolved?" Closed questions can confirm that progress has been made.

Questions to Avoid

Leading questions: "Don't you think the company's offer is reasonable?" These push toward a particular answer, compromising neutrality.

Multiple questions: "What happened, and why, and what did you do?" These overwhelm and confuse. Ask one question at a time.

Accusatory questions: "Why did you break the agreement?" These can assume guilt. Instead, try: "Help me understand what happened with that agreement."

Rhetorical questions: "How could anyone think that's fair?" These create an argument rather than seek information.

- "Why" questions: "Why did you do that?" These can feel accusatory and need to be used with caution and care, especially with resistant parties (see Chapter 14). Consider reframing: "What led to that decision?" or "Help me understand your thinking."

> **Caution: Interrogation Mode**
>
> Avoid rapid-fire questions that feel like cross-examination. Ask a question, wait for the full answer, acknowledge what you've heard, then ask a follow-up if needed. Effective mediation occurs when the pace feels like conversation rather than investigation.

4.4 Reframing

Reframing transforms inflammatory or positional statements into constructive, problem-solving language. The mediator preserves the essential meaning while removing blame, softening absolutes, or highlighting interests rather than positions. Reframing is also a powerful tool for breaking impasses (see Chapter 13) by shifting how parties perceive problems.

In conflict, people naturally communicate in ways that escalate rather than resolve disputes. They blame, accuse, exaggerate, and speak in absolutes. Left unchallenged, such statements harden positions and inflame the other party. By directly challenging them, the mediator can appear to take sides. Reframing offers a third path.

Effective reframing accomplishes several things simultaneously:

- Defuses inflammatory language: "They're poisoning our children" becomes "There are serious concerns about health impacts on children." The core concern is preserved while the accusatory edge is softened.
- Shifts from positions to interests: "We want them to shut down the mine" becomes "You need to see significant changes in how the mine operates." This identifies the underlying interest that might be addressed in multiple ways.

- Moves from past to future: "They destroyed our water supply" becomes "The water supply needs to be restored and protected going forward." Energy redirects from the unchangeable past to an actionable future.
- Reduces absolutism: "They never listen" becomes "There have been times when you've felt unheard." This creates space for nuance and movement.
- Makes concerns hearable: Sometimes one party's statement is so loaded that the other cannot hear the legitimate concern within it. Reframing expresses that concern in terms that the other party can engage with productively.

Key Concept: Timing Your Reframe

Reframe too early, and parties feel unheard. Reframe too late, and negative framing has already shaped the conversation. The optimal moment is after you have demonstrated understanding through paraphrasing but before the other party responds defensively.

Removing Blame While Preserving Concern

Strip out accusations while keeping the core issue:

Original Statement	Reframed Version
"The company lied to us and stole our land."	"You feel that commitments weren't honored and that the land transfer process wasn't fair."
"These people are just trying to extort money from us."	"You're concerned that the demands may exceed what's justified by actual impacts."
"They don't care about our children's health."	"There are serious concerns about health impacts, especially on children, and you need to see those concerns taken seriously."
"They're just greedy; they only care about profit."	"You're concerned that business priorities may be overriding community well-being."

Shifting from Position to Interest

Reframe specific demands to reveal underlying needs.

> **Sample Dialogue**
>
> *Community member: "We refuse to accept anything less than $10 million!"*
>
> *Mediator: "So addressing the harm your community has experienced is extremely important, and you need to be confident that any agreement actually makes a meaningful difference in people's lives."*
>
> *Company representative: "We will never agree to a community veto over our operations!"*
>
> *Mediator: "The company needs operational certainty, and you're concerned about how consultation processes might affect your ability to function effectively."*

Notice how the reframes acknowledge what each party cares about (meaningful remedy, operational certainty) without endorsing the specific position (dollar amount, veto). This opens space for exploring how to address interests without being locked into positions.

Softening Absolutes

Words like "always," "never," and "impossible" close down conversation. Soften them to create doors where walls exist:

Absolute Statement	Softened Version
"They never listen."	"There have been times when you've felt unheard."
"This is impossible."	"This seems very difficult given current constraints."
"They always break their promises."	"There have been commitments that weren't fulfilled."
"We will never trust them."	"Trust has been seriously damaged, and rebuilding it will take significant effort."
"That's completely unacceptable."	"There are serious concerns about that approach."

Reframing from Past to Future

When parties are stuck in blame about what happened, redirect toward what can happen.

Sample Dialogue

Community member: "They destroyed our sacred grove. We can never forgive that."

Mediator: "The loss of the sacred grove was a devastating harm that can't be undone. What would help your community honor that place and find a way forward from here?"

Company representative: "They blocked our trucks for three weeks. That cost us millions."

Mediator: "Those disruptions had a significant financial impact. Looking ahead, what would help ensure operations can continue smoothly while community concerns are being addressed?"

Practical Tip: Validating Your Reframe

After reframing, always check with the speaker: "Did I capture that correctly?" or "Is that what you're saying?" This ensures you haven't distorted their meaning and shows respect for their voice. If they correct you, incorporate their correction.

Caution: Reframing Should Not Sanitize

Reframing should clarify and de-escalate, not sanitize or minimize. Don't reframe away legitimate grievances or downplay real harm. A reframe that makes the speaker feel their concern has been diminished will backfire. The goal is constructive communication, not denial of genuine problems.

A matrix of examples showing how inflammatory, accusatory, or positional statements can be reframed into neutral, forward-looking language.

4.5 Summarizing

Summarizing involves concisely restating the key points that have emerged in the discussion. While paraphrasing responds to individual statements, summarizing pulls together multiple points across time into a coherent overview.

Summarizing serves multiple important functions:

- Confirms understanding: Demonstrates that the mediator has been listening and accurately grasps key issues. Parties recognize their concerns have been understood and become more willing to move forward.
- Creates shared reference: In complex disputes, parties have different understandings of where things stand. A summary creates a common picture visible to all.
- Organizes complexity: Discussions often jump between topics and revisit old ground. Summaries bring structure to chaos, organizing scattered points into coherent themes.
- Marks transitions: Summaries signal movement from one phase or topic to another, creating a clear process structure.
- Identifies common ground: Summaries can highlight areas of agreement that might otherwise be overlooked amid disagreements.
- Shows progress: When parties feel stuck, summarizing accomplishments can restore momentum.

Figure 6 demonstrates the range of summarizing techniques that help mediators capture key points and move discussions forward.

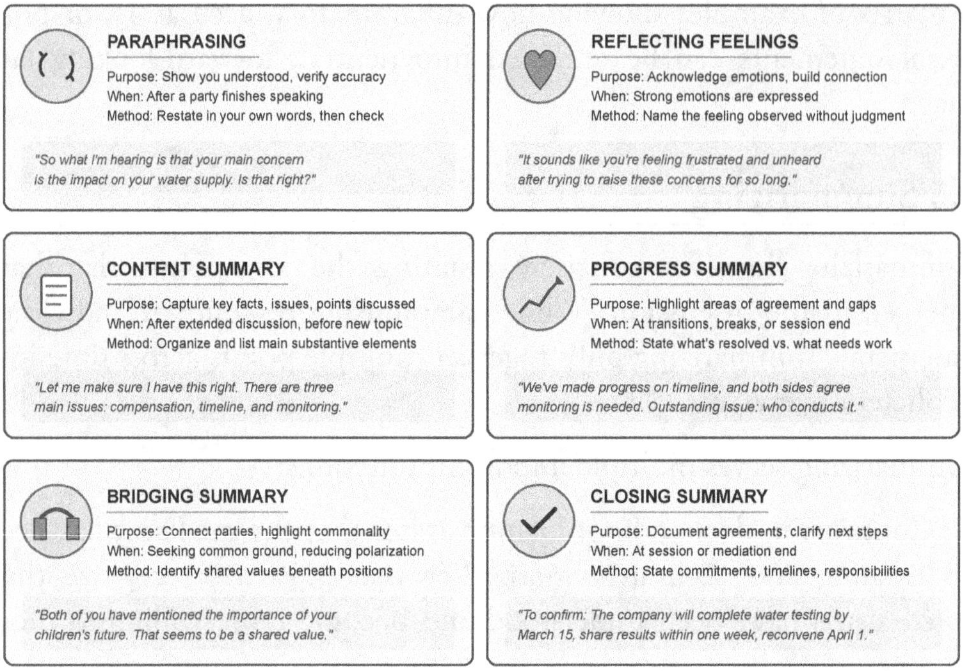

Figure 6: An overview of summarizing techniques that help mediators capture key points, check understanding, and move discussions forward.

These techniques are the bridge between listening and understanding, allowing you to demonstrate that you have truly heard what was said and checking whether your interpretation aligns with the speaker's intent.

When to Summarize

Strategic moments for summarizing include:

- After each party's opening statement, to show you've listened and create a starting point
- Before moving to a new agenda item, to close one topic before opening another
- When the discussion becomes confused or circular, to reset the conversation
- After generating options, before evaluation begins
- Before ending a session, to capture what's been accomplished and what remains

- When checking whether agreement exists, before assuming consensus
- When energy is flagging, to restore motivation by noting progress made

How to Summarize Effectively

A good summary is concise and captures essentials without repeating everything. In other words, distill, don't reiterate. Balanced summaries represent all parties fairly, giving appropriate weight to each perspective while using neutral language to avoid appearing as though you are taking sides. A good summary also needs to be effectively organized, grouping related points rather than listing them chronologically. At the same time, it clearly indicates issues that have been resolved and those that remain in dispute. Lastly, a good summary invites correction by ending with, "Did I capture that correctly?" or "What did I miss?"

Example: Comprehensive Summary

Mediator: "Let me pull together what I've heard this morning. The community's primary concerns center on three areas: water quality, which you believe has been affected by mining operations; employment, specifically that promises to hire locally haven't been kept; and feeling excluded from decisions that affect your lives. The company has acknowledged challenges with water management, though you believe the causes may be more complex. You've confirmed that local hiring hasn't met targets and explained some of the reasons why. Both sides have said they want to find a way forward and avoid continued conflict. Have I captured the key points fairly?"

> **Practical Tip: Writing Down Complex Summaries**
>
> For complex issues, write summaries down. Seeing key points on a flipchart or whiteboard helps everyone stay aligned, reduces misremembering, and provides a record. You can also share written summaries between sessions to confirm understanding.

4.6 Facilitation Techniques

Beyond specific communication skills, mediators need techniques for managing the overall flow and dynamics of sessions. Facilitation is the art of guiding group process so that it serves resolution. Good facilitation creates an environment where productive communication can happen.

Establishing and Enforcing Ground Rules

Ground rules create the container that makes safe, productive dialogue possible. Establishing them at the outset with party input and enforcing them consistently throughout helps ensure psychological safety. Common ground rules include:

- One person speaks at a time: This prevents chaos, ensures everyone can be heard, and slows conversation to create space for listening.
- Respectful language: No personal attacks, insults, or threatening language. Critique positions, not people.
- Speak for yourself: Use "I" statements rather than claiming to speak for all. This encourages ownership and allows for different perspectives.
- Listen to understand: Try to understand the other's perspective before responding.
- Confidentiality: What's said in mediation stays in mediation.
- Good faith participation: Come prepared to genuinely seek resolution, not to posture or score points.
- Breaks as needed: Anyone can request a break at any time without having to explain why.

When rules are violated, intervene promptly but without drama:

Mediator: "I need to pause us here. We agreed to avoid personal characterizations. I can hear that you're frustrated, but I'd ask that we focus on the issues rather than making judgments about each other. Can you tell me what you're concerned about in terms of the issues at hand?"

Beyond managing what is said, skilled mediators also manage what is not said. Silence is one of the most powerful yet underused tools in a mediator's repertoire. The following figure provides guidance on when and how to use silence deliberately as a facilitation technique.

Figure 7: Guidance on using silence as a deliberate facilitation tool, including when to allow pauses and how to read their meaning.

The strategic use of silence requires confidence and practice, but once mastered, it becomes one of the most effective tools for allowing parties to reflect and move toward their own insights.

Managing Balanced Participation

Effective facilitation ensures all voices are heard, not just the loudest or most powerful:

- Track who has and hasn't spoken. Some people need an explicit invitation to share.
- Explicitly invite quieter participants: "Maria, we haven't heard your perspective yet. What are your thoughts?"
- Use structured formats when needed: Round-robin sharing ensures everyone contributes.

- Limit dominant speakers tactfully: "Thank you, that's helpful. I want to make sure we hear other perspectives, too."
- Consider smaller breakouts: Some people speak more freely in groups of three than in groups of fifteen.
- Watch for internal dynamics: Notice if some defer to others, if younger people wait for elders, or if women are silent in mixed groups.

Caution: Over-Structuring Can Feel Controlling

Too much structure can feel controlling. If you find yourself constantly redirecting, interrupting, or managing the conversation, step back. Sometimes parties need space to engage directly with each other, even if the conversation becomes somewhat messy.

Managing Time and Agenda

Keep the process moving without rushing important discussions. You can do this by setting realistic expectations at the outset about time and goals, while building in buffers for unexpected issues. You may also consider using an agenda as a roadmap. Share it and get agreement, but hold it flexibly. Be sure to monitor progress. If one topic is consuming disproportionate time without resolution, decide whether to continue or move on, and don't be afraid to table issues when needed. Simply say, "Let's note where we are and come back to this with fresh perspectives." Checking in with both parties as the end of the session nears by saying, "We have about thirty minutes left. How might we use it?" On the same note, if you said you'd finish at 5:00, finish at 5:00, or explicitly renegotiate. Respecting time builds trust.

Using Breaks and Caucuses

Breaks serve multiple purposes:

Purpose	When to Use
Cooling down	When emotions are too high for productive discussion
Consultation	When parties need to confer with constituencies or advisors
Processing	After receiving difficult information or a surprising proposal
Relationship building	Sometimes, more progress happens during breaks when people interact as humans

Caucuses (private meetings between the mediator and one party) serve different purposes:

Purpose	Example
Exploring positions candidly	"Just between us, what do you really need from this?"
Reality testing	"What happens if you can't reach an agreement here?"
Coaching	"How might you present that proposal in a way they could hear?"
Venting	Letting a party express frustration in a safe space.
Generating ideas	"What if you proposed . . . ? How would that work?"

Caution: Transparency in Caucuses

Use caucuses transparently. Explain that you'll meet with each side separately and that you won't share anything without their permission. Spend roughly equal time with each side to maintain the appearance of impartiality.

Practical Tip: Strategic Use of Breaks

Call breaks not just when tensions are high, but also when momentum is building positively. A break after a breakthrough allows parties to absorb progress, consult privately, and return refreshed to build on the positive moment.

Using Visual Aids

Visual tools help organize and clarify complex discussions. Flipcharts, whiteboards, lists, tables, timelines, and diagrams all serve different purposes.

Visual Tool	Function
Flipcharts/whiteboards	Capture key points where everyone can see them
Lists	Track issues, options, concerns, and agreements
Tables	Compare options against criteria or party interests
Timelines	Map history or proposed implementation schedules
Diagrams	Show relationships between parties or processes

Writing things down creates a shared reference visible to all. It depersonalizes issues by putting them "out there" rather than leaving them owned by one person. Documentation prevents repetition, provides a record for later reference, engages visual learners, and slows the process in useful ways.

4.7 Building Rapport and Trust

Effective communication depends on building relationships. Parties who trust the mediator and feel a personal connection will engage more openly and give the process the benefit of the doubt when things get difficult.

Information flows more freely when people feel connected. Suggestions carry more weight when the mediator has earned trust. The mediator's rapport with each party can model the kind of relationship-building parties might eventually develop with one another. And when tensions rise or progress stalls, trust in the mediator keeps parties at the table.

Key Concept: Asymmetric Rapport

You may build a strong rapport with one party and struggle with another. This asymmetry is natural but dangerous. The party with a weaker rapport may perceive you as biased. Actively invest in relationship-building with the party you find it more difficult to connect with.

Small actions, such as those outlined below, accumulate to build a connection.

Practice	Why It Matters
Use names correctly	Learning and correctly pronouncing names conveys respect and attention
Show genuine interest	Ask about people's lives and concerns with authentic curiosity, not pro forma questions
Find common humanity	Natural points of connection remind everyone of their shared humanity
Be fully present	Give your full attention; presence communicates value
Follow through consistently	Keep every commitment, no matter how small; reliability builds trust
Be appropriately warm	Create an atmosphere of goodwill without being falsely friendly
Respect their expertise	Acknowledge that they understand their situation better than you do

Cultural Considerations

Rapport-building norms vary across cultures. Some cultures expect formal address and titles; others prefer informality. Some build rapport through extended conversation before business; others prefer getting straight to work. Gift-giving, tea-sharing, or meals together may be important in some contexts. Physical greeting norms and appropriate use of humor differ significantly. When uncertain, observe how people interact and adapt accordingly. When really unsure, ask.

Key Concept: Rapport Is Not Friendship

Rapport is not friendship. Maintain professional boundaries while being warm and human. The goal is trust and connection sufficient for productive work, not personal relationships. Be friendly without being a friend.

4.8 Integrating Communication Skills

In practice, these skills don't operate in isolation. At any given moment, a mediator might be actively listening while also noting emotional cues, formulating a clarifying question, considering how to reframe what's being said, and deciding when to summarize. With practice, this integration becomes fluid and intuitive.

Integrated Response Example

A community member says, "The company is destroying everything we've worked for. They promised jobs, but my sons can't get hired. They promised clean water, but look at the river now. They promised to consult us, but they never listen. Why should we believe anything they say now?"

The mediator's integrated response:

"I can hear how frustrated and betrayed you feel. It sounds like multiple commitments weren't kept, around jobs, water, and consultation, and that's deeply damaged your trust. Of all these concerns, which weighs most heavily right now?"

This single response demonstrates:

- Active listening through the accurate capture of the message
- Empathy through acknowledging feelings
- Strategic questioning through focusing on priorities

The skills in this chapter are foundational. They enable everything else in mediation. No clever process design can compensate for poor listening. No analytical framework helps if parties believe they have been ignored. Conversely, strong communication skills can salvage even the most difficult situations by creating moments of genuine understanding.

Continuing Your Development

Communication skills improve with deliberate practice. Below are some ways to continue practicing your listening and response skills.

Development Strategy	Description
Practice in daily life	Listen to friends, family, and colleagues with full attention. Practice paraphrasing and reflecting feelings in ordinary conversations.
Record and review	With appropriate permissions, record mediations and review them. Notice patterns and opportunities.
Seek feedback	Ask co-mediators, observers, or parties what helped and what didn't.
Role-play difficult scenarios	With colleagues, practice having someone play the role of a hostile party.
Study skilled practitioners	Watch mediators you admire and analyze what they do differently.
Keep a reflection journal	After sessions, write about what worked, what didn't, and what you'd do differently.
Pursue ongoing training	Attend workshops, take courses, and read about communication and mediation.

Practical Tip: Post-Session Self-Reflection

After each mediation, ask yourself: What questions opened things up? What did I miss? When did I listen well? When was I distracted or triggered? What would I do differently? This self-reflection is the fastest path to improvement.

4.9 Skill Progression Framework

Mediation skills develop through deliberate practice, reflection, and experience. This framework outlines three levels of competency for each core skill, helping practitioners assess their current abilities and identify areas for growth. Keep in mind, movement between levels is not strictly linear; mediators may demonstrate advanced capability in some areas while still developing others.

Key Concept: Skill Integration

Expert practice is not simply doing basic skills faster. It involves integrating multiple skills simultaneously, adapting fluidly to changing dynamics, and knowing when to deploy which approach. The expert mediator makes complex interventions look effortless because the underlying skills have become internalized.

BASIC	ADVANCED	EXPERT
Active Listening		
Maintains eye contact and avoids interrupting. Can paraphrase content accurately. Demonstrates basic nonverbal attentiveness.	Reflects both content and emotion accurately. Notices inconsistencies between verbal and nonverbal communication. Uses silence strategically.	Listens at multiple levels simultaneously. Models listening that transforms how parties hear each other. Identifies underlying interests through patterns.
Empathy and Emotional Intelligence		
Acknowledges emotions when expressed directly. Remains calm when parties become upset. Uses basic validation statements ("I can see this is difficult").	Reads emotional undercurrents before they surface. Names emotions accurately without triggering defensiveness. Manages own emotional responses to maintain neutrality. Recognizes when emotion indicates deeper interests.	Creates conditions for emotional expression that advance understanding. Facilitates empathy between parties. Holds space for intense emotion without rushing resolution. Recognizes collective and intergenerational trauma patterns.

BASIC	ADVANCED	EXPERT
Effective Questioning		
Uses open-ended questions to gather information. Avoids leading questions. Asks clarifying questions when confused. Distinguishes between open and closed question types.	Sequences questions strategically to move from positions to interests. Uses hypothetical questions to test possibilities. Asks reflexive questions that promote insight. Times questions for maximum impact.	Crafts questions that shift paradigms and create breakthroughs. Uses questions to help parties discover their own solutions. Adapts questioning style to cultural context. Knows when questions help and when silence serves better.
Reframing		
Removes inflammatory language while preserving meaning. Converts accusations into concerns. States positions in neutral terms. Separates people from problems.	Reframes positions as interests. Identifies common ground within opposing statements. Uses reframing to shift from past blame to future focus. Finds shared values beneath conflicting positions.	Creates narrative shifts that transform how parties understand the conflict. Reframes issues in ways that reveal new solution possibilities. Helps parties reframe their own stories. Maintains cultural authenticity while enabling new perspectives.
Summarizing		
Accurately restates key points after each party speaks. Checks for confirmation of accuracy. Uses summaries to transition between topics. Captures main issues without excessive detail.	Creates joint narratives from divergent perspectives. Uses summaries strategically to highlight progress and common ground. Summarizes in ways that set up productive next steps. Tracks complex multi-issue discussions accurately.	Crafts summaries that are themselves interventions, shifting understanding. Integrates content, emotion, and process in summaries. Uses summaries to help parties hear themselves differently. Creates summaries that parties adopt as their shared understanding.

BASIC	ADVANCED	EXPERT
Facilitation and Process Management		
Establishes and enforces ground rules. Manages speaking turns fairly. Knows when to call breaks. Follows a structured process from opening to closure.	Adapts process to emerging needs while maintaining structure. Uses caucuses strategically. Manages multiple agenda items and tracks agreements. Handles disruptions without losing momentum.	Designs processes tailored to specific conflict dynamics and cultural contexts. Manages complex multi-party, multi-issue mediations. Knows when to abandon structure and when structure is essential. Makes the process invisible so parties focus on the substance.
Building Rapport and Trust		
Demonstrates warmth and respect. Uses names appropriately. Maintains confidentiality. Treats all parties with equal consideration. Explains the process clearly.	Builds trust with skeptical or hostile parties. Adapts communication style to different personalities. Maintains trust when delivering difficult messages. Recovers when trust is damaged.	Builds trust across severe power asymmetries and deep historical mistrust. Uses presence to create safety without conscious effort. Facilitates trust-building between parties. Maintains credibility in politically charged environments.

4.10 Self-Assessment Guide

Use these reflection questions to assess your current level in each skill area:

Basic Level Indicators

Can you answer "yes" to these questions?

Question
Can you consistently apply the technique when consciously focused on it?
Do you recognize when you have failed to use the skill after the fact?

Question
Can you explain the technique and its purpose to others?
Do you need to think deliberately before applying the skill?

Advanced Level Indicators

Question
Can you adapt the technique to different situations and personalities?
Do you notice in real-time when the skill is needed?
Can you combine this skill with others fluidly?
Do you recognize the limitations and risks of the technique?

Expert Level Indicators

Question
Does the skill feel natural and effortless in most situations?
Can you innovate and create new applications of the underlying principles?
Do you intuitively know when to use the skill and when to set it aside?
Can you effectively teach and mentor others in this skill?

4.11 Development Strategies by Level

Moving from Basic to Advanced

Strategy	Description
Practice with feedback	Use role-plays with observers who provide specific feedback on technique
Record and review	With permission, record sessions and analyze your interventions
Focus on one skill	Select one skill area per month for concentrated development

Strategy	Description
Seek diverse cases	Expose yourself to different conflict types and cultural contexts
Find a mentor	Work with an experienced mediator who can observe and guide your practice

Moving from Advanced to Expert

Strategy	Description
Take on complex cases	Seek mediations that challenge your current abilities
Study underlying theory	Deepen understanding of psychology, conflict theory, and cultural dynamics
Teach others	Train others to clarify and deepen your own understanding
Cross-train	Learn from related disciplines such as therapy, negotiation, and facilitation
Reflect systematically	Maintain a practice journal; analyze patterns across cases
Embrace uncertainty	Expert practice means being comfortable with not knowing and adapting in real-time

Practical Tip: Deliberate Practice for Skill Growth

Moving from basic to advanced requires deliberate practice: identifying specific skills to develop, seeking feedback, reflecting on performance, and incrementally increasing difficulty. Moving from advanced to expert requires extensive experience across diverse situations, mentorship from experts, and deep reflection on underlying principles. Most mediators reach an advanced level in some skills while remaining basic in others. Honest self-assessment enables targeted development.

5.

UNDERSTANDING CONFLICT DYNAMICS AND ESCALATION

While communication skills equip mediators to facilitate dialogue (see Chapter 4), those skills require grounding in a deep understanding of conflict dynamics. Grasping how conflicts arise, evolve, and escalate proves essential. Company-community disputes often have deep roots and can intensify over time if not addressed. This chapter provides a framework for understanding conflict dynamics, enabling diagnosing situations accurately, choosing interventions, and navigating conflict dynamics.

Conflict analysis differs fundamentally from academic theory. When a mediator walks into a room where a community delegation is confronting company representatives after years of broken promises and environmental damage, theoretical knowledge must translate into practical insight: What is really driving this conflict? Why has it escalated to this point? What interventions might de-escalate tensions? What psychological dynamics are at play? These answers shape every mediation decision.

Key Concept: Conflict Analysis as Ongoing Practice

Conflict analysis is not a one-time exercise but an ongoing practice. Skilled mediators continuously observe, reflect, and adjust based on evolving understanding of conflict dynamics. Hold your initial analysis tentatively and remain open to new information throughout the mediation process.

5.1 The Three Dimensions of Conflict

Every conflict operates on three interconnected dimensions: substance, emotion, and process. Understanding all three is essential for effective intervention. Mediators who focus only on the substantive issues while ignoring emotions will find their carefully crafted agreements undermined by unaddressed resentment. Those who attend only to emotions without addressing legitimate concerns will provide comfort without resolution. And even when substance and emotion receive attention, a flawed process can delegitimize the outcome.

The Substantive Dimension

Substantive issues focus on what the conflict is truly about at its most concrete level: the disputed resources, the contested decisions, the incompatible interests. In company-community disputes, substantive issues typically include:

- **Resource allocation:** Who gets access to land, water, minerals, or other resources? How are benefits distributed? These tangible questions form the core of the visible dispute.
- **Compensation and remediation:** What compensation should parties provide for damages? How should environmental harm be repaired? Who should receive what, and how much?
- **Operational impacts:** How do company activities affect daily life? Issues like noise, dust, traffic, and work schedules create friction when company operations disrupt community routines.
- **Employment and economic opportunity:** What local jobs will the company create? What wages will be paid? Will local businesses benefit from procurement?
- **Environmental protection:** How will the company protect air, water, and soil quality? What happens when environmental harm occurs?

Parties typically articulate substantive issues first when discussing the conflict. However, they rarely tell the complete story. Focusing exclusively on substantive issues leads to bargaining over positions rather than understanding underlying needs.

Practical Tip: Probing Beneath Surface Demands

When parties present a substantive demand, always probe deeper. Ask: "What would that accomplish for you?" or "Why is that important?" The answer reveals emotional or process concerns that the substantive demand only partially addresses.

The Emotional Dimension

Emotional dimensions include the feelings, relationships, and psychological experiences entangled in conflict. Emotions are not peripheral to "real" issues. Emotions are themselves central issues parties must address for meaningful and lasting resolution.

In company-community conflicts, common emotional dynamics include:

- **Anger and resentment:** Communities carry deep anger about past harms, broken promises, or perceived disrespect. This anger accumulates over years and erupts unpredictably when triggered by new incidents.
- **Fear and anxiety:** Both parties operate from fear. Communities fear for their livelihoods, health, cultural survival, or displacement. Companies fear for project viability, reputation, or employee safety.
- **Grief and loss:** When communities have lost land, traditional practices, clean water, or community members to accidents or illness, grief underlies their engagement. This grief deserves acknowledgment, not dismissal.
- **Humiliation and dignity:** Feeling disrespected, ignored, or treated as obstacles rather than people creates wounds that no compensation package can heal. Dignity is a fundamental human need.
- **Betrayal and mistrust:** Broken promises, whether real or perceived, create a sense of betrayal that colors all subsequent interactions. Once parties break trust, they view every company action with suspicion.
- **Hope and disappointment:** Initial hopes for partnership and mutual benefit transform into cynicism and hostility when betrayed. Parties resist new overtures because they have dashed previous hopes.

Example: Emotional Undercurrents

In a mining dispute in West Africa, community representatives focused their formal complaints on water contamination. Yet in private conversations, what emerged most strongly was their sense of humiliation. They spoke of company executives arriving in helicopters, never stopping to greet community elders, and treating the village as if it did not exist. The water issue was real, but resolution required addressing the dignity wound as much as the technical problem.

The Process Dimension

Process dimensions shape how participants make decisions, communicate, and navigate disputes. Process issues are often invisible to those focused on substance, but they profoundly shape whether agreements feel legitimate and sustainable.

Process issues in company-community conflicts include:

- **Inclusion and participation:** Who is at the table? Whose voice counts? Communities may feel that decisions affecting them are made without their meaningful input. Even good outcomes feel imposed if the process excludes affected parties.
- **Information access:** Does the community have access to relevant information? Asymmetric information, where the company holds technical data that the community cannot access or understand, creates fundamental unfairness.
- **Communication channels:** How do parties communicate? Formal letters, community meetings, direct dialogue, media statements, and protests all represent different process choices with different implications.
- **Decision-making authority:** Who has the power to make commitments? Community frustration often grows when they negotiate with company representatives who lack the authority to agree to anything meaningful.
- **Implementation and follow-through:** How are agreements implemented? How is compliance monitored? Past implementation failures shape current process expectations.

Key Concept: Process Legitimacy

People care about process even when outcomes are unfavorable. Research consistently shows that parties accept adverse outcomes more readily when they believe the process was fair. Conversely, even favorable outcomes are seen as hollow when the process felt manipulated or exclusionary.

Interconnecting the Three Dimensions

These three dimensions continuously interact. Process failures generate emotional responses. Emotional states shape how parties receive substantive offers. Substantive disputes trigger process conflicts about how to resolve them. Attend to all three.

Example: Interconnected Dimensions

A company offers what it considers generous compensation for land acquisition (substantive). The community rejects it angrily. Why? The offer was announced publicly before consulting community leaders (process), making elders feel bypassed and disrespected (emotional). The substantive offer might have been acceptable, even welcomed, if delivered through an appropriate process that honored community authority.

Visualizing these three dimensions as an integrated system helps mediators assess which dimension needs attention in a given moment. The following figure shows how the three dimensions form a dynamic triangle, where attention to all three is necessary for lasting resolution.

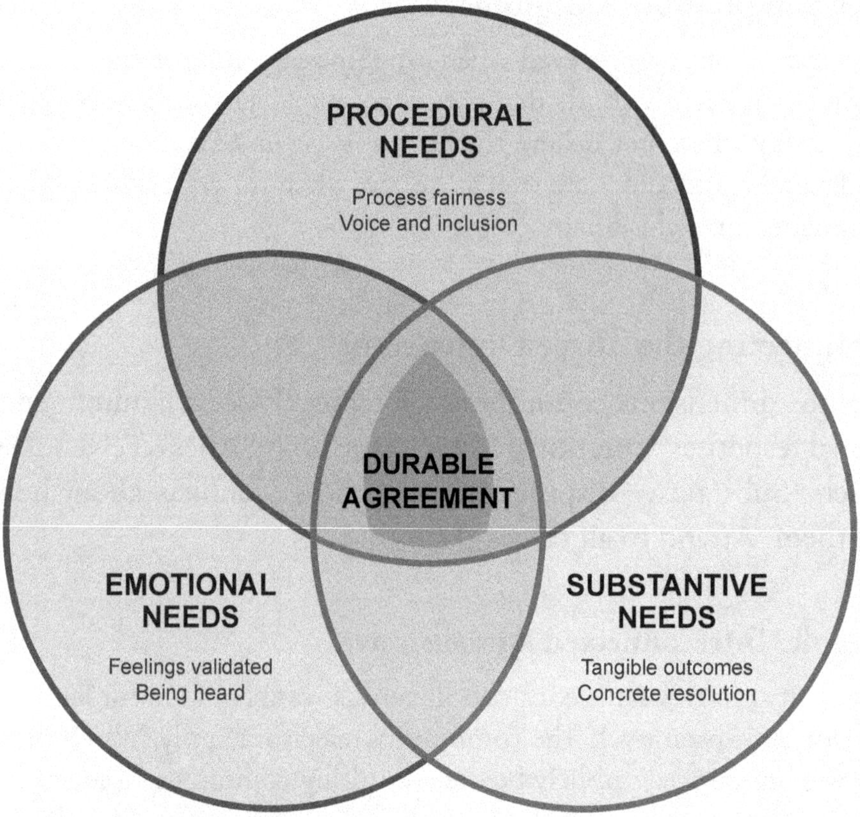

Figure 8: A model illustrating the three dimensions of conflict satisfaction: substantive (tangible outcomes), procedural (fair process), and psychological (recognition and respect).

When designing interventions in conflict, assess whether parties are satisfied with the substance of discussions, feel the process has been fair, and believe their concerns have been genuinely heard, as imbalance in any dimension creates instability.

Practical Tip: Dimension Diagnosis

When mediation stalls, ask yourself which dimension is blocking progress. Substantive impasse may require new options (see Chapter 13). Emotional blockage may need acknowledgment. Process concerns may require structural changes. Matching your intervention to the actual obstacle increases its effectiveness.

5.2 Root Causes of Company-Community Conflicts

Rather than erupting from single incidents, company-community conflicts grow from accumulated causes. They typically grow from underlying conditions that create vulnerability to conflict, with specific incidents serving as triggers that ignite accumulated grievances. Root cause analysis enables addressing fundamentals, not just symptoms. The following figure organizes the most common grievance categories that surface in company-community disputes, providing mediators with a diagnostic lens for identifying which root causes may be driving a particular conflict.

Figure 9 organizes common grievance categories that surface in company-community disputes, providing diagnostic lens for identifying root causes.

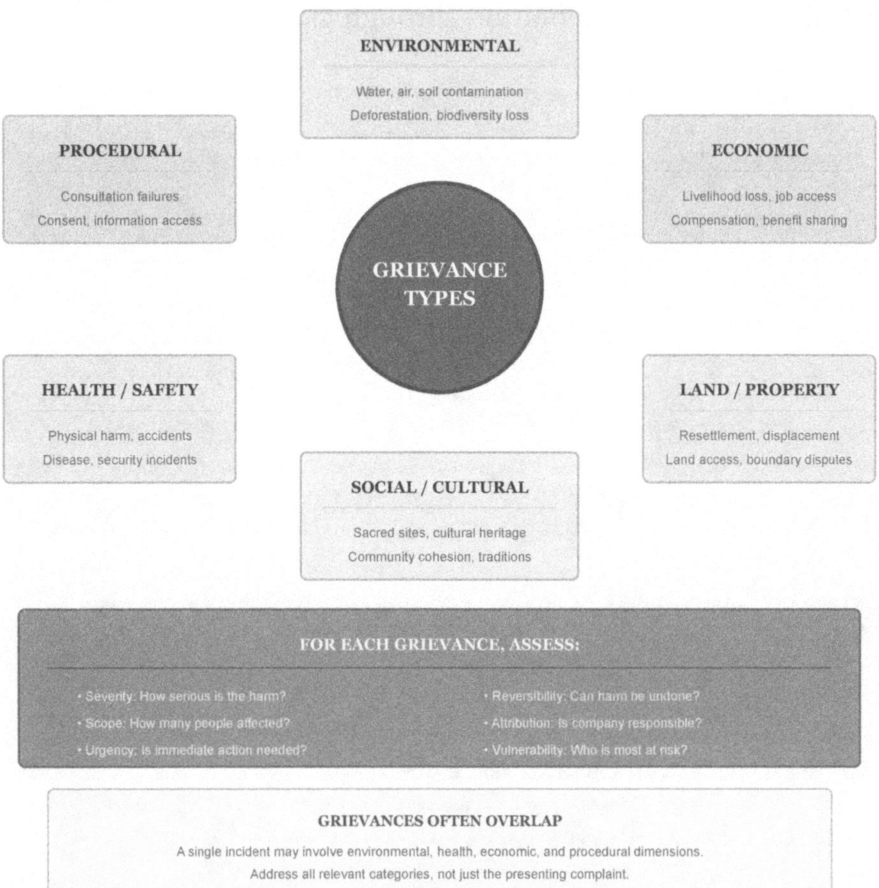

Figure 9: A classification of common grievance categories in company-community disputes, organized by type and frequency of occurrence.

Rather than treating grievances as isolated complaints, this categorization helps mediators understand the systemic roots of discontent and identify which types require different types of resolution approaches.

Resource Competition and Scarcity

Competition over limited resources lies at the heart of many company-community conflicts. These conflicts shift in nature as projects move through their lifecycle, from exploration through construction, operation, and eventual closure. The following figure maps the typical conflicts that emerge at each stage, helping mediators anticipate which grievances are most likely to surface depending on where a project stands.

Figure 10 maps the typical conflicts that emerge at each phase of the mining lifecycle, from exploration through closure.

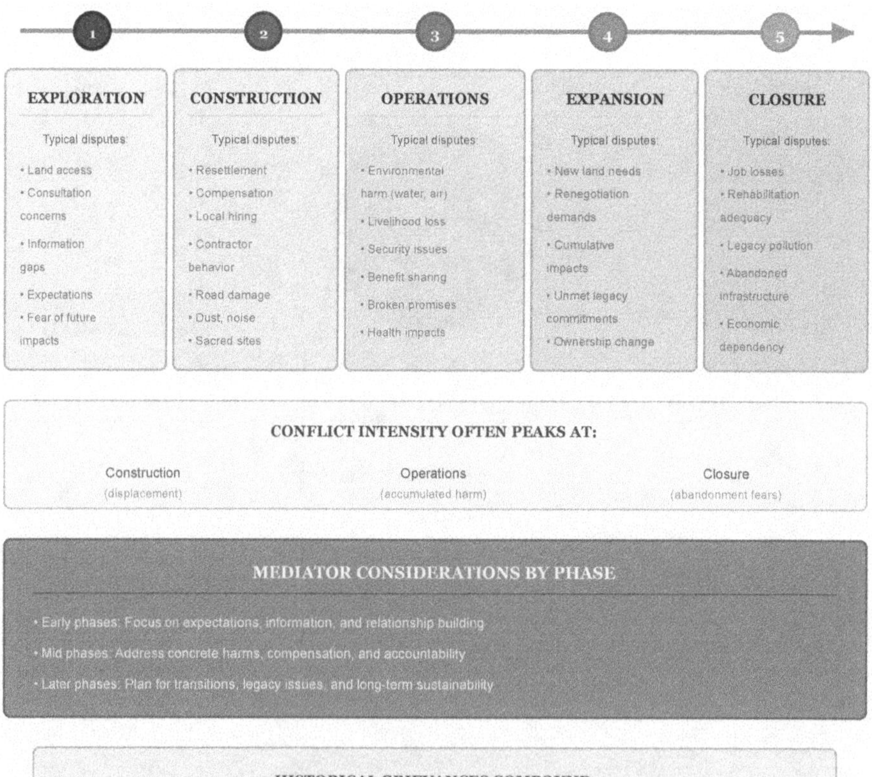

Figure 10: A mapping of typical conflicts that emerge at each phase of the mining lifecycle, from exploration and construction through to operation and closure.

Conflicts that appear identical in company-community disputes often have very different drivers depending on when they emerge, which is why timeline awareness is essential for appropriate intervention design.

When company operations affect resources that communities depend upon, conflict is almost inevitable.

- **Land displacement:** Mining, infrastructure, and energy projects often require land that communities live on, farm, or use for grazing. Displacement strikes at the fundamental human need for shelter, livelihood, and belonging. Even when relocation is handled carefully, the forced disconnection from ancestral land creates lasting grievance.
- **Water impacts:** Operations that affect water quality or quantity create existential threats. Communities that can no longer drink their water, irrigate their crops, or fish in their rivers face survival-level impacts that generate intense conflict.
- **Environmental degradation:** Air pollution, noise, dust, deforestation, and biodiversity loss diminish the quality of life and undermine traditional livelihoods. These impacts may be invisible in company reports but are experienced daily by affected communities.
- **Livelihood disruption:** Even without formal displacement, company operations may disrupt traditional livelihoods, such as when fishing grounds are affected by runoff, forests are cleared for access roads, or tourism potential is diminished by industrial presence.

Practical Tip: Uncovering Hidden Resource Impacts

When assessing resource conflicts, look beyond official company boundaries. Environmental and social impacts extend far beyond the project footprint. Communities experiencing these impacts have no formal standing in grievance mechanisms, creating significant frustration.

Broken Promises and Unmet Expectations

Perhaps no single factor generates more conflict than the gap between what communities expected and what they experienced. This gap may result from explicit broken promises, implicit misunderstandings, or the natural evolution of expectations over time.

- **Explicit commitments:** Companies often make specific promises during project approval processes, such as jobs, infrastructure, compensation, and environmental protection. When these promises are not kept, whether due to changed circumstances, different interpretations, or outright neglect, communities feel betrayed.
- **Employment expectations:** Companies typically promise job creation most prominently. When local hiring falls short, or when jobs prove temporary, low-skilled, or poorly paid, disappointment can be intense.
- **Infrastructure promises:** Commitments to build or improve roads, schools, clinics, or water systems may be delayed, scaled back, or abandoned. Partially built schools sitting empty become powerful symbols of broken faith.
- **Compensation disputes:** Disagreements over compensation amounts, eligibility, timing, or form generate conflict. Communities often feel that compensation was calculated unfairly, delivered late, or distributed to the wrong recipients.
- **Benefit-sharing gaps:** When communities see wealth extracted from their land while their own conditions remain unchanged or worsen, grievance is inevitable regardless of what was formally promised.

Example: Accumulated Broken Promises

In the Guinea mining case, which was resolved in 2024 after mediation, the community had accumulated grievances for years before mediation began. Initial promises of employment had not materialized as expected. Infrastructure improvements had been delayed repeatedly. Consultation processes had felt perfunctory rather than genuine. By the time formal mediation began, the community's list of unmet promises was long, and their trust was nearly exhausted. Resolution required addressing this entire history, not just current issues.

Communication Failures and Information Asymmetry

Conflict flourishes when communication breaks down. When information stops flowing, rumors fill the vacuum. When explanations are absent, assumptions take over. The resulting misunderstandings and suspicions compound underlying tensions.

- **Inadequate consultation:** Legal requirements for community consultation are often met minimally. Meetings are held, but at inconvenient times or locations. Information is provided, but technical language prevents communities from accessing it. Questions are heard, but not answered.
- **One-way communication:** Companies may issue statements without creating genuine dialogue. Communities hear about decisions after they are made, never feeling their input was sought or valued.
- **Language barriers:** When companies operate in communities speaking different languages, communication challenges multiply. Even with translation, technical concepts may not come across meaningfully.
- **Technical complexity:** Environmental impact assessments, financial projections, and engineering plans may be incomprehensible to communities without technical training. This creates information asymmetry that communities experience as disempowering.
- **Rumor and misinformation:** In information vacuums, rumors spread. Communities may assume the worst about the company's intentions because accurate information is unavailable. Companies may similarly misunderstand community concerns.

Caution: Information Asymmetry as a Power Tool

Information asymmetry is not neutral. When one party holds information that the other cannot access or understand, the power imbalance increases. Mediators should actively work to level information playing fields. One potential way to do this is to bring in neutral experts who can translate technical information for community understanding.

Power Imbalances

Power asymmetries between multinational corporations and rural communities shape every aspect of their relationship (see Chapter 12 for comprehensive strategies on managing power asymmetries). This imbalance manifests in multiple forms:

- **Economic power:** Companies command resources that dwarf community budgets. They can hire lawyers, consultants, and public relations firms that communities cannot afford. They can outlast communities in prolonged disputes simply by having deeper pockets.
- **Political access:** Companies often have relationships with government officials at levels communities cannot reach. They may influence regulatory decisions, enforcement priorities, and dispute-resolution processes.
- **Information power:** Technical expertise, legal knowledge, and data access give companies advantages in any negotiation or dispute. They can shape narratives, challenge community claims with technical arguments, and control what information becomes public.
- **Social power:** Companies may command respect from media, government, and international institutions in ways that marginalized communities do not. Their version of events may be presumed credible while community claims face skepticism.

Power imbalance does not mean communities are powerless. Communities can mobilize collective action, access media attention, invoke international norms, and impose costs through protest or legal action. But the asymmetry remains fundamental.

Government as Triple Actor: Regulator, Revenue Source, Political Player

In mining disputes, the government rarely occupies a simple role. It simultaneously functions as regulator (responsible for environmental and social standards), revenue beneficiary (dependent on mining taxes, royalties, and license fees), and political actor (responsive to both corporate lobbying and community pressure). This triple role creates fundamental conflicts of interest that mediators must understand and account for. A government that earns significant revenue from a mining operation has a financial incentive to ensure the mine continues operating, which may conflict with its regulatory obligation to enforce environmental standards or protect community rights. A governor who approved the mining concession has a political interest in defending that decision, even when evidence of harm mounts.

Assess carefully which governmental role is present at the table. Does the government representative have both authority and genuine inclination to remain neutral, or does participation risk tilting toward the company? In some cases, government involvement is essential, for example, when regulatory changes are needed to implement an agreement. In other cases, government participation may need to be limited to observer status, with specific issues referred to government through a structured process rather than allowing government actors to influence the direct negotiation between company and community.

Caution: When Government Is Not a Neutral Party

Be alert to signs that government actors are not functioning as neutral parties in the mediation. Warning indicators include: government officials discouraging the community from pursuing legal remedies or international mechanisms; government framing community resistance as a threat to "development" or "national interest"; government security forces being deployed to protect company operations rather than community safety; government officials receiving hospitality or benefits from the mining company; regulatory agencies failing to enforce environmental standards despite documented violations; and government mediators who have been appointed without community input or consent. When these dynamics are present, the mediator may need to address government bias directly or recommend that an independent mediator replace a government-appointed one.

Cultural and Value Clashes

Conflicts often reflect deeper clashes between worldviews, values, and ways of life. Cultural frameworks vary dramatically: reasonable from one perspective may appear incomprehensible or offensive from another.

- **Economic vs. traditional values:** Companies typically operate within market logic that measures value in monetary terms. Communities may hold values that resist monetization: sacred sites have no price, ancestral connections cannot be compensated for, and ways of life are not fungible.
- **Time horizons:** Corporate planning typically operates on quarterly or annual cycles. Community relationships with land and place may span generations. What seems like a temporary project disruption to a company may represent a permanent loss to a community.
- **Decision-making norms:** Corporate decision-making may be hierarchical and centralized. Community decision-making may be consensus-based and distributed. Each may find the other's approach illegitimate or inefficient.
- **Progress narratives:** Companies often frame their presence as bringing development and progress. Communities may experience the same presence as disruption, destruction, or dispossession. Neither framing is necessarily wrong, but they lead to very different evaluations.

Example: Cultural Clash

A mining company proposed relocating a community to new housing with modern amenities: electricity, running water, and paved roads. Company executives could not understand the community's resistance. From the community's perspective, the new site lacked the sacred groves where their ancestors were honored, the river where their children learned to swim, and the informal social spaces where community life happened. The houses were better by every measurable standard, but the place was wrong.

Historical Context and Colonial Legacy

Current conflicts occur within historical contexts that shape how parties interpret events and relate to each other. In many regions, extractive industry conflicts resonate with colonial histories of resource extraction that yielded no local benefit.

- **Colonial extraction patterns:** For communities whose lands were exploited under colonial rule, new extractive projects may feel like a continuation of the same dynamic: outsiders taking resources while locals bear the costs.
- **Historical dispossession:** Communities that lost land to previous projects may approach new ones with heightened suspicion, having learned that promises are not kept.
- **Generational trauma:** Past violence, displacement, or exploitation may create trauma that current generations inherit, shaping their responses to perceived threats.
- **Systemic distrust:** Repeated negative experiences with government, companies, or external actors may produce generalized distrust that makes any engagement difficult.

Key Concept: Systemic Causes

Some conflict causes lie beyond what individual parties can change, such as government policies, market forces, or historical patterns. Acknowledge these systemic factors explicitly. This validates frustrations that cannot be fully resolved in mediation while focusing energy on what can be addressed.

Caution: Surface vs. Root Issues

Parties often present surface issues (compensation amounts, specific incidents) while deeper causes (loss of dignity, historical betrayal, fear of the future) remain unspoken. An agreement that addresses only surface issues may not hold. Listen for hints of deeper concerns beneath the stated positions.

Key Concept: Historical Awareness

Mediators must understand that they are not working with blank slates. Parties bring histories that shape their responses. What seems like an overreaction to a current incident may be entirely proportional when viewed against accumulated historical experience.

5.3 Psychological Dynamics in Conflict

Beyond rational economics, conflicts engage fundamental human needs, cognitive biases, and psychological patterns. They are deeply psychological experiences that engage fundamental human needs, trigger cognitive biases, and shape behavior in predictable but often counterproductive ways. Understanding these psychological dynamics helps mediators anticipate parties' behavior and design interventions that address both psychological and substantive needs.

Practical Tip: Naming the Dynamic

Sometimes simply naming a psychological pattern can help parties step back from it. "I notice we might be in a cycle where each concession is seen as a weakness. What if we tried viewing offers as problem-solving rather than a surrender?" Making dynamics visible can reduce their power.

Fundamental Human Needs in Conflict

Conflict often intensifies when fundamental human needs are threatened. These needs operate below the level of expressed positions but powerfully shape what parties require for resolution:

- **Identity:** People need to maintain a coherent sense of who they are. When conflict threatens identity, whether individual or collective, responses intensify. A community whose identity is tied to traditional practices will resist changes that threaten those practices far more intensely than economic analysis would predict.

- **Security:** Both physical security and psychological security matter. Communities may feel physically unsafe due to company operations or security forces. They may feel psychologically unsafe when their future is uncertain.
- **Recognition:** People need to be seen, acknowledged, and treated as mattering. Conflicts often escalate not because of what was done, but because affected parties feel invisible or insignificant to those who make decisions.
- **Autonomy:** People need control over their own lives. This need is fundamental. When people feel that decisions are made about them without their input, they resist, regardless of whether the decisions are good or bad.
- **Fairness:** People have a deep need for fair treatment. Perceived unfairness triggers emotional responses that override rational calculation. Parties will reject favorable outcomes if they feel the process was unfair.
- **Meaning:** People need to understand why things happen. Unexplained events or decisions create anxiety and invite worst-case interpretations. Providing meaning, even for negative events, helps people cope.

Practical Tip: Decoding Disproportionate Reactions

When a party's response seems disproportionate to the substantive issue at stake, ask yourself which fundamental need might be threatened. Address the underlying need, and the substantive issue often becomes more manageable.

Cognitive Biases in Conflict

Human cognition is subject to systematic biases that intensify and prolong conflicts. Awareness of these biases helps mediators understand party behavior and design interventions that account for predictable distortions:

- **Confirmation bias:** People preferentially notice and remember information that confirms existing beliefs. In conflict, each party selectively attends to evidence supporting their view while dismissing contradictory information. Once parties have decided that the other side is untrustworthy, they will find evidence of it everywhere.

- **Attribution error:** People attribute others' negative behavior to character while attributing their own negative behavior to circumstances. The community sees company decisions as evidence of greed or callousness. The company sees community protests as irrational or manipulated. Neither recognizes the situational pressures driving the other's behavior.
- **Loss aversion:** People feel losses more intensely than equivalent gains. This means parties will fight harder to avoid losing what they have than to acquire something new. Framing proposals as preserving what parties already have rather than as gaining something novel can increase acceptance.
- **Anchoring:** Initial numbers or positions anchor subsequent judgments. The first compensation figure mentioned tends to define the range of discussion, regardless of its appropriateness. Mediators should be thoughtful about when and how numbers are introduced.
- **Reactive devaluation:** Proposals from adversaries are automatically devalued simply because of their source. The same offer might be accepted if proposed by a neutral party, but rejected if proposed by the opponent. Mediators can sometimes help by suggesting ideas rather than having parties propose them directly.
- **Overconfidence:** People typically overestimate the strength of their position and underestimate the other side's case. This leads parties to expect favorable outcomes from litigation or escalation when the reality may be much more uncertain.

Emotional Escalation Dynamics

Emotional escalation follows predictable patterns. Understanding these patterns helps mediators intervene before emotions spiral beyond management:

- **Anger spirals:** Anger expressed by one party triggers defensive anger in the other. Each round of angry exchange intensifies the next. What begins as frustration can escalate to rage. Intervening early in anger spirals is far easier than waiting for full escalation.

- **Fear contagion:** Fear spreads within groups and between them. When one community member expresses fear, others become afraid. When communities mobilize in fear, companies respond with their own fear-based actions (increased security, defensive communications), which confirms community fears.
- **Humiliation cycles:** Humiliation demands a response. When one party humiliates another, whether intentionally or not, the humiliated party must restore dignity. This often means humiliating the other in return, creating an escalating cycle.
- **Grief that becomes grievance:** Unacknowledged grief transforms into grievance. When losses are not mourned, when suffering is not witnessed, grief hardens into resentment that seeks targets. Creating space for acknowledgment can prevent this transformation.

Caution: Attribution Error

Parties typically attribute their own behavior to circumstances and others' behavior to character. The company sees its delay as unavoidable logistics. The community sees it as deliberate disrespect. Help both sides consider alternative explanations before assuming bad intent.

Example: Emotional Escalation

A community leader waited for two hours for a meeting with company executives who were running late from another engagement. The executives, upon arrival, moved quickly to business without acknowledging the wait. From their perspective, this was efficient. For the community leader, it was humiliating. He experienced being shown that his time did not matter, that he was not important enough to warrant an apology. His subsequent negotiating posture was shaped more by this humiliation than by the substantive issues on the agenda. The executives never understood why talks went badly.

Group Dynamics and Social Identity

Conflicts between communities and companies are fundamentally group conflicts, with all the dynamics that group membership introduces:

In-group/out-group thinking: Group membership creates boundaries. "We" think, feel, and act differently from "them." These boundaries can become rigid in conflict, making it harder to see shared humanity or common interests.

A related pattern is group polarization: Groups tend toward more extreme positions than individuals. When community members deliberate among themselves, initial moderate positions often shift toward extremes. The same occurs within company teams. This means the individuals you meet may hold more moderate views than they express on behalf of their group.

Representative accountability compounds this: Individuals negotiating on behalf of groups face pressure to prove their loyalty and toughness. They may see concessions as betrayal, making representatives less flexible than they might personally prefer.

At its most extreme, dehumanization risks emerge: In intense conflict, groups may dehumanize each other, using language that strips the other of human qualities. Once dehumanization takes hold, normal moral constraints relax, enabling behaviors that would otherwise be unthinkable. For practical strategies to counter dehumanization, including humanizing exercises and perspective-taking techniques, see Chapter 10: Trauma-Informed Approaches.

> **Caution: Warning Signs of Dehumanization**
>
> Watch for signs of dehumanization: language that portrays the other side as less than human, denies their legitimate interests, or frames them as entirely malicious. Such language signals dangerous escalation and should be gently challenged.

Trauma Responses in Conflict

Trauma often emerges in or is triggered by company-community conflicts. Understanding trauma responses is essential for mediators. We cover this in depth in Chapter 10: Trauma-Informed Approaches, but for now, the key points include:

- **Hypervigilance:** Traumatized individuals and communities may be constantly alert to threat, interpreting ambiguous events in worst-case terms.
- **Re-triggering:** Events or discussions that recall past trauma can trigger intense emotional responses that seem disproportionate to the immediate situation.
- **Avoidance:** Trauma survivors may avoid discussing specific topics, participating in certain processes, or engaging with certain people, even when doing so would serve their interests.
- **Numbness:** Chronic trauma can produce emotional numbness that masks the depth of feeling. This means that apparent calm may conceal deep pain.

5.4 Understanding Conflict Escalation

Predictable escalation patterns emerge, with each stage exhibiting distinct dynamics, behaviors, and intervention needs. Understanding these stages helps mediators assess where a conflict stands and what approaches are likely to be effective. The model presented here adapts Friedrich Glasl's influential escalation model to the company-community context.

Figure 11 traces the predictable stages through which conflicts escalate, from initial disagreement to potential crisis.

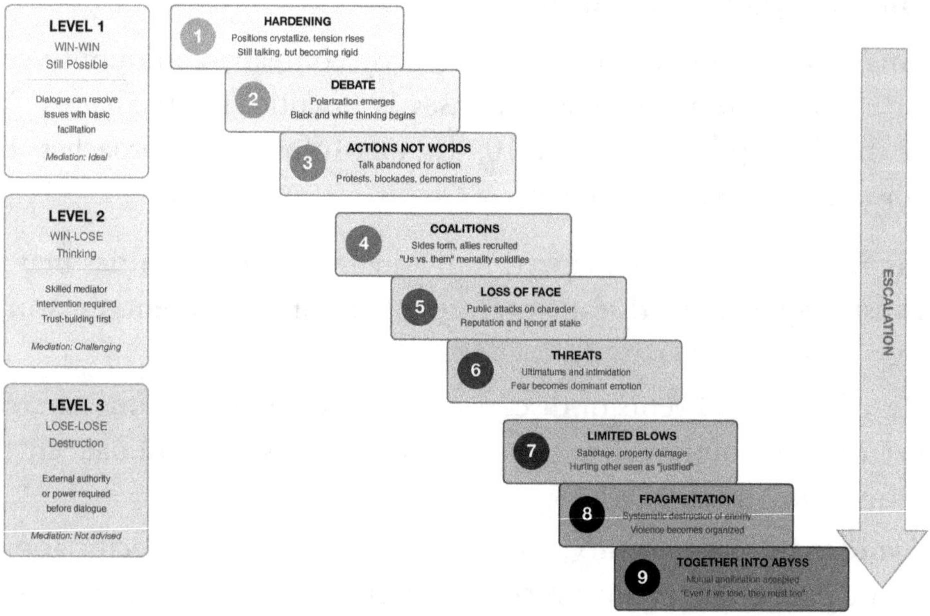

Figure 11: A model showing the stages of conflict escalation, from initial disagreement through polarization to potential crisis, with indicators at each stage.

Recognizing which stage a conflict has reached allows you to select the right intervention intensity, avoiding the common mistake of applying heavy-handed approaches to early-stage disagreements or underestimating the momentum of advanced escalation.

> **Key Concept: Escalation Asymmetry**
>
> Parties often perceive their own escalatory actions as defensive responses while viewing the other's actions as aggressive provocations. Both sides may genuinely believe they are merely reacting to the other's aggression. Help parties see how their "defensive" moves appear threatening to others.

Stage 1: Tension and Discomfort

In this earliest phase, tension exists without conviction that cooperation is lost. Communication continues, though it may become strained. Parties are aware of their differences but have not yet hardened into adversarial positions.

- **Characteristics:** Occasional friction, mild complaints, some misunderstandings. Parties still generally assume good intentions on the other side.
- **Communication:** Regular but sometimes uncomfortable. Issues are raised, but may be avoided if they are too sensitive.
- **Relationship:** Fundamentally intact. Parties may be frustrated, but are not yet adversaries.
- **Intervention approach:** Prevention and early problem-solving. Address issues before they accumulate. Strengthen communication channels. Build relationships. This is the easiest stage for resolution, but often the hardest to access because parties do not yet see the need for intervention.

> **Practical Tip: Early Detection of Latent Conflict**
>
> Conflicts at this stage often remain invisible to outsiders, failing to trigger formal grievance mechanisms. Proactive relationship-building and open communication channels catch issues at this stage before they escalate.

Stage 2: Debate and Polarization

Increased tension pushes parties toward opposing positions. Debate replaces dialogue. Each side develops arguments supporting its view while dismissing the other's perspective. Trust begins to erode.

- **Characteristics:** Formal positions emerge. Arguments become repetitive. Each side becomes convinced of its rightness. Stereotypes of the other begin forming.
- **Communication:** More formal, more argumentative. Parties talk past each other. Listening declines as advocacy increases.
- **Relationship:** Strained but not broken. Parties still engage, but with increasing frustration.
- **Intervention approach:** Facilitated dialogue focusing on interests beneath positions. Active listening training. Joint problem-solving on minor issues to rebuild trust. Reality testing of positions.

Stage 3: Actions Speak Louder Than Words

When dialogue fails to produce progress, frustrated parties turn to action. The community may stage protests, blockades, or media campaigns. The company may increase security, seek legal remedies, or apply political pressure. Each action triggers a reaction, accelerating escalation.

- **Characteristics:** Tactical maneuvering. Each side tries to strengthen its position. Actions replace words as the primary means of communication. Events take on symbolic significance.
- **Communication:** Public statements replace private dialogue. Communication becomes performative, aimed at audiences rather than at the other party.
- **Relationship:** Adversarial. Parties see each other as opponents to be overcome rather than partners to work with.
- **Intervention approach:** De-escalation becomes the priority. Cooling-off periods may be needed. Third-party intermediaries become essential since direct communication has broken down. Address immediate actions before underlying issues. (see also Chapter 13, Navigating Impasses and Rebuilding Cooperation)

Stage 4: Images and Coalitions

Hardening into rigid negative images, parties seek allies to strengthen their position. The community mobilizes NGO support, attracts media attention, and frames the company as a villain. The company activates government relationships, engages PR firms, and frames the community as unreasonable.

- **Characteristics:** Rigid stereotypes. Zero-sum thinking. Coalition building. Public narratives become weapons. Internal dissent on both sides is suppressed in favor of unified fronts.
- **Communication:** Largely through intermediaries or public channels. Direct dialogue is rare and unproductive when it occurs.
- **Relationship:** Deep adversarial. Each party defines itself partly in opposition to the other.

- **Intervention approach:** Humanization becomes the priority. Create opportunities for parties to see each other as people rather than stereotypes. Work with coalitions, not just principals. Address narratives, not just issues. Consider separate preparatory work before joint sessions.

Example: Coalition Dynamics

In the Stuttgart 21 infrastructure dispute, what began as a local concern evolved into a major confrontation involving political parties, environmental groups, urban planning organizations, and national media. Both supporters and opponents built coalitions that extended far beyond the original stakeholders. Resolving the dispute required engaging this entire ecosystem, not just the railway company and immediate neighbors.

Stage 5: Loss of Face

Concern with face, dignity, and reputation becomes paramount as conflict intensifies. Neither party can afford to be seen backing down. This concern with appearance often outweighs substantive interests, making compromise feel like humiliation.

- **Characteristics:** Public posturing. Dramatic gestures. Concern with appearance dominates substance. Concessions become impossible because they would signal weakness.
- **Communication:** Performative and often hostile. Statements designed more for internal and external audiences than for the other party.
- **Relationship:** Broken. Parties may refuse to be in the same room. Contact is maintained only through intermediaries.
- **Intervention approach:** Face-saving mechanisms become essential. Design processes that allow both parties to claim victory or at least avoid obvious defeat. Private channels for exploring options. Public framing that honors both parties.

Stage 6: Strategies of Threat

Escalation shifts to coercion: threats become the primary tool to force compliance. The community may threaten to shut down operations, pursue international campaigns, or take legal action. The company may threaten closure, legal retaliation, or political intervention.

- **Characteristics:** Ultimatums. Deadlines. Contingent threats. Demonstration of capability to impose costs.
- **Communication:** Dominated by threats and counter-threats. Genuine dialogue is nearly impossible.
- **Relationship:** Hostile. Each party actively seeks to harm the other's interests.
- **Intervention approach:** De-escalation of threats becomes the priority. Help parties understand the costs of following through. Create face-saving paths away from ultimatums. Focus on interests that threats theoretically serve rather than the threats themselves.

Stage 7: Limited Destructive Blows

Parties begin inflicting actual harm, though still with some restraint. The community may sabotage equipment. The company may cut off benefits or pursue aggressive legal action. Each blow invites retaliation.

- **Characteristics:** Calculated harm. Proportional retaliation. Damage is still limited by some remaining calculation of the consequences.
- **Communication:** Largely through actions. Words may continue, but carry little weight.
- **Relationship:** Actively hostile. Causing harm to the other is now a goal, not just a means.
- **Intervention approach:** Crisis intervention. Establishing ceasefires or standstills. Separating parties. Addressing immediate safety concerns. Substantial preparatory work is needed before any joint process.

Stage 8: Fragmentation

Each party seeks to destroy the other's capacity to function. The community attempts to shut down operations entirely. The company attempts to remove or marginalize community opposition. Harm inflicted becomes an end in itself. At this stage of escalation, mediation may no longer be appropriate, and mediators should assess whether proceeding is ethical (see Chapter 8).

- **Characteristics:** Systematic attacks on the other's capacity. Dehumanization complete. All-or-nothing thinking.
- **Communication:** Interactions cease to function as communication. Statements are weapons, not exchanges.
- **Relationship:** Non-existent in any constructive sense.
- **Intervention approach:** External intervention likely required. Third-party peacekeeping or enforcement may be necessary before mediation is possible. Extensive shuttle diplomacy. Very gradual rebuilding.

Stage 9: Together Into the Abyss

At the extreme, parties become willing to destroy themselves if it means destroying the other. Project cancellation, community displacement, violence, and destruction become acceptable if they inflict sufficient harm on the opponent.

- **Characteristics:** Self-destructive behavior is acceptable if it harms the enemy. No calculation of costs, only commitment to destruction. This stage is rarely reached in company-community disputes, but it is not unheard of.
- **Intervention approach:** Crisis intervention by powerful external parties. Mediators cannot intervene effectively until parties establish basic safety. Focus on preventing catastrophe rather than resolution.

Key Concept: Conflict Stage Oscillation

While most conflicts never reach extreme stages, many oscillate between them 3 through 6. Understanding where a conflict sits helps mediators design appropriate interventions. Techniques suitable for stage 2 may be dangerously inadequate for stage 6.

5.5 Recognizing Early Warning Signs

Conflicts are easier to resolve early, before positions harden and escalation dynamics take hold. Recognizing early warning signs allows for preventive intervention. Companies, communities, and mediators should watch for indicators that conflict may be developing or intensifying.

> **Practical Tip: Monitoring Between Sessions**
>
> Conflicts can escalate between mediation sessions. Establish a simple check-in system, perhaps a brief phone call or message, to monitor developments. Learning that the community held a protest or the company issued a press release allows you to address new tensions before they derail progress.

Communication Warning Signs

Decreasing communication: Parties who used to talk regularly now avoid each other. Meetings become less frequent or are canceled. Phone calls go unanswered. Silence often precedes escalation.

The tone of communication shifts: Once cordial communication becomes formal, curt, or hostile. Language becomes more legalistic or adversarial. People stop using first names.

Parties may begin communicating through intermediaries: Parties stop talking directly and communicate through lawyers, media, or government officials. This formalization signals a deteriorating relationship.

Public statements become another signal: Issues that were discussed privately are now raised in the media, community meetings, or public forums. Going public often represents escalation.

Finally, rumors and misinformation spread: When accurate information stops flowing, rumors fill the vacuum. Increasing rumor circulation suggests a communication breakdown.

Behavioral Warning Signs

- **Position hardening:** Parties that once seemed flexible now express rigid positions. "Non-negotiable demands" appear. Phrases like "final offer" or "never" increase.
- **Mobilization:** Parties begin organizing for conflict. The community forms action committees, contacts NGOs or lawyers, and prepares protest materials. The company increases security, hires crisis consultants, and prepares legal responses.
- **Testing behavior:** Parties probe each other's limits through small provocations. Minor incidents that might previously have been overlooked are now challenged.
- **Withdrawal from joint activities:** Parties who previously participated in joint committees, community events, or shared initiatives withdraw from these engagements.
- **Historical grievances resurface:** Old complaints that seemed resolved return to discussion. Past incidents are reinterpreted as part of a pattern.

Emotional Warning Signs

- **Rising anger:** Statements become more heated. Calm discussions give way to angry accusations. Physical signs of anger appear in meetings.
- **Expressions of hopelessness:** Parties express belief that resolution is impossible, that the other side will never change, or that nothing short of confrontation will work.
- **Dehumanizing language:** References to the other party become more negative, abstract, or dehumanizing. They become "the company" rather than people with names.
- **Fear indicators:** Statements suggesting fear of what the other side might do. Security concerns increase. People worry about retaliation.

Structural Warning Signs

- **Leadership changes:** New leaders, whether in company management or community representation, who take harder positions may signal escalation.
- **External involvement:** Entry of new actors, such as NGOs, lawyers, politicians, or media, often correlates with escalation, as does withdrawal of moderating influences.
- **Deadline approach:** Approaching deadlines, such as permit renewals, elections, or project milestones, create pressure that can trigger escalation.
- **Precedent concerns:** When parties begin framing the dispute as setting precedent for other situations, the stakes increase, and flexibility decreases.

> **Practical Tip: Monitoring Escalation Warning Signs**
>
> Create monitoring systems to track these warning signs systematically. Regular community association, grievance mechanism data analysis, and relationship health checks can identify problems early when intervention is still easy.

5.6 De-Escalation Strategies

Just as conflicts escalate through predictable patterns, mediators can de-escalate them through deliberate strategies. De-escalation does not mean resolving the conflict. It means reducing intensity, slowing spirals, and creating conditions that make constructive engagement possible.

Figure 12 outlines practical de-escalation techniques for high-tension moments.

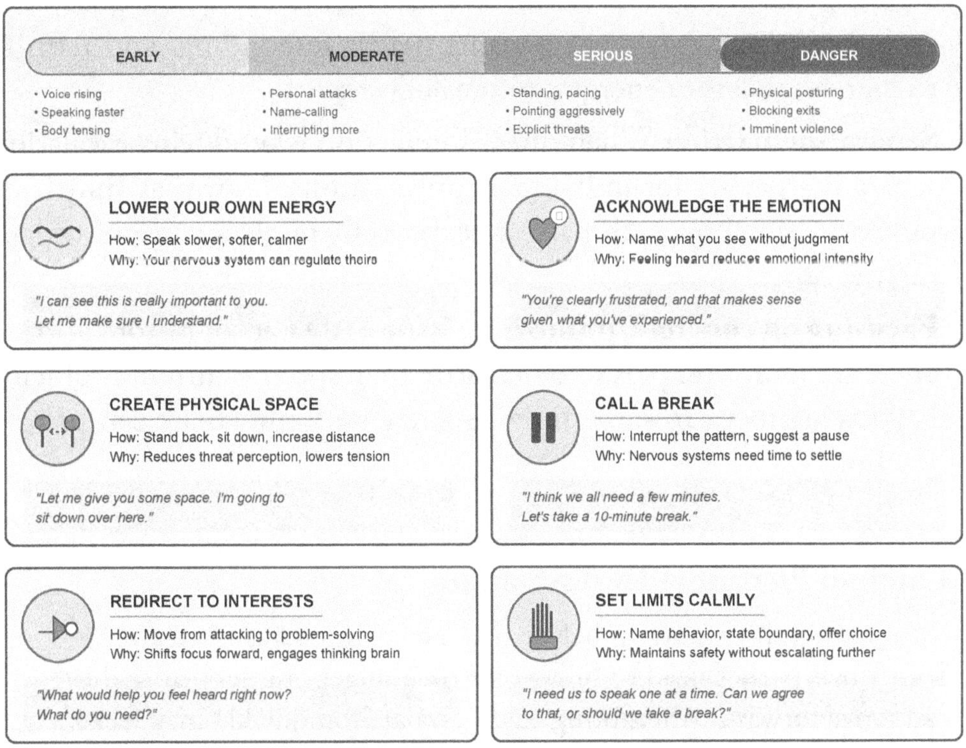

Figure 12: A collection of practical de-escalation techniques that mediators can use to reduce tension, slow momentum, and create space for dialogue.

De-escalation is not about eliminating emotion or suppressing legitimate concerns, but rather about creating the conditions where emotion does not drive the conversation and rationality can resurface.

Immediate De-Escalation Techniques

- **Creating space:** Physical and temporal space can reduce intensity. Calling a break in heated discussions, moving to a different location, or simply slowing the pace of interactions allows emotions to settle. Sometimes the most effective intervention is simply stopping.
- **Acknowledging emotions:** Saying "I can see you're very angry about this," or "This has clearly caused real pain" validates emotional experience without agreeing or disagreeing with positions. Acknowledgment alone can reduce intensity.

- **Slowing down:** Conflict tends to accelerate. Slowing the pace of an exchange, speaking slowly, pausing before responding, and refusing to match escalatory energy can break cycles.
- **Separating parties:** When direct interaction is producing escalation, separating parties for individual conversations, known as shuttle diplomacy, can allow each party to express themselves without triggering the other.
- **Focusing on concrete, immediate issues:** Abstract or historical grievances are more complex to de-escalate than specific current problems. Narrowing focus to something concrete and immediate can provide traction.

Caution: Premature De-Escalation

Rushing to calm emotions before they are expressed can backfire. Sometimes parties need to fully voice their anger or grief before they can move forward. Attempting to de-escalate too quickly may feel dismissive and actually increase frustration.

Structural De-Escalation Strategies

- **Establishing communication channels:** Creating reliable, trusted ways for parties to communicate can prevent the spiral of misunderstanding that drives escalation. Regular meetings, designated liaisons, and established protocols provide structure.
- **Introducing neutral parties:** Third parties, whether mediators, ombudsmen, or respected community figures, can absorb some of the relational tension and provide face-saving paths to de-escalation.
- **Creating joint projects:** Collaboration on non-contentious issues can rebuild working relationships. If parties can cooperate on something, they begin to see each other differently.
- **Standstill agreements:** Formal or informal agreements to pause escalatory actions create breathing room. For example, the community agrees to suspend protests, and the company agrees to suspend the

disputed activities. Neither concedes the underlying issue, but both step back from confrontation.

- **Graduated reciprocation:** Small, unilateral de-escalatory gestures, if reciprocated, can begin a positive spiral. A company might release information as a goodwill gesture. The community might suspend criticism. Each reciprocation builds toward larger de-escalation.

Example: De-Escalation Through Acknowledgment

In a South American mining dispute, tensions had escalated to the point of threatened blockades. A new company manager was advised to begin meetings with a simple acknowledgment: "I know this company has not always kept its promises. I know you have reason to be skeptical. I'm not asking you to trust us, but I am asking you to test us." This acknowledgment, though it committed to nothing concrete, shifted the dynamic. By acknowledging the community's justified skepticism rather than defending against it, the manager created space for engagement.

Trust-Building as De-Escalation

Trust rebuilding is central to de-escalation. Trust grows through consistent, predictable behavior over time, including:

- **Small commitments kept:** Making small promises and keeping them demonstrates reliability. It is better to promise a little and deliver than to promise too much and fail.
- **Transparency:** Sharing information proactively, especially information that is not flattering, builds trust. Parties trust those who share inconvenient truths.
- **Consistency:** Saying the same thing to different audiences, behaving predictably, and following through on stated intentions all build trust.
- **Accountability:** Acknowledging mistakes, explaining what happened, and describing corrective action builds trust even after failures.

Addressing Dignity

De-escalation requires attention to dignity. Mediators can build dignity by:

- **Avoiding humiliation:** Even when a party is wrong, public humiliation prevents de-escalation. Finding face-saving ways for parties to shift positions is essential.
- **Honoring both parties:** Processes and outcomes that allow both parties to claim success, or at least avoid obvious defeat, are more sustainable than clear wins and losses.
- **Private channels:** Providing ways for parties to explore options privately, without public commitment, allows flexibility that public positions do not.
- **Acknowledgment and apology:** Genuine acknowledgment of the harm caused, with or without a formal apology, addresses dignity needs that substantive remedies cannot reach.

5.7 Conducting Conflict Assessment

Before intervening, conduct systematic assessment to understand the situation. An assessment is not a single event but an ongoing process of gathering information, testing hypotheses, and refining understanding.

> **Practical Tip: Conflict Mapping Updates**
>
> Create your initial conflict map before mediation begins, but update it as new information emerges. Stakeholders, relationships, and issues shift; a map that was accurate in pre-mediation may be outdated by session three. Regular updates keep your analysis current.

Key Assessment Questions

A thorough conflict assessment addresses:

- **Parties:** Who are the parties to this conflict? Who has a stake in the outcome? Who has the power to influence the resolution? Who may be affected but not represented? Are there factions within parties?

- **Issues:** What are the substantive issues in dispute? What are the underlying interests behind stated positions? What emotional issues are wrapped up with substantive ones? What process issues exist?
- **History:** How did this conflict develop? What key events shaped the current situation? What previous attempts at resolution have been made? Why did they succeed or fail?
- **Dynamics:** What stage has the conflict reached? Is it escalating, de-escalating, or stable? What drives escalation? What moderates it?
- **Power:** How is power distributed? What sources of power does each party have? How do power dynamics affect the conflict (see Chapter 12)?
- **Context:** What broader factors affect the conflict? What political, economic, cultural, and legal contexts? What external actors influence the situation?
- **Ripeness:** Is this conflict ripe for resolution? Are parties motivated to seek agreement? What would increase readiness?

Assessment Methods

- **Document review:** Examine available documents: correspondence, agreements, media coverage, reports. These provide a factual foundation and reveal how parties frame issues.
- **Key informant interviews:** Speak with knowledgeable individuals from each party and neutral observers. Listen for different perspectives and underlying concerns.
- **Site visits:** See the situation firsthand. Physical context reveals dynamics that descriptions miss.
- **Stakeholder mapping:** Create visual maps of parties, their relationships, and their interests. Mapping reveals complexity and identifies gaps in understanding.
- **Timeline construction:** Build chronological accounts of key events. Timelines reveal patterns, triggers, and turning points.

Assessment Tools

Several analytical tools support conflict assessment, including:

Tool	Purpose	Application
Stakeholder Analysis	Identify all relevant parties and their interests	List stakeholders, their stakes, power, and relationships
Conflict Mapping	Visualize relationships and dynamics	Diagram parties, alliances, and tensions
Timeline Analysis	Understand historical development	Chart key events, decisions, and turning points
BATNA/WATNA	Assess alternatives to agreement	Identify the best and worst alternatives for each party
Escalation Analysis	Determine conflict stage	Match current dynamics to escalation model stages

Practical Tip: Continuous Assessment During Mediation

Assessment continues throughout mediation. Initial assessments are hypotheses to be tested and refined as you learn more. Stay curious and update your understanding as new information emerges.

5.8 Applying Conflict Analysis in Practice

Conflict dynamics are fundamentally practical, not academic. It directly informs every mediator decision, including how to structure the process, what issues to address first, when to meet jointly versus separately, how to frame proposals, and how to navigate emotional moments.

From Analysis to Strategy

- **Match intervention to stage:** A conflict at stage 2, still characterized by dialogue despite polarization, requires a different intervention than one at stage 5, where dignity concerns dominate. Techniques appropriate for early stages may fail or backfire later.

- **Address root causes, not just symptoms:** If underlying resource competition is not addressed, resolving current disputes will only create temporary respite. Lasting resolution requires engaging the fundamental drivers.
- **Attend to all three dimensions:** Purely substantive agreements that ignore emotional needs and process concerns will not hold. Design processes that address all three dimensions.
- **Anticipate psychological dynamics:** Knowing that reactive devaluation will cause parties to dismiss each other's proposals, a mediator can propose ideas themselves or structure idea generation to obscure the sources.
- **Monitor for escalation:** Throughout mediation, watch for warning signs that the conflict is escalating. An early response to an escalation is far easier than managing a full-blown crisis.

Beyond Analysis: From Understanding to Action

While analysis is essential, it has limits, including:

- **Analysis is not neutral:** Every framework highlights some aspects while obscuring others. Your analysis reflects your perspectives and biases.
- **Parties may resist analysis:** Being analyzed can feel dehumanizing. Share analytical frameworks carefully, and always prioritize each party's own understanding.
- **Analysis does not resolve conflict:** Knowing why conflict exists does not automatically create resolution. Analysis informs action but does not replace it.
- **Conflicts surprise:** No matter how thorough your analysis, conflicts will surprise you. Hold your conclusions tentatively and remain adaptive.

This chapter has provided a framework for understanding conflict dynamics. It covered the dimensions of conflict, root causes common in company-community disputes, psychological patterns that shape conflict behavior, escalation stages, assessment tools, warning signs, and de-escalation strategies. With this analytical foundation, mediators are better equipped to design interventions suited to specific situations and navigate the complex dynamics they will encounter.

The chapters that follow build on this foundation, addressing how to design and conduct mediation processes, handle specific challenges such as power imbalances and trauma, and navigate impasses when they arise. Throughout, the conflict analysis skills developed here remain essential since understanding why conflicts exist and how they behave is the foundation for helping parties resolve them.

6.

DESIGNING MEDIATION PROCESSES

Understanding conflict dynamics (see Chapter 5) prepares mediators to design processes that respond to these realities rather than impose generic templates. Process design creates a roadmap from conflict to resolution. A clear structure gives parties confidence that the process is fair and comprehensive, while flexibility ensures their specific context is respected. This chapter provides a detailed, step-by-step guide to designing and conducting mediation processes, from initial grievance intake through to benefit-sharing agreements or other resolutions.

Process quality directly shapes outcomes. A well-designed process creates psychological safety for participants, ensures all voices are heard, and builds the trust necessary for parties to take risks in negotiation. Conversely, a poorly designed process can reinforce power imbalances (see Chapter 12), trigger defensive behaviors, and doom the mediation before substantive discussions even begin.

This chapter expands on each phase of the mediation process, explaining not only what to do but why each element matters and how to adapt it to different contexts. The real-world examples, practical tips, and sample dialogues in this chapter help illustrate the concepts in action.

Key Concept: The Six Phases of Mediation

The mediation process consists of six interconnected phases: (0) Preparation and Pre-Mediation, (1) Opening Session, (2) Agenda Setting, (3) Exploring Interests and Needs, (4) Generating Options, (5) Negotiation and Bargaining, and (6) Reaching Agreement.

Each phase builds on the previous one, and the effort invested in early phases often determines whether later phases succeed. Skipping or rushing preparation is the most common mistake in mediation process design.

The following sections illustrates how these six phases connect and flow from preparation through to conclusion.

6.1 Phase 0: Preparation and Pre-Mediation

Thorough preparation, often called "Phase 0," encompasses everything that happens before the parties formally come together. Preparation effort often determines whether mediation succeeds or fails. Poor preparation leads to misunderstandings, process breakdowns, and missed opportunities for resolution.

Understanding the Purpose of Pre-Mediation

Pre-mediation serves multiple critical functions that shape everything that follows. Understanding these purposes helps mediators invest preparation time wisely and avoid common shortcuts that undermine later success.

Building Initial Trust

Parties often arrive at mediation with deep skepticism. Communities may have experienced broken promises from companies or ineffective grievance processes. Companies may have encountered what they perceive as unreasonable demands or bad-faith negotiations. The mediator's first task is establishing themselves as a trustworthy, competent guide through a process that can feel risky.

In mining and extractive-industry disputes, trust deficits are acute and specific. Communities may have experienced abandoned site reclamation, broken benefit-sharing agreements, or regulatory bodies that approved mining licenses without enforcing environmental conditions. Companies may have faced operational disruptions or harassment campaigns. Acknowledging these sector-specific grievances, rather than treating trust as an abstract concept, is essential to credible process design.

Pre-mediation meetings allow the mediator to demonstrate impartiality, explain how the process protects each party's interests, and begin building the rapport that will be essential during difficult moments. When parties enter formal mediation having already met the mediator and feeling understood, they start from a position of cautious openness rather than defensive suspicion.

Assessing Feasibility

Not every dispute suits mediation. Pre-mediation assessment determines whether conditions for success exist. Key questions include: Are the parties genuinely willing to participate, or is one side participating only to appear cooperative while planning to undermine the process? Do decision-makers have sufficient authority to reach an agreement? Are there external factors, such as pending litigation, political pressures, or safety concerns, that would prevent meaningful engagement?

If significant obstacles exist, the mediator should address them before proceeding, delay mediation until conditions improve, or recommend an alternative approach entirely.

Gathering Intelligence

Pre-mediation is the mediator's opportunity to understand the dispute's full dimensions. This includes the formal issues (compensation, environmental impacts, employment), as well as the underlying dynamics that shape them. What is the history of the relationship? What previous attempts at resolution have been made, and why did they fail? What cultural factors influence how parties communicate? Who holds power, and how is it exercised?

This understanding enables tailored process design rather than generic templates. It also helps anticipate challenges, prepare for emotional moments (see Chapter 10 for trauma-informed approaches), and identify potential areas of common ground that parties themselves may not yet recognize.

Practical Tip: Pre-Mediation Preparation Checklist

Create a pre-mediation checklist that includes: stakeholder mapping, power analysis, conflict history, prior resolution attempts, cultural considerations, and potential spoilers.

Schedule separate pre-mediation meetings with each party. Use these meetings to build rapport, explain the process, and gather intelligence about interests and concerns that may not be raised in joint sessions.

Stakeholder Identification and Analysis

Determining who participates in mediation is more complex than it first appears (see Chapter 9 for detailed stakeholder analysis tools and techniques). Missing stakeholders can doom agreements; too many participants make dialogue unmanageable. Thoughtful stakeholder analysis balances inclusivity with practicality.

Extractive-industry stakeholder maps carry unique complexity. A government environment ministry may officially support mediation while a mining regulator encourages continued operations. Indigenous communities may include members economically dependent on mine employment alongside those opposing the project to protect ancestral lands. Artisanal miners whose livelihoods are threatened by industrial-scale operations create additional stakeholder layers not immediately apparent in initial mapping.

Practical Tip: Stakeholder Completeness Check

Before finalizing participant lists, ask each party: "Who else should be involved?" and "Whose support will be needed to implement any agreement?" Missing stakeholders can torpedo implementation. Better to identify them early, even if their inclusion complicates the process.

To conduct this stakeholder analysis systematically, a mapping template provides a structured framework for identifying all relevant parties and their relationships to the dispute.

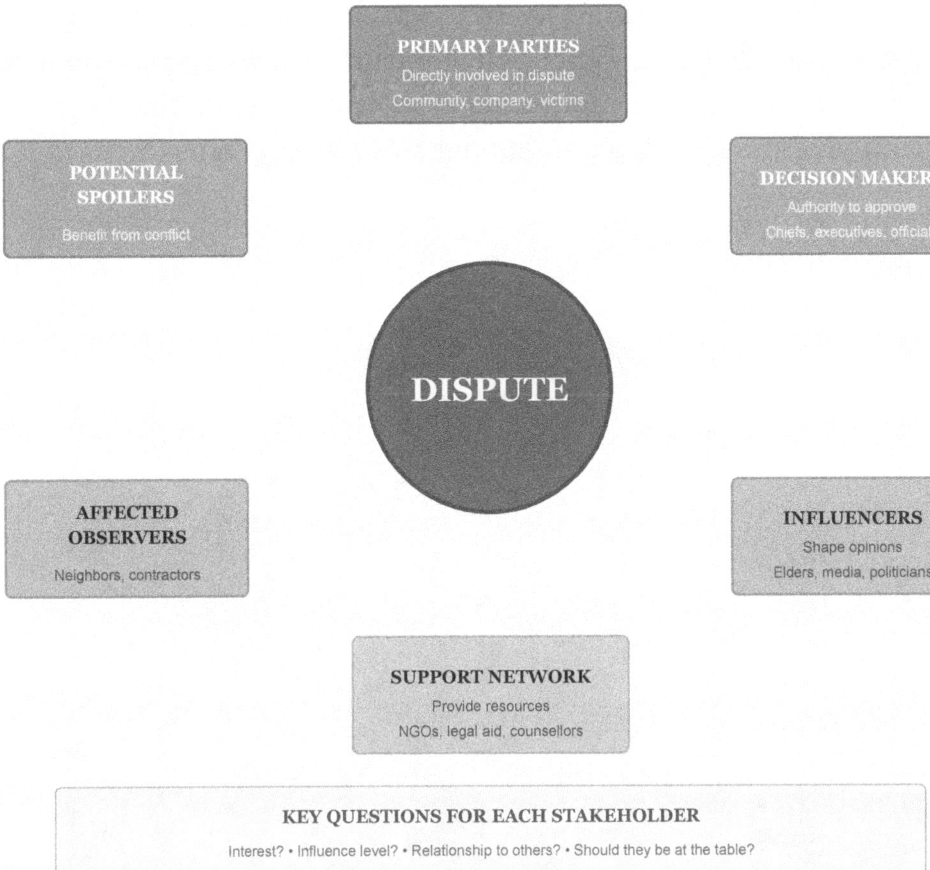

Figure 13: A template for identifying and mapping all relevant stakeholders, their interests, influence levels, and potential impact on the mediation process.

A complete stakeholder map reveals not only who sits at the table but who influences decisions from off-stage, which is critical because mediation often succeeds or fails based on managing these invisible networks.

Identifying Primary Parties

Primary parties are those directly involved in the dispute and whose agreement is needed for resolution. In company-community conflicts, primary parties typically include:

- Company representatives: Identify which company officials have both the knowledge to understand community concerns and the authority to make commitments. A community relations officer may understand the issues but lack the authority to commit resources; a CEO may have the authority but lack detailed knowledge. Often, a team is needed. The figure below illustrates how decision-making authority is typically distributed across corporate structures, and why identifying the right level of representation strengthens the process.

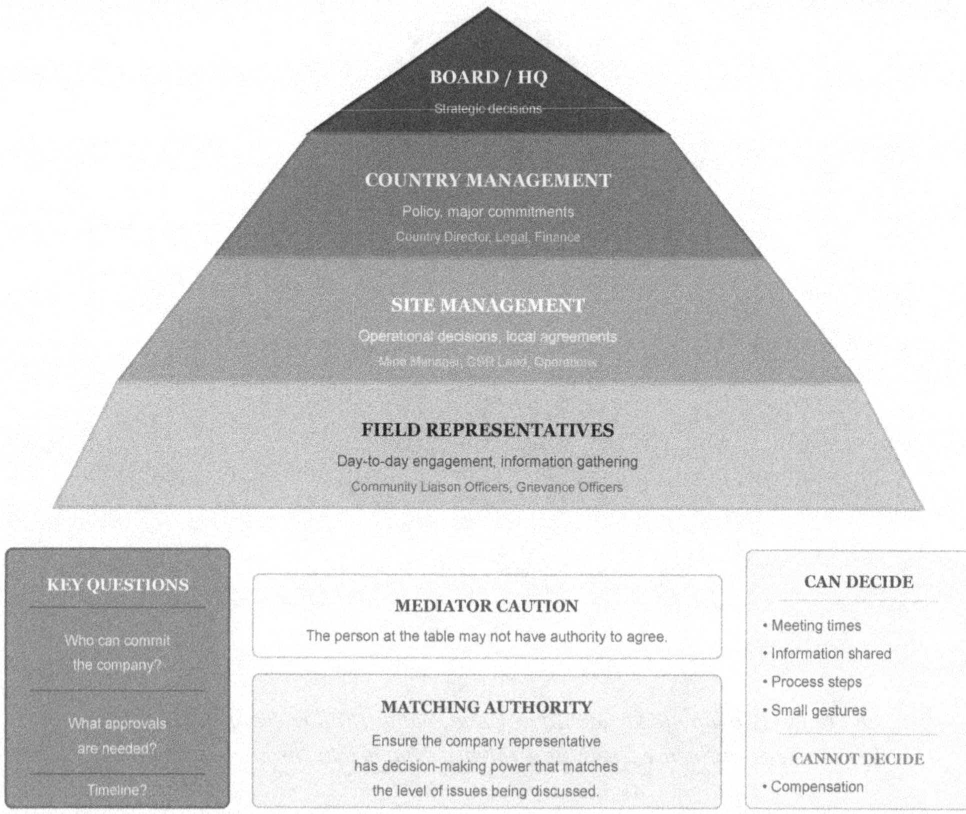

Figure 14: A diagram showing the different levels of decision-making authority within corporate structures and their relevance to the mediation process.

Understanding how authority flows through organizational hierarchies ensures that the decision-makers you engage are actually empowered to commit to agreements, avoiding the common trap of negotiating with those who can only report back.

- Community leaders: Both formal leaders (elected officials, traditional chiefs) and informal leaders (respected elders, activists, religious figures) may need to participate. Agreements that lack buy-in from influential community members often fail during implementation. Understanding how decisions are actually made within a community is essential for identifying the right representatives, as shown below.

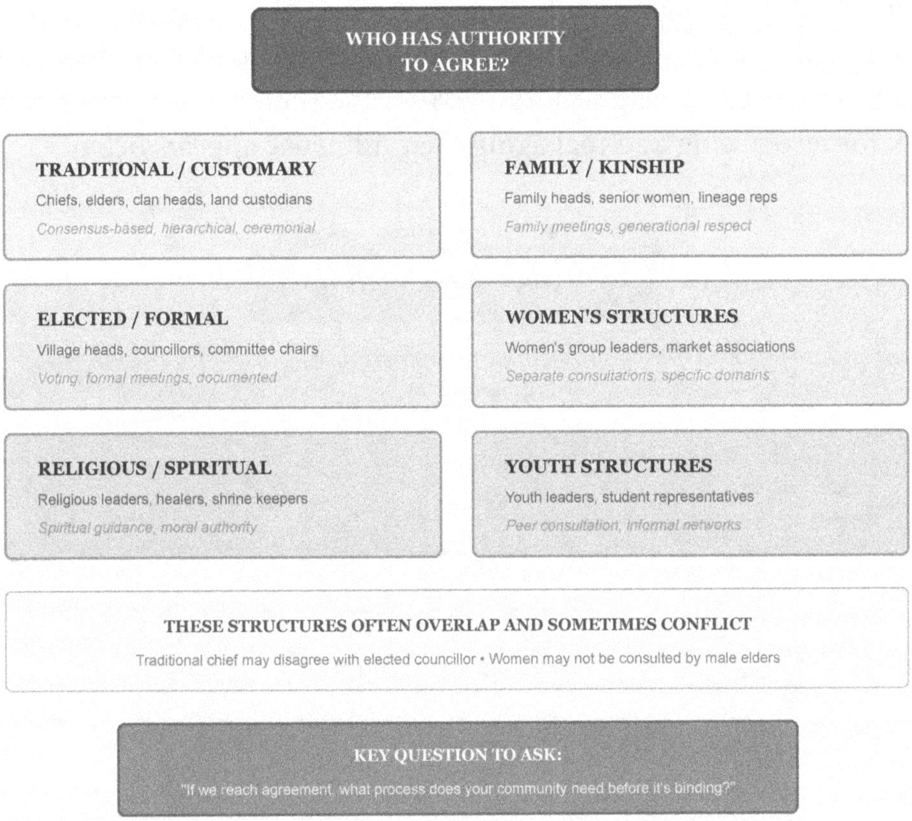

Figure 15: A visual representation of typical community governance and decision-making structures, including formal and informal leadership roles.

Community decision-making is rarely linear or top-down, and respecting these structures, even when they seem inefficient to outsiders, is essential for building legitimacy and ensuring community members feel ownership of the process.

Affected sub-groups: Communities are not monolithic. Women, youth, specific occupational groups, such as farmers and fishers, or neighboring villages may have distinct interests. Ensure these voices are represented, either directly at the table or through consultation mechanisms.

Identifying Secondary Stakeholders

Secondary stakeholders are those who influence the dispute or are affected by its outcome but may not participate directly in negotiations. Understanding their positions and interests is essential because they can support or undermine any agreement reached. Among the most important secondary stakeholders to identify early are potential spoilers: individuals or groups who may actively seek to obstruct the process. A practical framework for recognising and managing their influence appears below.

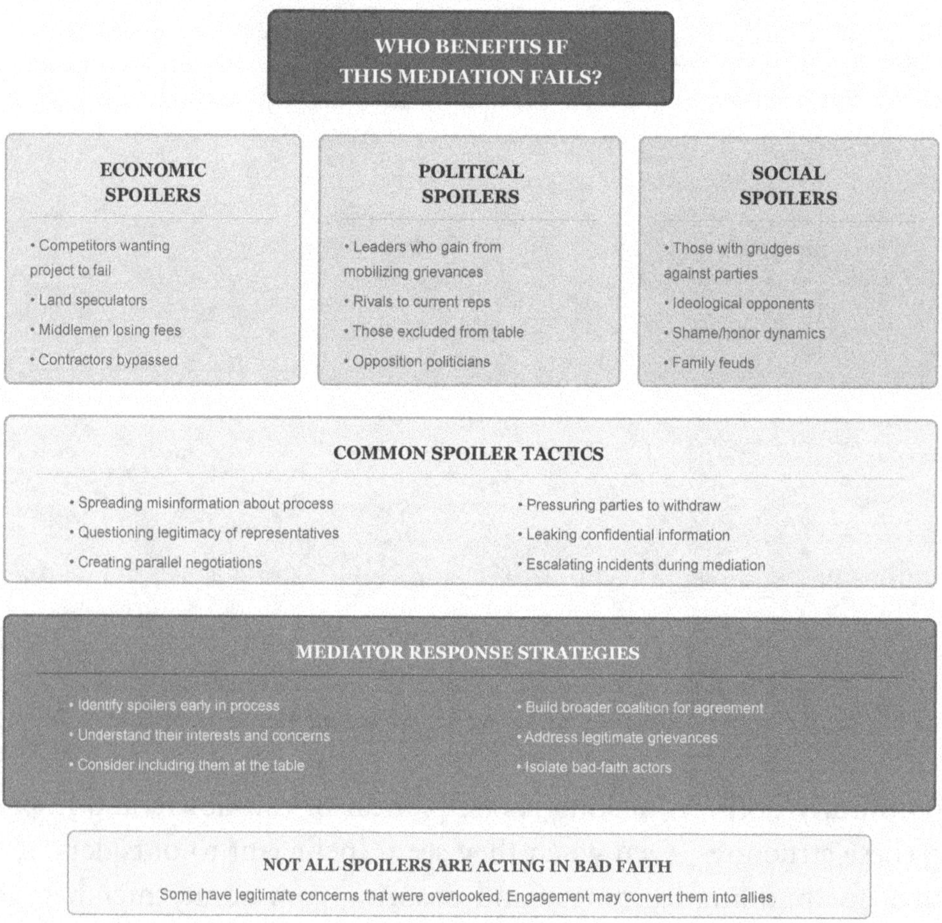

Figure 16: A framework for identifying individuals or groups who seek to obstruct, undermine, or sabotage the mediation process, and strategies for managing their influence.

Spoilers often appear as rational actors pursuing their own interests, which means the most effective strategy is often not confrontation but acknowledging their interests and finding whether there is a role they can play in success.

- Government agencies: Local, regional, or national authorities may have regulatory responsibilities, political interests, or implementation roles. Their support may be necessary for the agreement terms to be enforceable.
- NGOs and civil society: Organizations supporting the community may provide resources, expertise, or mobilization capacity. Their endorsement of an agreement can strengthen community confidence; their opposition can undermine it.
- Media: Media coverage shapes public perception and can create pressure on both parties. Understanding media dynamics helps manage communications during and after mediation.
- Investors and lenders: Financial stakeholders may impose conditions that constrain the company's flexibility or create incentives for resolution. International financial institutions, such as the World Bank and IFC, may have grievance mechanisms or standards that influence the process.

Stakeholder Mapping Tools

Create a visual map of stakeholders showing:

1. Interest level: How much does this stakeholder care about the outcome?
2. Influence level: How much power does this stakeholder have to affect the outcome?
3. Position: What outcome does this stakeholder favor?
4. Relationships: How does this stakeholder relate to other parties?

Stakeholders with high interest and strong influence require the most attention. Those with strong influence but low interest may become problematic if they feel excluded. Effective mediators develop strategies for engaging each stakeholder appropriately.

Example - Stakeholder Analysis in a Mining Dispute

In a dispute between a gold mining company and a community in West Africa, stakeholder analysis revealed:

The community was not unified. Village elders favored negotiation; youth activists demanded more aggressive action. Women, who bore primary responsibility for water collection, had specific concerns about contamination that male leaders had not prioritized.

The company's local management wanted a resolution but felt constrained by their headquarters' policies, which were developed without local context. Identifying the right headquarters decision-makers and involving them early proved essential.

An international NGO supporting the community had significant influence over community positions. Including them in the process design (though not necessarily at the negotiating table) helped ensure their support for the eventual agreement.

Gender-Inclusive Process Design

Mining operations disproportionately affect women in ways that are often invisible in formal mediation processes. Women in mining-affected communities frequently bear the primary burden of water collection, which becomes more difficult when mining operations contaminate or deplete water sources. Women manage household food production on agricultural land that may be taken for mine expansion.

Women experience the social disruption of resettlement differently, losing the social networks and economic relationships that sustain their families. Yet in many cultural contexts, women are excluded from the community delegations that negotiate with the company, and their specific concerns are subsumed under general "community interests" articulated by male leaders.

> **Practical Tip: Ensuring Women's Participation**
>
> Design the mediation process to include women's voices from the outset. This may involve separate preliminary consultations with women's groups before joint sessions. Propose that community delegations include women representatives, while being sensitive to the cultural dynamics this may raise. Schedule sessions at times and locations that are accessible to women with caregiving responsibilities. When discussing compensation, explicitly ask how proposed measures will affect women's livelihoods, water access, and food production. If cultural norms prevent women from speaking in mixed groups, create formal mechanisms for their input to be documented and presented by a trusted representative.

Adapting Process Design for Low-Resource Contexts

Many company-community disputes occur in settings where professional mediation infrastructure is limited or nonexistent. In remote mining regions of sub-Saharan Africa, Southeast Asia, or Latin America, challenges multiply: trained mediators may not exist within hundreds of kilometers, suitable conference facilities may be absent, translation services are limited, and formal mediation traditions do not exist as dispute resolution mechanisms. Mediators must design processes that work within these constraints rather than importing models developed for well-resourced urban settings.

Practical adaptations for low-resource contexts include using existing community gathering spaces (schools, religious buildings, community halls) rather than requiring purpose-built venues. Consider how agricultural cycles, market days, and seasonal access constraints that may make travel impossible during parts of the year.

Where professional interpreters are unavailable, trusted bilingual community members can serve as interpreters, though the mediator must assess whether their social position creates bias. Documentation may need to rely on oral summaries and audio recordings where literacy is limited, with visual aids and diagrams replacing written position papers.

Practical Tip: Working Without Professional Support

When mediating in low-resource settings without access to professional support services, consider these adaptations. For legal support: contact university law clinics, legal aid organizations, or international NGOs that provide pro bono counsel to communities in extractive sector disputes. For technical expertise: international organizations such as the IFC, UNDP, or sector-specific NGOs may provide or fund independent technical assessments. For trauma support: identify local health workers, religious leaders, or community counselors who can provide culturally appropriate support, even if they lack formal trauma training. For documentation: use smartphone audio and video recording (with consent) to create accessible records. For follow-up: establish a simple communication protocol using whatever technology is reliably available, whether mobile phone calls, WhatsApp messages, or periodic in-person check-ins (see Chapter 16 for digital mediation approaches).

Regardless of the resources available, one question must always be answered before mediation begins: is this process perceived as legitimate by all parties? The following checklist helps mediators evaluate whether the conditions for perceived legitimacy and credibility are in place.

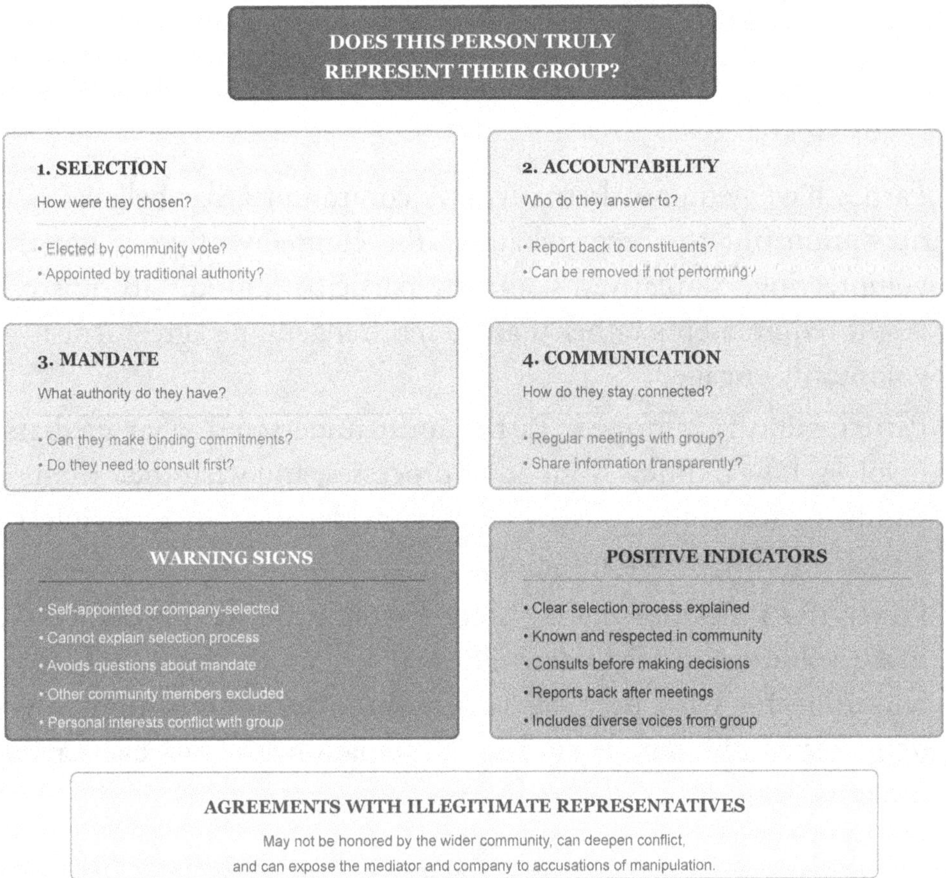

Figure 17: A checklist for evaluating whether the mediation process and the mediator are perceived as legitimate and credible by all parties involved.

Legitimacy assessments conducted early prevent the common scenario where parties engage in a process they do not believe in, only to withdraw their support at critical moments when trust has not been properly established.

Assessing Readiness and Voluntariness

Before proceeding, the mediator must confirm that parties are genuinely willing and ready to engage in mediation. This assessment goes beyond simply asking "Do you want to mediate?" to exploring whether the conditions for meaningful participation exist.

Elements of Genuine Voluntariness

True voluntariness requires more than the absence of explicit coercion. Assess whether:

- Parties have genuine alternatives: A community that believes it has no option but to accept whatever the company offers is not truly volunteering. Similarly, a company participating only to satisfy investor requirements rather than to reach a genuine agreement is not voluntarily engaged.
- Participation is informed: Parties must understand what mediation involves, how it differs from other processes, and what their rights are within it. Informed consent requires explanation in accessible language, possibly with translation.
- Power dynamics are manageable: Extreme power imbalances can make voluntary participation illusory. If community members fear retaliation for what they say, or if the company can simply impose its preferred outcome regardless of mediation, the process may lack integrity.

Caution: Detecting Coerced Participation

Watch for signs that participation is not genuinely voluntary, such as the following:

Parties who agree to mediate but set preconditions that effectively prevent dialogue participate in bad faith.

If one party appears to be using mediation as a delay tactic while pursuing aggressive actions elsewhere, address this directly before proceeding.

Community representatives who cannot speak freely due to internal power dynamics or fear of retaliation require special attention to ensure their genuine voice is heard.

Assessing Readiness to Negotiate

Beyond voluntariness, parties must be ready to engage constructively. Warning signs of unreadiness include:

- Preconditions that effectively prevent dialogue: Statements such as "We will only talk if they first admit wrongdoing" or "We will participate, but compensation is off the table" may indicate a party is not genuinely ready to negotiate.
- Active escalation: If parties are simultaneously pursuing aggressive actions, such as protests, legal filings, and media campaigns, they may not be ready to shift into a collaborative mode.
- Internal division: If the community is deeply divided about whether to negotiate or if company decision-makers are not aligned, mediation is premature.
- Insufficient authority: Participants must be able to make commitments. Sending junior staff who must seek approval for every decision undermines the process.

Pre-Mediation Conversations

Pre-mediation conversations with each party help establish rapport and clarity. These "shuttle diplomacy" meetings serve multiple purposes, including:

1. Explaining the process: Many participants have never experienced mediation. A clear explanation of what to expect, the mediator's role, and the rights of participants within the process builds confidence.
2. Hearing initial perspectives: Understanding each party's view of the dispute, their core concerns, and their hopes for mediation helps the mediator design an effective process.
3. Addressing concerns about participating: Parties often have fears about mediation. "Will what I say be used against me?" "What if the other side is not sincere?" Addressing these concerns early helps parties engage more openly.
4. Securing initial commitments: The mediator may seek agreement to pause hostile actions during mediation to create space for dialogue.
5. Beginning relationship-building: These early conversations establish the mediator's credibility and begin building the trust that will be essential later.

Sample Dialogue: Pre-Mediation Meeting with Community Representatives

Mediator: "Thank you for meeting with me today. Before we bring everyone together, I wanted to understand your perspective and explain how this process works. First, I want to be clear that participation is entirely voluntary. You're not committing to anything by talking with me, and you can withdraw from mediation at any time. My role is not to judge who is right or wrong, but to help both sides understand each other and find solutions. What questions do you have about the process?"

Community leader: "How do we know the company won't just use this to delay while they continue operations that are harming us?"

Mediator: "That's an important concern, and I've heard it from other communities in similar situations. One thing we can discuss is whether to request that certain actions be paused during mediation. We can also set clear timelines so the process doesn't drag on indefinitely. If at any point you feel the company is not participating in good faith, you remain free to pursue other options. What would help you feel confident that this process is worth trying?"

Building trust in the process, as illustrated in the dialogue above, is only one dimension of preparation. The mediator must also ensure that the process is practically accessible to all participants. The following assessment tool helps identify and address barriers to participation before they undermine the mediation.

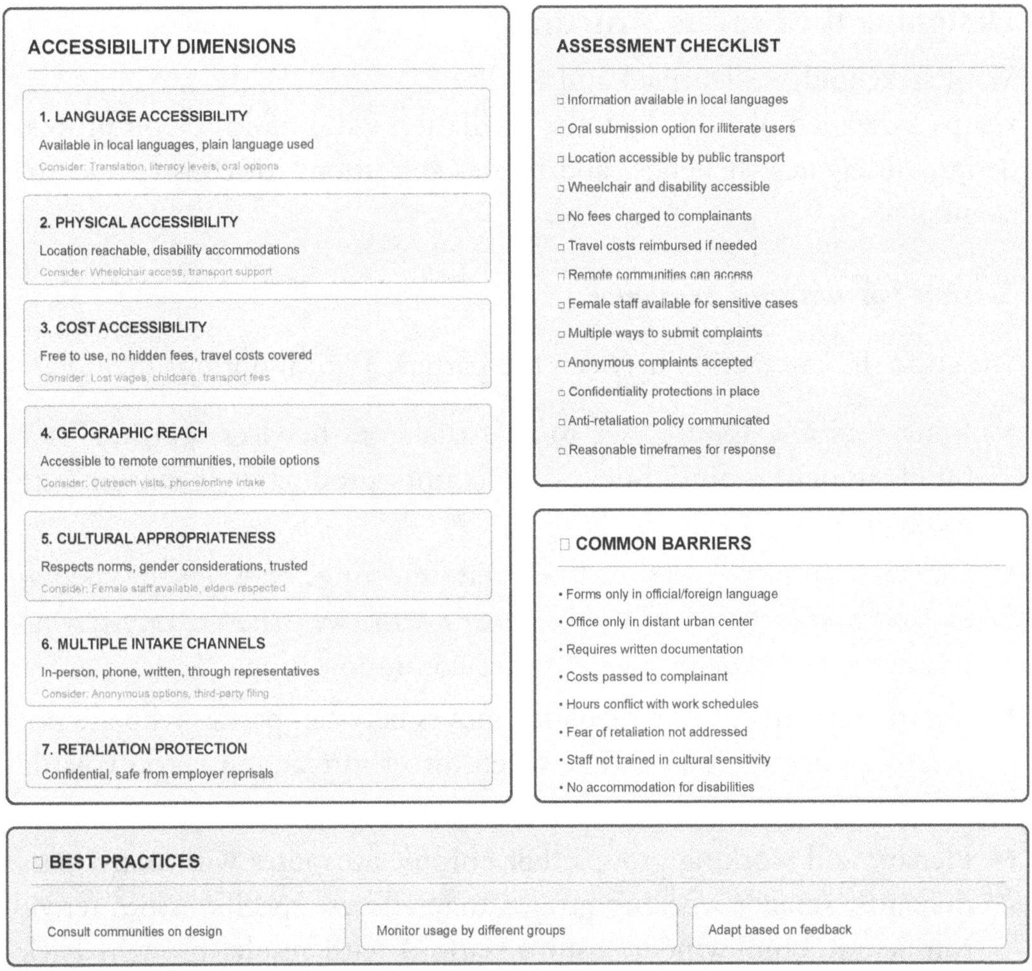

Figure 18: A tool for assessing whether the mediation process and venue are accessible to all participants, including considerations for disability, language, and cultural barriers.

Accessibility goes far beyond providing transportation. It includes ensuring that all participants can engage with the process, understand what is being discussed, and contribute on equal terms regardless of background or circumstance.

> **Caution: Pre-Mediation Promises**
>
> Be careful what you promise during pre-mediation conversations. Statements like "I think we can resolve this quickly" or "The company seems willing to compromise" create expectations that may prove inaccurate. Keep pre-mediation communications realistic and non-committal about outcomes.

Designing the Process Structure

With stakeholders identified and readiness confirmed, the mediator develops a detailed plan for how the mediation will unfold. Good process design anticipates challenges and creates conditions for constructive dialogue.

Session Format and Sequence

Structure the interaction between the parties. Typical options include:

- Joint sessions: Direct face-to-face dialogue between parties. This builds understanding, but can be counterproductive if tensions are too high.
- Caucuses (private meetings): Separate meetings between the mediator and one party. Useful for exploring sensitive issues, reality-testing positions, and coaching on effective communication.
- Shuttle diplomacy: The mediator moves between parties who are not meeting directly. Appropriate when direct interaction is too volatile or when parties are geographically separated.
- Plenary and working groups: For complex disputes with many participants, smaller working groups may address specific issues (environmental, employment, compensation) with results brought back to the whole group.

Most mediations use a combination of formats. A typical sequence might begin with caucuses to prepare each party, move to joint sessions for opening statements and agenda-setting, use working groups or caucuses for detailed exploration of the issues, and return to joint sessions for negotiation and agreement. For a detailed discussion of caucusing techniques, shuttle diplomacy, joint fact-finding, and other process management tools, see Chapter 9: Tools and Competencies in the Mediator's Toolbox.

Timeline and Pacing

Establish a realistic timeline that balances urgency with thoroughness. Several tips can help:

- Number of sessions: Simple disputes resolve in one or two sessions. Complex multi-issue conflicts require multiple sessions over weeks or months. Some disputes require years of engagement and multiple interim agreements (see Case Study A in Chapter 17).
- Session length: Full-day sessions (6 to 8 hours with breaks) allow deep engagement but can be exhausting. Half-day sessions maintain energy but may feel rushed. Consider participants' other commitments, especially community members who may have farming or family responsibilities.
- Spacing between sessions: Allow time for parties to reflect, consult constituents, and gather information, but not so much time that momentum is lost. Weekly or bi-weekly sessions work well for many disputes.
- Milestones and deadlines: External deadlines (project phases, regulatory requirements, seasonal factors) may create natural pressure points. Internal milestones, such as "We aim to complete agenda-setting by session two," help maintain progress.

Venue Selection

The physical setting significantly influences mediation dynamics. Key considerations include:

- Neutrality: Avoid venues associated with either party. A company's conference room puts community members at a psychological disadvantage; a community hall may make company representatives feel like outsiders. Neutral third-party venues, such as hotels, government facilities, and religious institutions, are often preferable.
- Accessibility: Ensure all participants can reach the venue without undue burden. Consider transportation, accessibility for those with disabilities, and safety.

- Privacy: Confidential discussions require a space where conversations cannot be overheard. Ensure rooms for caucuses are available.
- Comfort: Adequate lighting, temperature control, seating arrangements, and refreshments contribute to productive discussion. Uncomfortable participants become irritable participants.
- Symbolic meaning: Some venues carry symbolic significance. A site of previous conflict or trauma may not be appropriate. Conversely, a location associated with peace or community pride may set a positive tone.

To weigh these considerations systematically, a structured set of criteria for selecting an appropriate venue appears in the figure below.

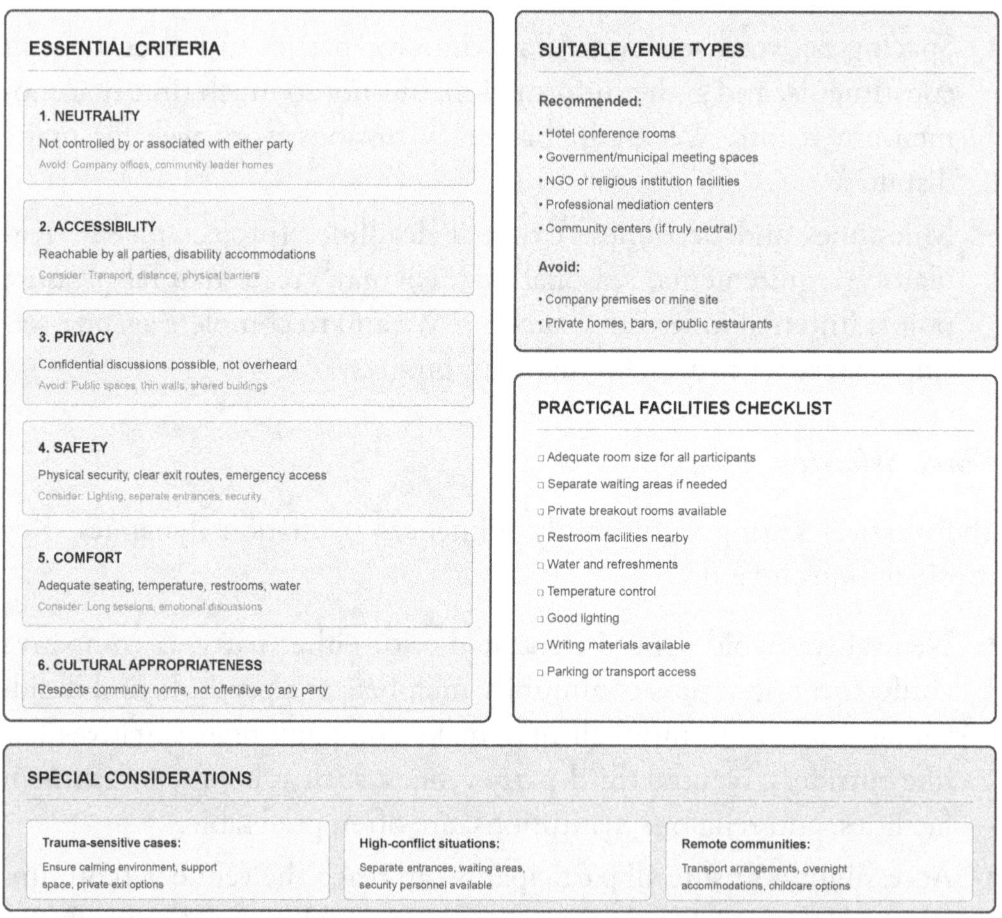

Figure 19: A set of criteria for selecting an appropriate mediation venue, considering neutrality, accessibility, symbolic meaning, and practical logistics.

The venue itself communicates a message about neutrality and respect, which is why choosing carefully matters as much as how you prepare the room once parties arrive.

Practical Tip: Seating Arrangements Matter

Seating arrangements matter more than most people realize. Circular or U-shaped arrangements promote equality and dialogue. Rectangular tables with parties on opposite sides can reinforce adversarial dynamics.

Position the mediator equidistant from both parties, not aligned with either side. If using visual aids such as flipcharts or screens, position them so all participants have equal visibility.

Establishing Ground Rules and Agreements

Ground rules create the container for productive dialogue. They establish expectations for behavior, protect participant safety, and provide a framework for managing difficult moments.

Core Ground Rules

Most mediations include some version of the following ground rules:

- Confidentiality: What is said in mediation stays in mediation. Parties agree not to disclose discussions outside the process and not to use mediation statements in legal proceedings if mediation fails. Clearly state exceptions, such as mandatory reporting requirements or threats of harm.
- Respectful communication: One person speaks at a time. No interrupting. No personal attacks. Focus on issues, not personalities. Use respectful language.
- Good faith participation: Parties commit to engaging honestly, providing accurate information, and genuinely seeking resolution rather than using mediation as a tactical delay.
- Voluntary participation: Parties may withdraw at any time without penalty. No one will be pressured into an agreement they do not genuinely accept.

- No retaliation: Parties agree that nothing said in mediation will result in retaliation against the speaker. This matters most for community members who may fear consequences for criticizing a powerful company.

Additional Ground Rules for Company-Community Disputes

Depending on the specific context, additional ground rules may be needed, including:

- Pause on external actions: Parties may agree to pause protests, legal proceedings, media campaigns, or expansion activities during mediation to create space for dialogue.
- Information sharing: Parties may agree to share relevant documents or data during mediation that they might otherwise keep confidential.
- Consultation rights: Representatives may need time to consult with constituents before making commitments. Ground rules can establish how this will work.
- Media communications: Parties may agree on how (or whether) to communicate about the mediation to the media and external stakeholders.

Key Concept: Co-Creating Ground Rules

Ground rules are most effective when parties participate in creating them. The mediator typically proposes a starting set, then invites additions and modifications. This collaborative development gives parties ownership of the rules, surfaces concerns the mediator may not have anticipated, and provides practice for later substantive negotiations.

An agreement on ground rules represents the first collaborative success in the mediation process.

Cultural and Contextual Considerations

Process design must be adapted to the cultural context. Approaches that work in one setting may be inappropriate or ineffective in another.

Incorporating Cultural Protocols

Many cultures have protocols for beginning important discussions, such as:

- Opening rituals: Prayer, blessing, libation, or ceremonial greetings may be expected before substantive discussion begins. It strengthens the process to inquire about appropriate protocols and invite community elders or religious leaders to lead them.
- Forms of address: Some cultures require formal titles or elaborate greetings before business discussions. Failure to observe these can be perceived as disrespectful.
- Hospitality customs: Sharing food or drink may be an important part of relationship-building. Build time for this into the schedule rather than treating it as an inconvenient delay.
- Decision-making processes: Some cultures make decisions by consensus, requiring extended consultation. Others defer to elders or chiefs. The mediation timeline must accommodate these processes.

Communication Style Differences

Cultural differences in communication style can cause misunderstandings in the following ways:

- Direct vs. indirect communication: Some cultures value directness; others consider it rude. Indirect speakers may say "that's interesting" when they mean "I disagree." Mediators must learn to read these cues.
- Silence: In some cultures, silence indicates thoughtful consideration. In others, it signals disagreement. Effective practice involves pausing before filling silences, to understand their meaning.
- Emotional expression: Some cultures encourage open emotional expression; others value restraint. A mediator must create space for different styles without judging either.
- Storytelling: In many cultures, points are made through extended stories rather than direct statements. Allow time for this and listen for the underlying message.

Caution: Gender Dynamics Across Cultures

Gender dynamics vary significantly across cultures. In some contexts, women may not speak in mixed-gender settings or may be excluded from formal negotiations.

The mediator may need to create separate opportunities for women's voices to be heard. Avoid imposing gender norms from one culture onto another, but also ensure that power imbalances within communities are not simply reproduced in the mediation.

6.2 Phase 1: Opening Session

The opening session marks the formal beginning of mediation. It sets the tone for everything that follows, establishes the mediator's credibility and the process's legitimacy, and gives each party an initial opportunity to be heard. A well-conducted opening creates the psychological foundation for productive dialogue; a poorly handled one can doom the process before substantive discussion begins.

Purpose and Importance of the Opening

The opening session accomplishes several critical objectives, outlined below.

Establishing the Mediator's Role and Authority

Participants may be unclear about what a mediator does and how mediation differs from other processes, such as arbitration, court, and negotiation without a facilitator. The opening clarifies that the mediator will guide the discussion and ensure fairness but will not impose solutions. This understanding is essential for parties to engage appropriately. If they expect the mediator to decide who is right, they will argue their case rather than explore solutions. If they see the mediator as an advocate, they will be confused by impartial facilitation.

Key Concept: First Impressions

The opening moments set the tone for everything that follows. A warm, professional, confident opening builds credibility. A disorganized or anxious start undermines trust in the process. Rehearse your opening statement until it feels natural, and arrive early to ensure smooth logistics.

Creating Psychological Safety

Parties enter mediation feeling vulnerable. They may fear being judged, manipulated, or pressured into unfavorable outcomes. The opening establishes that mediation is a safe space where concerns can be voiced, where participation is voluntary, and where confidentiality protects what is shared. This safety is a prerequisite for the honest communication that resolution requires.

Humanizing Participants

Before substantive discussion, participants often see each other through the lens of conflict. The "company" is a faceless corporation; the "community" is an irrational mob. The opening provides an opportunity to see each other as human beings with names, roles, and lives beyond this dispute. Personal introductions, even brief ones, begin to break down stereotypes and lay the interpersonal foundation for dialogue.

Providing Catharsis

Parties come to mediation with accumulated frustration, anger, and even pain. Opening statements provide an opportunity to express these feelings. Being heard, truly heard, is itself therapeutic. Parties who feel they've had a chance to tell their story are better able to shift into problem-solving mode. Rushing past this cathartic function in pursuit of "getting to the issues" often backfires, as unexpressed emotions resurface disruptively later.

Key Concept: Four Functions of the Opening Session

The opening session serves four essential functions: establishing the mediator's role, creating psychological safety, humanizing participants, and providing catharsis.

Rushing through the opening is a common mistake. The relational and emotional work done in the opening phase is essential groundwork for the substantive work that follows.

Welcoming and Introductions

Before participants arrive, ensure the physical space is ready. Arrange the seating area appropriately (typically in a circle or around a table, with the mediator equidistant from each party), and set out name tents or place cards if participants don't know each other. Position flipcharts, markers, and other materials appropriately, then test them. Provide water and refreshments, set up and test translation equipment if needed, and identify breakout rooms for caucuses.

As participants arrive, the mediator should greet each warmly and ensure they are comfortable. This pre-session interaction continues the relationship-building begun in the pre-mediation meetings. If the parties have not met before, the mediator may facilitate brief informal introductions as people arrive.

Once everyone is seated, the mediator will formally open the session. If cultural protocol calls for a prayer, blessing, or other ceremonial opening, this occurs first. The mediator then welcomes everyone and invites participants to introduce themselves. Throughout these opening exchanges and the discussions that follow, the mediator must capture key information without disrupting the flow of dialogue. The following framework offers a structured approach to note-taking during mediation sessions.

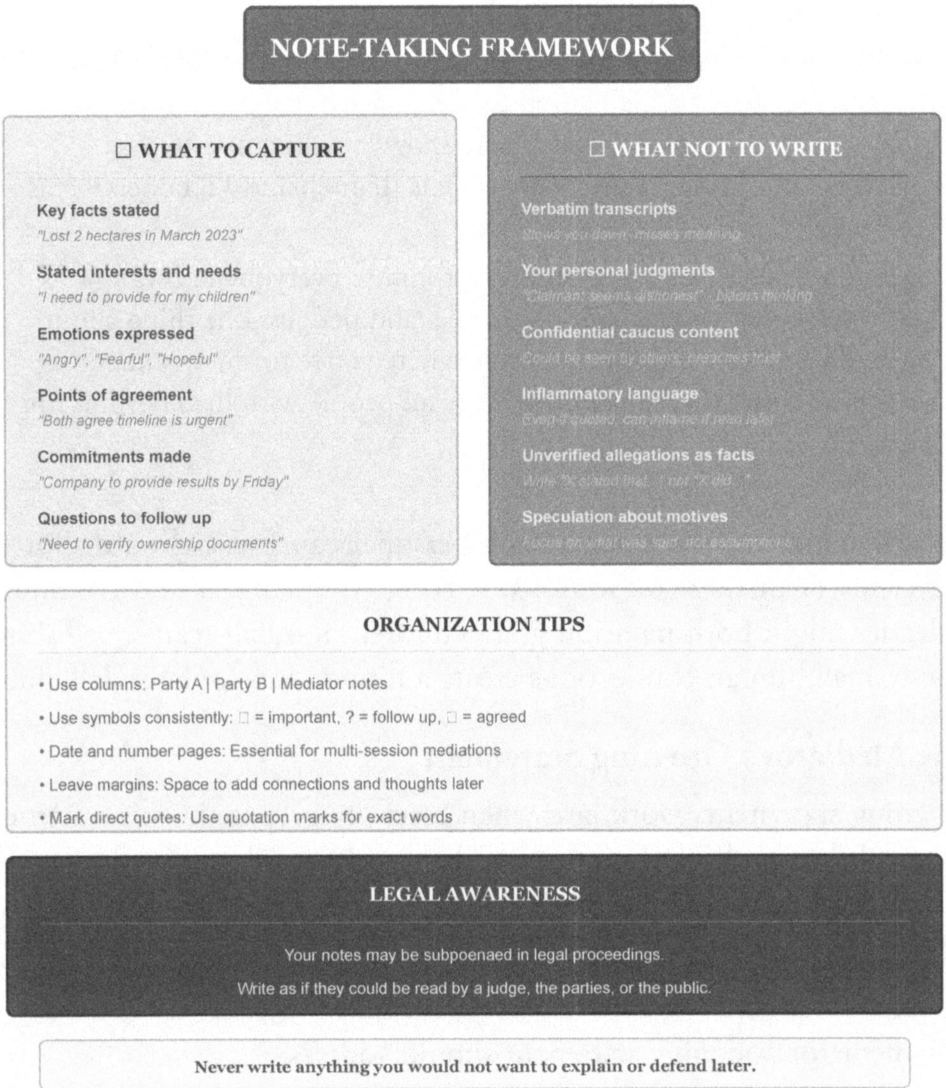

Figure 20: A structured framework for documenting key points during mediation sessions, including issues raised, agreements reached, and action items.

Clear note-taking practices allow parties to verify that their positions have been accurately captured and reduces the common source of frustration where people leave the table unsure whether their concerns were truly understood.

Sample Opening and Introductions

Mediator: "Good morning, and thank you all for being here. I know that coming to this table has required courage and commitment from each of you. The fact that you're here shows a willingness to seek solutions, and I respect that. My name is [name], and I'll be serving as your mediator.

"Before we begin, let's go around the room so everyone knows who is here. Please share your name, your role, and perhaps one thing about yourself beyond this dispute. Maybe where you're from, or something you enjoy doing. Let's remember we're all people with lives beyond this room."

This invitation to share something personal can feel awkward, but often yields surprising connections. A company manager and community leader might both mention grandchildren, football teams, or fishing. These small human connections create a foundation for later dialogue.

The Mediator's Opening Statement

Opening statements work best when carefully prepared. This statement accomplishes multiple functions and should be tailored to the specific situation while covering essential elements.

Essential Elements

The mediator's opening statement should address:

1. Role clarification: Explain that the mediator facilitates but does not decide. "My job is to help you communicate effectively and explore solutions. I won't tell you what to do or who is right. Any agreement will be your agreement, not mine."
2. Voluntariness: Emphasize that participation is by choice. "You're here voluntarily, and you can leave at any time. Nothing will be decided without your agreement."
3. Confidentiality: Explain confidentiality rules. "What is said here stays here. We've all agreed not to disclose our discussions outside this room or use them in any legal proceeding. This allows us to speak honestly without fear."

4. Ground rules: Review agreed ground rules. "We've agreed on some guidelines: one person speaks at a time, we'll only use respectful language, and we'll focus on issues, not personalities. I may remind us of these if needed."
5. Process overview: Explain what will happen. "We'll begin by giving each side a chance to share their perspective. Then we'll identify the issues to address, explore underlying interests, and work together toward solutions."
6. Questions: Invite clarification. "Before we begin, do you have any questions about how this will work?"

Sample Mediator Opening Statement

"Thank you all for being here. I want to start by acknowledging that coming to this table has not been easy. You've had a difficult history, and there is real pain and real frustration in this room. The fact that you're here despite that tells me you're serious about finding a better path forward.

"Let me explain my role. I'm not a judge, and I won't decide who is right or wrong. I'm not here to take sides. My job is to help you have a productive conversation, ensure everyone has a chance to be heard, and explore options that might address everyone's concerns. Any agreement that comes out of this process will be your agreement, based on what you decide is workable, not on what I think you should do.

"This process is entirely voluntary. You chose to be here, and you can leave at any time. Nothing will be decided without your consent. If you ever feel uncomfortable or need a break, just let me know.

"Everything said here is confidential. We've all agreed not to share our discussions with outsiders or use anything said here in court if we don't reach an agreement. This allows us to speak honestly, explore ideas without commitment, and understand each other without worrying about how it might be used against us later.

"We've also agreed on some ground rules: one person speaks at a time using only respectful language while focusing on issues rather than attacking individuals. If I think we're straying from these, I may gently bring us back.

"Here's how we'll proceed. First, I'll give each side a chance to share its perspective on this situation without interruption. Then we'll identify the specific issues we need to address. We'll explore what's really important to each of you, not just your positions but your underlying interests and needs. And then we'll brainstorm options and work toward solutions that address as many of those interests as possible.

"Do you have any questions before we begin?"

Practical Tip: Opening Statement Personalization

While maintaining consistent core content, adapt your opening to each specific mediation. Reference the particular context, acknowledge the journey parties have taken to reach this point, and signal understanding of their specific situation. Generic openings feel impersonal.

Opening Statements by Parties

After the mediator's opening, each party has an opportunity to present their perspective without interruption. This is often the most emotionally charged part of the mediation, and skillful facilitation is essential.

Purpose of Opening Statements

Opening statements serve several purposes, including:

- Catharsis: Parties have been waiting to tell their story. Being heard is itself valuable.
- Information gathering: The mediator learns about issues, concerns, and emotional valence.
- Mutual education: Each party hears how the other experiences the situation.
- Issue identification: Key topics for the agenda often emerge from opening statements.

Managing Difficult Moments

Opening statements can become heated. Some practical strategies for managing difficult moments include:

- Allow emotion without letting it derail: Anger and tears are natural and often necessary. Validate the emotion ("I can see this is very painful") without getting drawn into content disputes during opening statements.
- Redirect personal attacks: If statements become accusatory ("You people are liars"), gently redirect ("I hear your frustration. Can you tell us more about the specific incident that concerns you?").
- Use breaks strategically: If emotions become overwhelming, a brief break allows everyone to compose themselves ("Let's take five minutes. We'll resume shortly.").
- Prevent escalation: If the listening party's body language signals they're about to erupt, make eye contact and silently signal patience.

> **Practical Tip: Managing Opening Statements**
>
> During opening statements, effective facilitation involves setting a time limit (typically 10 to 15 minutes per party), listen actively with eye contact and nodding, protect the speaker from interruptions, note key points (such as issues, interests, emotions, and potential common ground), and watch the nonverbal cues of all participants.
>
> If emotions become overwhelming, offer a brief pause. Sometimes simply acknowledging the emotion ("I can see how much this has affected you") is enough to allow the speaker to continue.

Transitioning to Dialogue

Moving from opening statements to collaborative dialogue is a key transition moment. This transition is crucial: it shifts the dynamic from "taking turns talking at each other" to "working together on shared problems."

Summarizing and Synthesizing

Summarizing both parties' perspectives, highlighting common themes and framing differences constructively.

Sample Transition Summary

"Thank you both for sharing so openly. Let me see if I've understood. The community has expressed concerns about water quality, employment opportunities, and a feeling of being excluded from decisions that affect your lives. You've experienced broken promises in the past, and trust has been damaged as a result.

"The company has shared the pressures you face from regulations, market conditions, and headquarters expectations. You want to be a responsible neighbor, but you feel your efforts haven't been recognized, and your constraints aren't understood.

"Both of you have mentioned wanting a peaceful, productive relationship going forward. Did I capture that fairly?

"So we have some real differences to work through, but I also heard some common ground. Both of you want stability. Both of you want to be treated fairly. The challenge is figuring out how to get there. Rather than continuing to argue about the past, I'd like us to focus on the future. What can we build together that addresses the community's concerns while working within the company's constraints? I'm optimistic we can find solutions neither of you has thought of yet."

6.3 Phase 2: Agenda Setting

Once the opening phase establishes the foundation for dialogue, the next task is to identify and organize the issues to be addressed. Agenda setting provides structure and ensures that all concerns receive attention. A well-constructed agenda transforms an overwhelming conflict into manageable pieces and creates a roadmap for the discussions to follow.

The Purpose of Agenda Setting

Agenda setting serves multiple essential functions in the mediation process, the most important of which are covered in detail below.

Creating Manageable Structure

Complex disputes often involve numerous grievances that can feel overwhelming. A community may have a hundred complaints against a company spanning many years. Breaking these into a manageable number of agenda items (typically five to ten) makes the challenge feel surmountable. It also prevents discussions from becoming chaotic, with participants jumping from topic to topic.

Ensuring All Concerns Are Addressed

Formally listing agenda items ensures that no key issue is overlooked or avoided. This matters especially for protecting weaker parties. Without an explicit agenda, more powerful parties may steer discussion away from uncomfortable topics. An agreed-upon agenda creates accountability: "These are the things we committed to addressing."

Building Agreement Early

Agreeing on an agenda, even a tentative one, represents the first collaborative success. Parties are not yet agreeing on solutions, just on what needs to be discussed. This relatively low-stakes agreement builds momentum and models the collaborative process that will be needed later.

Collecting and Organizing Issues

The mediator invites each party to identify the topics they want addressed, writing each issue on a flipchart visible to all. Once issues are collected, reframe them in neutral language that does not presume fault or predetermine solutions.

Original Statement	Neutral Framing
"The company poisoned our river."	Water quality and health concerns
"The company broke all their promises."	Past commitments and future expectations
"The community makes impossible demands."	Understanding community needs and priorities

Original Statement	Neutral Framing
"We're not getting our fair share of jobs."	Local employment opportunities
"They never consult us before making decisions."	Communication and consultation processes

When reframing, explain what you're doing: "I'm going to write this in a way that captures your concern without taking sides. Let me know if this wording works for you."

Multiple grievances often cluster around common themes. Grouping them creates a more manageable agenda. Consider grouping concerns as follows: environmental cluster (water quality, dust, noise, deforestation); economic cluster (employment, local procurement, business impacts); relationship cluster (communication, consultation, respect, trust); and compensation cluster (land, property damage, livelihood losses).

Caution: Hidden Agendas

Parties may agree to a formal agenda while harboring unstated goals. A community might publicly seek compensation while privately seeking the termination of a company executive. Watch for issues that generate disproportionate emotion, as these often signal hidden agenda items that need surfacing.

Hidden agendas are often linked to hidden parties: individuals or groups who exert significant influence behind the scenes without being directly present at the mediation table. The following mapping tool helps mediators identify these invisible actors and develop strategies for managing their impact on the process.

Identifying parties who exert influence from behind the scenes is one of the most valuable investments you can make in process design.

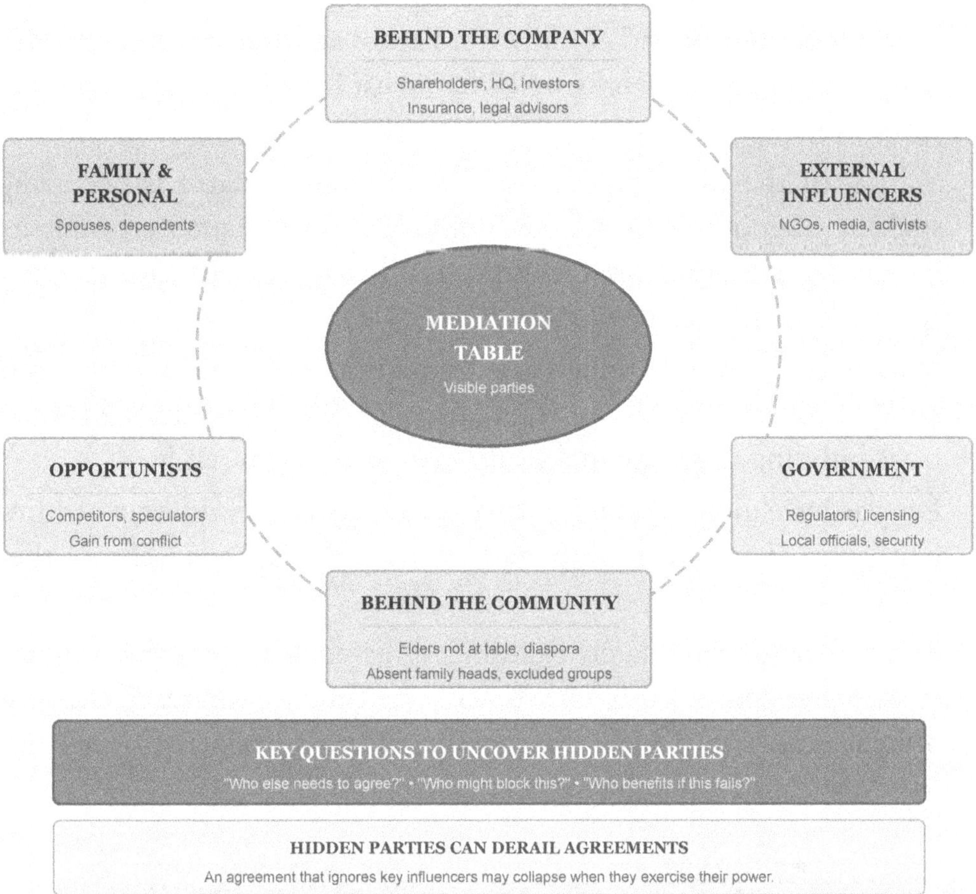

Figure 21: A mapping tool for identifying parties who exert influence behind the scenes but may not be directly present at the mediation table.

Hidden parties often represent the greatest risk to implementation success, as their unaddressed interests can quietly undermine agreements that appeared solid at the table.

Prioritizing and Sequencing

Once issues are identified and organized, parties typically benefit from deciding which to tackle first. The sequence can significantly affect the dynamics and success of mediation. Different sequencing approaches have different advantages. Below are some common methods along with their benefits and uses:

- Start with the easiest issue: Resolving a relatively simple issue first builds momentum and confidence. Parties see that agreement is possible. This approach works well when trust is low and parties need an early win.
- Start with the most urgent issue: If immediate harm is occurring, such as ongoing pollution or imminent displacement, addressing it first demonstrates responsiveness and may be necessary to create space for broader discussions.
- Start with the foundational issue: Sometimes one issue underlies others. If broken trust is the foundation of all grievances, addressing trust-building first may make other issues easier to resolve.
- Let parties choose: Asking parties which issue they'd like to address first gives them ownership and ensures the agenda reflects their priorities.
- Save the hardest for later: Building agreements on easier issues first creates investment in the process. By the time parties reach the most difficult issue, they have the momentum to sustain them and may have developed enough trust to make progress.

Key Concept: Interconnected Issues in Complex Disputes

In complex disputes, issues are often interconnected. A party may want to link their concession on one issue to receiving something on another. Acknowledging linkages while maintaining progress:

"I understand that these issues are connected for you. Let's explore them one at a time, keeping in mind that the agreement is not final until we've addressed the whole package."

6.4 Phase 3: Exploring Interests and Needs

This phase is often the heart of mediation. Here, the mediator helps parties move beyond their stated positions to understand the underlying interests, needs, and concerns that drive them. This deeper understanding is essential for generating creative solutions that satisfy all parties.

Understanding Positions vs. Interests

The distinction between positions and interests is fundamental to interest-based negotiation and effective mediation.

What Are Positions?

Positions are the specific demands or solutions that parties present. They are what people say they want. Positions are often framed in terms of outcomes: "We want one million dollars in compensation," "We refuse to relocate," "We can only offer 100,000 dollars."

Positions are visible and concrete, making them easy to articulate and argue for. However, they are also typically rigid and often incompatible with each other. When negotiations focus on positions, they tend to become adversarial, with each side defending its own demands while attacking the other party's.

What Are Interests?

Interests are the underlying needs, desires, concerns, and fears that motivate positions. They are why people want what they say they want. Interests are often less visible than positions, and sometimes parties themselves may not have fully articulated them.

Figure 22 illustrates the critical distinction between what parties demand (positions) and what they actually need (interests).

ASPECT	POSITIONS	INTERESTS
Definition What it is	Specific demands or solutions *What parties say they want*	Underlying needs, desires, concerns *Why they want it*
Example (Mining context)	"The mine must cease operations" "We want €500,000 compensation"	"Protect our water supply" "Secure our children's future"
Flexibility Room to move	Rigid and binary *Either/or, win/lose framing*	Flexible and often overlapping *Multiple ways to satisfy*
Solution Potential What's possible	Limited, zero-sum thinking *One party's gain = other's loss*	Creative, mutually beneficial *Both parties can gain*
Mediator Focus Where to look	Surface level *Stated demands only*	Root causes *Underlying motivations*
	VISIBLE (Above the surface)	HIDDEN (Below the surface)

Figure 22: A visual comparison illustrating the difference between stated positions (what parties demand) and underlying interests (what parties actually need).

The distinction between positions and interests is perhaps the single most important conceptual tool for opening movement in stuck conflicts, as it allows you to validate what parties care about while creating space for creative solutions.

Behind a community's demand for one million dollars might be interests in security for displaced families, acknowledgment of harm suffered, resources for children's education, and justice for wrongs committed. Behind a company's refusal to pay that amount might be interests in financial viability, avoiding precedents that invite more claims, and fairness to shareholders and other stakeholders.

Key Concept: Positions vs. Interests

Positions are often incompatible, while interests can frequently be reconciled. A community demanding one million dollars and a company offering 100,000 dollars appear to have irreconcilable positions.

But when underlying interests are explored, creative solutions may emerge that neither party initially envisioned. The possibilities expand dramatically when interests rather than positions become the focus.

Practical Tip: Interest Verification

When you believe you have identified an underlying interest, test it: "It sounds like what matters most is not the specific amount, but ensuring your children's future is secure. Is that right?" Verification prevents building solutions on misunderstood foundations.

From Positions to Interests: Examples

Position	Underlying Interests	Deeper Needs
We want $1M in compensation	Displaced families need resources to rebuild; children need education; the community needs infrastructure	Security, dignity, hope for the future, acknowledgment of harm
We can only pay $100K	Financial viability matters; avoiding precedent for future claims; fairness to shareholders	Predictability, responsibility to multiple stakeholders, and sustainability
We refuse to relocate	This is ancestral land; livelihoods depend on specific location; cultural sites are irreplaceable	Identity, continuity, respect for heritage, control over destiny
Hire fifty locals immediately	Youth need employment; families need income; communities benefit when they gain meaningful advantages from projects	Dignity of work, economic participation, fairness, hope

Techniques for Uncovering Interests

Uncovering interests requires skillful questioning and deep listening. Parties often have not fully articulated their interests even to themselves, so the mediator helps them discover and express what truly matters.

The "Why" Question

The simplest technique is asking "why": "Why is that important to you?" "Why do you need that?"

Repeated "why" questions peel back layers to reveal deeper interests.

Figure 23 uses the iceberg model to show how visible positions sit above deeper interests, needs, fears, and values.

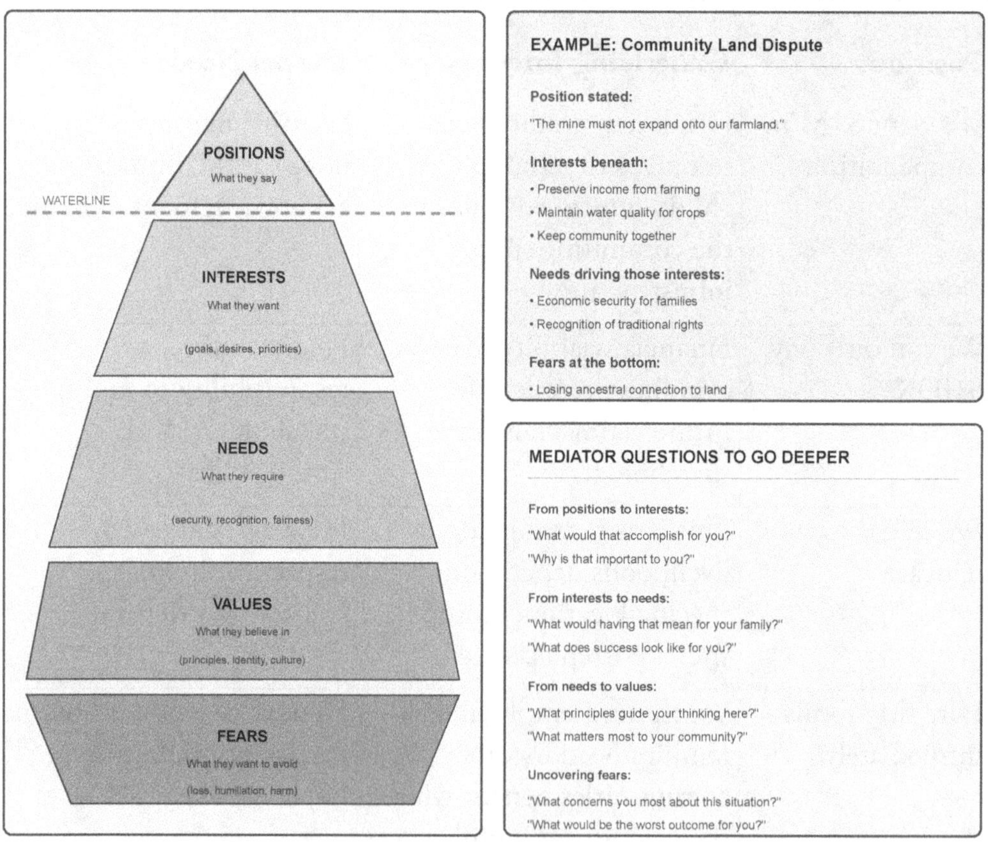

Figure 23: An iceberg model showing how visible positions sit above the surface while deeper interests, needs, fears, and values lie beneath.

The iceberg model illustrates why surface agreement often fails, because agreements that address positions without touching the deeper interests, values, and fears underlying them tend to collapse under implementation pressure.

The "Five Whys" Technique

Community: "We need the company to build us a new road."

Mediator: "Why is the road so important?"

Community: "Because our village is isolated."

Mediator: "And why does isolation concern you?"

Community: "We can't get our crops to market, and the children can't get to school easily."

Mediator: "So your underlying concerns are about economic opportunity and education access?"

Now the discussion can focus on how to address access and opportunity. A road is one solution, but others might include a market facility closer to the village, school transportation, or telecommunications infrastructure that reduces the need for physical travel.

The "What Would That Give You" Question

When "why" feels too direct, ask what achieving the position would provide. This reveals interests: "If you received that compensation, what would you do with it?" The answer discloses what the money is really for, opening the possibility of addressing those needs in different ways.

Identifying Common and Compatible Interests

Amidst divergent interests, there are often shared concerns that can anchor agreement. The mediator actively looks for and highlights these.

Shared Interests

Some interests are genuinely common to both parties. These include:

- Stability: Both the community and company typically want a stable, predictable environment. The community wants life to be undisrupted; the company wants operations to be uninterrupted.
- Reputation: Both may care about how they are perceived. The company has corporate reputation concerns; the community has pride and dignity concerns.
- Avoiding escalation: Neither typically wants the conflict to worsen into violence, protracted litigation, or international attention.
- Future relationship: If the company will operate in the area for years or decades, both parties have an interest in establishing a workable long-term relationship.

Explicitly noting alignments helps parties recognize their common ground: "I'm hearing that both sides want the community to thrive and the project to succeed. The disagreement is about how to make that happen and who contributes what. That's actually encouraging, because it means we're not working at cross-purposes on fundamental goals."

Acknowledging Intangible Interests

Some of the most important interests are intangible: respect, acknowledgment, justice, dignity, and trust. These often matter more than material issues but are easier to overlook because they cannot be quantified.

> **Key Concept: Interest Layers**
>
> Interests often exist in layers. Surface interests (compensation) may cover deeper interests (security), which may mask even deeper needs (dignity, recognition). Keep probing. The most sustainable solutions address the deepest layer of genuine interest.

Caution: The Weight of Intangible Interests

Intangible interests like respect, acknowledgment, and dignity often matter more than material outcomes but are frequently overlooked because they cannot be quantified.

Communities that have suffered harm often need the harm to be acknowledged before they can move forward. This acknowledgment may be as important as compensation, sometimes more so. Surfacing underlying interests explicitly supports deeper problem-solving.

6.5 Phase 4: Generating Options

Once interests are understood, the mediation shifts to brainstorming potential solutions. This phase is often more optimistic than earlier ones, as parties begin to see opportunities to address their concerns. The goal is to generate a wide range of options before evaluating them, separating invention from decision. A collection of creative techniques that mediators can use to facilitate this brainstorming process appears below.

Figure 24 presents a collection of creative techniques for generating potential solutions and expanding options beyond initial positions.

Figure 24: A collection of creative techniques for generating potential solutions, including brainstorming approaches and lateral thinking methods.

Option generation is not primarily about finding the perfect solution, but rather about demonstrating to parties that solutions exist and that creative thinking can transform what appeared to be zero-sum conflict into mutual gain.

Principles of Effective Brainstorming

Separate Invention from Decision

The most crucial principle of brainstorming is to keep idea generation separate from idea evaluation. When options are criticized as soon as they're proposed, creativity shuts down. Parties stop suggesting anything that might be rejected, and the range of possible solutions narrows dramatically.

The mediator needs to establish this norm explicitly: "We're going to brainstorm options now. The rule is that any idea is welcome, no matter how unconventional. We won't evaluate them yet. That comes later. For now, let's just generate as many possibilities as we can."

> **Caution: Premature Evaluation**
>
> The quickest way to kill brainstorming is to allow evaluation during idea generation. Even subtle reactions like a raised eyebrow or a skeptical "hmm" can signal judgment and shut down creativity. Maintain enthusiastic neutrality toward all ideas during the generation phase.

Encourage Creativity and Volume

Quantity leads to quality in brainstorming. The more options generated, the more likely a truly creative solution will emerge. Encouraging unconventional thinking: "What if we approached this completely differently?" "What would a solution look like if money weren't a constraint?" "What would your grandmother suggest?"

> **Practical Tip: Visual Documentation in Brainstorming**
>
> During brainstorming, write all ideas on a flipchart for everyone to see. This creates a shared inventory and prevents ideas from being lost. It also depersonalizes the ideas so that they can be evaluated on merit rather than ownership.
>
> Aim to generate at least three options for each agenda item. This prevents binary thinking ("Either we do it their way or ours") and opens space for creative alternatives that neither party initially envisioned.

Techniques for Generating Options

Interest-Based Option Generation

The interests uncovered in Phase 3 become the starting point for options. For each key interest, ask: "What are all the ways this interest might be addressed?" For example, if the community's interest is children's education, options include direct cash payments to families, scholarship programs, building or improving schools, teacher training, school supplies, transportation to existing schools, or tutoring programs.

Using Objective Criteria

Introducing external standards can generate and legitimize options. "What do international standards suggest?" "What have other companies done in similar situations?" "What does the government require?" These criteria provide neutral reference points that move discussions beyond "what I want" versus "what you want."

Creative Solution Frameworks

Expanding the Pie

Some options create value that neither party could achieve on its own. A community development fund jointly governed by the community and the company, for example, may attract additional investment from the government or donors, creating benefits beyond what either party could provide independently.

Trading Across Differences

Parties often value things differently. The company may find it easier to provide in-kind benefits (using its equipment and expertise to build infrastructure) than cash. The community may value specific outcomes (a school, a clinic) more than equivalent cash. Identifying these differences creates opportunities for mutually beneficial trades.

In the mining industry, there are a number of options and creative solutions that can be found and discussed, and which go far beyond monetary issues. Below is a diagram of multiple options that are typically discussed, depending on the nature of the dispute.

ACCOUNTABILITY	SUPPORT	PREVENTION	COMMUNITY
Acknowledgment of impact and harm	**Counselling** access to services	**Enhanced Training** staff education	**Infrastructure** schools, roads, health
Apology sincere, appropriate	**Healthcare** medical support	**Policy Revisions** updated procedures	**Empowerment** programs, initiatives
Compensation financial restitution	**Mental Health** ongoing resources	**Independent** oversight, monitoring	**Education** awareness campaigns
Personnel Changes reassignment, action	**Advocacy** legal, social support	**Reporting Systems** improved mechanisms	**Local Programs** community benefit

CROSS-CUTTING ELEMENTS

Documentation • Long-term Commitments • Regular Reviews • Community Input

IMPLEMENTATION REQUIREMENTS

All agreements documented in writing • Signed by all parties

Clear timelines established • Accountability measures defined

Figure 25: A menu of possible resolution options commonly used in company-community disputes, organized by type and scope.

Having a menu of resolution options available helps parties visualize what success could look like and prevents the common dynamic where mediation stalls because parties cannot imagine any outcome other than total victory or defeat.

> **Example - Creative Solutions in Practice**
>
> In a mediation over mining impacts, the community initially demanded cash compensation for land damage. The company resisted, fearing precedent and cash flow impacts.
>
> Interest exploration revealed the community wanted the compensation to build a community center. The company had construction expertise and idle equipment between projects.

The creative solution: the company would build the community center directly, providing value worth more than the cash demanded (because of their construction efficiencies) while costing the company less than the cash payout. Both parties gained more than they would have from the original positions.

Practical Tip: Quantity Before Quality

Push for more options than seem necessary. Ask "What else could work?" even when parties seem satisfied with the existing ideas. The best solutions often emerge late in brainstorming, after obvious options are exhausted and creative thinking kicks in.

6.6 Phase 5: Negotiation and Bargaining

After generating options, parties move into negotiation, choosing and refining the solutions that will make it into the final agreement. This stage is about making decisions and often involves compromise. The mediator's role shifts from facilitating exploration to facilitating decision-making.

Evaluating Options

The mediator helps parties evaluate which options best meet the core interests identified earlier. For each option, consider:

- Feasibility: Can this actually be implemented? Does the party have the resources, authority, and capability to deliver?
- Interest satisfaction: How well does this option address each party's key interests?
- Acceptability: Is this something both parties can live with?
- Durability: Will this solution hold over time, or will it create new problems?

Reality Testing

The mediator helps parties think realistically about their options, including what happens if no agreement is reached. This is where BATNA (Best Alternative to a Negotiated Agreement) and WATNA (Worst Alternative to a Negotiated Agreement) become essential tools.

Key Concept: Understanding BATNA

BATNA: What is the best outcome a party can achieve if mediation fails?

WATNA: What is the worst outcome if mediation fails?

Clarifying these alternatives helps parties assess whether proposed solutions are better than their alternatives. Often, both parties realize their alternatives are unattractive, which increases motivation to reach an agreement.

Reality testing is typically done in caucus, where the mediator can ask candid questions.

Sample Reality Testing in Caucus

Mediator: "You've said you won't accept anything less than one million dollars. Let me ask you to think about what happens if we don't reach an agreement here. What will you do?"

Community: "We'll go to court."

Mediator: "And how long might that take? What are the costs? What's the range of possible outcomes?"

Community: "It could take years. We'd need lawyers. We might win, or we might not."

Mediator: "So your best alternative involves significant time, cost, and uncertainty. The company has offered 400,000 dollars plus the community development fund. How does that compare to the uncertain outcome of litigation?"

This is not pressure to accept, but helping the community make an informed decision about whether the offer on the table is better than their realistic alternatives.

Building Package Agreements

In complex disputes with multiple issues, parties often need to see the complete package before committing to individual elements. This is sometimes called "nothing is agreed until everything is agreed." The mediator helps parties build and evaluate comprehensive packages that address all agenda items.

Package deals allow trade-offs across issues. A party might accept less on one issue in exchange for more on another. The mediator might say, "The company is offering X on employment, Y on compensation, and Z on environmental monitoring. Looking at the whole package, does this address your core interests?" When compensation is a central element of the package, mediators benefit from knowing the full range of options that are typically available. An overview of financial, in-kind, and developmental compensation approaches that parties may consider is presented below.

Figure 26 presents a range of compensation approaches, spanning financial, in-kind, and developmental options for resolving disputes.

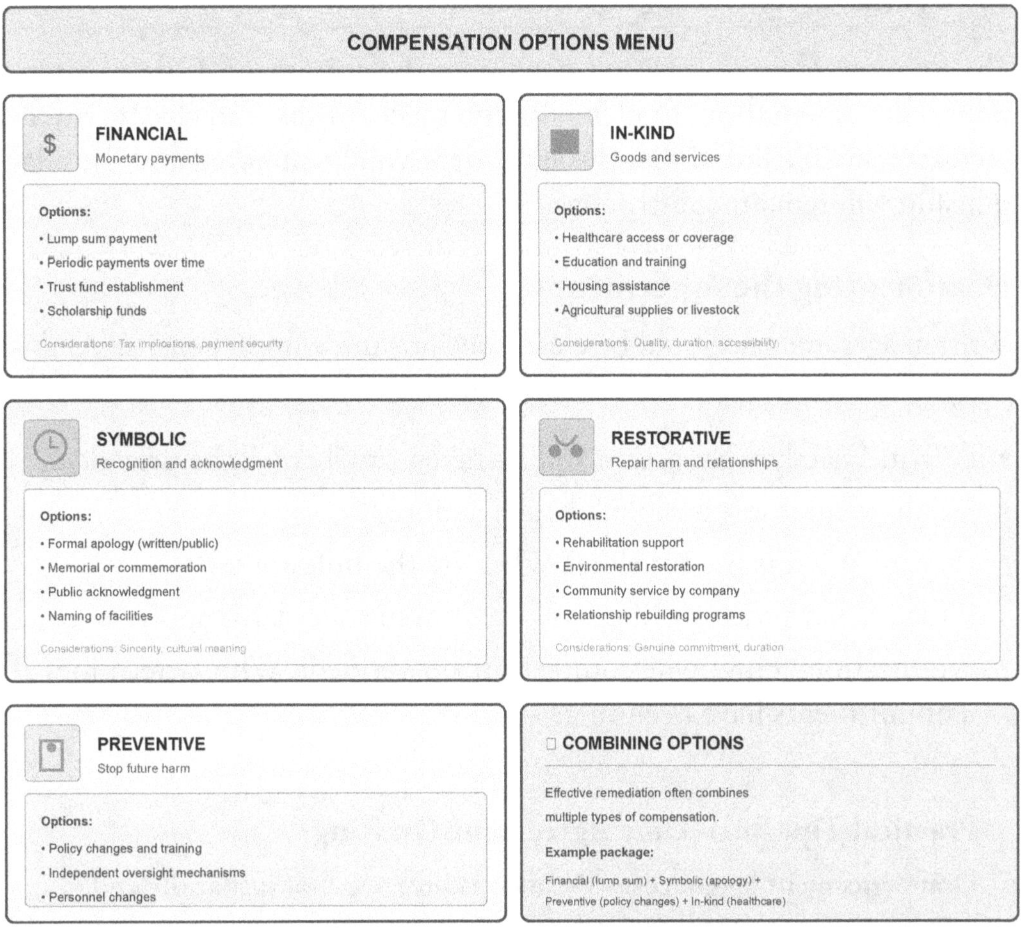

Figure 26: An overview of different compensation options available in dispute resolution, including financial, in-kind, and developmental approaches.

> **Key Concept: Package Deals**
>
> Trading across issues often unlocks solutions that single-issue negotiation cannot. If the community cannot move on the compensation amount and the company cannot move on the timeline, then link them: a higher amount with a longer timeline, or a lower amount with faster payment. Packages create flexibility.

6.7 Phase 6: Reaching Agreement

The final phase formalizes and concludes the agreement. Careful attention to documentation, implementation mechanisms, and closure rituals increases the likelihood that the agreement will be honored and the relationship will remain constructive.

Documenting the Agreement

Written agreements should be clear, specific, and comprehensive. Ambiguity invites later disputes. For each commitment, specify:

- What: Exactly what action will be taken or what will be provided?
- Who: Who is responsible for each action?
- When: What is the timeline? What are the milestones?
- How: What process will be followed? What standards apply?
- Verification: How will completion be verified? Who determines if commitments have been met?

Practical Tip: Real-Time Agreement Drafting

Draft agreement language as discussions progress, not just at the end. This ensures clarity and surfaces misunderstandings immediately.

Read the agreement aloud before signing. This catches ambiguities and ensures all parties understand the same thing.

If parties speak different languages, prepare the agreement in all relevant languages and ensure translations are accurate.

Practical Tip: Implementation Reality Check

Before finalizing any commitment, walk through implementation: "Who exactly will do this? By what date? How will we know it is done? What happens if circumstances change?" Vague agreements with clear intentions often fail. Specific agreements with clear responsibilities succeed.

Closure and Signing

The signing of an agreement is a significant moment that deserves appropriate recognition. Consider:

- Acknowledgment: Recognize the hard work and good faith that led to the agreement
- Symbolic gestures: Handshakes, shared meals, gift exchanges, or other culturally appropriate symbols of reconciliation
- Witnesses: Presence of respected community members, company officials, or external observers adds weight to commitments
- Documentation: Photographs or video can serve as a record and reminder

> **Caution: Agreement Fatigue**
>
> After lengthy negotiations, parties often agree to unclear or unrealistic terms just to reach the finish line. Watch for signs of exhaustion-driven agreement. It is better to pause and return fresh than to sign an agreement that parties will later regret or fail to implement.

Planning for Implementation and Monitoring

Agreements succeed or fail during implementation. Building accountability mechanisms into the agreement increases the likelihood that commitments will be honored.

Joint Monitoring Mechanisms

Establish mechanisms for both parties to monitor implementation together, including:

- Joint monitoring committees: Regular meetings with representatives from both parties to review progress
- Progress reports: Periodic written updates on implementation status
- Site visits: Joint inspections of project sites
- Third-party verification: Independent monitoring by neutral parties where trust is limited

Dispute Resolution Mechanisms

Include provisions for handling disagreements about implementation, including:

- Direct discussion: First attempt to resolve through direct communication
- Return to mediation: If direct resolution fails, reconvene the mediation process
- Escalation procedures: Clear path for escalating unresolved issues

6.8 Process Design Checklist

Before formal mediation begins, use this comprehensive checklist to ensure thorough preparation.

Stakeholder Preparation

✓ All key stakeholders identified (primary parties, secondary influencers)
✓ Parties confirmed willing and ready to participate voluntarily
✓ Decision-makers identified and confirmed to have authority
✓ Pre-mediation meetings completed with each party
✓ All participants understand the mediation process

Process Design

✓ Format determined (joint sessions, caucuses, working groups)
✓ Timeline established (number of sessions, overall timeframe)

To visualise how these elements fit together over the course of a mediation, a template below lays out the major phases and milestones from initial preparation through to final agreement.

Figure 27 offers a template for planning and scheduling the phases and milestones of the mediation process from start to completion.

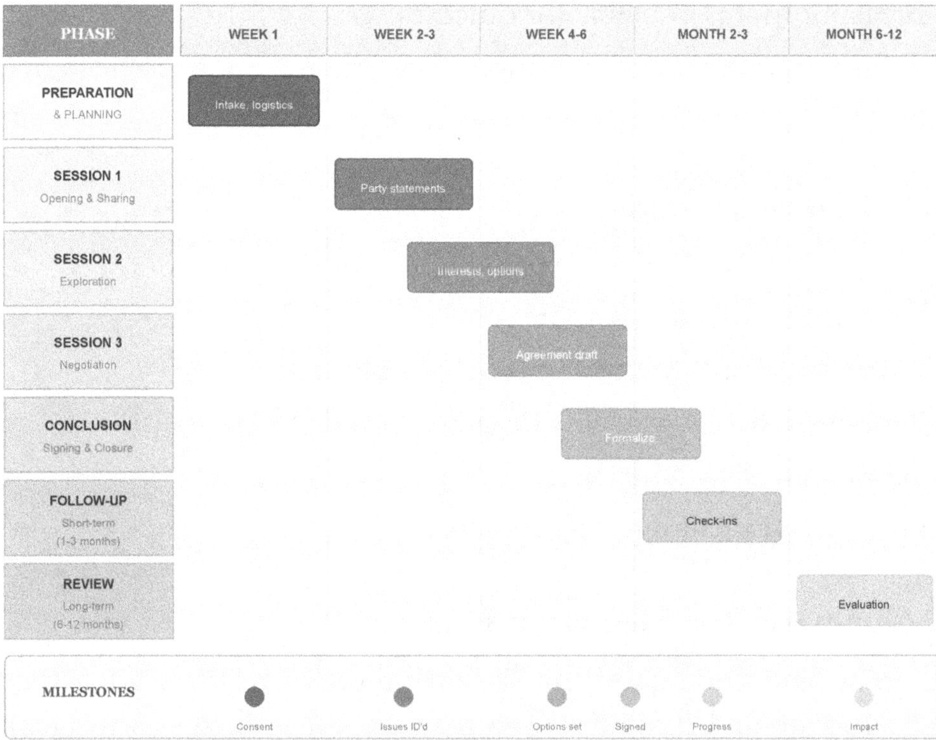

Figure 27: Mediation Timeline Template

A realistic timeline communicates respect for the time required for genuine dialogue and prevents the common mistake of rushing toward agreement before parties have actually shifted their understanding of the problem.

✓ Ground rules drafted and agreed
✓ Confidentiality provisions established
✓ Agreement to Mediate prepared if appropriate

Logistics

✓ Neutral venue selected and booked
✓ Seating arrangements planned
✓ Translation and interpretation arranged if needed
✓ Materials prepared (flipcharts, markers, name tents, documents)
✓ Refreshments and meals arranged

✓ Breakout rooms available for caucuses
✓ Transportation and accommodation arranged for participants if needed

Special Considerations

✓ Cultural protocols identified and incorporated
✓ Trauma considerations addressed
✓ Power imbalance mitigation strategies planned
✓ Support resources available (legal, technical, psychosocial)
✓ Safety concerns addressed
✓ Gender considerations incorporated

6.9 Summary: The Mediation Journey

Designing and conducting mediation processes requires attention to both structure and flexibility. The six phases described in this chapter provide a roadmap, but every mediation is unique. Skilled mediators adapt the process to the specific situation, culture, and parties involved.

Key principles that strengthen process design include:

1. Invest in preparation: The effort put into Phase 0 often determines whether mediation succeeds. Thorough stakeholder analysis, careful readiness assessment, and thoughtful process design create the conditions for productive dialogue.
2. Create psychological safety: Parties must feel safe to speak honestly, take risks, and explore options. This safety comes from clear ground rules, consistent facilitation, and demonstrated impartiality.
3. Focus on interests, not positions: The shift from positional bargaining to interest-based problem-solving is the heart of effective mediation. Help parties understand what they and the other side truly need.
4. Generate options before choosing: Separate invention from decision. Brainstorm widely before evaluating. Creative solutions often emerge from unexpected combinations.

5. Document carefully: Clear, specific agreements prevent future disputes. Build in monitoring and dispute resolution mechanisms.
6. Plan for implementation: An agreement is only as good as its implementation. Build accountability mechanisms from the start.

The following matrix consolidates these responsibilities, showing how the mediator's role shifts across the different phases of the process, from preparation through to follow-up and implementation support.

Figure 28 outlines the mediator's core responsibilities across the different phases of the process, from preparation through follow-up.

Figure 28: A matrix outlining the core responsibilities of the mediator across different phases of the mediation process, from preparation through to follow-up.

This matrix clarifies that mediator responsibilities are not static but evolve as the process moves forward, shifting from information-gathering to facilitation to implementation support, and this clarity helps you remain focused and avoid role confusion.

Key Concept: Process Integrity Builds Trust

When parties see the mediator consistently uphold fairness, enforce ground rules equally, give equal time and respect to all perspectives, and manage the process with integrity, they develop trust in the process, even when trust between the parties remains limited.

This process of trust enables parties to take risks, explore options, and ultimately make commitments they would not make in a less-trustworthy environment. Process integrity is not just procedurally correct; it is strategically essential for reaching an agreement.

7.

POST-AGREEMENT IMPLEMENTATION

The mediation process described in Chapter 6 culminates in agreement, but an accord does not guarantee lasting resolution. The true test of any mediation lies in the successful implementation of the agreed-upon terms. In company-community disputes, implementation failure commonly reignites conflict, leaving communities more disillusioned and companies facing greater operational disruptions. This chapter provides comprehensive guidance on translating agreements into lasting change through robust monitoring systems (including strategies to address power imbalances discussed in Chapter 12), clear accountability mechanisms, and strategies for addressing challenges that arise during implementation.

7.1 Why Implementation Matters: The Risk of Agreement Failure

A signed agreement represents a moment of hope and possibility. Both parties have invested time, emotional energy, and, often, considerable compromise to reach common ground. However, research and field experience consistently show that a substantial proportion of mediated agreements fail during implementation. When agreements collapse, the consequences extend well beyond the original conflict.

The Costs of Implementation Failure: When a company fails to deliver on promised infrastructure, compensation, or employment commitments, or when a community does not uphold its side of the agreement, several destructive dynamics emerge:

1. **Deepened Mistrust:** Communities that experience broken promises during implementation become far more resistant to future dialogue. The narrative shifts from "they didn't understand us" to "they deliberately deceived us." This cynicism can persist for generations and spread to neighboring communities.
2. **Escalated Conflict:** Failed implementation triggers conflict more intense than the original dispute. Communities feel they have tried the "peaceful route" and resort to more disruptive tactics such as blockades, legal action, or international campaigns. The company loses its opportunity to resolve matters quietly.
3. **Damaged Credibility of Mediation:** When agreements fail, communities may lose faith in the specific company and in mediation as a dispute-resolution mechanism. This makes future conflicts harder to address through dialogue.
4. **Financial and Operational Costs:** Companies face renewed operational disruptions, reputational damage, potential legal liability, and the need to negotiate again from a position of diminished trust. The cost of implementation failure almost always exceeds the cost of proper implementation.
5. **Personal Harm to Individuals:** Community members who advocated for the mediated solution may face criticism or lose standing within their community. Company representatives who championed dialogue may face internal consequences. These personal costs discourage future leaders from taking risks for peace.

Key Concept: The Implementation Gap

Between written agreements and ground-level reality lies the implementation gap, a distance that emerges from unclear language, inadequate resources, changing circumstances, staff turnover, and the absence of accountability mechanisms. These factors prevent what parties commit to from actually occurring. Active management, not passive hope, drives successful implementation.

Root Causes of Implementation Failure: Understanding why agreements fail helps mediators and parties design implementation systems that succeed. Common causes include:

- **Vague or Ambiguous Agreement Language:** Terms like "adequate compensation," "meaningful consultation," or "timely implementation" mean different things to different parties. Without specificity, disputes about interpretation can arise.
- **No Clear Responsibility Assignment:** Agreements may specify what will happen, but not who will make it happen. Accountability then diffuses until no one feels responsible.
- **Unrealistic Timelines or Budgets:** In the enthusiasm to reach an agreement, parties may commit to timelines or costs that are infeasible. When reality sets in, missed deadlines erode trust.
- **Staff Turnover and Institutional Memory Loss:** The company representatives who negotiated the agreement may move to other positions, and new staff may not feel ownership of commitments they did not make. Similarly, community leadership may change.
- **Changing Circumstances:** Economic downturns, commodity price fluctuations, political changes, or unexpected events can render commitments originally feasible difficult to honor.
- **Absence of Monitoring Mechanisms:** Without systematic tracking, problems go unnoticed until they escalate into crises. Small slippages accumulate into major failures.
- **Lack of Consequences for Non-Compliance:** If there are no repercussions for missed commitments, the incentive to prioritize implementation diminishes, especially when other pressures compete for attention and resources.

7.2 Designing Agreements for Implementation Success

Successful implementation begins during the drafting phase of the agreement. As discussed in Chapter 6, experienced mediators guide parties toward language and structures that increase the likelihood of implementation. The SMART criteria, adapted from project management, provide a useful framework: agreements should be Specific, Measurable, Achievable, Relevant, and Time-bound.

Specificity and Clarity

Clarity emerges when each commitment answers: What exactly will be done? Who will do it? For whom? Where? By when? How will completion be verified?

Compare these two versions of the same commitment:

Vague (Problematic)	Specific (Better)
"The company will improve water access for the community."	"The company will construct three boreholes equipped with hand pumps in locations jointly selected with the Community Water Committee, meeting WHO water quality standards. Construction will be completed by December 31, 2025. The company will provide maintenance training to five community members and supply spare parts for two years."

The specific version prevents misinterpretation and establishes clear completion criteria.

Measurable Indicators

Each commitment requires measurable success criteria. Quantitative indicators work best where applicable, though qualitative indicators can work if clearly defined. Build these into your agreement:

- **Output Indicators:** What tangible things will be produced?
    - Examples: Number of jobs created, kilometers of road repaired, amount of compensation paid

- **Outcome Indicators:** What changes will result?
    - Examples: Percentage of households with water access, reduction in travel time to market, community satisfaction levels
- **Process Indicators:** How will the process be conducted?
    - Examples: Number of consultation meetings held, response time to grievances, frequency of joint committee meetings

Realistic Commitments

Reality-testing commitments before finalizing the agreement. Questions to consider:

- Does the company actually have the budget authority to make this commitment?
- Are the proposed timelines realistic given procurement processes, seasonal constraints, and other factors?
- Does the community have the capacity to fulfill its obligations?
- What external factors could prevent implementation? How will these be addressed?
- Have similar commitments been made and kept in the past? If not, what will be different this time?

> **Practical Tip: The Implementation Stress Test**
>
> Before finalizing an agreement, conduct a mental stress test: Imagine it is one year from now and the agreement has failed. What went wrong? Walk through each commitment and identify potential failure points. Then build safeguards against those failures into the agreement itself. This pessimistic exercise reveals gaps that optimism during negotiations overlooks.

Built-in Flexibility and Adaptation Mechanisms

Circumstances change, and rigid agreements may fail to accommodate unforeseen developments. Consider including:

- **Amendment Procedures:** Clear processes for modifying the agreement when both parties agree, without requiring a return to full mediation.
- **Force Majeure Clauses:** Provisions addressing situations in which extraordinary circumstances (natural disasters, major economic crises, political instability) prevent implementation.
- **Review Points:** Scheduled opportunities to assess whether commitments remain appropriate and achievable, with the option to adjust by mutual consent.
- **Substitution Options:** Where appropriate, allow for equivalent alternatives if the original commitment becomes impossible. For example, "If the planned school site becomes unavailable, the company will identify an alternative site acceptable to the community."

7.3 Establishing Monitoring and Oversight Systems

Systematic tracking of implementation progress serves multiple purposes: early warning of problems, accountability creation, confidence building through demonstrated progress, and documentation that prevents disputes about what actually occurred. A comprehensive monitoring system combines internal mechanisms, joint structures, and external oversight (addressing common mistakes in implementation discussed in Chapter 15).

Joint Implementation Committees

A Joint Implementation Committee (JIC) brings together representatives of both parties to oversee the implementation of the agreement. This structure has several advantages, including maintaining communication channels, providing a forum for addressing problems before they escalate, and creating shared ownership of implementation success.

Composition: Joint Implementation Committees function best when they include individuals with the authority to make decisions and the operational knowledge to assess implementation. A typical structure might include:

- Two to four company representatives (including someone with budget authority and someone with operational responsibility)
- Two to four community representatives (representing different stakeholder groups within the community)
- Possibly an independent chair or facilitator, especially in the early stages when trust is still fragile
- Technical advisors as needed for specific issues

Functions: The JIC typically:

1. Reviews progress against each commitment at regular intervals.
2. Identifies obstacles to implementation and develops solutions.
3. Addresses emerging grievances or concerns before they escalate.
4. Makes minor adjustments to implementation approaches by mutual consent.
5. Communicates progress to wider stakeholders.
6. Escalates significant problems to higher authorities when needed.

Meeting Frequency: Initially, conduct monthly meetings. As implementation stabilizes and trust builds, move to quarterly meetings. Always have mechanisms for emergency meetings to enable rapid response.

> **Caution: Power Dynamics in Joint Committees**
>
> Joint committees can reproduce the same power imbalances present in the original conflict. Company representatives may have more time, resources, and technical expertise. Community representatives may feel intimidated or lack the information needed to ask probing questions. Leveling the playing field in committee structures strengthens balanced representation, potentially including capacity building for community representatives, provision of independent technical support, and clear procedures that give community members equal voice.

External Auditors and Third-Party Monitors

In disputes where trust is low or the stakes are high (particularly when power asymmetries exist, as discussed in Chapter 12), external monitoring provides crucial credibility. Third-party monitors bring independence, technical expertise, and perceived objectivity that internal mechanisms may lack.

Types of External Monitors:

1. **Independent Accountability Mechanisms:** Organizations like the IFC's Compliance Advisor Ombudsman (CAO), which facilitated and monitored the Guinea mining mediation, can provide ongoing oversight. Their involvement signals commitment to accountability and provides an avenue for communities to raise concerns if implementation falters.
2. **Professional Auditing Firms:** For financial commitments (compensation payments, community development fund contributions), independent auditors can verify that funds were disbursed as agreed and used appropriately.
3. **Technical Experts:** For environmental commitments, independent environmental consultants can conduct monitoring and report on whether standards are being met. Water quality testing, air monitoring, and environmental impact assessments benefit from independent verification.
4. **Civil Society Organizations:** Respected NGOs with relevant expertise can serve as monitors, though care must be taken to select organizations perceived as neutral by both parties.
5. **Academic or Research Institutions:** Universities or research centers can provide an objective assessment while building local capacity for ongoing monitoring.

Designing Effective External Monitoring:

- **Clear Terms of Reference:** Define precisely what the monitor will assess, what standards they will apply, and what access they require.
- **Joint Selection:** Joint selection of external monitors enhances their perceived independence.
- **Funding Arrangements:** Typically, the company funds external monitoring, but financial arrangements work best when they prevent

financial dependence from compromising independence. Escrow arrangements or multi-year contracts can help.

- **Reporting Requirements:** Specify how often monitors will report, to whom reports will be submitted, and whether reports will be public.
- **Access Provisions:** Ensure that monitors have the necessary access to company facilities, documents, personnel, and community members.

Practical Tip: Combining Internal and External Monitoring

The most robust monitoring systems combine internal and external elements. Internal monitoring (by the company and community themselves) provides frequent, low-cost tracking of routine implementation. External monitoring provides periodic, independent verification of overall progress and handles sensitive assessments where perceived objectivity is essential, and specifying how these elements relate to each other ensures a coherent system.

The following framework brings these monitoring and verification elements together into a single structured system, showing how internal tracking and external review can be coordinated to ensure that agreement commitments are being fulfilled as intended.

Figure 29: A framework for establishing monitoring and verification systems to ensure that agreement commitments are being fulfilled as intended.

Robust monitoring systems transform agreements from paper documents into living commitments by creating accountability mechanisms and early warning systems that allow you to intervene before small implementation gaps become major relationship breakdowns.

7.4 Communication Infrastructure for Accountability

Implementation succeeds or fails through countless daily interactions, decisions, and communications. A well-designed communication infrastructure facilitates information flow between parties, enables the rapid identification and resolution of problems, and demonstrates ongoing commitment to the relationship.

Regular Reporting Mechanisms

Structured reporting creates predictability and ensures that progress (or the lack thereof) is documented and shared.

Progress Reports: Progress reports function effectively when clearly specifying who produces them, how often they are to be submitted, and to whom they are submitted. Typical elements include:

- Status of each commitment (completed, in progress, delayed, not started)
- Key activities completed since the last report
- Challenges encountered and how they were addressed
- Activities planned for the next reporting period
- Financial information (expenditures against commitments)
- Issues requiring attention or decision

Report Format Considerations: Reports should be accessible to all stakeholders. This may involve producing versions in multiple languages, using visual formats (charts or photos of completed work) for communities with varying literacy levels, and avoiding excessive technical jargon. Accompanying detailed reports with brief summaries enhances accessibility.

Public Reporting: Public reporting enhances accountability, though confidentiality concerns may apply. Public reporting can build broader community support, but may also raise sensitivities about confidential business information or require careful management of expectations.

Designated Liaison Points

Designating liaison officers helps maintain communication channels. These liaison officers serve as the first point of contact for questions, concerns, or emerging issues.

Characteristics of Effective Liaisons:

- **Accessible:** They can be reached through multiple channels (phone, email, in person) and respond promptly.
- **Authorized:** They have sufficient authority to address routine matters without constant escalation.
- **Knowledgeable:** They understand the full scope of the agreement and current implementation status.
- **Trusted:** They have credibility with their own stakeholders and, ideally, have built some personal rapport with their counterpart.
- **Consistent:** Maintaining the same liaisons throughout implementation supports relationship continuity.

Grievance and Feedback Channels

Even with the best intentions, problems arise during implementation. Communities need clear, accessible, and safe channels to raise concerns without fear of retaliation. These channels serve as a release valve, allowing issues to be addressed before they escalate.

Design Principles for Grievance Mechanisms:

1. **Accessibility:** Multiple submission methods (in person, by phone, in writing, or through community leaders). Accessibility increases when location and timing do not create barriers. Consider literacy levels and language needs.
2. **Predictability:** Clear steps and timelines for the processing and resolution of grievances.
3. **Transparency:** Acknowledging grievances and providing regular updates builds trust in the process.
4. **Safety:** Ensuring protection against retaliation enables safe grievance submission. This may include confidential submission options.
5. **Rights-Compatibility:** Grievance mechanisms work best when they complement, rather than replace, other remedial options, such as courts or regulatory complaints.

6. **Learning:** Using grievance patterns to inform improvements strengthens both implementation and company practices.

> **Key Concept: The Complaint-to-Trust Pathway**
> A well-handled grievance can actually strengthen trust. When community members raise a concern and see it addressed promptly and fairly, they gain confidence that the company takes the relationship seriously. Conversely, ignored or poorly handled grievances damage trust far more than the original problem would have. View every complaint as an opportunity to demonstrate commitment.

7.5 Early Warning Systems: Reading the Relationship Barometer

The oversight process extends beyond commitment compliance to track the company-community relationship itself. Relationship deterioration often signals emerging implementation problems, while relationship improvements suggest successful progress. Several indicators reveal relationship health.

Spontaneous Engagement Tracking

Voluntary, informal interactions between the company and the community reveal relationship health most clearly. When relationships are healthy, community members readily approach company personnel to share information, ask questions, or flag potential problems early; they attend company-hosted events and engage in casual conversation. When relationships are strained, these spontaneous interactions diminish or disappear entirely.

What to Track:

- **Frequency of Informal Visits:** How often do community members come to company offices or sites for reasons other than formal grievances? A decline may signal growing discomfort.

- **Attendance at Voluntary Events:** When the company hosts community meetings, open houses, or social events, who attends? Declining attendance or absence of key leaders is a warning sign.
- **Quality of Informal Interactions:** When interactions do occur, are they warm or cold? Do community members seem comfortable or guarded?
- **Information Flow:** Are community members proactively sharing information that may be useful to the company (e.g., alerting the company to a road washout or a potential security concern)? A willingness to share reflects trust.
- **Response to Company Staff in the Community:** How do community members react when they encounter company employees in community spaces? Avoidance or hostility indicates relationship problems.

Creating a Spontaneous Engagement Log: Maintaining logs of informal interactions helps track relationship health. This need not be onerous. Key information includes the date, the initiator of contact, the nature of the interaction, and any issues raised. Over time, this log reveals patterns. A month with significantly fewer entries than usual may warrant investigation.

Practical Tip: The Coffee Test

A simple question that company staff can ask themselves: "Would community members be comfortable sitting down for coffee with us right now?" If the answer is uncertain or no, something is wrong. This informal "coffee test" can prompt reflection on relationship health beyond formal metrics.

Community Sentiment Indicators

Beyond tracking direct interactions, monitoring should capture broader community sentiment about the company and the agreement.

Formal Sentiment Assessment:

- **Periodic Surveys:** Simple surveys, conducted annually or semi-annually, can track community perceptions. Questions might address satisfaction with implementation progress, trust in the company, the sense that their voices are heard, and expectations for the future. Independent surveys encourage honest responses.
- **Focus Groups:** Periodic focus group discussions with different community segments (women, youth, elders, different geographic areas) can yield richer qualitative information on concerns and perceptions.
- **Key Informant Interviews:** Regular conversations with trusted community figures who have their finger on the pulse of community opinion can provide early warning of brewing discontent.

Informal Sentiment Indicators:

- **Social Media and Local Media Monitoring:** Where relevant, track how the company is discussed on social media and in local press. Shifts in tone can signal changing sentiment.
- **Rumors and Misinformation:** The spread of false rumors about the company often indicates a breakdown in communication and trust. Tracking and addressing rumors is important.
- **Community Meeting Dynamics:** At public meetings or consultations, note the tone of questions and comments. Are people constructive or hostile? Do they seem to expect positive engagement, or are they bracing for confrontation?

Implementation Performance Indicators

These indicators track the technical aspects of whether commitments are being met.

Indicator Category	Examples	Warning Signs
Timeline Adherence	Percentage of milestones met on time	Multiple missed deadlines, pattern of delays

Budget Execution	Funds disbursed vs. committed, spending rate	Significant underspending, funds redirected
Quality Standards	Water quality test results, construction standards	Failed tests, complaints about quality
Grievance Patterns	Number, types, and resolution rates of grievances	Rising grievance numbers, repeat complaints, low resolution
Meeting Attendance	JIC meeting attendance, community meeting participation	Declining attendance, key parties not showing up

7.6 Compliance Mechanisms and Accountability

Identifying whether commitments are being met matters only if consequences follow. Compliance mechanisms provide incentives for success and penalties for failure. Without accountability, monitoring becomes documentation rather than a performance driver.

Positive Incentives for Compliance

Compliance is more likely when both parties see continued benefit from honoring the agreement.

- **Public Recognition:** Successful implementation can be celebrated through joint announcements, ceremonies, or media coverage. This provides reputational benefits and builds an institutional memory of success.
- **Progressive Benefits:** Agreements can structure benefits to increase as trust builds. For example, a community development fund might grow if initial implementation milestones are met, creating an incentive for continued cooperation.
- **Relationship Dividends:** As implementation succeeds, the improved relationship itself becomes a resource. A community that trusts the company may provide early warning of potential problems, support the company during regulatory processes, or speak positively about the company to outside parties.

- **Operational Benefits:** Companies that successfully implement agreements often experience reduced security costs, lower staff turnover (as working in a supportive community is more attractive), and smoother regulatory relationships.

Consequences for Non-Compliance

While positive incentives are preferable, there must also be meaningful consequences when commitments are not kept.

Graduated Response Framework: A graduated response framework, escalating with severity and persistence, provides proportionate accountability:

1. **Informal Reminder:** For minor delays or oversights, a direct communication from the liaison officer may suffice.
2. **Formal Notice:** A written notification of non-compliance is delivered, documenting the issue and requesting corrective action within a specified timeframe.
3. **JIC Review:** The committee formally reviews the non-compliance, requests an explanation, and agrees on remedial steps.
4. **External Review:** If the matter remains unresolved, refer to external monitors or an independent body for assessment and recommendation.
5. **Public Reporting:** The non-compliance is disclosed to the public, which carries reputational consequences for the non-compliant party.
6. **Suspension of Reciprocal Obligations:** The compliant party may suspend its own obligations until the other party addresses the breach.
7. **Legal Remedies:** As a last resort, pursue legal enforcement where the agreement has been structured to be legally binding.

> **Caution: Asymmetric Consequences**
>
> In company-community disputes, the parties often have very different capacities to absorb consequences. A company can weather reputational damage and continue operating; a community may have few

alternatives if the company withdraws. When designing consequences, ensure they create meaningful accountability without inadvertently harming the very community the agreement was meant to protect.

Escrow and Financial Security Mechanisms

Financial commitments require security mechanisms to ensure funds actually exist when needed:

- **Escrow Accounts:** Funds are deposited with a neutral third party and released upon meeting milestones. This protects community interests if the company later faces financial difficulties or changes leadership.
- **Bank Guarantees or Bonds:** The company provides a financial institution guarantee that can be called upon if commitments are not met.
- **Trust Funds:** Long-term community development commitments can be placed in independently managed trust funds, thereby insulating them from the company's financial difficulties.
- **Performance Bonds:** Third-party insurance or bonds that pay out if specific commitments are not met.

7.7 Managing Implementation Challenges

Even with well-designed agreements and monitoring systems, challenges inevitably arise. The key is addressing them promptly before they escalate into renewed conflict.

Common Implementation Obstacles

Staff Turnover: When the company representatives who negotiated the agreement leave, their successors do not understand or feel ownership of commitments. Mitigate through comprehensive documentation, formal handover procedures, and institutional (rather than personal) accountability structures.

Budget Constraints: Economic downturns or internal budget pressures may make commitments harder to honor. Early warning systems can identify this before commitments are missed, allowing for renegotiation rather than silent default.

Technical Difficulties: Infrastructure projects may encounter unforeseen challenges (poor soil conditions, supply chain problems, regulatory delays). Transparent communication about difficulties, along with revised timelines, can maintain trust if handled well.

Community Leadership Changes: New community leaders may not feel bound by agreements negotiated by their predecessors, or they may face pressure to renegotiate them. Inclusive original processes that engage broad community segments, rather than just leaders, help ensure durability.

Scope Creep: Communities may expect the agreement to address issues beyond its original scope, leading to disappointment when these expectations are not met. Clear communication about what the agreement does and does not cover is essential.

External Interference: Third parties (political actors, NGOs, competing interests) may attempt to undermine the agreement for their own purposes. Maintaining strong direct communication between the company and the community can help resist such interference.

Adaptive Management Approaches

Successful implementation requires adaptation as circumstances change. Core principles include:

- **Distinguish Substance from Method:** The core commitment (e.g., providing water access) should remain fixed, whereas the method of achieving it (e.g., specific well locations, technology used) can adapt. Flexibility on method while maintaining commitment to outcomes builds trust.
- **Transparent Problem-Solving:** When obstacles arise, share information openly with the other party and engage them in finding solutions. Communities are often more understanding of difficulties than companies expect, provided they are informed and involved.
- **Document Changes:** Documenting modifications in writing ensures clarity and integration with monitoring.

- **Maintain Regular Communication:** Maintaining regular meetings, even during periods of steady progress, preserves relationship momentum. These meetings build the relationship capital that sustains cooperation when problems arise. Even with the best intentions, however, implementation can fail.

The following figure identifies the most common risk factors that lead to implementation failure and suggests preventive measures for each.

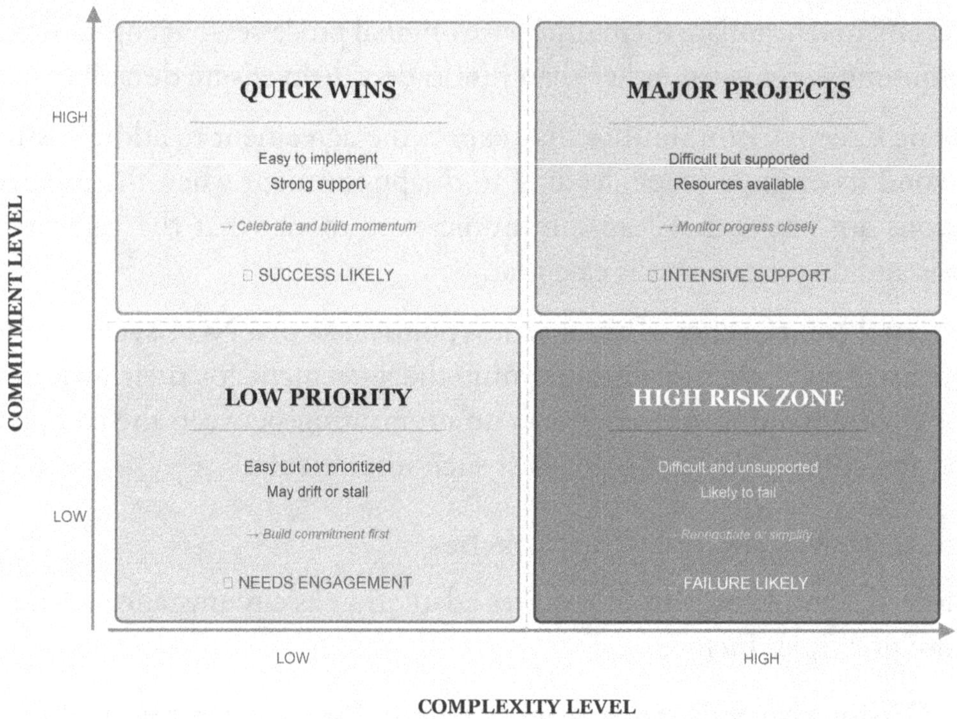

Figure 30: Implementation Failure Risk Assessment

Understanding the risk factors that could derail implementation allows you to design preventive measures and contingency plans in the moment you reach agreement, rather than scrambling to salvage a failed commitment months later.

> **Practical Tip: The Problem-Solving Partnership**
> When implementation challenges arise, frame them as shared problems to be solved together rather than as one party failing the other. The

language used matters: "We have a challenge with the water project" is more constructive than "The company has not delivered the water project." Collaborative framing maintains the relationship even while addressing difficulties.

7.8 When Agreements Break Down: Re-Engagement Strategies

Despite best efforts, some agreements fail. Recognizing breakdown early and responding appropriately can prevent the complete collapse of the relationship and create an opportunity for recovery.

Recognizing Agreement Breakdown

Signs that an agreement is failing include:

- Multiple significant commitments are missed without adequate explanation or remediation.
- JIC meetings are repeatedly canceled or become unproductive.
- Grievance numbers spike, or grievances go unaddressed for extended periods.
- Community members express that the agreement has "failed" or was "never real."
- Conflict activities resume (protests, blockades, legal filings).
- Key parties disengage from implementation structures.
- External parties publicly declare the agreement as a failure.

Graduated Response to Breakdown

Proportionate responses matched to breakdown severity guide escalation decisions.

Early Warning Response: When initial signs of trouble appear, request an emergency JIC meeting to address concerns. Then, engage external monitors or the original mediator for assessment, seek frank conversation with counterparts about what is going wrong, and identify quick wins that can demonstrate recommitment.

Active Deterioration Response: When problems are clearly worsening, immediately escalate to senior leadership on both sides. Consider bringing in the original mediator or a new neutral party, conduct an honest assessment of whether the original agreement is still salvageable, and explore whether renegotiation of specific elements could address the concerns.

Breakdown Response: When the agreement has effectively collapsed, conducting lessons-learned analysis helps identify what led to breakdown. Assess whether the conditions for renewed dialogue exist, and consider whether different representatives or structures are required. Then determine the minimum confidence-building measures required before new talks and, if both parties are willing, begin a fresh mediation process.

Renegotiation Versus Fresh Start

When agreements fail, a key question is whether to renegotiate specific elements or start fresh with a new process.

Renegotiation may be appropriate when:

- The overall agreement structure remains sound, but specific commitments need adjustment
- Both parties acknowledge the problem and express willingness to address it
- The relationship between key individuals remains functional
- The failure resulted from changed circumstances rather than bad faith

A fresh start may be necessary when:

- Trust has been deeply damaged by perceived bad faith or deception
- The original agreement was fundamentally flawed in its design
- Key representatives have changed, and new parties want to define their own relationship
- Circumstances have changed so substantially that the original agreement no longer makes sense

Caution: The Broken Promise Burden

When entering renewed negotiations after a failed agreement, the burden on the previously non-compliant party is substantially higher. Communities that experienced broken promises will require more concrete assurances, stronger monitoring, and potentially different personnel before they are willing to trust again. Re-engagement succeeds when companies acknowledge past failures honestly and demonstrate through actions, not just words, that this time will be different.

7.9 Sustaining Long-Term Success

The ultimate goal is not merely to implement specific commitments but to transform a conflictual relationship into a sustainable partnership. This requires attention to institutional sustainability, capacity building, and eventual transition from mediated to self-sustaining relationship management.

Figure 31 outlines strategies for sustaining positive long-term relationships between companies and communities after formal mediation concludes.

Figure 31: Guidance on sustaining positive long-term relationships between companies and communities after formal mediation has concluded.

The relationship work does not end when the formal mediation concludes. In fact, the quality of the post-agreement relationship often determines whether the agreement itself survives its first major test.

Institutionalizing the Relationship

Agreements survive personnel changes only when relationships become institutionalized.

Embed in Corporate Systems: Integrating commitments into corporate systems ensures they become standard operations. They should not depend on the goodwill of particular managers; rather, they should be standard operating procedures.

Build Community Institutions: Strengthening community institutions enables them to function effectively regardless of changes in individual leadership.

Create Succession Plans: Planning for leadership transitions supports relationship continuity. Incoming leaders should receive briefings on the agreement history and rationale, introductions to their counterparts, and clear expectations for maintaining the relationship.

Document Institutional Memory: Maintain clear records not only of what was agreed but also of why. Understanding the interests and concerns that shaped the agreement helps future parties maintain its spirit, not just its letter.

Capacity Building

Long-term success often requires building capabilities that did not exist at the time of the original agreement.

- **Community Capacity:** Training community members in negotiation, financial management, project oversight, and technical skills enables them to engage as equal partners. This might include supporting community members to obtain formal qualifications or providing ongoing technical assistance.
- **Company Capacity:** Company staff may need training in community engagement, cross-cultural communication, and conflict sensitivity. Companies that treat community relations as a specialized professional function, rather than an add-on to other roles, generally perform better.
- **Joint Capacity:** Building shared skills through joint training, collaborative projects, and opportunities to work together on challenges outside the original dispute can strengthen the overall relationship.

Exit Strategy for External Support

If the original mediation involved external parties (mediators, accountability mechanisms, supporting NGOs), planning for their eventual exit is important.

Gradual exit of external parties allows time for capacity transition. This might mean transitioning from active facilitation to observer status, with periodic check-ins to complete the exit over months or years. Transferring external functions to local institutions ensures sustainability.

Define what conditions would indicate that the parties are ready for independent relationship management. This provides transparency and helps both parties work toward self-sufficiency. Even after the formal exit, external parties may remain available for consultation if significant new challenges arise. This safety net can give parties confidence to proceed independently.

7.10 Implementation Success: A Case Example

The Guinea mining mediation (2017-2024) offers instructive lessons about sustained implementation success. Over nearly seven years, the CAO facilitated a process between the Kintinian community and the Société AngloGold Ashanti de Guinée (SAG) that not only reached agreement but successfully implemented a series of commitments.

Key Implementation Success Factors:

1. **Phased Approach:** Rather than pursuing a single comprehensive agreement, the parties reached multiple interim agreements over the years, each building on prior successes. Agreements in 2019 addressed water, schooling, and consultation. Additional agreements in 2022 and 2023 addressed further issues. Each delivered tangible benefits that built trust for the next phase.
2. **Visible Results:** Implementation produced visible improvements in community life, including infrastructure (market, health center, roads) that community members could see and use. These tangible results demonstrated that mediation was working.
3. **External Monitoring:** CAO continued to monitor implementation throughout the process, providing independent verification that commitments were being kept. The two-year monitoring period following the final agreement ensured continued oversight.

4. **Sustainable Structures:** The final agreement included the establishment of a Sustainable Development Fund managed with community involvement and IFC technical support. This created institutional continuity beyond the mediation process itself.
5. **Relationship Transformation:** Both parties expressed commitment to ongoing collaboration. The conflict transformed from adversarial confrontation into a partnership for community development and peaceful coexistence.

This case demonstrates that with patience, structured monitoring, demonstrated results, and genuine commitment from both parties, the parties can transform even deeply rooted conflicts through sustained implementation of mediated agreements.

7.11 Conclusion: From Agreement to Lasting Change

Post-agreement implementation determines whether the promise of mediation falters or becomes reality. The signing ceremony marks not an ending but a beginning, and the work that follows determines whether the conflict is truly resolved or merely postponed.

Successful implementation requires deliberate design: agreements crafted for clarity and realism, monitoring systems that provide early warning and accountability, communication infrastructure that keeps parties connected, and compliance mechanisms that create genuine incentives. It requires sustained attention over time, not only in moments of crisis but also through patient, consistent relationship-building.

When implementation challenges arise, as they inevitably will, the response matters more than the problem itself. Transparent problem-solving, adaptive management, and sustained communication can transform obstacles into opportunities to demonstrate commitment.

Success ultimately depends not on whether parties fulfilled specific commitments, but on whether the underlying relationship has transformed. When former adversaries become partners who can address new challenges together without returning to conflict, the mediation has truly succeeded.

Mediators must understand that agreement signing marks a midpoint, not an endpoint. Designing robust implementation systems, remaining available during implementation, and building capacity for sustainable relationship management extend the mediation function in necessary ways.

Companies and communities face this reality: agreements succeed only through committed implementation. Invest in monitoring, maintain communication, address problems early, and approach relationships as long-term partnerships rather than one-time transactions.

Sustained implementation separates temporary relief from genuine resolution.

Implementation Readiness Checklist

Before finalizing an agreement, verify that these implementation elements are in place.

Agreement Design:

- Each commitment specifies what, who, for whom, where, when, and how
- Measurable indicators are identified for key commitments
- Timelines are realistic given known constraints
- Budgets are confirmed, and authority to spend is secured
- Amendment and adaptation procedures are included

Monitoring Systems:

- Joint Implementation Committee composition and procedures are defined
- External monitoring arrangements are established where appropriate
- Reporting requirements and formats are specified
- Early warning indicators are identified

Communication Infrastructure:

- Both parties designate liaison officers
- A grievance mechanism is designed and operational
- A meeting schedule is established
- Communication channels are accessible to all stakeholders

Accountability Mechanisms:

- Consequences for non-compliance are defined
- Escalation procedures are specified
- Financial security mechanisms are in place where appropriate
- Dispute resolution procedures for implementation disagreements are available

Long-Term Sustainability:

- Institutional embedding of commitments is planned
- Capacity building needs are identified and resourced
- Succession planning is considered
- An exit strategy for external support is defined

All of these implementation considerations presuppose that mediation was the right approach in the first place. The next chapter examines the equally important question of when mediation should not proceed at all, and why the willingness to decline is itself a mark of professional integrity.

8.

WHEN MEDIATION SHOULD NOT PROCEED

Professional wisdom requires knowing not only how to facilitate dialogue, but also when mediation is inappropriate, ineffective, or harmful. Previous chapters equipped you with tools and techniques for voluntary mediation. This chapter addresses a different question: When should a mediator decline to proceed, suspend a process, or recommend an alternative path entirely?

Mediation has value, but it is not a universal remedy. In some situations, mediation causes more harm than good, by legitimizing wrongdoing, endangering vulnerable parties, or failing to deliver justice. Declining mediation when appropriate reflects ethical maturity and professional integrity.

This chapter examines five critical scenarios where mediation should not proceed. These include situations involving genocide, war crimes, or crimes against humanity; ongoing violence that makes mediation dangerous or unethical; severe power asymmetry combined with demonstrable bad faith; mediator capture or manipulation by one party; and decision-makers absent from the table. Each section provides indicators, ethical considerations, and practical guidance for mediators facing these challenging circumstances. (See Chapter 12 for strategies to address power asymmetries when mediation does proceed.)

Key Concept: The Ethical Duty to Decline

Mediators have an affirmative ethical obligation not only to facilitate fair processes but also to refuse to participate in processes that would be fundamentally unfair, harmful, or inappropriate. This duty, grounded in the core principles discussed in Chapter 3, exists regardless of external pressure, financial considerations, or the parties' expectations. Declining to mediate in inappropriate circumstances protects the integrity of mediation as a practice and prevents the mediator from becoming complicit in injustice.

8.1 Genocide, War Crimes, and Crimes Against Humanity: When Accountability, Not Mediation, Is Required

Some acts are so grave that they fall outside the scope of what voluntary mediation can effectively address. Genocide, war crimes, and crimes against humanity represent the most serious violations of international law. These are not merely disputes between parties with differing interests. They are fundamental breaches of human dignity that demand accountability, not negotiation.

Understanding the Legal and Moral Threshold

International law recognizes certain acts as so fundamentally wrong that they cannot be subject to compromise or negotiated settlement without formal accountability mechanisms. These include:

- **Genocide:** Acts committed with the intent to destroy, in whole or in part, a national, ethnic, racial, or religious group, including killing members of the group, causing serious bodily or mental harm, deliberately inflicting conditions calculated to bring about physical destruction, imposing measures to prevent births, or forcibly transferring children.
- **War Crimes:** Serious violations of the laws and customs of war, including intentional killing of civilians, torture, taking hostages, deliberately attacking civilian infrastructure, using prohibited weapons, sexual violence as a weapon of war, and conscripting child soldiers.

- **Crimes Against Humanity:** Widespread or systematic attacks directed against civilian populations, including murder, extermination, enslavement, deportation, torture, sexual violence, persecution, enforced disappearance, and apartheid.

When a company is alleged to have participated in, facilitated, or benefited from such acts, whether directly or through complicity with state actors, security forces, or militias, the appropriate response is not mediation but formal legal accountability.

> **Caution: The Risk of Legitimizing Impunity**
> Entering mediation over allegations of mass atrocities signals that such acts are negotiable matters rather than non-derogable violations. It allows perpetrators to avoid criminal accountability by reaching a private settlement. It retraumatizes survivors by reducing their suffering to a bargaining chip. Mediators must be vigilant against becoming instruments of impunity.

Why Mediation Is Inappropriate in These Cases

Several fundamental principles explain why mediation should not proceed when serious international crimes are alleged, including:

1. **Non-Derogable Rights:** International human rights law establishes certain rights as non-derogable, meaning they cannot be suspended or traded away under any circumstances. The right to life, freedom from torture, and freedom from slavery fall into this category. Mediation, by its nature, involves compromise. But some violations do not warrant compromise.
2. **The Duty to Prosecute:** States have a duty under international law to investigate and prosecute serious crimes. Private mediation cannot fulfill this duty and may actually obstruct it by creating confidential settlements that prevent evidence from reaching prosecutors.
3. **Collective and Intergenerational Harm:** Mass atrocities affect not just individual victims but entire communities and future generations.

No small group of representatives can validly negotiate away the rights of those not at the table, including those yet to be born.

4. **The Symbolic Function of Justice:** Public acknowledgment of wrongdoing through formal legal processes serves critical societal functions, including establishing a historical record, deterring future violations, and affirming the dignity of victims. Private mediation cannot fulfill these functions.

Indicators That You May Be Facing Such a Situation

In company-community disputes, allegations of the most serious crimes may emerge gradually or be obscured by the parties. Awareness of indicators that war crimes, genocides, crimes against humanity, and other serious offenses have taken place is critical. Reports of multiple deaths connected to the company's operations, especially involving security forces, or allegations of systematic sexual violence by company personnel or security contractors are serious claims that need to be investigated.

Claims of forced displacement of entire communities signal a need for intervention beyond mediation. So does evidence of the company providing logistical support to armed groups or government forces committing abuses. International human rights organizations documenting serious abuses connected to the project send the same signal.

Considering existing or pending investigations by international tribunals, national prosecutors, or UN bodies helps mediators make informed decisions before continuing.

Practical Tip: When to Refer to Accountability Mechanisms

If you encounter allegations of genocide, war crimes, or crimes against humanity during the assessment phase, do not proceed with mediation. Instead, inform the parties that formal accountability mechanisms are the appropriate avenue. This may include national courts, international tribunals such as the International Criminal Court, United Nations human rights bodies, or regional human rights courts. You may also refer parties to legal aid organizations specializing in international criminal law or transitional justice. Document your decision and reasoning carefully.

What the Mediator Should Say

When declining to mediate because the situation involves potential crimes under international law, effective mediators communicate clearly and compassionately.

Sample Dialogue

Mediator: *"I have carefully reviewed the information provided by both parties and conducted my own assessment of this situation. Based on what I have learned, I am not able to proceed with mediation in this matter."*

Community Representative: *"But we were told this process could help us. Why are you refusing?"*

Mediator: *"I understand your frustration, and I want to be clear that this is not a reflection on you or your community's decision to seek resolution. The allegations here describe acts that, if substantiated, would constitute serious crimes under international law. Mediation is designed for disputes where parties can negotiate in good faith toward mutually acceptable solutions. But some acts, such as mass killings or systematic violence against civilians, are not matters for negotiation. They require accountability through formal legal processes."*

Company Representative: *"We dispute these characterizations entirely. Shouldn't we have a chance to present our side?"*

Mediator: *"I am not making a determination of guilt or innocence. That is precisely why a court, not a mediator, is the appropriate venue. The seriousness of the allegations means that any resolution must come with the safeguards, transparency, and authority that only formal legal processes can provide. I would be doing a disservice to everyone, including your company, by proceeding with a process that cannot deliver true accountability or lasting peace."*

8.2 Ongoing Violence: When Mediating During Active Conflict Escalation Is Dangerous or Unethical

Mediation requires a minimum baseline of physical safety for participants. When violence is ongoing, escalating, or imminent (as discussed in Chapter 5 on conflict dynamics), proceeding with mediation may expose participants to danger, may be used by perpetrators as cover to continue violence, or may create false hope that obscures the need for immediate protective action.

Before proceeding, conduct a thorough safety assessment to determine whether physical risks are too severe for mediation to proceed safely.

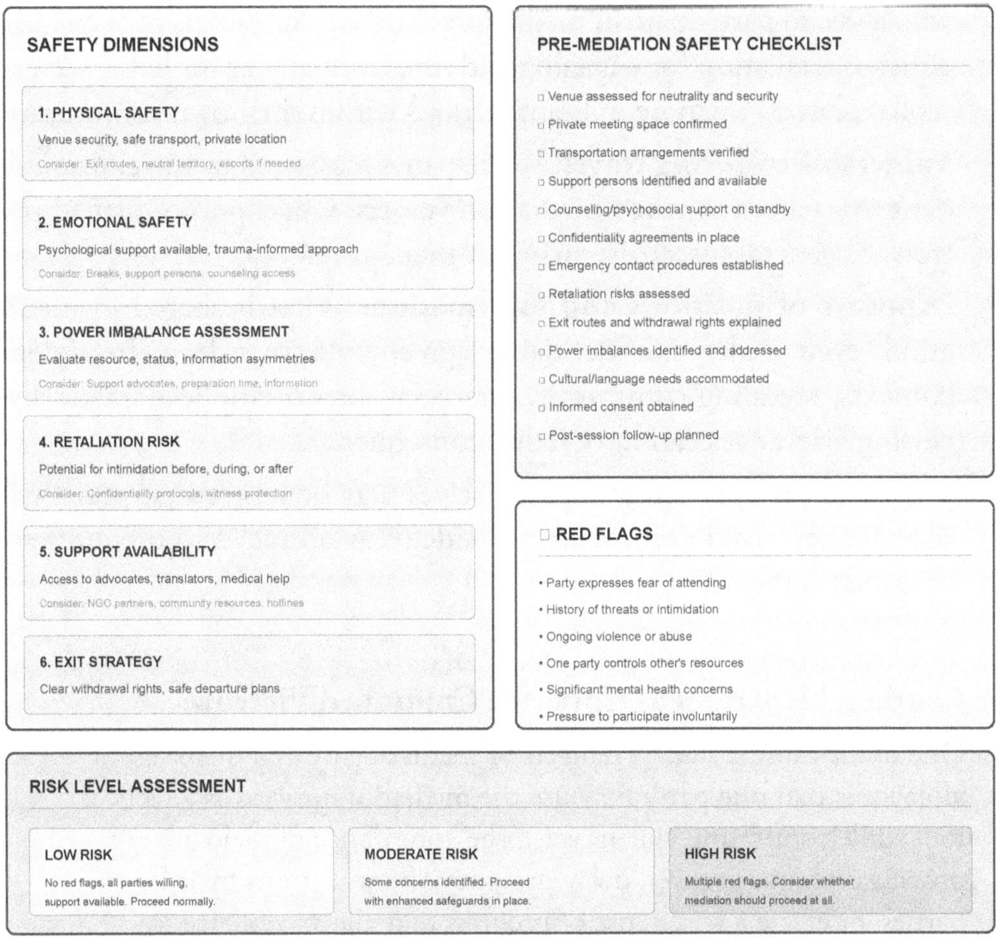

Figure 32: A framework for assessing whether physical safety risks exist that would make mediation inadvisable, including violence indicators and protective factors.

A safety assessment conducted with care and transparency allows you to acknowledge real risks while deciding whether mediation can proceed safely, and this honest assessment protects both parties and the integrity of the process.

The Safety Imperative

The principle of "do no harm" requires that mediators ensure the process does not endanger participants. In situations of ongoing violence, several risks emerge:

- **Physical danger to community participants:** Community members who agree to participate in mediation may become targets for violence, either as retaliation for engaging with the company or for being seen as "collaborators" by more militant factions within their own community.
- **Vulnerability during travel:** Participants may need to travel through dangerous areas to reach mediation venues. Checkpoints, armed patrols, or general insecurity may put them at risk.
- **Exposure of positions and information:** What is shared in mediation, even under confidentiality agreements, may leak. In violent contexts, revealing community strategies, identifying leaders, or disclosing grievances can have lethal consequences.
- **Mediator safety:** Mediators themselves may be targeted, especially if they are perceived as favoring one side or as obstacles to the interests of armed actors.

> **Caution: Mediation as Cover for Continued Violence**
>
> One of the most insidious dangers of mediating during ongoing violence is that one party may use the mediation process as a tactical tool while continuing violent acts. The appearance of dialogue can provide diplomatic cover, delay protective interventions by third parties, or create a false sense of progress that allows violence to continue unchecked. Mediators must be vigilant against being instrumentalized in this way.

Distinguishing Ongoing Violence from Historical Grievances

Many company-community disputes involve past violence that has subsided. Mediating historical grievances is appropriate and often necessary for reconciliation. The distinction lies in whether violence is currently occurring or is imminently threatened. Consider the following questions:

1. When did the most recent incident of violence occur?
2. Are there credible threats of imminent violence from any party?
3. Are security forces or armed groups actively deployed in the area?
4. Has there been a cessation of hostilities, ceasefire, or stabilization?
5. Do participants feel safe enough to travel to and attend mediation sessions?
6. Are there protective mechanisms in place for participants if tensions escalate?

Types of Violence That Should Halt Mediation

Mediation is generally inappropriate when specific conditions exist, such as:

- Active armed conflict in the project area, whether between state forces, non-state armed groups, or company security
- Recent killings, beatings, or other physical attacks on community members related to the dispute
- Credible death threats against community leaders, company personnel, or the mediator
- Deployment of security forces in a manner that intimidates or restricts community movement
- Detention of community members or activists related to the dispute
- Escalating protest and counter-response that shows signs of spiraling toward violence

Practical Tip: Establishing Preconditions for Mediation

When violence is ongoing but parties express interest in dialogue, consider establishing preconditions that must be met before mediation can begin. These might include a ceasefire or standstill agreement, the withdrawal of security forces from contested areas, the release of detained community members, a commitment from all parties to refrain from violence during the process, and agreement on safe passage for participants. Document these preconditions clearly and monitor compliance before scheduling mediation sessions.

The False Hope Problem

Beginning mediation during ongoing violence can create false hope that dialogue alone will resolve the crisis. Community members may reduce their vigilance or advocacy efforts, believing that the mediation will address their concerns. International attention may shift away from protective measures, assuming that a resolution is imminent. Meanwhile, the violence continues.

This false hope can have tragic consequences. When mediation ultimately fails to stop violence, or when it becomes clear that one party was using talks as a delay tactic, the community may end up in a worse position than before. They may have lost momentum for other protective strategies, alienated potential allies, or revealed information that puts them at greater risk.

Sample Dialogue

Community Leader: *"We need to talk. People are being hurt. Can you mediate now before this gets worse?"*

Mediator: *"I share your urgency, and I deeply appreciate your courage in reaching out during such a dangerous time. However, I have to be honest with you. Mediation while violence is actively occurring is not safe for you or effective in creating lasting solutions."*

Community Leader: *"But if we don't do something now, more people will suffer."*

Mediator: *"I understand, and your concern for your community is exactly right. What I can do is help you connect with organizations that specialize in protective measures during active crises, including human rights monitors, journalists, and diplomatic actors who can apply pressure for the immediate cessation of violence. Once there is a genuine reduction in violence and safety can be reasonably assured, I am committed to facilitating a mediation process. But I will not put you in a room to negotiate while your community is still under threat, because that would not protect you, and any agreement reached under such duress could not be trusted."*

Example: Mining-Specific Violence Indicators

In mining contexts, ongoing violence takes distinctive forms that mediators must recognize. These include clashes between artisanal miners and company security forces, community blockades of access roads met with forcible dispersal, intimidation of community leaders who oppose the project, and environmental sabotage or retaliatory destruction of company equipment. When security forces employed by a mining company have used lethal force against community members, or when community protests have resulted in deaths, the conditions for voluntary mediation are fundamentally compromised. The mediator must assess whether the violence is truly in the past or whether the threat of its recurrence shapes every interaction at the table.

8.3 Severe Power Asymmetry Combined with Bad Faith

Power imbalances exist in virtually all company-community disputes. Chapter 12 of this handbook addresses strategies for managing such imbalances within the mediation process. However, there are situations in which the power differential is so extreme and combined with demonstrable bad faith by the more powerful party that mediation cannot function as a fair process, regardless of the mediator's skill.

Distinguishing Manageable Asymmetry from Fatal Imbalance

The question is not simply whether one party is more powerful than the other. It is whether the imbalance is so severe, and accompanied by such bad faith, that the weaker party cannot meaningfully protect their interests through dialogue. Certain severity levels of power asymmetry, combined with bad faith, may preclude meaningful mediation, as explored in the table below.

Manageable Asymmetry	Fatal Imbalance
The stronger party has a genuine interest in the resolution	The stronger party seeks only to delay, exhaust, or legitimize a predetermined outcome

Manageable Asymmetry	Fatal Imbalance
The weaker party has some leverage (BATNA, public support, allies)	The weaker party has been systematically stripped of all alternatives
Both parties can walk away if talks fail	Walking away means disaster for the weaker party alone
The stronger party engages transparently and honestly	The stronger party lies, withholds information, or acts deceptively
Power imbalance can be partially corrected through process design	Process adjustments cannot overcome fundamental coercion

Indicators of Bad Faith

Bad faith is not simply aggressive negotiation or hard bargaining. It refers to a fundamental lack of genuine willingness to reach a fair agreement. Indicators include:

- **Pattern of broken promises:** A history of agreements that were never implemented, or were implemented only partially before being abandoned.
- **Simultaneous contrary actions:** While publicly engaging in dialogue, the party is taking actions that undermine the stated purpose of mediation, such as continuing disputed activities, pursuing legal action, or lobbying against community interests.
- **Deliberate deception:** Providing false information, hiding material facts, or misrepresenting capabilities or intentions.
- **Procedural manipulation:** Using the mediation process to gather intelligence, delay legal proceedings, or create the appearance of good faith for external audiences while having no intention to reach an agreement.
- **Ultimatums presented as negotiation:** Demanding that the weaker party accept predetermined terms with no genuine room for discussion.

- **Targeting the other party's representatives:** Attempting to co-opt, intimidate, or undermine community leaders who are participating in mediation.

Key Concept: The Purpose of Mediation Is Not Process, But Justice

Mediation is a means to an end, not an end in itself. The purpose is to achieve a fair resolution that both parties can live with. When one party is participating in bad faith, the process cannot accomplish this purpose, no matter how well it is conducted. Continuing mediation under such circumstances gives the appearance of fairness while producing fundamentally unjust outcomes.

When Coercion Masquerades as Consent

A particularly dangerous scenario arises when a community appears to "consent" to mediation and its outcomes, but that consent is obtained through coercion rather than free choice. This can occur when the community faces immediate threats to their survival, such as loss of land, water, or their livelihoods, if they do not agree, or when community members who oppose mediation have been arrested, threatened, or silenced.

This can also happen when the company has captured local institutions, including the government, police, or local courts, that might otherwise protect the community. When no alternative dispute resolution mechanism exists or is accessible to the community, or when time pressure is artificially created to force hasty decisions, they may not be in a position to give valid consent.

In such circumstances, proceeding with mediation lends legitimacy to what is essentially extortion. The mediator becomes complicit in dressing up coercion as voluntary agreement.

Sample Dialogue

Company Representative: *"The community has agreed to mediate. We are ready to begin."*

Mediator: *"Before we proceed, I need to understand the circumstances of that agreement. Can you tell me what options the community has if they choose not to mediate?"*

Company Representative: *"Well, if they don't participate, our project will proceed anyway. We have all the necessary permits."*

Mediator: *"I see. And what happens to community members who have publicly opposed the project?"*

Company Representative: *"That's not really relevant to the mediation."*

Mediator: *"I'm afraid it is. For mediation to be meaningful, participation must be genuinely voluntary. If the community is participating because they have no other choice, and particularly if those who object have been marginalized, then any agreement we reach will lack legitimacy. I need to speak with community representatives privately to assess whether the conditions for fair mediation exist."*

Practical Tip: Assessing Genuine Consent

Before proceeding with mediation in a context of significant power imbalance, conduct private conversations with community members away from any company presence. Ask open-ended questions about why they are participating, what alternatives they considered, whether any community members oppose mediation, what has happened to them, and whether they feel free to walk away. If you detect coercion, do not proceed. Consider the steps that might be needed before genuine voluntary mediation could take place.

Example: When a Multinational Faces an Indigenous Community

Consider a scenario where a multinational gold mining company holds a government-granted concession over land that an indigenous community has occupied for generations but holds no formal legal title. The company has a team of lawyers, environmental consultants, and government allies. The community has traditional leaders, limited literacy in the national language, and no access to independent legal counsel. The power asymmetry here is not merely about resources. It is structural: the legal system itself does not recognize the community's most fundamental claim. In such cases, mediation risks legitimizing an unjust status quo unless the mediator can first ensure that the community has access to independent legal and technical advice, and that the legal framework itself is not the subject being mediated.

8.4 Mediator Capture: When You Realize You Are Being Manipulated

Even experienced mediators can be manipulated by sophisticated parties. "Mediator capture" occurs when a mediator, often without fully realizing it, becomes an instrument of one party's strategy rather than a neutral facilitator. Recognizing and responding to mediator capture is essential for maintaining the integrity of the mediation process.

How Mediator Capture Happens

Mediator capture is rarely the result of overt bribery or corruption, though these do occur. More commonly, it happens through subtle mechanisms that exploit normal human psychology and professional relationships, including:

1. **Financial Dependence:** If the mediator's income depends significantly on one party (for example, a company that regularly hires the mediator for multiple disputes), there is inherent pressure to maintain that relationship. The mediator may unconsciously favor outcomes that keep the paying client satisfied.
2. **Information Asymmetry:** One party (often the company) may provide the mediator with extensive briefings, technical information, and context that shapes the mediator's understanding of the dispute before the other party speaks. The mediator may not realize how much the other party's silence has influenced their framing of issues.

3. **Social Relationships:** Mediators may develop personal or professional relationships with representatives of one party through repeated interactions, shared social circles, or common backgrounds. These relationships create unconscious affinity and can bias the mediator's perceptions.
4. **Flattery and Deference:** Sophisticated parties may strategically flatter the mediator, defer to their expertise, or make them feel valued in ways that create a sense of loyalty or obligation.
5. **Shared Worldview:** Mediators from business, legal, or international development backgrounds may share assumptions with corporate representatives about the value of development, the legitimacy of property rights, or the nature of progress that community members do not share. These shared assumptions can lead to unconscious bias.
6. **Strategic Information Disclosure:** One party may selectively share information with the mediator in caucus, knowing that even if the mediator cannot reveal specifics, their negotiation strategy will be influenced. The mediator becomes an unwitting conduit for the manipulating party's interests.

Caution: The Subtlety of Capture

Mediator capture remains invisible to the mediator. You believe you are being fair and neutral, while your judgment has been systematically influenced. Be especially vigilant if you find yourself consistently sympathizing with one party's perspective, making excuses for one party's behavior, or feeling irritated by one party's positions. These emotional responses signal that your neutrality has been compromised.

Warning Signs of Mediator Capture

Ongoing self-reflection helps mediators recognize warning signs of capture or manipulation:

- You find yourself internally arguing one party's case, even when not speaking aloud.

- You feel personally invested in the success of one party's project or objectives.
- You accept information from one party without verification while questioning information from the other.
- You spend significantly more time with one party outside formal sessions.
- You find one party's representatives more "reasonable" or "professional" than the other.
- You receive hospitality, gifts, or favors from one party, even small ones.
- You have financial interests (such as future work or reputation) that align with one party's success.
- Party representatives express concern that you are favoring the other side.

Responding to Mediator Capture

If you recognize that you have been captured or that your neutrality is compromised, you have an ethical obligation to address the situation. Depending on the severity, responses may include:

1. **Self-Correction:** If you recognize subtle bias early, you may be able to consciously correct your approach. This might involve spending more time with the party you have neglected, being more skeptical of information from the party you have favored, or actively seeking perspectives that challenge your assumptions.
2. **Disclosure:** Transparency can sometimes cure bias. Disclosing to all parties the nature of your relationship with one party, the information you have received, or your own background may allow them to decide whether to continue with you as the mediator.
3. **Co-Mediation:** Bringing in a co-mediator who is closer to the other party (for example, someone with deep community experience if you have been captured by the company) can help balance perspectives and maintain neutrality.
4. **Recusal:** In severe cases, the only ethical response is to withdraw from the mediation. This is difficult but may be necessary to protect the integrity of the process and the interests of the disadvantaged party.

Practical Tip: Building Structural Safeguards

Prevent mediator capture through structural safeguards. Ensure that your compensation does not depend on any single client. Maintain strict protocols about gifts and hospitality. Use co-mediators or peer supervision, especially in high-stakes cases. Seek feedback from both parties throughout the process about their perception of your neutrality. Document your decision-making process so that you can review it for bias. Consider engaging a mentor or supervisor to confidentially discuss your internal reactions and concerns.

Sample Dialogue

Mediator (internal reflection): *"I've noticed that I keep finding reasons to agree with the company's timeline concerns. They've been so accommodating and reasonable. But wait, I've also been attending their receptions, having coffee with their legal team, and relying heavily on their technical briefings. The community hasn't had the same access to me. I need to address this."*

Mediator (to both parties): *"Before we continue, I want to be transparent about something. I have realized that I have had significantly more informal contact with company representatives than with community representatives. I am concerned that this may have affected my perspective, even unconsciously. To address this, I propose that we pause for a few days so that I can spend equivalent time with community representatives, hearing their full context and concerns. I also want both parties to feel free to tell me if, at any point, you feel I am favoring one side."*

Caution: Mediator Capture in Mining Disputes

In mining disputes, mediator capture often follows a predictable pattern. The company funds the mediation process, provides logistical support, and may have recommended the mediator. Over time, the mediator develops a professional relationship with company staff, accepts hospitality during site visits, and begins unconsciously framing issues from the company's perspective. Warning signs include: finding yourself explaining the company's constraints to the community more than the reverse, feeling irritation when the community raises new demands, accepting the company's timeline as the default, and socializing primarily with company representatives between sessions. If you realize capture has occurred, the ethical response is disclosure and, in most cases, withdrawal.

8.5 Hidden Decision-Makers: When the Person at the Table Has No Authority

Effective mediation requires that the people at the table have genuine authority to make decisions and commit their organizations. When the actual decision-makers are hidden behind delegates who lack authority, the mediation becomes a charade. Agreements cannot be made, or if made, cannot be honored. The process wastes time, raises false hopes, and may even be a deliberate tactic to delay or manipulate.

The Authority Problem

Authority issues can arise on either side of a company-community dispute, though they manifest differently.

Company-Side Authority Gaps:

- The local manager attends mediation, but all decisions require approval from distant headquarters
- Legal counsel participates but cannot authorize anything without board approval
- A subsidiary or contractor participates, but the parent company or client makes real decisions
- The representative has authority only within narrow parameters that exclude the issues in dispute

Community-Side Authority Gaps:

- Representatives are appointed by external NGOs rather than genuinely chosen by the community

- Traditional authority structures have not authorized the participants to speak for the community
- Different factions within the community have not agreed on who represents them
- Key stakeholders, such as women, youth, and neighboring communities, are excluded from representation

Key Concept: Authority Is Not the Same as Attendance

A warm body at the table does not equal decision-making authority. True authority means the capacity to commit the organization to specific actions, to agree to compromises, and to ensure implementation of agreements. Without this authority, mediation yields only tentative understandings that may be rejected by those absent.

Why Parties Send Representatives Without Authority

Understanding why this happens helps mediators address the problem:

1. **Information Gathering:** The party wants to learn about the other side's positions, evidence, and strategies without committing to anything. This is especially common when litigation is ongoing or contemplated.
2. **Delay:** Participating in mediation without authority to conclude allows a party to delay resolution while appearing cooperative. This can be useful for running out the clock on legal deadlines, completing disputed activities, or waiting for changed circumstances.
3. **Public Relations:** A company may want to be seen as engaging constructively with community concerns without actually changing its behavior. Sending a representative to mediation creates a narrative of good faith.
4. **Internal Politics:** Within a company or community, there may be genuine disagreement about whether to mediate or what outcomes are acceptable. Sending a representative without full authority may reflect unresolved internal conflicts.

5. **Testing the Waters:** A party may genuinely be uncertain about mediation and want to see what emerges before committing. While understandable, this still undermines the process if not disclosed.

Detecting Authority Gaps

Assessing authority during preparation and remaining alert throughout the process is essential. Warning signs include:

- The representative frequently says, "I need to check with (headquarters/my supervisor/the board)."
- Tentative agreements are later rejected by parties not at the table.
- The representative cannot answer questions about the organization's bottom line or limits.
- The party's position changes only after caucuses with external phone calls.
- The representative speaks in terms of "recommendations" rather than "decisions."
- Key issues are declared "off the table" because the representative cannot negotiate them.

Practical Tip: Authority Verification During Preparation

Before mediation begins, explicitly ask each party: "Who has authority to make binding decisions on the issues we will discuss? Will that person be at the table? If not, what is the approval process, and how will it work during our sessions?" Get specific answers. If a company says decisions require board approval, ask when the board meets and whether there is a mechanism for emergency approvals. If community representatives say they need to consult their members, discuss how and when the consultation will take place.

Addressing Authority Gaps

When you identify an authority gap, several responses are possible, including:

1. **Require Decision-Makers at the Table:** Pause mediation until those with genuine authority can participate. This may mean bringing senior executives from headquarters or ensuring that community assemblies have mandated their representatives.
2. **Adjust the Process:** If decision-makers cannot be physically present, build approval processes into the mediation structure. This might mean scheduled consultation breaks, hybrid meetings with decision-makers joining remotely at key moments, or a two-stage process in which negotiation occurs first, followed by ratification.
3. **Clarify Limits:** If authority is partial, make those limits explicit to all parties. Clarity about decision-making authority helps participants have realistic expectations. This prevents false expectations and wasted effort on issues beyond the participants' authority.
4. **Terminate If Authority Is Unavailable:** If genuine authority cannot be secured and the authority gap appears intentional, you may need to conclude that mediation is not viable under current conditions. Proceeding without authority wastes resources and builds frustration.

Sample Dialogue

Mediator: *"Before we begin today's session, I want to confirm something important. We discussed during preparation that decisions would require approval from your regional director. Is that still the case?"*

Company Representative: *"Yes, I can negotiate, but final approval rests with the regional director. She's been briefed."*

Mediator: *"I appreciate your honesty. However, I'm concerned because we spent two full days in the last session reaching a tentative agreement, only to have it rejected by the regional director. The community representatives took significant risks to participate, and they are understandably frustrated."*

Company Representative: *"I understand. But she was concerned about setting precedents."*

Mediator: *"Let me be direct. For this mediation to continue productively, we need either the regional director at the table or you need clear authority to make final decisions within defined parameters. Can we arrange either of those? If not, I am not certain that mediation can proceed effectively, because the community cannot continue negotiating with someone who cannot commit to outcomes."*

Caution: Gender-Based Violence as a Bar to Mediation

When allegations of gender-based violence by company personnel or security forces are part of the dispute, the mediator must assess whether mediation is appropriate at all. Survivors of sexual violence face unique risks in mediation: re-traumatization through retelling their experience, intimidation by the perpetrators or their associates, and community stigma if their experience becomes known. Mediation should not proceed unless: survivors have given genuine, informed consent to participate; adequate support services are available; confidentiality protections are robust; and the mediation will not be used to pressure survivors into accepting inadequate remedies in exchange for silence. When these conditions cannot be met, mediators typically recommend alternative accountability mechanisms.

Example: The Corporate Headquarters Problem

A common authority gap in mining disputes occurs when the local site manager participates in mediation but lacks authority to commit to significant concessions. The community negotiates in good faith, believing they are speaking with decision-makers, only to learn that "headquarters needs to approve" every substantive agreement. This pattern is sometimes deliberate: companies may send representatives without authority to test community positions, delay commitments, or create the appearance of engagement without the substance. Effective mediators establish authority parameters before mediation begins, asking directly: "What decisions can you make at this table without further approval? What requires headquarters approval, and how long does that process take?"

8.6 Making the Decision to Decline: Ethical Considerations and Communication

Deciding not to proceed with mediation is never easy. There may be pressure from parties who have invested time and resources, from organizations that have arranged the process, or from your own professional desire to help. But proceeding with inappropriate mediation is not helping. It may harm vulnerable parties and undermine the legitimacy of mediation as a practice. Note that declining mediation because of inappropriateness (Chapter 8) differs from responding to party resistance during a process (Chapter 14).

Ethical Framework for Declining

When considering whether to decline or terminate a mediation, ask yourself:

- **"Can this process produce a fair outcome?"** If structural conditions make fairness impossible, proceeding legitimizes an unfair result.
- **"Is participation genuinely voluntary?"** If coercion is present, consent is illusory.
- **"Am I capable of being neutral?"** If you have been captured or compromised, you cannot serve the process.
- **"Could proceeding cause harm?"** If mediation puts participants at risk or forecloses better options, it violates the "do no harm" principle.
- **"Is there a better alternative?"** If formal legal accountability, protective interventions, or other mechanisms are more appropriate, recommending those serves the parties better.
- **"What precedent does proceeding with mediation set?"** If continuing legitimizes inappropriate mediation, it harms future parties in similar situations.

The figure below highlights the most common mistakes mediators make during this decision and the harm they cause. Recognizing these pitfalls is the first step toward avoiding them.

AVOID	WHY IT CAUSES HARM
Victim-blaming or judging Suggesting survivor is responsible	Retraumatizes survivor, discourages communication, destroys trust
Invasive or inappropriate questions Asking overly detailed questions	Violates privacy, causes distress, irrelevant to mediation goals
Minimizing or dismissing Downplaying severity or impact	Invalidates survivor, undermines trust, prevents safe dialogue
Questioning credibility Expressing skepticism about account	Creates invalidation, discourages participation, causes trauma
Rushing the process Pressuring for quick decisions	Leads to poor outcomes, incomplete healing, regret
Taking a biased position Displaying favoritism or taking sides	Compromises fairness, undermines credibility and process integrity
Forcing participation Pressuring when not ready	Removes agency, violates voluntary principle, causes further harm
Offering legal advice Providing guidance on legal matters	Exceeds mediator role, may be inaccurate, creates liability

Figure 33: A guide to common mistakes and inappropriate actions that mediators benefit from avoiding when deciding whether to decline or proceed with mediation.

Learning from the mistakes of others accelerates your growth as a mediator and helps you avoid repeating patterns that damage trust and derail processes.

Communicating Your Decision

When you decide not to proceed, communicate your decision with clarity, compassion, and professionalism:

- **Explain your reasoning:** Parties deserve to understand why mediation is inappropriate. Be honest about your concerns without assigning blame unnecessarily.
- **Provide alternatives:** Where possible, suggest other avenues that may be more appropriate, whether legal processes, protective mechanisms, or different types of facilitated dialogue.
- **Identify conditions for future mediation:** If the barriers are potentially temporary, explain what would need to change for mediation to become viable.
- **Document your decision:** Create a written record of why you declined, both for your own protection and to inform any future mediators who may be approached.
- **Support the vulnerable party:** The party in the weaker position may have invested hope in mediation. Acknowledge this and, where appropriate, help connect them with resources for alternative paths.

Key Concept: Professional Integrity

The willingness to say "no" is a hallmark of professional integrity. Mediators who proceed with inappropriate cases undermine not only the specific process but the legitimacy of mediation itself. By declining when conditions are not right, you protect the parties, protect yourself, and protect the field. This is not a failure of mediation. It is mediation practice at its most ethical.

Summary: The Five Scenarios Where Mediation Should Not Proceed

Scenario	Why Mediation Is Inappropriate
Mass Atrocities	Genocide, war crimes, and crimes against humanity require formal accountability. These acts are non-negotiable, and mediation risks legitimizing impunity.
Ongoing Violence	Active violence endangers participants, may provide cover for continued harm, and creates false hope that diverts from protective action.

Scenario	Why Mediation Is Inappropriate
Power + Bad Faith	When severe power asymmetry is combined with demonstrable bad faith, the process cannot produce fair outcomes. Consent becomes coercion in disguise.
Mediator Capture	When the mediator is compromised by one party through financial ties, information asymmetry, or relationship dynamics, neutrality is impossible.
No Authority	When decision-makers are hidden, and representatives lack the authority to commit, agreements cannot be made. The process becomes theater rather than negotiation.

The decision tree below guides you through the key readiness indicators for each of these five scenarios.

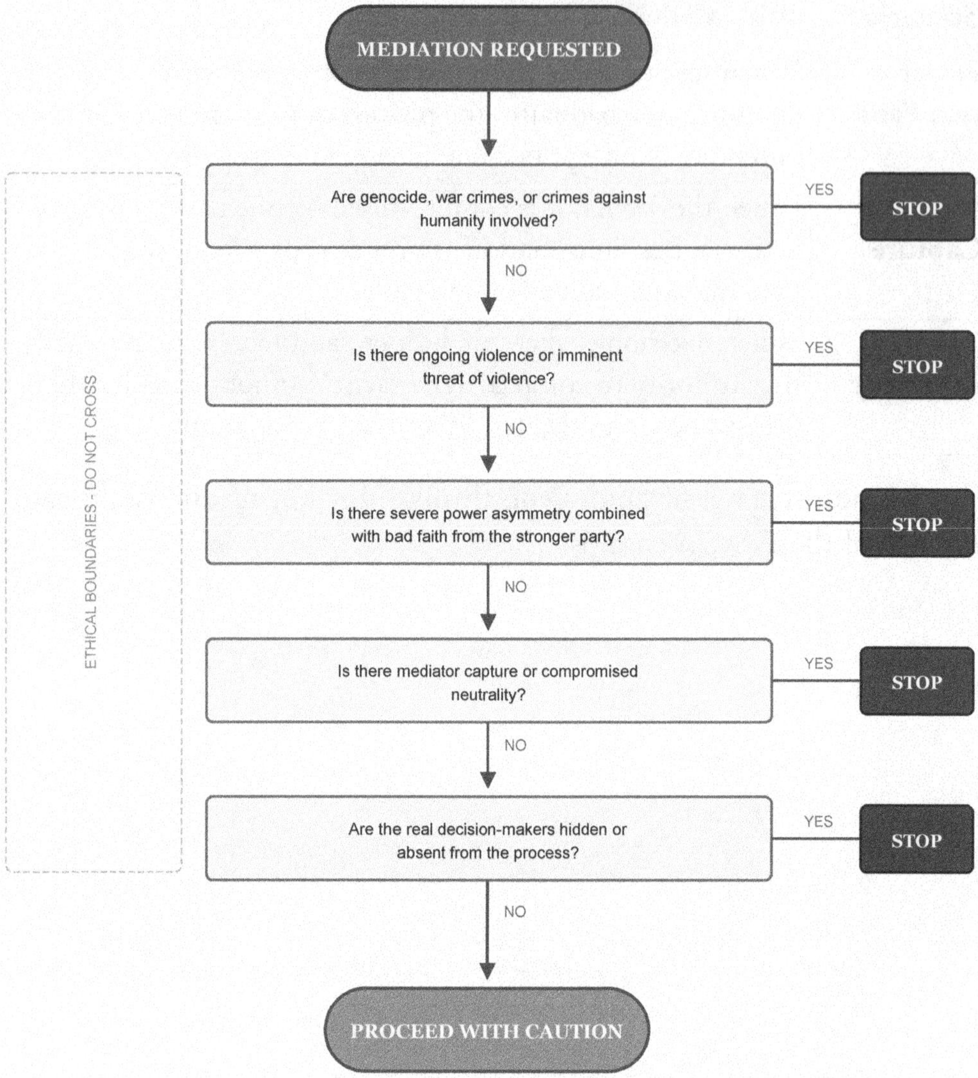

Figure 34: A decision tree to help practitioners assess whether conditions are appropriate for mediation to proceed, based on key readiness indicators.

This decision tree helps you avoid the trap of either proceeding with mediation regardless of conditions or abandoning a process prematurely when creative approaches could still succeed.

Knowing when to say "no" is not the end of a mediator's responsibility. Rather, it marks the beginning of different kind of help. The mediator points parties toward paths that actually serve their needs. She protects vulnerable communities from processes that would harm them. She preserves the integrity of mediation for situations where it can genuinely make a difference.

The courage to decline inappropriate mediation is professional wisdom at its finest.

Key Takeaways

- Mediators have an ethical duty to decline cases involving genocide, crimes against humanity, or systematic violence, regardless of organizational or political pressure.
- Five scenarios warrant refusal: international crimes, active ongoing violence, severe power imbalances with no mitigation, bad faith participation, and mediator capture by a dominant party.
- The decision to decline is not a failure. It is an act of professional integrity that protects both the process and the affected communities.
- Safety assessment must be continuous, not a one-time evaluation. Conditions can change during a mediation, requiring reassessment at every stage.
- When declining, mediators should document their reasoning and, where possible, refer parties to more appropriate mechanisms such as legal accountability processes or human rights bodies.

Reflection Questions

1. Have you encountered a case where you felt pressured to proceed despite warning signs? What factors influenced your decision?
2. What would your process look like for assessing bad faith? What specific indicators would you watch for?
3. How would you communicate a decision to decline mediation to a referring organization or funding body?
4. Consider a scenario involving serious human rights violations that fall short of formal international crimes. Where would you draw the line?
5. What support structures do you have in place for the emotional weight of refusing a case where communities are suffering?

9.

TOOLS AND COMPETENCIES IN THE MEDIATOR'S TOOLBOX

Having established both what effective mediation looks like and when it should not proceed, we now examine the specific tools and competencies that enable practitioners to work effectively. Every mediator brings to the table a set of tools and personal competencies that enable them to navigate conflicts effectively. In complex disputes between companies and communities, mediators need a versatile toolkit, ranging from analytical tools like conflict mapping to interpersonal skills like patience and cultural fluency. This chapter outlines essential techniques, tools, and qualities that form the mediator's "toolbox."

These are practical instruments, tested and refined through real-world mediations across diverse contexts, from mining disputes in West Africa to infrastructure conflicts in Europe. A skilled mediator learns to select the right tool for each situation, much like a surgeon choosing instruments during an operation. The goal is to become fluent in multiple approaches so you can respond effectively to whatever challenges arise during the mediation process.

9.1 Analytical Tools

Before entering the mediation room, a mediator must understand the conflict's landscape. Analytical tools help mediators systematically examine the dispute, identify hidden dynamics, and prepare effective strategies. These tools transform complex, emotionally charged situations into structured information that can guide decision making throughout the process.

> **Practical Tip: Tool Selection**
>
> Selecting tools based on specific situations often works better than using every tool. A straightforward two-party dispute may need only basic process management. A multi-party, multi-issue conflict may require extensive mapping, stakeholder analysis, and phased approaches.

Conflict Mapping

Conflict mapping creates a visual or written representation of the dispute's key elements. This technique, rooted in peacebuilding practice (Lederach, 1997), has proven invaluable in corporate-community disputes where multiple parties, historical grievances, and complex relationships intersect. The purpose of conflict mapping is to make the invisible visible, revealing patterns and connections that might otherwise remain hidden.

A thorough conflict map addresses:

- **Primary parties:** Who is directly involved in the dispute? In a mining conflict, this typically includes the company management, affected community leaders, and possibly government representatives. Identifying primary parties seems straightforward, but conflicts often reveal unexpected stakeholders.
- **Secondary parties:** Who influences the situation without being directly involved? NGOs, media outlets, investors, neighboring communities, or political actors may shape the conflict's trajectory.

- **Issues:** What are the main points of contention? Common issues include environmental impacts, employment opportunities, compensation for land use, infrastructure development, and respect for cultural sites.
- **Relationships:** How do parties relate to each other? What is their history? Understanding relational history helps mediators anticipate reactions and design appropriate trust-building measures.
- **Dynamics:** What patterns of interaction exist? Are there escalation cycles where each party's actions provoke increasingly aggressive responses from the other? Recognizing these patterns helps mediators interrupt destructive cycles.

Practical Tip: Mapping Relationships Visually

Draw a simple diagram with circles representing the parties and lines showing the relationships. Use solid lines for positive relationships and dotted lines for tense or broken ones. Add notes about each party's primary concerns. Color-code issues by urgency or complexity. This visual representation helps identify hidden influencers, relationship patterns, and potential entry points for dialogue. Share a simplified version with parties to validate your understanding.

Stakeholder Analysis

In mining disputes, the stakeholder landscape is typically more complex than a simple bilateral negotiation. A typical mapping reveals a triangular dynamic between the company, the affected community, and government actors who may simultaneously serve as regulator, revenue beneficiary, and political actor. Secondary stakeholders often include artisanal and small-scale miners who may lose access to deposits. Downstream communities may face impacts from water use or contamination, while environmental advocacy organizations, international development agencies, and the company's investors and lenders may have their own social responsibility requirements. Each of these actors brings different interests, different forms of power, and different timelines to the dispute.

When mapping stakeholders in mining disputes, mediators should disaggregate "government" into its component parts, as different government actors may have conflicting interests and different degrees of power. The national mining ministry may prioritize production and foreign investment. The environmental agency may be responsible for enforcement but lack resources or political backing to act. Local government may depend on the mine for employment and tax revenue. The judiciary may be independent or may be influenced by political pressure. Traditional governance structures, where they exist, may have legal standing or may be marginalized by the formal legal system. Each of these actors requires separate analysis: what are their interests, what power do they hold, what is their relationship with the company and the community, and how will they respond to different mediation outcomes?

While conflict mapping provides an overview, stakeholder analysis goes deeper into understanding each actor's motivations, constraints, and alternatives. This tool helps mediators anticipate behavior, identify leverage points, and craft proposals that address genuine needs rather than surface demands.

For each stakeholder, analyze:

- **Interests:** What do they really want and why? Interests lie beneath stated positions. Understanding interests opens the door to creative solutions.
- **Power:** What resources, authority, or influence do they possess? Power takes many forms: financial resources, legal authority, political connections, media access, moral legitimacy, or the ability to mobilize collective action.
- **Position:** What are they publicly demanding? Positions are the stated solutions that parties advocate. Understanding positions helps you recognize when parties are moving toward compromise.
- **Needs:** What underlying needs drive their position? Needs are often non-negotiable human requirements such as safety, dignity, recognition, and security. Addressing needs rather than positions enables breakthroughs.

- **BATNA:** What will they do if mediation fails? Understanding each party's Best Alternative to a Negotiated Agreement helps assess their willingness to compromise.

> **Caution: Analysis Paralysis**
>
> Extensive analysis can delay action indefinitely. At some point, you know enough to begin. Additional analysis yields diminishing returns. Trust your preparation and start the process, remaining open to learning and adjusting as you go.

Sample Stakeholder Analysis Matrix:

Stakeholder	Interests	Power/Influence	BATNA
Community leaders	Jobs, clean water, respect, future for children	Can mobilize protests, media attention, political allies	Legal action, blockades, international advocacy
Company management	Stable operations, reputation, investor confidence	Financial resources, government relationships, legal team	Security enforcement, legal proceedings, government intervention
Local government	Tax revenue, social stability, political support	Regulatory authority, permits, police/security	Impose solution, revoke permits, force negotiations

BATNA/WATNA Analysis

One of the most powerful tools in a mediator's arsenal is helping parties realistically assess their alternatives. BATNA/WATNA analysis (Fisher and Ury, 1981), provides a framework for evaluating what happens if mediation fails. This analysis often proves transformative because parties frequently overestimate their alternatives or underestimate risks.

In extractive-industry mediation, BATNA and WATNA analysis is sector-specific. A community's best alternative may include litigation for water contamination damages, appeals to international mining standards bodies, or campaigns targeting the company's supply chain. A company's worst alternative may involve operational shutdown, license revocation, or loss of social license to operate. Mediators must assess whether these alternatives are genuinely available to the weaker party or merely theoretical.

The framework includes three assessments:

- **BATNA (Best Alternative to Negotiated Agreement):** What is the best possible outcome if talks fail? BATNAs are often overly optimistic.
- **WATNA (Worst Alternative to Negotiated Agreement):** What is the worst that could happen? WATNAs inject a sobering reality into negotiations.
- **MLATNA (Most Likely Alternative to Negotiated Agreement):** What will probably happen? The MLATNA helps parties understand that a negotiated agreement they help shape is usually preferable to an imposed outcome.

Key Concept: Using BATNA to Create Realistic Options

When both sides realize their alternatives are unattractive, they often become more willing to compromise. A community's BATNA of prolonged litigation and a company's BATNA of continued conflict both involve significant costs, uncertainty, and potential damage. Mediators use BATNA analysis not to threaten, but to inject realism. The question becomes: Is the proposal on the table better or worse than what will likely happen without an agreement?

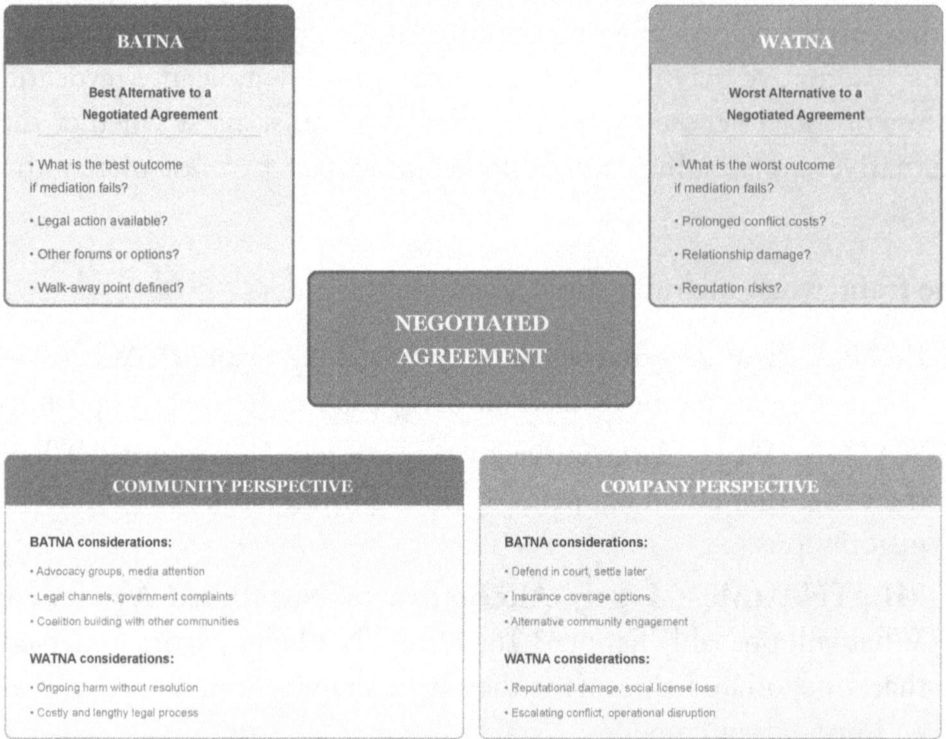

Figure 35: A tool for analyzing the Best Alternative to a Negotiated Agreement (BATNA) and Worst Alternative to a Negotiated Agreement (WATNA) to inform realistic decision-making.

BATNA and WATNA analysis grounds parties in reality and shifts the conversation from abstract ideals to concrete alternatives, which often creates surprising openness to settlement when parties recognize their no-deal alternatives are worse.

Sample Mediator Language: *"If we don't reach an agreement here, what will you do? What's the best you could hope for in that scenario? And what's the worst that could happen? Sometimes looking at those alternatives helps clarify whether the proposals on the table are worth considering."*

Key Concept: BATNA Evolution

BATNAs are not static. As mediation progresses, alternatives change. A community that initially had no legal options may find a lawyer willing to take their case. A company facing a deadline may find its BATNA worsening. Periodically reassess how alternatives are shifting.

> **Practical Tip: BATNA Reality Testing**
>
> Parties often overestimate the attractiveness of their alternatives. Gentle reality testing helps: "If you do pursue litigation, what is the realistic timeline and cost? What are the chances of winning? What happens to the community in the meantime?" Help parties see alternatives clearly.

To help parties engage in this reality testing systematically, mediators can draw on the following structured set of questions.

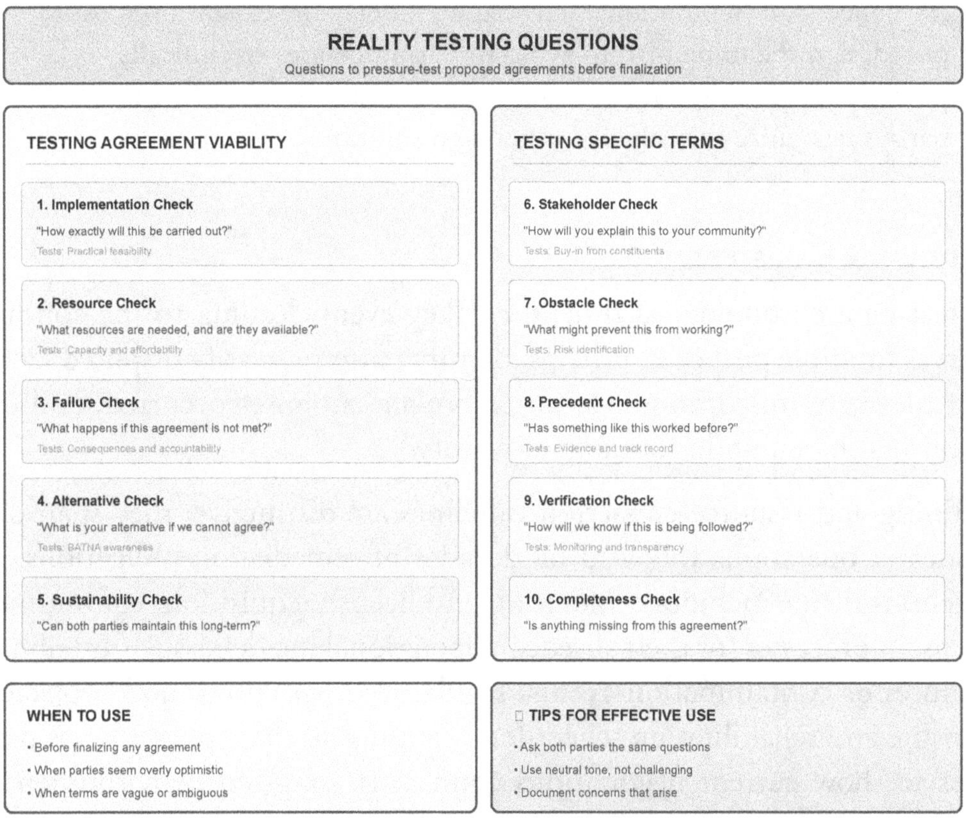

Figure 36: A set of probing questions designed to help parties assess whether their positions and expectations are realistic and achievable.

Reality testing questions are not about advocating for settlement or suggesting what parties should accept, but rather helping them stress-test their assumptions and develop more sophisticated understanding of feasibility.

Example: BATNA/WATNA in a Mining Dispute

Consider a community opposing a copper mine's expansion into their agricultural land. The community's BATNA might include: filing a legal challenge (costly and uncertain, but potentially effective), organizing a sustained protest campaign (high personal cost, uncertain outcome), or seeking support from international NGOs to pressure the company's investors. The community's WATNA is that the expansion proceeds without any negotiation, with minimal or no compensation. The company's BATNA is to seek government intervention to enforce the concession (reputationally damaging), delay the expansion (costly), or redesign the mine plan to avoid the disputed area (technically possible but expensive). Mapping these alternatives honestly helps both parties recognize the value of negotiated solutions.

Timeline Construction

Creating a chronological timeline of key events leading to the conflict serves multiple purposes. It helps identify patterns, clarify disputed facts, reveal where miscommunication or broken promises occurred, and establish a shared understanding of history.

Mining and resource-extraction timelines are distinctive: they span decades of operations followed by decades of remediation obligations. A useful timeline includes exploration and license acquisition, community consent processes (or their absence), operational incidents such as tailings failures or contamination events, regulatory inspections, and projected closure and rehabilitation schedules. Mapping all these phases helps parties see how current negotiations connect to long-term environmental commitments.

A detailed timeline should include:

- **Project milestones:** When did exploration begin? When did construction start? When did operations commence?
- **Commitments made:** What promises were made, by whom, and when? Document verbal commitments, written agreements, and public statements.

- **Problems emerging:** When did concerns first arise? Were they reported? How did the company respond?
- **Escalation events:** What incidents intensified the conflict? Protests, violent confrontations, media campaigns, or legal filings often mark turning points.
- **Resolution attempts:** What previous efforts were made to resolve the dispute? Why did they fail?

> **Practical Tip: Co-Creating Timelines with Parties**
>
> Create timelines jointly with both parties rather than presenting a finished version. Ask each side to identify key dates and events. Where their accounts differ, note both versions without judgment. The process of constructing the timeline together often reveals misunderstandings and helps to create a new shared understanding.

9.2 Process Management Tools

Beyond analyzing the conflict, mediators need tools to manage the mediation process itself. These process management tools help maintain productive dialogue, overcome obstacles, and move parties toward agreement.

Caucusing

A caucus is a private meeting between the mediator and one party, away from the other side. Caucusing is one of the mediator's most versatile tools, serving multiple purposes throughout the mediation process.

Purposes of caucusing include:

- **Allowing confidential venting:** Parties often need to express frustration, anger, or fear that they would not voice in front of the other side.
- **Exploring flexibility:** Parties may have more room for compromise than they reveal publicly.

- **Reality-testing proposals:** Before a party makes an offer publicly, the mediator can privately test whether it is likely to be accepted.
- **Coaching parties on communication:** Mediators can help parties frame their concerns more constructively.
- **Breaking deadlocks:** When joint sessions reach an impasse, caucuses provide a way to explore underlying barriers without the pressure of the other side watching.

> **Caution: Protecting Confidentiality in Caucuses**
>
> *Caucuses must be used transparently. Explain to all parties at the outset that you may meet privately with each side, and that anything shared in caucus remains confidential unless they give explicit permission to convey something. Never carry information between parties without consent. If one side suspects the mediator is sharing their confidential information, trust in the entire process collapses.*

Shuttle Diplomacy

When direct interaction has broken down or tensions are too high for productive face-to-face dialogue, shuttle diplomacy serves a critical function. In this approach, the mediator physically moves between parties in separate rooms, carrying messages, proposals, and responses.

Shuttle diplomacy techniques include:

- **Presenting proposals without revealing their source:** "I've been thinking about a possible approach" allows the mediator to test an idea without attribution.
- **Testing reactions before formal offers:** The mediator can gauge responses to hypothetical scenarios.
- **Allowing face-saving:** By attributing ideas to the mediator, parties can accept proposals without appearing to capitulate.
- **Building gradually toward acceptable positions:** Through iterative exchanges, parties can move toward each other in small steps.

Caution: Caucus Frequency Balance

Too many caucuses can make parties feel the real negotiation is happening without them. Too few can leave important information undiscovered. Find the balance for each situation. Some disputes benefit from extensive shuttle diplomacy, while others work best in joint sessions.

Practical Tip: Caucus Transitions

When returning from caucus to joint session, briefly summarize what can be shared publicly: "In our separate conversations, both parties expressed commitment to finding a solution. We discussed some new possibilities that I'd like to explore together." This maintains momentum and transparency.

Joint Fact-Finding

Disputes often stall because parties disagree about facts. Is the water actually contaminated? How many jobs were promised versus delivered? Joint fact-finding addresses this problem by creating a shared evidentiary basis for discussion.

Approaches to joint fact-finding include:

- **Agreeing on an independent expert:** Both sides jointly select a neutral expert whose findings they agree in advance to accept.
- **Forming joint investigation committees:** Representatives from both sides work together to gather information.
- **Commissioning studies with shared oversight:** Both parties review the methodology and monitor the research process.
- **Conducting joint site visits:** Seeing conditions together creates a shared experience.

Sample Mediator Language: *"You disagree about whether the water is actually contaminated. Rather than continue arguing about it, would you both* *accept findings from an independent environmental laboratory? We could jointly select the lab and agree in advance to accept their results as the basis for our discussion."*

Key Concept: From Adversaries to Partners Through Fact-Finding

Joint fact-finding not only produces better information, but it also transforms adversarial dynamics into collaborative problem-solving. When parties work together to investigate facts, they begin to see each other as partners rather than opponents. The process of agreeing on methodology, selecting experts, and reviewing findings builds relationship muscles that carry over into negotiating solutions.

Practical Tip: Joint Fact-Finding in Mining Disputes

Mining disputes frequently involve contested technical claims: the community says the water is contaminated; the company says it meets regulatory standards. Joint fact-finding resolves this by engaging mutually agreed independent experts to test water quality, assess environmental impact, or evaluate compensation values. For this to work, both parties must agree on the expert, the methodology, the sampling locations, and how results will be shared. The mediator's role is to facilitate these agreements and ensure the community understands the technical process. The community should have access to its own technical advisor who can explain findings in accessible language and challenge methodology if needed.

Visual Aids and Documentation

Visual tools help parties see the problem objectively, keep discussions focused, and create a shared record. They transform abstract discussions into concrete, visible elements that everyone can reference.

Practical Tip: Collaborative Visuals

Rather than presenting completed diagrams, create visuals collaboratively. Ask parties to help draw the stakeholder map or list the issues. Collaborative creation builds ownership and often reveals insights that would not emerge from a one-sided presentation.

Effective uses of visual aids include:

- **Writing the agenda where everyone can see it:** A visible agenda keeps discussions on track and allows parties to see progress.
- **Listing issues and tracking status:** Create columns for "Not discussed," "In progress," "Tentatively agreed," and "Finalized."
- **Mapping options against interests:** Create a matrix showing which proposed solutions address which underlying interests.
- **Creating timelines and process diagrams:** Visual representations of implementation schedules help parties understand what will happen when.
- **Recording agreement language as it develops:** Writing tentative agreement text where everyone can see it catches misunderstandings immediately.

Practical Tip: Always Bring Visual Tools

Always carry flipcharts, markers, and tape to every mediation session, even if you don't plan to use them. Visual tools are invaluable when discussions become circular or confusing. Writing something down often clarifies it. Ask parties: "Can I write that down to make sure I understand correctly?" The act of committing words to paper usually leads to more careful formulation.

9.3 Personal Competencies

Tools and techniques are only as effective as the person using them. The most sophisticated analytical framework or process design will fail if the mediator lacks the personal competencies to implement it skillfully. The communication skills discussed in Chapter 4 form the foundation of this competency development.

> **Key Concept: Competency Gaps**
>
> Every mediator has strengths and weaknesses. Some excel at emotional attunement but struggle with technical details. Others manage complex logistics brilliantly but miss relational cues. Know your gaps and compensate through preparation, co-mediation, or deliberate skill development.

The following framework identifies the core competencies that effective mediators develop and maintain throughout their careers. Research on mediator practice (Kolb and Associates, 1994) identifies these competencies as distinguishing effective mediators from those who merely follow procedural steps.

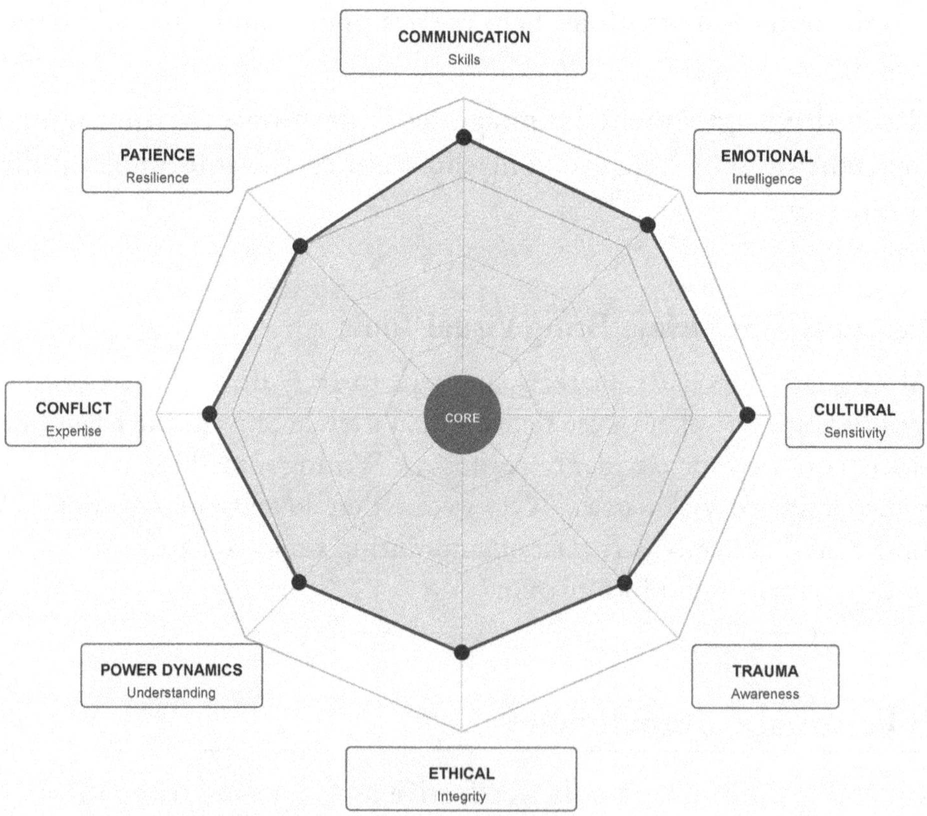

Figure 37: An overview of the knowledge, skills, and personal qualities that make up the core competency profile of an effective mediator.

These core competencies form an integrated profile rather than a checklist, as the strongest mediators are those who combine technical knowledge with emotional intelligence and personal humility.

Emotional Intelligence

Emotional intelligence (EI) is the capacity to recognize, understand, and manage emotions, both in oneself and others. In mediation, high emotional intelligence enables practitioners to navigate the intense emotional currents that flow through conflict situations.

Components of emotional intelligence for mediators include:

- **Self-awareness:** Recognizing your own emotional reactions, biases, and triggers.
- **Self-regulation:** Remaining calm when parties are angry, frustrated, or hostile.
- **Empathy:** Understanding and sharing the feelings of others without losing objectivity.
- **Social awareness:** Reading the room, noticing when someone is withdrawn, agitated, or disengaged.
- **Relationship management:** Building rapport, managing conflict, and facilitating cooperation.

Sample Mediator Language: *"I can see this is bringing up strong feelings. That's completely understandable given what you've experienced. Would a short break help, or would you prefer to continue? Either way, I want you to know that your feelings are valid and there's space here to express them."*

Patience and Persistence

Conflicts that have simmered for years will not be resolved in minutes. As discussed in Case Study A (Chapter 17), complex disputes can take years to reach a comprehensive agreement. Mediators must prepare for long journeys.

Patience manifests in multiple ways:

- **Allowing adequate time for expression:** Parties, especially those who feel historically silenced, need time to tell their stories fully.
- **Tolerating repetition:** People often need to say things multiple times before they feel truly heard.
- **Persisting through setbacks:** Negotiations often take two steps forward and one step back.
- **Maintaining optimism:** When progress is slow, parties look to the mediator for reassurance.
- **Recognizing that trust-building takes time:** Trust destroyed over years cannot be rebuilt in hours.

> **Key Concept: Patience as Active Engagement**
>
> Patience is not passive waiting. It is active engagement with a distant horizon. Patient mediators continue probing for interests, testing options, and building relationships even when immediate progress is not visible. They understand that every interaction, even difficult ones, contributes to the eventual resolution. As one experienced mediator noted, "The most important breakthroughs often come after hours that seemed wasted."

Cultural Competence

In company-community disputes, mediators often work across significant cultural divides, including working with communities who have experienced trauma (discussed in Chapter 10). Effective mediators develop cultural competence, the ability to understand, communicate with, and work effectively across cultural differences.

Cultural competence includes:

- **Understanding local customs and hierarchies:** Who are the respected figures whose blessing matters? Are decisions made by consensus or by designated leaders?

- **Adapting communication styles:** Some cultures favor direct communication; others prefer indirect approaches.
- **Respecting gender dynamics:** Mediators must find ways to ensure all voices are heard while respecting cultural norms.
- **Learning key phrases:** Being able to recite even a few greetings in the local language signals respect.
- **Incorporating appropriate rituals:** Starting with a prayer, sharing a meal, or conducting a ceremony builds legitimacy.

In mining-affected communities, traditional land tenure systems often conflict fundamentally with state-granted concession frameworks. Colonial and post-colonial power structures have shaped how community authority is recognized, and mediators must navigate this historical legacy. Additionally, women in mining-affected communities are often excluded from traditional authority structures even though they are frequently the primary users of water and subsistence resources directly affected by mining operations. Building cultural competence requires understanding these intersecting power dynamics (discussed further in Chapter 12) and finding ways to include marginalized voices in decisions that affect them.

> **Caution: Avoiding Cultural Stereotypes**
>
> Avoid cultural stereotypes. Cultures are not monolithic, and individuals vary. A young, university-educated community member may communicate very differently from an elder who has never left the village. Ask respectful questions when uncertain: "Could you help me understand how decisions are usually made in your community?" Let the parties guide you rather than making assumptions based on generalizations.

Impartiality in Practice

Impartiality is the bedrock of mediation credibility. If either party perceives the mediator as biased, they will not trust the process or accept its outcomes.

Practical impartiality requires:

- **Equal time and attention:** Track speaking time and meeting arrangements to ensure balance.
- **Balanced language:** The words you choose can subtly signal favor. Use consistent language for both sides.
- **Acknowledging valid points from everyone:** When a party makes a legitimate argument, acknowledge it explicitly.
- **Checking your assumptions and biases:** Reflect on your own predispositions before and during mediation.
- **Ensuring process fairness:** Meeting times, venues, and procedures should not systematically provide an advantage to one side.

In extractive-industry disputes, maintaining genuine impartiality requires acknowledging structural asymmetries that pure procedural balance cannot correct. Mining companies typically have legal teams, technical consultants, and substantial financial resources for extended negotiations. Communities often have neither. Companies control data while communities control only lived experience. Companies can sustain lengthy processes while communities often face urgent livelihood pressures. True impartiality means recognizing these imbalances and, where possible, helping communities access information and expertise so they can negotiate from a less unequal footing.

Creativity and Problem-Solving

The best mediators think creatively. When parties are stuck in zero-sum thinking, in which one side's gain seems to require the other's loss, creative problem-solving can reveal solutions that satisfy everyone.

Creative approaches include:

- **Expanding the pie:** Look for ways to increase total value rather than just dividing existing resources.
- **Combining elements from different proposals:** Each party's proposal may contain valuable components that can be reworked into a single, more favorable agreement.

- **Introducing new options:** Parties locked in their positions may not see possibilities that an outsider can perceive.
- **Reframing problems:** How parties define a problem shapes what solutions appear possible.
- **Finding connections between issues:** Trade-offs across issues create opportunities for both parties to claim victories.

Creative solutions in extractive-industry mediation require understanding mine closure timelines, rehabilitation commitments, and the distinction between short-term compensation and long-term sustainable development. Solutions that work in general mediation, such as splitting the difference or time-limited trials, may be inadequate in mining disputes. When mining operations permanently alter landscapes and deplete finite resources, split-the-difference compromises may satisfy neither side, and time-limited solutions create uncertainty during the years when environmental impacts emerge. Mediators must help parties envision creative solutions that reflect the permanent nature of mining's footprint and the timescales across which communities will live with its consequences.

Sample Mediator Language: *"I'm wondering if there's a way to address both concerns at once. The community wants jobs, and the company needs skilled workers. What if we combined a hiring commitment with a training program that the company helps design? That way, the community gets employment opportunities, and the company gets qualified candidates."*

Credibility and Trustworthiness

Trust is a mediator's most precious asset. Parties enter mediation wary, often with histories of broken promises and failed negotiations.

Trust-building practices include:

- **Following through on every promise:** If you say you will send meeting notes by Friday, send them by Friday.
- **Maintaining strict confidentiality:** Never share information from caucuses without explicit permission.
- **Being honest about limitations:** Admit what you don't know. Clarify what mediation can and cannot achieve.

- **Treating everyone with equal respect:** Dignity must be accorded regardless of status, education, or eloquence.
- **Demonstrating competence through preparation:** Parties trust mediators who clearly understand the dispute and context.
- **Acknowledging mistakes:** If you misunderstand something, acknowledge it promptly. Honesty often strengthens trust.

> **Practical Tip: Continuous Learning Habit**
>
> After each mediation, spend fifteen minutes reflecting: What worked well? What would I do differently? What surprised me? Brief reflection converts experience into learning. Keep a journal of insights to review before future mediations.

9.4 Documentation and Organization

Complex mediations generate enormous amounts of information. Effective documentation and organization transform this raw material into usable resources that support the mediation process.

Note-Taking

Mediator notes serve multiple functions. They capture important information for future reference, help identify patterns across sessions, provide the basis for drafting agreements, and create a record for consultation.

Effective notes capture:

- **Key interests and concerns:** What does each party really care about?
- **Proposals and counter-proposals:** Track the evolution of offers and responses.
- **Areas of agreement:** Document tentative agreements immediately, even if they aren't final.
- **Sticking points and barriers:** Identify not just what remains unresolved but why.

- **Action items and commitments:** What did each party agree to do before the next session?

> **Practical Tip: Note-Taking Without Disruption**
> Take notes in a way that doesn't disrupt the flow of the conversation. Use brief keywords and shorthand rather than transcribing everything. Maintain eye contact with speakers as much as possible. Review and expand your notes between sessions while the discussions are fresh in your mind.

Issue Tracking

For complex mediations involving multiple issues, systematic tracking prevents important matters from slipping through the cracks.

An effective issue tracking system includes:

- **Master issue list:** Comprehensive inventory of all issues that must be resolved.
- **Status tracking:** Categories might include: "not yet discussed," "under discussion," "tentatively agreed," or "finalized."
- **Linkages and dependencies:** Map connections between interconnected issues.
- **Obstacle analysis:** Document what is blocking progress on stuck issues.

Agreement Drafting

Drafting agreement language as discussions progress, rather than waiting until the end, prevents misunderstandings and builds momentum toward completion.

Best practices for agreement drafting include:

- **Write points of agreement on a visible surface:** Visibility creates ownership and enables immediate correction.

- **Check understanding in real time:** After writing, ask explicitly: "Is this what you're agreeing to?"
- **Use clear, specific language:** Avoid ambiguity. "The company will construct two water wells meeting WHO standards in Villages X and Y by December 2025" is better than "The company will improve water access."
- **Include verification mechanisms:** Specify how compliance will be verified for each commitment.

> **Key Concept: Package Integrity vs. Progressive Agreement**
>
> The principle "nothing is agreed until everything is agreed" protects parties from piecemeal commitments that disadvantage them. However, documenting tentative agreements creates useful building blocks and demonstrates progress. Label preliminary agreements clearly as "agreed in principle, subject to final package" so parties understand they retain flexibility until parties finalize the complete agreement.

9.5 Developing Your Competencies

Mediation competencies are not innate talents but developed skills. Even experienced mediators continually refine their capabilities.

Pathways for Development

- **Training programs:** Participate in advanced mediation courses, especially those focused on community disputes or trauma-informed practice.
- **Practice and simulation:** Skills develop through repetition. Use role-play exercises regularly.
- **Mentorship and observation:** Learn from experienced practitioners. Observe their sessions when possible.
- **Reflective practice:** After each mediation, systematically assess your performance.
- **Knowledge building:** Stay current on negotiation research and best practices.

- **Self-care and resilience:** Mediation is emotionally demanding work. Develop practices that sustain your well-being. For detailed guidance on managing vicarious trauma, preventing burnout, and building long-term resilience, see Chapter 11: Mediator Health and Well-Being.

Summary: The Mediator's Toolbox

Tool Category	Key Elements
Analytical Tools	Conflict mapping, stakeholder analysis, BATNA/ WATNA assessment, timeline construction
Process Tools	Caucusing, shuttle diplomacy, joint fact-finding, visual aids
Personal Competencies	Emotional intelligence, patience, cultural competence, impartiality, creativity, trustworthiness
Documentation	Note-taking, issue tracking, agreement drafting, organizational systems
Development	Training, practice, mentorship, reflection, knowledge building, self-care (Chapter 11)

A well-stocked toolbox and honed skills mean you can pivot to the approach that best serves the parties at any given moment. The goal is to become a multi-dimensional professional: part communicator, part analyst, part facilitator, part empathetic listener. Each dispute may call for a different emphasis. Having diverse tools and skills ensures the mediator can respond effectively to whatever challenges emerge during the process.

Tools are means, not ends. The most elegant analysis or skillful technique is worthwhile only when it serves the parties' underlying needs and enables constructive relationships going forward.

Key Concept: Building a Comprehensive Toolbox

As the saying goes, "If your only tool is a hammer, every problem looks like a nail." By developing a comprehensive toolbox of analytical frameworks, process techniques, personal competencies, and organizational systems, mediators ensure they have the right instrument for every situation. Continuous learning and reflective practice keep those tools sharp and ready for use.

The pathways illustrated in Figure 38 show how you can systematically develop these competencies throughout your career.

Figure 38: A guide to developing and strengthening mediator competencies through continuous learning, practice, and reflective growth.

Competency development is an ongoing practice, not a destination, and the willingness to continuously assess your own strengths and growth areas is perhaps the most important quality of effective mediators.

Technical Literacy for Mining Mediators

Mediators working in the mining sector need not be geologists or environmental scientists, but they must develop sufficient technical literacy to follow the substance of disputes. This requires understanding several key areas. Mediators should grasp the mining lifecycle (exploration, development, operation, closure, and rehabilitation) and common environmental impacts (acid mine drainage, tailings storage, water table drawdown, dust and noise).

They should also understand land tenure and concession systems in the relevant jurisdiction, compensation valuation methods for land, crops, and livelihoods, and the regulatory framework governing mining operations, environmental protection, and community consultation. Without this foundation, mediators cannot assess whether proposed solutions are technically feasible, whether expert opinions are credible, or whether one party is using technical complexity to obscure a simple injustice.

Understanding commodity economics strengthens technical competence. Mediators must grasp price cycles, investment timelines that span from exploration through closure and rehabilitation, and how global market conditions affect a company's willingness to negotiate.

A mining operation becomes less profitable as ore grades decline, commodity prices fall, or regulatory costs rise. When mediators understand these economic pressures, they can assess whether a company's refusal to accept a remedial commitment reflects genuine economic infeasibility or strategic positioning.

Assessing the feasibility of proposed remedies requires evaluating whether commitments in draft agreements are technically and economically achievable. Can the company actually construct the proposed water treatment system within the stated timeframe? Are rehabilitation targets grounded in realistic soil science, or are they aspirational? Mediators who can identify engineering constraints, cost implications, and regulatory limitations help parties reach agreements that will endure rather than collapse when implementation reveals impracticality.

Interpreting environmental monitoring data strengthens mediation practice. Mediators should understand baseline studies, water quality measurements, air quality reports, and how to identify when data gaps or methodological choices obscure real impacts. A company may conduct baseline monitoring during a favorable season or use measurement methods that underestimate impacts. Mediators who can recognize these methodological vulnerabilities help communities understand whether data truly shows low risk or simply reflects incomplete measurement.

Finally, mediators must develop the capacity to distinguish genuine technical impossibility from strategic claims. Companies may argue that a requested water quality standard is "technically impossible" when what they really mean is "expensive." Communities may claim that mine-induced subsidence poses "insoluble" risks when engineering solutions exist but haven't been presented. Mediators with sufficient technical knowledge can probe these claims, ask for evidence, and identify when "technical" objections mask unwillingness to invest in mitigation.

Managing Asymmetric Information in Extractive-Industry Disputes

In extractive-industry disputes, information asymmetries are often profound and structural. Mining companies typically control environmental baseline data, operating cost data, regulatory compliance records, and production projections. Communities, by contrast, possess oral histories, lived experience of past company behavior, and traditional ecological knowledge.

Neither party begins with complete information, but the distribution is far from equal. Companies employ teams of data scientists, hydrologists, and accountants. Communities often lack access to technical experts or financial resources to hire them.

The mediator's role is to help level this information landscape without compromising neutrality. This involves advocating for balanced information access, recommending independent technical experts who can review company data on behalf of the community, and facilitating access to relevant documents.

Many jurisdictions have laws requiring disclosure of environmental baseline data, and mediators can help communities understand and exercise these rights. Mediators can also suggest that parties jointly commission studies or retain independent experts, transforming the process from one where each side battles over data to one where both sides invest in getting accurate information.

Finally, mediators should recognize when persistent information gaps suggest bad faith rather than legitimate confidentiality concerns. If a company repeatedly refuses to disclose costs, citing commercial confidentiality, yet those same costs have been disclosed in other disputes or financial filings, the refusal likely masks strategic positioning. By noting patterns and inconsistencies, mediators can push parties toward transparency without having to verify each claim independently.

Practical Tip: Mediator Competencies in Low-Resource Settings

When working in contexts with limited professional infrastructure, mediators need additional competencies beyond those required in well-resourced settings. These include the ability to improvise process design using available materials and spaces, cultural fluency sufficient to understand local conflict resolution traditions that may complement or substitute for formal mediation techniques, practical skills in managing logistics (transport, food, accommodation) that would typically be handled by support staff, and the judgment to know when a dispute exceeds what can be safely mediated without professional backup and when to refer parties to other mechanisms.

10. TRAUMA-INFORMED AND CULTURALLY SENSITIVE APPROACHES

Few competencies matter more than the ability to recognize and respond to trauma and cultural dynamics that shape how parties experience conflict. These two dimensions are deeply intertwined: cultural context determines how trauma is expressed, understood, and healed, while trauma itself can fracture the cultural structures that communities depend on for resilience. A mediator who addresses trauma without cultural awareness risks applying frameworks that do not fit, and one who attends to culture without recognizing trauma risks overlooking the psychological undercurrents that drive behavior at the table. This chapter treats trauma-informed and culturally sensitive practice as inseparable elements of effective mediation in company-community disputes.

Company-community disputes are not merely technical disagreements about compensation or resource allocation. They involve people's fundamental sense of safety, identity, dignity, and place in the world. Trauma and culture intersect at every stage: a community's cultural relationship to land shapes the depth of trauma caused by displacement. Cultural norms around gender determine how survivors of violence can seek redress, and a community's collective memory of historical injustice amplifies the psychological impact of current grievances. Mediators who overlook these interconnected dimensions risk causing harm, deepening mistrust, and producing agreements that collapse because they never addressed what truly mattered.

10.1 Understanding Trauma in Conflict

Trauma occurs when events overwhelm a person's capacity to cope, leaving lasting psychological impacts on thought, emotion, and relationships. Understanding trauma helps mediators interpret responses that appear confusing or obstructive without a trauma-informed lens. Apparent unwillingness to engage may reflect a survival response triggered by the mediation environment.

> **Practical Tip: Trauma Screening**
>
> You cannot always know who carries trauma. Assume that any participant in a serious Company-Community dispute may have a history of trauma, and design your process accordingly. This universal precaution ensures you do not inadvertently harm those whose trauma is not visible.

Sources of Trauma in Company-Community Disputes

In company-community disputes, trauma may result from various experiences, each carrying its own psychological weight and requiring specific sensitivity from mediators:

Forced Displacement or Loss of Homes and Land

When communities are relocated for mining or infrastructure projects, the loss extends far beyond physical property. People lose their connection to ancestral lands where generations lived and died, to sacred sites where they practiced spiritual traditions, and to the social networks that gave meaning to their daily lives. For many indigenous and rural communities, land is not merely an economic asset but the foundation of cultural identity. Forced displacement can trigger grief responses similar to the death of a loved one, combined with feelings of powerlessness and injustice. In the Guinea mining mediation case, community members affected by resettlement carried years of accumulated pain from losing their homes, which had to be acknowledged before substantive negotiations could proceed meaningfully.

Violence from Security Forces or During Protests

When communities experience violence, whether from company security guards, police, or clashes during protests, the psychological scars can persist for years. Survivors may experience flashbacks, hypervigilance, and difficulty trusting authority figures. Violence also creates collective trauma within communities, where even those who did not directly experience the violence feel its effects through shared fear and broken trust. In several mining disputes across Africa, past violent confrontations between security forces and community protesters have created lasting barriers to dialogue that mediators must carefully navigate.

Environmental Disasters Affecting Health and Livelihoods

When pollution contaminates water sources, destroys crops, or causes illness, communities experience both immediate harm and ongoing fear about their future. The uncertainty of not knowing whether the water is safe to drink or whether children will develop health problems creates chronic stress that compounds the trauma of tangible losses. Communities living near mining operations often report anxiety about invisible threats they cannot see or control, adding a layer of psychological burden to their physical and economic challenges.

Sexual Assault or Gender-Based Violence

When gender-based violence is part of the conflict context, the mediator faces decisions that require specialized knowledge and careful ethical reasoning. The first question is whether mediation is appropriate at all. If the violence is ongoing, if perpetrators will be present or represented at the table, or if survivors face retaliation for participating, mediation should not proceed until these safety concerns are addressed. If mediation does proceed, it must be structured around safety: survivors should never be required to confront perpetrators directly, their identities should be protected, and their participation must be genuinely voluntary at every stage.

The mediator must understand the distinction between their role and that of an investigator or therapist. The mediator is not conducting a criminal investigation, establishing fault, or providing trauma therapy. The mediator's role is to facilitate a process in which the community's experience of gender-based violence is acknowledged as part of the broader harm, and in which remedies address both individual survivors' needs and systemic failures that enabled the violence. This may include commitments to reform security force conduct, establish independent complaint mechanisms, fund survivor support services, and implement training programs.

Caution: Preventing Secondary Victimization

Secondary victimization occurs when the mediation process itself causes additional harm to survivors. This can happen when survivors are pressured to share details of their experience before a group, when their credibility is questioned during negotiations, when proposed remedies are framed as "generous" rather than as obligations, or when confidentiality is breached. The mediator must establish clear protocols: no survivor is required to testify or share details; the fact of violence is established through other evidence (medical records, reports, witness statements); discussions of remedy focus on needs and accountability rather than re-litigating events; and all participants sign enhanced confidentiality agreements that specifically protect survivor identities.

Practical Tip: Structuring Mediation Around GBV

When gender-based violence is part of the dispute, consider these structural adaptations: engage a female co-mediator or support person; hold separate, confidential sessions with survivors before any joint process; ensure survivors have independent legal counsel and psychosocial support; establish a separate track for GBV-related issues that can proceed with enhanced confidentiality protections; agree in advance that no settlement will require survivors to waive future legal claims; and connect survivors with specialized services regardless of the mediation's outcome. The mediator should also consult with organizations experienced in GBV response before designing the process.

Sexual violence perpetrated by company agents, security personnel, or enabled by the disruption that accompanies large projects creates particularly deep trauma. Survivors often face stigma, shame, and isolation from their own communities in addition to the psychological impact of the assault itself. Mediating such cases requires specialized approaches that prioritize the safety, autonomy, and dignity of survivors above all other considerations. The impact extends beyond individual survivors to affect families and entire communities, creating complex dynamics that mediators must navigate with extreme care.

Given the complexity of these cases, a structured assessment is essential before any mediation process begins. The following framework provides a step-by-step approach for evaluating whether mediation is appropriate, focusing on survivor safety, readiness indicators, and the support mechanisms that must be in place.

This assessment framework specifically addresses the complex dynamics of sexual assault cases, where survivor safety must be the first priority before any mediation process can begin.

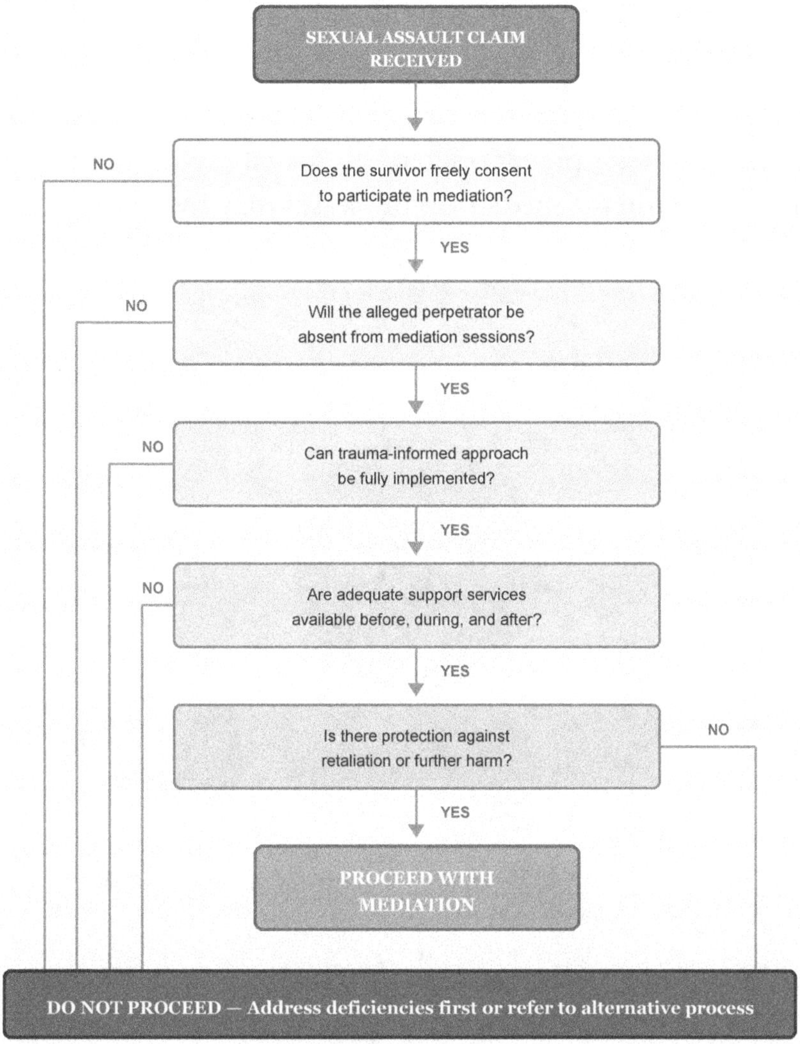

Figure 39: A specialized assessment framework for mediations involving allegations of sexual assault or gender-based violence, with safety-first protocols.

Sexual assault and gender-based violence cases require assessment frameworks that center safety without retraumatizing parties, and this specialized approach differs fundamentally from how mediators assess other sensitive disputes.

Sexual assault cases also involve layered power dynamics that the mediator must recognize and actively address. Institutional authority, economic dependence, and social stigma can all work against survivors, making genuine voluntary participation difficult unless these imbalances are named and mitigated.

Understanding these layered power dynamics is essential before proceeding, as the specific ways power operates in sexual assault cases reveal vulnerabilities that standard mediation processes may overlook.

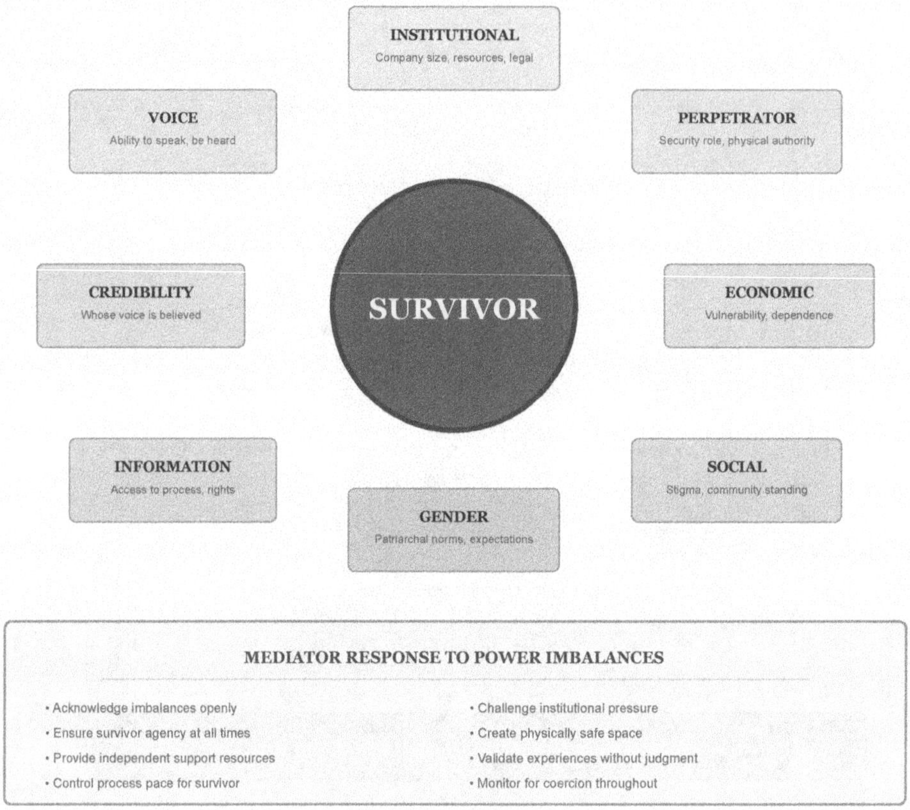

Figure 40: An analysis of the power dynamics present in cases involving sexual assault, highlighting vulnerability factors and protective measures for mediation.

Power dynamics in sexual assault cases are never simple, and understanding the specific vulnerability factors present allows you to design processes that provide genuine protection rather than just symbolic safeguards.

Loss of Loved Ones or Community Members

When community members have died as a result of accidents, violence, or health impacts related to company operations, the grief and anger can make dialogue extremely difficult. Grieving families may feel that no compensation or agreement can address their loss, and they may view the mediation process with suspicion or hostility. Mediators must create space for this grief to be expressed and acknowledged before any productive discussion of a resolution can occur.

Prolonged Uncertainty and Powerlessness

Even without discrete traumatic events, living for years under conditions of uncertainty about one's future, combined with a sense of powerlessness to influence decisions that profoundly affect one's life, creates chronic stress that functions similarly to trauma. Communities waiting for years to learn whether they will be relocated, what compensation they will receive, or whether their health concerns will be addressed experience ongoing psychological harm that affects their capacity to engage constructively in mediation.

Historical Injustices and Collective Trauma

Many communities bring to the mediation table not just grievances about the specific company involved, but layers of historical trauma from colonialism, exploitation, and discrimination. A community's response to a current mining dispute may be shaped by memories of how their ancestors were treated by previous extractive operations or by colonial authorities. Understanding this historical context helps mediators recognize why communities may approach negotiations with deep suspicion, even when the current company has made genuine efforts to engage respectfully.

> **Key Concept: Trauma Is Cumulative**
>
> A community may have experienced multiple types of trauma over many years, with each new incident building on previous wounds. What appears to be an overreaction to a minor issue may actually reflect accumulated pain from many sources.

Caution: Vicarious Trauma

Mediators repeatedly exposed to trauma narratives can develop vicarious trauma themselves. Monitor your own well-being. Symptoms include emotional numbness, cynicism, difficulty sleeping, and intrusive thoughts about cases. Seek supervision, peer support, or professional help when needed.

Recognizing Trauma Responses

Trauma manifests differently in different people, and mediators benefit from learning to recognize these varied responses without judgment. The four primary trauma responses, often called the "four Fs," are survival mechanisms that evolved to protect humans from danger. Understanding these responses helps mediators interpret behaviors that might otherwise seem puzzling or counterproductive.

Response Type	Signs You May Observe	What It Means
Fight	Anger outbursts, aggression, confrontational behavior, blaming, raised voice, threatening posture, hostile statements	The person feels threatened and is attempting to protect themselves or others. The intensity may not match the current situation because they are responding to accumulated threats.
Flight	Wanting to leave the room, restlessness, fidgeting, avoiding certain topics, repeatedly changing the subject, making excuses to end early	The person's nervous system is signaling danger, and their instinct is to escape the situation. They may not be able to articulate what feels threatening.

Response Type	Signs You May Observe	What It Means
Freeze	Shutting down, inability to speak or respond, blank expression, dissociation, appearing "checked out" or distant, difficulty remembering what was said	The person is overwhelmed, and their system has shut down as a protective measure. This is not defiance or disinterest but an involuntary response to perceived threats.
Fawn	Over-agreeing with everything, excessive people-pleasing, difficulty expressing their own needs or disagreement, apologizing unnecessarily, going along to avoid conflict	The person has learned to survive by appeasing others, often through experiences in which asserting themselves led to harm. Agreements made in this state may not reflect their true needs.

Key Concept: Trauma Responses Are Survival Mechanisms

Trauma responses are survival mechanisms, not character flaws. A community member who freezes when asked about an incident is not being uncooperative. They may be experiencing a trauma response that makes it impossible to respond in that moment. Understanding this prevents misinterpretation and allows the mediator to respond helpfully rather than with frustration.

Recognizing these responses in the mediation room allows mediators to adjust their approach accordingly. A person showing fight responses may need acknowledgment of their anger and assurance that their concerns will be taken seriously before they can engage constructively. Someone in flight mode may benefit from a break or reassurance about their safety and control in the process. A freeze response calls for patience, gentleness, and, if needed, a pause to allow the person's nervous system to reset. Fawn responses are particularly important to recognize because the person may agree to outcomes that do not serve their interests, leading to unstable agreements that unravel later.

10.2 Principles of Trauma-Informed Mediation

Trauma-informed mediation is not a separate technique but a lens through which mediators must view and conduct all mediation activities. It involves understanding how trauma affects behavior and decision-making, adapting practices to minimize the risk of retraumatization, and creating conditions that support healing alongside dispute resolution. The following principles provide a framework for trauma-informed practice.

These principles are not abstract ideals but practical guides for every interaction and decision mediators make in trauma-sensitive contexts.

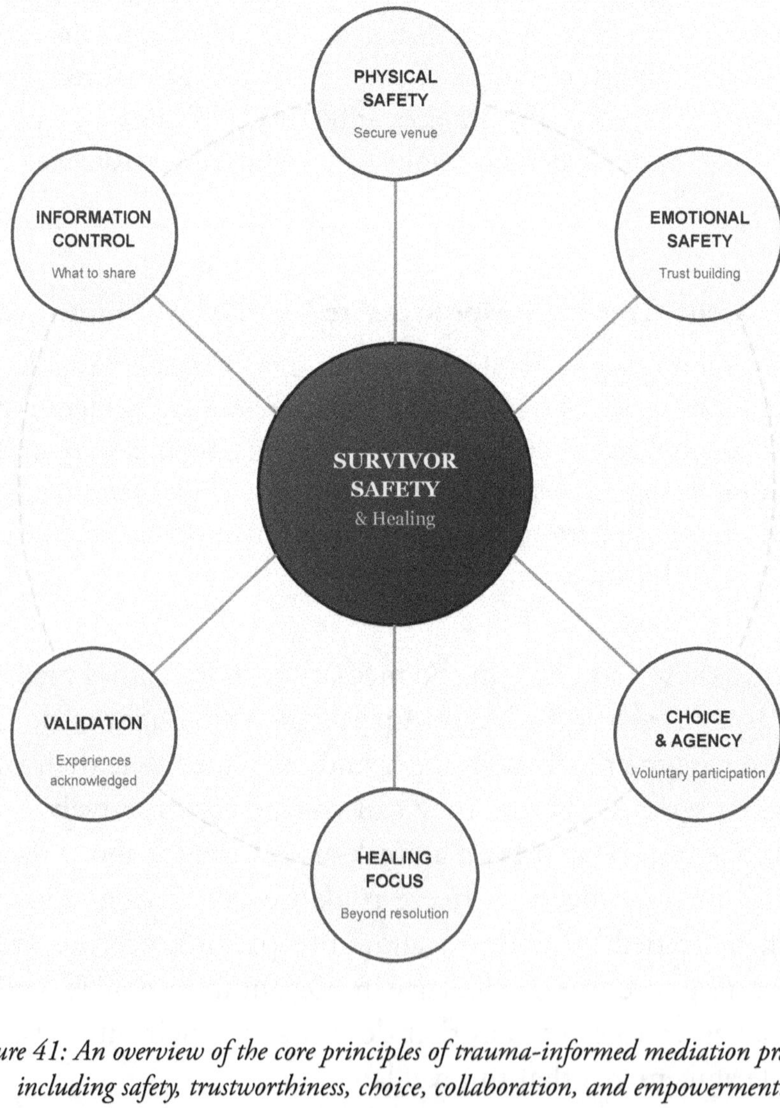

Figure 41: An overview of the core principles of trauma-informed mediation practice, including safety, trustworthiness, choice, collaboration, and empowerment.

Applying these principles consistently transforms them from abstract ideals into habits that shape every interaction, from how you greet parties to how you structure confidentiality discussions.

> **Key Concept: Trauma-Informed vs. Trauma-Focused**
>
> Trauma-informed mediation adapts the process to accommodate trauma without requiring disclosure or treatment. Trauma-focused therapy addresses trauma directly. Mediators are not therapists. Our role is to create conditions where traumatized participants can engage effectively, not to heal their trauma.

Safety First

Safety is the foundation of all trauma-informed work. Without a genuine sense of safety, traumatized individuals cannot access the cognitive resources needed for problem-solving and negotiation. Safety has multiple dimensions, including:

- Physical Safety and Venue Selection: Choose neutral venues away from trauma sites and locations associated with negative experiences. For example, a community member who was assaulted by company security guards will not feel safe meeting at the company's offices, even in a conference room far from where the incident occurred.
- Psychological Safety Through Predictability: Traumatized individuals often experience the world as unpredictable and threatening. Creating psychological safety requires clear explanations of what will happen, when, and why. Before sessions begin, explain the process, the ground rules, and what participants can expect.
- Protection from Retaliation: Many community members fear that speaking honestly in mediation will lead to retaliation by the company, local authorities, or even within their own community. Establish clear ground rules prohibiting retaliation and explain how confidentiality will be maintained.
- Support Person Availability: Allow survivors and vulnerable participants to bring a chosen support person to sessions. This person might

be a family member, friend, advocate, or counselor who can provide emotional support.

- Crisis Resources on Standby: Have mental health professionals or crisis support available, either on-site or accessible by phone, in case participants become overwhelmed. This is particularly important when mediating cases involving sexual assault, violence, or loss of life.

Sample Mediator Dialogue:
"Before we begin, I want to make sure everyone feels safe here. This is a confidential space where nothing said will be used against you in any other proceeding. You can take breaks whenever you need them by simply raising your hand or stepping out. A counselor is available in the next room if anyone wants to speak privately at any time. We have agreed on ground rules that prohibit all types of retaliation. Does anyone have safety concerns that we should address before we proceed?"

Choice and Control

Fundamentally, trauma involves a loss of control. Events happened that the person could not prevent or escape. Restoring a sense of agency and control is therefore central to trauma recovery and to effective trauma-informed mediation. Every aspect of the process should offer choices where possible, reinforcing that participants have power and autonomy. You can do this by ensuring:

- Process Choices: Offer choices about how the mediation will proceed whenever feasible. Would the participant prefer to speak first or second? Would they rather have an initial private meeting with the mediator or go directly to a joint session?
- Information Sharing Boundaries: Never force disclosure or participation in discussions that participants are not ready for. Make clear that they can set boundaries on what they share.
- Pace Control: Let participants set the pace as much as possible. Check in regularly about whether they need a break, want to change topics, or need more time to consider something.

Avoiding Retraumatization

One of the most critical aspects of trauma-informed practice is ensuring that the mediation process itself does not cause additional harm. Retraumatization occurs when the process triggers traumatic memories or recreates aspects of the original traumatic experience. Use these guidelines to avoid retraumatization:

- Do Not Probe for Graphic Details: Mediators do not need to know every detail of what happened. Focus on understanding the impact and what participants need going forward, not on gathering detailed accounts of traumatic events.
- Avoid Victim-Blaming Questions: Questions that imply the participant could have prevented what happened, or that probe why they did not respond differently, can be deeply harmful. Never ask questions like "Why didn't you report it sooner?" or "What were you doing there?"
- Do Not Pressure Forgiveness: While forgiveness and reconciliation may ultimately benefit survivors, pressuring them to forgive before they are ready can be harmful. Forgiveness is a personal journey with its own timeline, and it is not a requirement for successful mediation.

Empowerment Focus

Trauma-informed mediation should actively contribute to survivors' empowerment and recovery, not merely avoid causing harm. This means designing processes and outcomes that help participants regain a sense of agency, dignity, and hope. Mediators can do this by:

- Validating Their Right to Be Heard: Many trauma survivors have had experiences of being dismissed, not believed, or ignored. The mediation process can be healing simply by providing a space where they are listened to respectfully and taken seriously.
- Designing Active Roles in Solutions: When developing resolution options, look for ways to give survivors active rather than passive roles. For example, an agreement where "a community-managed fund will

administer compensation payments" is more empowering than one where "the company will pay compensation to the community."

- Recognizing Strengths and Resilience: Trauma survivors are not defined by their trauma. They have survived difficult experiences and often demonstrated remarkable strength in doing so. Acknowledge this resilience.

Trust and Transparency

Trauma destroys trust in others, in institutions, and sometimes in oneself. Rebuilding trust is both a goal and a method of trauma-informed mediation. Mediators build trust through their own consistent, transparent behavior, which can then create conditions for trust to develop between parties. To help establish trust, mediators convey trust through:

- Consistent, Predictable Behavior: Be reliable in every aspect of your conduct. If you say you will do something, do it. If you commit to maintaining confidentiality, maintain it without exception.
- Clear Explanations: Explain what is happening and why at every stage of the process. Do not assume participants understand procedural steps that may be familiar to you.
- Honesty About Limitations: Do not promise what you cannot deliver. If there are aspects of the situation you cannot change or outcomes you cannot guarantee, say so clearly.

10.3 Practical Trauma-Informed Techniques

Beyond these general principles, mediators need specific techniques they can employ when working with traumatized participants. These practical tools help translate trauma-informed principles into concrete actions.

Pacing and Breaks

The pace of mediation significantly affects traumatized participants' ability to engage effectively. Traditional mediation scheduling, with long sessions aimed at maximizing progress, may be counterproductive when trauma is involved.

The following can help ensure trauma survivors can participate effectively in mediation:

- Schedule Longer Sessions with More Breaks: Rather than packing a session with continuous discussion, plan for substantial break time. A three-hour session might include two fifteen-minute breaks plus flexibility for additional pauses.
- Watch for Fatigue and Emotional Overload: Pay attention to signs that participants are tiring or becoming overwhelmed, such as decreased engagement, irritability, difficulty concentrating, or physical signs of stress.
- Offer Breaks Proactively: Do not wait for participants to ask for breaks. Many people are reluctant to request breaks, fearing they will appear weak or obstruct progress.
- Consider Multiple Shorter Sessions: Rather than marathon sessions, spread mediation over multiple shorter sessions across several days or weeks. This gives participants time to process between meetings.

Grounding Techniques

When someone becomes overwhelmed during mediation, grounding techniques can help them return to the present moment and regain their capacity to participate. The following techniques work by redirecting attention from traumatic memories or overwhelming emotions to immediate sensory experience:

- Speak Calmly and Slowly: When someone is distressed, your calm presence can be stabilizing. Lower your voice, slow your speech, and use simple, clear language.
- Use Physical Grounding: Suggest simple physical awareness exercises. "Can you feel your feet on the floor? Press them down a little and notice the sensation."
- Offer Water: The simple act of drinking water can help someone ground in the present moment. It also provides a pause for collecting themselves without the awkwardness of prolonged silence.

- Take a Break and Change the Environment: If someone is seriously overwhelmed, suggest stepping outside or moving to a different space. A change of environment can help reset the nervous system.
- Respect Physical Boundaries: Do not touch participants without explicit permission, even with well-intentioned gestures like a hand on the shoulder. For trauma survivors, unexpected touch can be triggering.

Sample Mediator Dialogue:

"I notice this is bringing up a lot. Would you like to take a moment? Sometimes it helps to take a few deep breaths or feel your feet on the ground. There is no rush here. We can pause as long as you need. Would you like some water, or would you prefer to step outside for a few minutes?"

Practical Tip: Grounding Techniques

Learn simple grounding techniques to share with participants who become overwhelmed, such as deep breathing, noticing five things you can see, and feeling your feet on the floor. Having these tools available allows you to help participants regulate without stopping the process entirely.

Language Matters

The words mediators use can either create safety and respect or trigger distress and alienation. Trauma-informed language is sensitive, non-blaming, and follows participants' lead. Best practices include:

- Mirror Participant Language: Pay attention to how participants describe their experiences and use their language when discussing those experiences. If someone uses the phrase "what happened at the river," you should also use the phrasing "what happened at the river."
- Avoid Legal or Clinical Jargon: Terms that sound neutral to professionals may sound cold, dismissive, or threatening to participants.

Use plain language that acknowledges reality without sounding technical or legalistic.

- Be Careful with Labels: Do not refer to people as "victims" unless they explicitly prefer that word. Some people find that term disempowering and prefer "survivor." Others may not want either label. When in doubt, ask.

Support Resources

Mediation alone cannot address all the needs of traumatized participants. Ensuring that appropriate support resources are available and that participants know how to access them. You can do this by:

- Having Counselors or Psychosocial Support on Standby: For mediations involving severe trauma, arrange for mental health professionals to be available, either in an adjacent room or by phone.
- Providing Referrals to Ongoing Support: Prepare information about counseling services, support groups, legal aid, and other resources that participants may need beyond the mediation.
- Checking in After Difficult Sessions: Follow up with participants after particularly intense sessions to see how they are doing. This might be a brief phone call the next day or an email checking in.

> **Practical Tip: Preparing a Resource List**
>
> Before the mediation begins, compile a resource list appropriate to the context, including local counseling services, support organizations, legal aid, and emergency contacts. Ensure this information is available in languages participants can read and includes culturally appropriate, accessible services.

10.4 Where Trauma and Culture Intersect

The preceding sections presented trauma-informed principles and practical techniques as though they operate in a culturally neutral space. In reality, every aspect of trauma, from how it is experienced to how it can be addressed, is filtered through cultural context. Before turning to cultural sensitivity as a distinct competency, it is worth pausing to examine how trauma and culture interact, because this intersection is where mediators most often misjudge what is happening at the table.

Cultural Shaping of Trauma Expression

The "four Fs" described in Section 10.1 are universal survival mechanisms, but culture profoundly shapes how they manifest. In some communities, vocal expression of grief and anger is expected and even encouraged, so a fight response may look like passionate protest that a mediator unfamiliar with the culture could mistake for aggression. In others, stoic composure is a deeply held value, and a freeze response may be indistinguishable from cultural deference to authority. A mediator trained to watch for Western markers of distress, such as tears, visible agitation, or verbal disclosure, may completely miss trauma responses that take culturally specific forms. These include withdrawal into silence, somatic complaints like headaches or stomach pain, or spiritual explanations for suffering that a secular framework would not recognize as trauma at all.

Cultural Pathways to Healing

Western trauma frameworks emphasize individual therapy conducted by trained professionals. Many communities, however, process trauma collectively through ceremony, storytelling, communal mourning, or spiritual practice. A mediator who responds to visible trauma only by offering referrals to individual counseling may miss what the community actually needs. The community may require a collective acknowledgment of harm, a ceremony of restoration, or the involvement of traditional healers alongside mental health professionals. The practical techniques from Section 10.3, particularly grounding and pacing, work best when adapted to culturally appropriate forms. A grounding exercise that asks participants to "notice five things you can see" may feel alien in a context where a brief prayer or a shared moment of silence would accomplish the same regulatory function more naturally.

When Trauma Fractures Culture

Displacement, prolonged conflict, and violence do not only traumatize individuals. They can break down the very cultural structures that would normally support healing. When a community is forcibly relocated, it may lose access to sacred sites, traditional gathering places, and the social networks through which elders transmit knowledge and resolve disputes. The result is a compounding effect: people lose both their sense of safety and the cultural resources that would help them recover. Mediators encountering this situation face a particular challenge, because the cultural practices they might draw on to build trust and legitimacy may themselves have been damaged by the conflict they are trying to resolve. Recognizing this dynamic is essential. It means the mediation process may need to create space not only for resolving the immediate dispute but also for beginning to rebuild the cultural fabric that the conflict has torn.

10.5 Cultural Sensitivity in Mediation

Culture profoundly shapes how people understand conflict, express emotions, make decisions, and expect resolution to occur. A mediation process that ignores cultural context risks alienating participants, missing crucial information, and producing outcomes that do not work within the participants' social reality. Adapting the approach to honor cultural contexts while still upholding the core principles of fair, voluntary mediation.

Understanding Cultural Context

Before entering any mediation with a community, invest time in understanding their cultural context. This does not mean becoming an expert in the culture, but instead developing enough understanding to be respectful and to recognize when cultural factors may be affecting the process. You can do this by:

- Researching the Community's Cultural Background: Learn about traditions, social structures, and historical experiences. Understand who holds authority, how decisions are traditionally made, and what values are particularly important.

- Consulting Cultural Insiders: Seek guidance from people who know the culture well, whether community members willing to advise, local NGOs with community ties, or cultural liaisons.
- Considering Using a Cultural Co-Mediator: In some cases, working with a co-mediator from the community or with deep cultural knowledge can significantly enhance the process.
- Learning Appropriate Greetings and Protocols: Simple gestures like learning proper greetings, understanding how to address elders respectfully, and knowing the significance of certain practices demonstrate respect.
- Understanding Spiritual and Religious Dimensions: Sacred sites, spiritual practices, and religious beliefs may be central to the dispute or to how resolution is understood.

Practical Tip: Learning Community Customs

Ask community members directly: "Could you help me understand how important decisions are usually made in your community?" and "Are there customs I should know about to show proper respect?" People usually appreciate genuine curiosity and are willing to help outsiders navigate their cultural context appropriately.

While these individual suggestions provide starting points for cultural learning, the following checklist offers a more systematic approach to ensuring that cultural considerations are not overlooked.

Language and Communication

Language differences present obvious challenges, but addressing them requires more than simple translation. Through the following techniques, mediators can ensure that clear communication is genuinely accessible and that the nuances important for mediation are not lost:

- Use Qualified Interpreters: When interpretation is needed, use qualified interpreters who understand both the languages involved and the mediation context. Brief interpreters on their role and the importance of faithful translation.

- Avoid Technical Jargon: Legal, technical, and procedural language that may be clear to professionals can be opaque or intimidating to community members, especially when translation is involved.
- Use Local Metaphors and Proverbs: When culturally appropriate, incorporating local metaphors, proverbs, or ways of expressing ideas can increase understanding and show respect for the culture.
- Check Understanding Frequently: Do not assume that silence or nodding indicates understanding. Regularly check that participants have understood what was communicated.

Incorporating Cultural Practices

Where appropriate, incorporating culturally significant practices into the mediation process can increase its legitimacy and effectiveness. This requires sensitivity and genuine collaboration with participants rather than superficial adoption of cultural elements. Mediators can accomplish this through:

- Opening Rituals: In many cultures, important gatherings begin with prayers, blessings, or other rituals. Offering to incorporate such openings, if desired by participants, can create a more comfortable environment.

Sample Mediator Dialogue:
"I understand that in your tradition, important discussions often begin with a blessing. Would you like to start our session that way today? We want this process to feel right to everyone involved."

- Involvement of Traditional Authorities: Respected elders, chiefs, or traditional authorities may have essential roles in legitimizing agreements and ensuring community buy-in.
- Traditional Reconciliation Practices: Many cultures have traditional practices for reconciliation that go beyond Western concepts of agreement and compensation, including ceremonies of forgiveness or symbolic acts of restoration.

- Shared Meals and Relationship-Building: In many cultures, sharing food together is an important element of relationship-building and reconciliation.
- Ceremonies Marking Agreement or Closure: The way an agreement is formalized can affect its perceived legitimacy. In one case, community and company representatives planted a tree together to symbolize the growth of a new relationship.

Ensuring Inclusive Participation

Cultural norms may systematically silence certain voices within a community. While respecting culture, mediators must also ensure that all affected parties have a meaningful opportunity to participate. This can be done by:

- Creating Opportunities for Women's Input: If cultural norms inhibit women's participation in mixed-gender settings, consider holding separate sessions with women. Their input can then be communicated to the broader mediation.
- Including Youth Perspectives: In cultures with strong elder authority, younger community members may not feel able to speak freely. Create opportunities for youth input through separate sessions or designated representatives.
- Using Small Group Discussions: Breaking into smaller groups can enable participation from people who are uncomfortable speaking in larger settings.
- Collecting Anonymous Input: In situations where people may fear speaking openly, anonymous mechanisms such as written submissions or suggestion boxes can be valuable.

Understanding Corporate Culture

Cultural sensitivity extends to understanding both corporate and community cultures. Company representatives operate within organizational constraints and cultures that shape what they can offer and how they communicate, including:

- Decision-Making Chains and Authority: Understand who at the table has authority to make commitments and what must be referred to higher levels.
- Pressures from Headquarters or Investors: Company negotiators often face pressure from corporate headquarters, shareholders, or investors that constrain their flexibility.
- Corporate Values Worth Drawing On: Many companies have stated commitments to corporate social responsibility that can be drawn on in mediation.
- Internal Constraints: Companies face budget cycles, regulatory requirements, and operational constraints that affect what is possible.

Caution: Cultural Stereotyping

Learning about cultural patterns helps, but it can also lead to stereotyping. Not every member of a culture follows its general patterns. Treat cultural knowledge as starting hypotheses to test, not fixed rules to apply. Ask individuals how they prefer to engage rather than assuming based on group membership.

Practical Tip: Cultural Informants

Before mediating in unfamiliar cultural contexts, consult with cultural informants. These might be community members not directly involved in the dispute, local NGO staff, or anthropologists who have studied the area. Their insights can prevent serious cultural missteps.

Key Concept: Cultural Humility

Cultural competence implies mastery, but no one can fully master another culture. Cultural humility means approaching each situation as a learner, acknowledging what you do not know, asking rather than assuming, and accepting correction gracefully when you make mistakes.

10.6 Psychological Dynamics in Conflict

Trauma and culture do not operate in isolation from the broader psychological forces that shape human judgment. Cognitive biases and emotional patterns affect everyone, but trauma amplifies them. A community that has been harmed in the past is more susceptible to confirmation bias when interpreting a company's actions, and cultural norms can reinforce or counteract tendencies like loss aversion. Understanding these dynamics helps mediators recognize when psychological patterns, rather than substantive disagreements, are impeding progress.

Common Cognitive Biases

Cognitive biases are systematic patterns in how humans process information that can lead to distorted perceptions and poor decisions. Understanding them helps mediators recognize when biases may be affecting negotiation. Common biases include:

- Confirmation Bias: People tend to notice and remember information that confirms their existing beliefs while overlooking information that contradicts them. Mediators can address confirmation bias by explicitly presenting information that challenges each side's assumptions.
- Loss Aversion: People feel losses more intensely than equivalent gains. Losing $100 feels "worse" than gaining $100 feels "good." Mediators can address loss aversion by reframing proposals in terms of what parties gain rather than what they lose.
- Anchoring: The first number or position stated in a negotiation tends to anchor subsequent discussion. Mediators can address anchoring by introducing multiple reference points and focusing on criteria rather than positions.

Sample Mediator Dialogue

"I notice we keep coming back to that initial figure from the first session. Let's step back and think about what actually makes sense based on comparable situations and the criteria we identified as fair, rather than being anchored to numbers from early in our discussions. What does similar compensation look like in other communities in this region?"

- Reactive Devaluation: Proposals are often valued less simply because they come from the other side. Mediators can address reactive devaluation by presenting options as jointly generated or by neutrally attributing ideas.
- Overconfidence: People tend to overestimate the strength of their own position and their alternatives if negotiation fails. Mediators can address overconfidence through reality testing.

Dehumanization and "Us vs. Them" Thinking

As discussed in Chapter 5 (Understanding Conflict Dynamics and Escalation), dehumanization is a hallmark of intensifying conflict. Parties stop seeing each other as individual human beings and instead perceive the other side as a monolithic enemy. Trauma deepens this tendency, because people who have been harmed by a group naturally generalize that threat to all members of it. Cultural differences compound the problem: unfamiliar customs, languages, and values make it easier to see the other side as fundamentally different rather than simply differently situated. Actively working to counter dehumanization and restore awareness of the people that exist on both sides requires attention to both these dynamics, through various means including:

- Encouraging Personal Stories: Create opportunities for participants to share personal stories and humanizing details. Personal storytelling in opening sessions can set a tone of mutual recognition.
- Pointing Out Common Ground: Explicitly identify and highlight shared values, concerns, or goals. Both sides may care about safety, about the community's long-term well-being, and about being treated fairly.
- Facilitating Perspective-Taking: Encourage parties to articulate the other side's perspective and concerns. Even if the answers are imperfect, the exercise can soften rigid adversarial thinking.
- Using Names Rather Than Labels: Refer to individuals by their names rather than their roles. Saying "Maria's concern" is more humanizing than "the community's complaint."

- Acknowledging Legitimate Concerns on All Sides: Explicitly acknowledge that all parties have legitimate concerns and interests, even when you do not agree with all their positions.

11.
MEDIATOR HEALTH

Chapter 10 addressed how mediators must support trauma-affected participants. This chapter turns to an equally critical question: who supports the mediator? Mediators working in company-community disputes occupy a unique psychological position. They absorb the pain of communities that have lost land, livelihoods, and sometimes lives. They witness the frustration of corporate representatives caught between headquarters pressure and community realities. They hold space for stories of violence, displacement, and betrayal, often for hours at a time, across months or years of engagement. And throughout, they must maintain the calm, neutral presence required by the process.

This work extracts a psychological cost. The mediation field largely ignores this reality, treating mediator well-being as a personal responsibility rather than a professional necessity. This chapter addresses that gap directly. It examines the specific psychological hazards of mediation work, provides concrete tools for recognition and response, and argues that caring for oneself is not separate from caring for parties but integral to it.

A mediator who ignores their own psychological state does not serve parties well. They serve them with diminished capacity, impaired judgment, and eventually, with harm. Understanding and actively managing one's psychological health is therefore not optional; it is a core professional competency within the broader competency framework described in Chapter 9.

Key Concept: The Wounded Healer Paradox

Empathy and the desire to help draw mediators to this work. Those same qualities make them vulnerable to absorbing the suffering they witness. The traits that make someone an excellent mediator also place them at heightened risk for vicarious trauma and burnout. Awareness of this paradox is the first step toward sustainable practice. (see also Chapter 15, Learning from Mediator Mistakes)

11.1 The Psychological Demands of Company-Community Mediation

Company-community disputes carry psychological demands that distinguish them from other mediation contexts. Understanding these specific demands helps mediators anticipate and prepare for the toll this work can take.

Exposure to Suffering and Injustice

Unlike commercial disputes over contracts or family mediations over custody schedules, company-community disputes frequently involve fundamental questions of justice, survival, and human rights. Mediators hear accounts of homes bulldozed, sacred sites desecrated, water sources poisoned, and violence perpetrated by security forces. They witness the grief of people who have lost everything and the frustration of those who feel invisible to power.

This exposure is not occasional but cumulative. A mediator might spend years on a single case, hearing variations of the same suffering repeatedly. Each joint session, each caucus, each interview adds to an internal archive of pain. The human psyche was not designed to process suffering at this volume without consequence.

The Burden of Neutrality

It is essential that professionals maintain neutrality even when one party's actions seem clearly harmful or unjust. This creates a particular psychological strain. When a community describes violence and the mediator cannot express outrage, or when a company offers inadequate remediation, and the mediator cannot advocate for more, the emotions that would naturally arise must be contained and managed.

This emotional containment is exhausting. The mediator experiences empathy, indignation, and frustration but cannot release these feelings in the normal ways. They must process them internally, without acknowledgment or support. Over time, this suppression creates psychological pressure that demands an outlet.

Moral Complexity and Uncertainty

Company-community disputes rarely present clear moral simplicity. Even when harm has occurred, questions of causation, responsibility, and remediation remain complex. A mediator might facilitate an agreement that provides tangible benefits to a community while knowing it falls short of full justice. They might help parties reach terms that both can live with while privately feeling that the outcome reflects a power imbalance rather than fairness.

This moral ambiguity creates what psychologists call "moral distress," the experience of knowing the right thing to do but feeling unable to do it. This repeated navigation of situations where their professional role constrains their moral agency. This creates a specific form of psychological burden that accumulates over time.

High Stakes and Limited Control

The stakes in company-community disputes are existential for one or both parties. Communities fight for their survival as distinct cultural entities. Companies face reputational, financial, or operational crises. This high-stakes environment creates pressure that mediators absorb even though they cannot control outcomes.

The Isolation Factor

While mediators can influence outcomes, they cannot determine results. They facilitate effectively, manage processes skillfully, and create conditions for agreement, but ultimately, the parties decide. When mediation fails, when communities accept inadequate terms under pressure, when agreements collapse during implementation, mediators feel responsible despite their limited control. This combination of high stakes and limited control is a recipe for psychological strain.

> **Caution: The Isolation Factor**
> Many mediators working in company-community disputes operate in relative isolation. They may be the only mediator on a case, working in remote locations, across cultures and languages different from their own. This isolation removes the natural support systems that buffer psychological stress. Colleagues who understand the work are distant. Debriefing opportunities are rare. The mediator carries their psychological burden alone, which significantly amplifies its weight.

11.2 Vicarious Trauma: Understanding the Invisible Wound

Vicarious trauma, sometimes called secondary traumatic stress or compassion fatigue, refers to the psychological impact of repeated exposure to others' traumatic experiences. Unlike direct trauma from firsthand experience, vicarious trauma develops through empathic engagement with survivors. For mediators working with communities that have experienced violence, displacement, or other severe harm, vicarious trauma is an occupational hazard that requires active management. (see Chapter 10 for guidance on trauma-informed approaches that also protect the mediator)

> **Key Concept: Vicarious Trauma Defined**
> Vicarious trauma transforms helpers through empathic engagement with trauma survivors and their material. It accumulates through repeated exposure, changing how helpers see themselves, others, and the world. Unlike burnout, which depletes emotional resources, vicarious trauma fundamentally alters cognitive schemas and worldview.

How Vicarious Trauma Develops

Vicarious trauma does not result from a single overwhelming exposure. It develops gradually through the accumulation of empathic connections with suffering. Each time a mediator truly listens to a community member describe violence, each time they absorb the pain in a survivor's voice, each time they hold space for grief and rage, small psychological deposits accumulate.

The brain processes witnessed trauma similarly to directly experienced trauma. Neuroimaging studies show that witnessing others' suffering activates the same neural circuits as experiencing pain oneself. For mediators, this means that years of empathic listening create neurological changes that mirror, in attenuated form, the trauma of those they have helped.

Certain factors accelerate vicarious trauma development. These include personal trauma history, high caseloads involving traumatic material, insufficient support and supervision, working in isolation, and strong identification with trauma survivors. Mediators working with communities that share their cultural background or personal experiences face heightened vulnerability.

Recognizing Vicarious Trauma: The Warning Signs

Vicarious trauma manifests across multiple dimensions. Monitor yourself for these symptom clusters:

Cognitive Changes:

- Persistent intrusive thoughts about cases or community members' experiences
- Difficulty concentrating or making decisions
- Cynicism about the possibility of justice or positive change
- Changed beliefs about human nature, seeing people as fundamentally cruel or exploitative
- Loss of hope or meaning in the work
- Persistent questioning of one's competence or effectiveness

Emotional Changes:

- Emotional numbing or detachment, feeling less than one used to
- Chronic anxiety, particularly about safety or the future

- Irritability or anger that seems disproportionate to triggers
- Persistent sadness
- Feelings of helplessness or powerlessness
- Guilt about not doing enough or not having prevented harm

Behavioral Changes:

- Social withdrawal, avoiding friends, family, or colleagues
- Increased use of alcohol or substances, or other numbing behaviors
- Changes in eating or sleeping patterns
- Neglecting self-care or personal relationships
- Hypervigilance or excessive concern about personal safety
- Avoidance of work tasks, particularly those involving traumatic material

Physical Symptoms:

- Chronic fatigue that is not relieved by rest
- Unexplained physical complaints (headaches, stomach problems, muscle tension)
- Weakened immune system, frequent illness
- Sleep disturbances, including nightmares about cases

Practical Tip: Keeping a Weekly Well-Being Log

Keep a brief weekly log noting your energy level, mood, sleep quality, and any intrusive thoughts about cases. Patterns often become visible in retrospect that are invisible in the moment. Review your log monthly to identify trends that might indicate developing vicarious trauma.

Worldview Shifts: The Deeper Impact

Beyond specific symptoms, vicarious trauma produces fundamental shifts in how mediators view the world. These shifts can be subtle, rationalized as wisdom or realism rather than recognized as trauma effects.

Trust may erode. Those who have witnessed corporations behave badly develop generalized distrust of institutions. Those who have seen communities manipulated question the authenticity of all collective action. This erosion of trust, while grounded in real experience, impairs professional effectiveness and personal well-being.

Safety assumptions change. After years of exposure to violence and harm, the world feels fundamentally unsafe. This hypervigilance develops, seeing danger everywhere. They develop excessive protective behaviors toward family members or become unable to relax in public spaces.

Intimacy and connection suffer. The emotional numbing that develops as a protective mechanism extends beyond work into personal relationships. Partners and friends feel the mediator has become distant or unavailable. The mediator feels unable to connect meaningfully with people who have not shared similar experiences.

Caution: Normalization Danger

Mediators normalize vicarious trauma symptoms as simply "part of the job." When colleagues share similar experiences, it reinforces the belief that these symptoms are unavoidable and acceptable. This normalization is dangerous. It prevents recognition and treatment while allowing symptoms to worsen. Just because a symptom is common among mediators does not mean it is healthy or acceptable.

11.3 Secondary Trauma from Specific Populations

While all company-community mediation carries psychological risk, certain case types present heightened exposure to traumatic material. Additional caution is warranted when approaching these cases; with additional preparation and support.

Sexual Violence Cases

Mediating claims involving sexual assault perpetrated by company agents creates particularly intense secondary trauma exposure. Sexual violence narratives carry unique psychological weight. They involve detailed accounts of physical violation, profound betrayal of trust, and lasting psychological harm.

Such cases present specific challenges for practitioners. They must maintain presence and composure while hearing graphic accounts of assault. They must manage their own emotional responses, which may include horror, rage, and disgust, while remaining neutral and supportive. They must avoid retraumatizing survivors through their questions or reactions while still gathering necessary information.

For mediators who have personal histories of sexual assault, these cases trigger their own trauma. Even without personal history, sexual violence cases resonate with deep fears and vulnerabilities. The intimate nature of the harm described creates psychological proximity that other trauma types may not.

Physical Violence and Security Force Abuses

Cases involving beatings, shootings, torture, or other physical violence by security forces present their own traumatic intensity. Practitioners may hear detailed accounts of brutality, see photographs of injuries, or witness lasting physical disabilities in survivors. They may encounter communities living in ongoing fear, where the perpetrators remain present and powerful.

The injustice element can be particularly acute in these cases. When violence has been perpetrated by those supposedly providing security, and when perpetrators have faced no consequences, mediators may struggle with rage that their neutral role does not permit them to express. This suppressed anger takes a toll.

Displacement and Loss of Homes

Mediating resettlement disputes involves repeated exposure to loss narratives. Communities describe leaving ancestral lands, losing access to sacred sites, watching homes demolished, and attempting to rebuild lives in unfamiliar places. These accounts involve not just material loss but loss of identity, community cohesion, and connection to the dead.

For mediators, displacement cases can trigger existential questions about belonging, security, and the fragility of what we take for granted. They may find themselves thinking differently about their own homes and feeling less secure in spaces that once felt permanent. The grief witnessed in these cases can seep into the mediator's own relationship with place and belonging.

Child Harm and Intergenerational Impact

Cases involving harm to children, whether through environmental contamination affecting child health, disruption of education, or direct violence, carry particular psychological weight. Mediators who are parents may find these cases especially difficult. The vulnerability of children and the long-term consequences of harm to developing bodies and minds can feel overwhelming.

Intergenerational trauma, where current disputes connect to historical injustices passed through families and communities, adds complexity. Mediators may feel they are witnessing not just current harm but the cumulative weight of decades or centuries of injustice. This historical dimension can make individual cases feel hopeless or irresolvable.

> **Practical Tip: Assessing Readiness for Trauma Cases**
>
> Before accepting any case involving traumatic content, honestly assess your current psychological state, personal history with similar trauma, and available support resources. It is not a weakness to recognize that a particular case at a particular time is not right for you; it is professional judgment.

11.4 Burnout in Mediation: Why It Happens Faster

Burnout, distinct from vicarious trauma, involves exhaustion, cynicism, and reduced professional efficacy resulting from chronic workplace stress. While burnout affects many professions, several factors make mediators particularly vulnerable to rapid burnout development.

The assessment tool in Figure 42 helps you identify when burnout risk factors are accumulating.

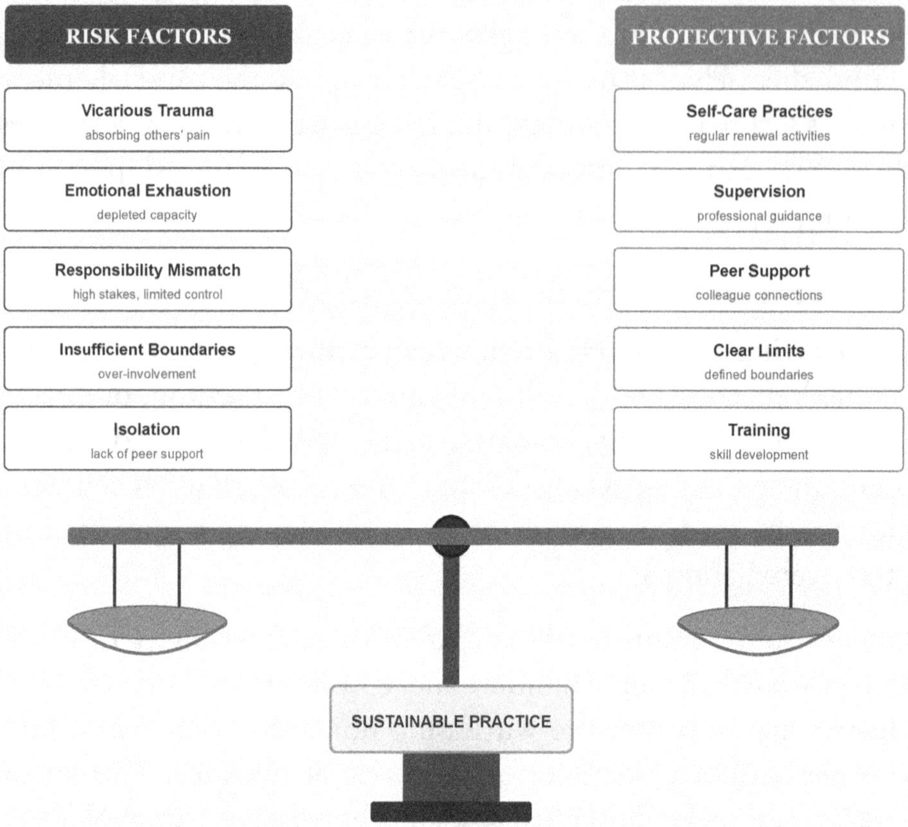

Figure 42: A tool for assessing the risk factors for mediator burnout, including workload indicators, compassion fatigue symptoms, and warning signs.

Burnout risk assessment tools help you recognize when the weight of mediation work is becoming unsustainable, allowing you to make conscious choices about workload, support systems, and boundary-setting before you reach crisis.

> **Key Concept: Burnout vs. Vicarious Trauma**
>
> Burnout and vicarious trauma co-occur but are distinct phenomena. Burnout is about exhaustion and depletion, the result of giving more than can be sustained. Vicarious trauma is about transformation and alteration, the result of absorbing traumatic material. Burnout can be addressed through rest and workload management. Vicarious trauma requires processing and integration of traumatic material. Both require attention, but the interventions differ.

The Emotional Labor Intensity

Mediation is among the most emotionally labor-intensive professions. For hours at a time, mediators must manage not only their own emotions but also the emotions of multiple parties in high-conflict situations. They must project calm when parties are angry, maintain hope when parties despair, and demonstrate engagement when they feel depleted.

This emotional labor, the gap between felt emotions and displayed emotions, requires constant effort. Unlike physical labor, which has clear limits, emotional labor can continue long past sustainable capacity. Mediators push through emotional exhaustion in ways they would never push through physical exhaustion, depleting reserves that take far longer to rebuild.

The Uncertainty and Lack of Closure

Many professionals experience completion and closure in their work. Surgeons finish operations. Lawyers conclude cases. Teachers see students graduate. Mediators, particularly in complex company-community disputes, work in ambiguity for extended periods. Cases drag on for years. Agreements may be reached, but then fail to be implemented. Mediators never learn the ultimate outcomes of their efforts.

This lack of closure creates a psychological burden. The human mind craves completion. When mediators accumulate numerous unfinished narratives, open questions, and unknown outcomes, it creates a kind of cognitive load that drains energy even during periods of rest. The mediator carries the weight of every unresolved case, every uncertain outcome.

The Responsibility-Control Mismatch

Mediators feel deeply responsible for outcomes they cannot control. They feel responsible for community well-being without the power to ensure it. They feel responsible for preventing further harm, yet lack the authority to require protective measures. This mismatch between felt responsibility and actual control is a classic recipe for burnout.

When mediations fail, mediators engage in extensive self-criticism. What could I have done differently? Did I miss something? Should I have pushed harder? This rumination, while sometimes productive for learning, becomes counterproductive self-blame that depletes psychological resources.

Recognizing Burnout: The Three Dimensions

Burnout manifests across three primary dimensions:

- **Exhaustion:** The depletion of emotional and physical resources. Signs include feeling drained before the workday begins, needing excessive recovery time after sessions, being unable to engage with previously enjoyable activities, and persistent fatigue that sleep does not resolve.
- **Cynicism:** The development of detached, negative attitudes toward the work and those involved. Signs include thinking of parties as problems rather than people, feeling that mediation does not really help anyone, losing interest in cases that previously engaged you, and making cynical jokes about the work.
- **Reduced Efficacy:** The sense that one is no longer competent or effective. Signs include doubting your skills despite evidence of competence, feeling that your contributions do not matter, finding it harder to generate creative solutions, and procrastinating on work tasks.

> **Caution: The Burnout Spiral**
>
> Burnout tends to be self-perpetuating. Exhaustion reduces performance, which increases cynicism about the value of efforts, which in turn reduces motivation, which further exacerbates exhaustion. Early intervention is critical because once the spiral establishes itself, breaking free becomes increasingly difficult. Pay attention to early warning signs and act before the spiral accelerates.

Gender and Mediator Wellbeing

Vicarious trauma and burnout do not affect all mediators equally, and gender is one dimension that shapes vulnerability. Female mediators working in contexts where sexual violence is part of the dispute may experience particularly intense secondary trauma, especially if they share aspects of identity with survivors. Male mediators may face different pressures: cultural expectations about emotional stoicism can discourage them from acknowledging distress or seeking support, allowing trauma responses to accumulate unrecognized. Mediators from marginalized communities who work on disputes affecting communities like their own may carry an additional emotional burden, as the professional distance that protects against vicarious trauma is harder to maintain when the suffering described mirrors experiences within one's own community.

Organizations that deploy mediators should be attentive to these dynamics. Case assignment should consider not only competence and availability but also the cumulative emotional load a mediator is carrying. Supervision and peer support structures should be designed to be accessible to mediators of all genders, recognizing that the barriers to seeking help differ. A male mediator may need explicit permission to discuss emotional impact; a female mediator may need assurance that doing so will not be interpreted as a lack of professional capability.

11.5 The Ethical Obligation to Step Back

Mediator self-care is not merely a personal choice. It is an ethical obligation. A mediator whose psychological state is compromised cannot serve parties adequately. They cannot listen fully. They cannot maintain true neutrality. They cannot hold the emotional space that effective mediation requires. To continue working in a compromised state is to provide substandard service to parties who deserve better.

Key Concept: The Professional Duty to Self-Monitor

Just as mediators have ethical obligations regarding neutrality, confidentiality, and informed consent, they have an ethical obligation to monitor their own fitness to practice. Continuing to practice while impaired is not dedication. It is a failure of professional responsibility. Stepping back when necessary is not a sign of weakness; it is a sign of integrity.

Recognizing When You Are Compromised

Honest self-assessment is difficult, particularly when mediators mobilize psychological defenses. The following signs suggest impairment that warrants stepping back:

- You find yourself unable to listen fully because you are preoccupied with your own distress
- You feel a strong identification with one party that compromises your neutrality
- You are having intrusive thoughts about cases that interfere with daily functioning
- You are dreading sessions with intensity that suggests more than normal pre-session nerves
- You notice yourself becoming impatient, dismissive, or irritable with parties
- You are making uncharacteristic errors in judgment or process management
- Colleagues, family members, or friends have expressed concern about your well-being
- You are using substances or other avoidance behaviors more than usual to cope

Forms of Stepping Back

Stepping back does not always mean complete withdrawal from practice. It can take various forms depending on the severity of impairment and the nature of the situation, including:

- **Temporary case reduction:** Reducing caseload to allow recovery while maintaining some practice. This might mean declining new cases while completing existing commitments, or handing off some cases to colleagues while retaining others.
- **Case-specific recusal:** Stepping back from particular cases that are triggering while continuing with others. A mediator might recognize that a specific case involving sexual violence is activating their own

history, and recuse from that case while remaining able to handle other matters.

- **Role modification:** Shifting to a co-mediator or support role rather than a lead role. This reduces responsibility and emotional load while maintaining connection to the work and contributing experience.
- **Complete pause:** Temporary cessation of practice to allow full recovery. This might last weeks or months, depending on severity. During this time, the mediator focuses entirely on healing without the demands of practice.
- **Permanent transition:** In some cases, the accumulated impact of trauma work may necessitate a permanent transition away from trauma-focused mediation. This is not failure. It is recognition of your personal limits after years of demanding service.

Managing the Transition

When stepping back from cases, mediators benefit from managing the transition in ways that protect parties while honoring their own needs. This requires honest communication with relevant stakeholders, appropriate handoff procedures, and attention to confidentiality.

> **Caution: The Harm of Pushing Through**
>
> The mediation field often celebrates those who push through difficulty, who take on the hardest cases, who never say no. This culture can pressure mediators to continue working when they should step back. Remember: a mediator who continues despite impairment does not serve parties well. They provide inferior service while potentially causing harm. The heroic choice is often to step back, not to push through.

11.6 Building Sustainable Resilience

Resilience is not merely the absence of psychological harm. It is the active capacity to engage with difficulty while maintaining well-being. Building resilience for mediation work requires intentional practices across multiple domains. The following practices have demonstrated effectiveness in helping trauma-exposed professionals sustain their work over time.

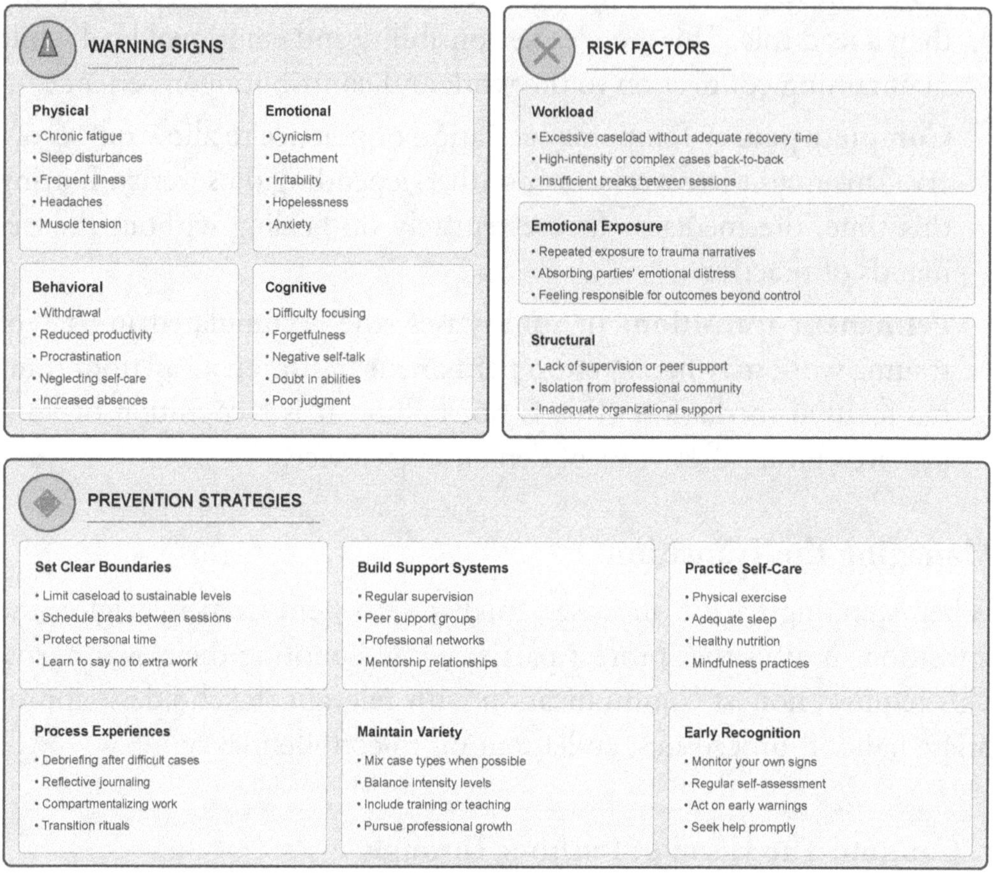

Figure 43: A collection of evidence-based strategies for preventing burnout and building sustainable resilience in mediation practice.

Prevention strategies are far more effective than crisis management, which is why implementing practices like regular peer consultation, adequate rest, and meaningful separation between cases becomes an investment in your long-term effectiveness.

Physical Foundation

Psychological resilience rests on physical well-being. The body and mind are not separate systems but interconnected aspects of a single organism. Neglecting physical health undermines psychological capacity. Prioritize physical health through:

- **Sleep:** Sleep deprivation profoundly impairs emotional regulation, cognitive function, and stress resilience. Prioritizing consistent sleep schedules, adequate sleep duration (typically seven to nine hours for adults), and good sleep hygiene. When work requires travel across time zones or sessions at unusual hours, build in recovery time.
- **Exercise:** Regular physical activity is one of the most effective interventions for stress management and emotional regulation. It need not be intense. Walking, swimming, yoga, or any consistent movement practice helps process stress hormones and maintain physical vitality. Build movement into your routine, not as optional but as essential.
- **Nutrition:** During intensive mediation periods, nutrition often suffers. Meals are skipped, convenience foods substitute for proper nourishment, and caffeine compensates for fatigue. These patterns undermine the physical foundation that psychological resilience requires. Plan for adequate nutrition during demanding periods.

Processing Practices

Traumatic material that enters through empathic engagement benefits from being processed and integrated rather than suppressed or accumulated. Several practices support this processing, including:

- **Regular Supervision:** Clinical supervision with a qualified professional provides a structured space for processing case material. Unlike peer support, supervision offers a professional perspective, clinical insight, and accountability for self-care. Regular supervision for mediators working with traumatic material represents a professional standard, not a sign of inadequacy.
- **Peer Debriefing:** Sharing experiences with colleagues who understand the work provides validation and perspective. Peer debriefing reduces isolation and normalizes difficult experiences without normalizing impairment. Establish regular debriefing relationships with trusted colleagues.
- **Journaling:** Writing about experiences helps organize thoughts and emotions, identify patterns, and externalize internal experiences. Many mediators find that brief journaling after difficult sessions helps

them process material that might otherwise accumulate. The writing need not be elegant. It is for processing, not publication.

- **Therapy:** Regular engagement with a therapist skilled in trauma provides deep processing support. This is not reserved for a crisis. Ongoing therapeutic support helps prevent accumulation and provides a consistent relationship for working through difficult material. Consider therapy part of professional maintenance, like continuing education.

Practical Tip: Creating a Transition Ritual

After particularly difficult sessions, implement a transition ritual before returning to regular life. This might be a short walk, a few minutes of breathing exercises, changing clothes, or any consistent practice that signals the shift from work to personal life. This ritual helps prevent work material from bleeding into personal time and relationships.

Boundary Practices

Clear boundaries between work and personal life help prevent traumatic material from infiltrating all domains of existence. Without boundaries, mediators find themselves always on, never fully present in personal life, and unable to recover. Important boundaries to set include:

- **Time Boundaries:** Establish clear work hours and protect personal time rigorously. Avoid checking work communications during personal time. When intensive periods require extended hours, build in compensating recovery time afterward.
- **Space Boundaries:** If possible, maintain physical separation between work and personal spaces. If working from home, have a dedicated workspace that can be closed off. The physical act of leaving a workspace helps signal a psychological transition.
- **Emotional Boundaries:** Practice intentional separation between the emotions of work and the emotions of personal life. This does not mean suppression but rather containment, the ability to engage fully with work emotions during work time and set them aside during personal time.

Connection and Meaning

Isolation is a significant risk factor for both vicarious trauma and burnout. Maintaining meaningful connections outside of work provides perspective, support, and a reminder of life beyond the pain encountered in mediation. You can find this connection through:

- **Personal Relationships:** Invest in relationships with family and friends who know you outside your professional role. These relationships ground you in your identity beyond the role of mediator. Protect time for these relationships even during demanding periods.
- **Community Involvement:** Participation in communities unrelated to work, whether religious, recreational, or interest-based, provides connection and perspective. These communities remind you that the world contains more than conflict and suffering.
- **Meaning Practices:** Maintain a connection to whatever provides your life with meaning beyond work accomplishment. This might be spiritual practice, creative expression, time in nature, or service in other domains. These practices provide a wellspring that sustains you through challenging work.

Professional Practices

Certain professional practices specifically support resilience in demanding mediation work, including:

- **Caseload Management:** Maintain realistic caseloads and avoid accumulating too many high-intensity cases simultaneously. Balance trauma-focused work with less demanding matters. Say no to new cases when your load is full.
- **Co-mediation:** Work with co-mediators when possible, particularly for demanding cases. Having a colleague in the room halves the emotional burden, provides real-time support, and enables immediate debriefing after sessions.
- **Continuing Development:** Ongoing learning and skill development counteract the sense of stagnation that contributes to burnout. It also

provides the community with opportunities to connect with other practitioners and to gain exposure to new perspectives.

- **Positive Case Tracking:** Actively maintain awareness of positive outcomes and contributions. The negativity bias of trauma work can obscure the real difference your work makes. Keep a file of positive feedback, successful outcomes, and meaningful contributions.

> **Key Concept: The Oxygen Mask Principle**
>
> Flight attendants instruct passengers to secure their own oxygen masks before helping others. This principle applies directly to mediator self-care. A mediator who neglects their own well-being will eventually be unable to help anyone. Self-care is not selfish. It is the foundation of sustained service. Taking care of yourself enables you to take care of others.

11.7 Organizational Responsibilities

While individual mediators bear responsibility for their own self-care, organizations that employ or engage mediators share responsibility for creating conditions that support psychological health. Individual resilience practices cannot compensate for organizational cultures that deplete psychological resources faster than mediators restore them.

What Organizations Should Provide

Access to Clinical Supervision: Funding regular clinical supervision for mediators working with traumatic material. This is not an optional benefit but a professional necessity. Supervision should be with qualified professionals who understand trauma exposure in helping professions.

Manageable Caseloads: Sustainable caseloads require honest assessment. This requires an honest assessment of case complexity and emotional demand, not just counting cases. A mediator handling three high-trauma cases may be more burdened than one handling ten routine matters.

Recovery Time: After intensive engagements, particularly those involving traumatic material, building in recovery time helps. Immediately assigning the next demanding case upon completion of a demanding case prevents necessary processing and recovery.

Mental Health Benefits: Employment benefits should include robust mental health coverage. Mediators should be able to access therapy, medication, or other treatments without financial barriers.

Culture of Permission: Organizations that normalize acknowledging difficulty and seeking support, rather than stigmatizing them, strengthen practice. Leaders should model vulnerability and self-care. Performance evaluations should consider sustainable practice, not just productivity.

Red Flags in Organizational Culture

Alertness to organizational cultures that undermine psychological health. Common signs include:

- Celebration of overwork, such as praise for those who never take breaks or who handle enormous caseloads
- Stigmatization of those who are struggling, such as implying that those who acknowledge difficulty are weak or uncommitted
- Insufficient resources, such as expecting mediators to handle traumatic cases without supervision or support
- Denial of impact, such as dismissing the psychological toll of the work as exaggeration or personal weakness
- Pressure to continue despite impairment, such as discouraging mediators from stepping back when they recognize their own compromised state
- Competition for suffering, such as cultures where people compete to demonstrate they have it worse rather than supporting each other

Caution: The Organizational Trap

Some mediators work within organizations that systematically undermine psychological health. If you find yourself in such an environment and advocacy for change is unsuccessful, consider whether remaining is compatible with your well-being. No job is worth your mental health. Sometimes, the most crucial boundary is deciding to leave a toxic organizational culture.

11.8 Treatment and Recovery

When prevention is insufficient and vicarious trauma or burnout develops, treatment and recovery require intentional effort. The earlier the intervention begins, the more quickly and completely recovery can occur.

Professional Treatment Options

Several evidence-based treatments have demonstrated effectiveness for vicarious trauma and burnout, including:

- **Trauma-Focused Cognitive Behavioral Therapy (TF-CBT):** This approach helps identify and modify thinking patterns that perpetuate distress while building coping skills for managing trauma responses.
- **Eye Movement Desensitization and Reprocessing (EMDR):** EMDR has shown effectiveness in processing traumatic material, including vicariously acquired trauma. It can help integrate difficult experiences that have not been fully processed.
- **Mindfulness-Based Stress Reduction (MBSR):** Structured mindfulness programs teach skills for managing stress and building psychological flexibility. These skills are both treatment for current distress and prevention against future impact.
- **Somatic Approaches:** Trauma is held in the body as well as the mind. Approaches such as Somatic Experiencing, yoga therapy, or body-based psychotherapy can help release physical tension and complete stress responses that had been interrupted.

The Recovery Journey

Recovery from vicarious trauma or burnout is not a linear process. It involves periods of progress and setbacks, moments of clarity and confusion. Understanding the typical patterns of recovery helps manage expectations and sustain hope.

Initial recovery often brings relief. Simply acknowledging the problem and beginning to address it can produce immediate improvement. Sleep may improve. The sense of being trapped may lift. Hope may return.

Middle phases often involve deeper work. As surface symptoms resolve, underlying material may emerge. Processing accumulated traumatic material can temporarily increase distress before integration brings relief. This is normal and does not indicate treatment failure.

Later recovery involves integration and growth. Many mediators who recover from vicarious trauma report eventual positive transformation. They develop deeper self-understanding, clearer boundaries, and more sustainable practices. Some describe a sense of having learned something essential about themselves and their work.

Practical Tip: Finding a Trauma-Informed Therapist
When seeking a therapist, look for someone with experience in treating helping professionals and an understanding of trauma exposure in professional contexts. Not all therapists understand the specific dynamics of vicarious trauma. A therapist who specializes in first responders, healthcare workers, or other trauma-exposed professions is likely to understand the unique challenges of mediation work.

Returning to Practice

After treatment and recovery, returning to practice requires thoughtful planning. The goal is not to return to previous unsustainable patterns but to establish a new relationship with the work that incorporates lessons learned.

Gradual reentry often works better than immediate return to full capacity. Start with less demanding cases. Build back slowly while monitoring for symptom recurrence.

Implement structural changes that address factors that contributed to the original problem. If overwork was a factor, establish firm caseload limits. If isolation was a factor, find ways to connect more regularly with colleagues.

Maintain treatment gains through ongoing practices. Continue therapy, supervision, or other support structures even when feeling better. Prevention is easier than treatment.

11.9 Conclusion: The Sustainable Mediator

The best mediators are not those who sacrifice themselves for the work but those who sustain themselves through it. A career in mediation that spans decades, maintains effectiveness and passion, and contributes profoundly to parties and the field requires intentional attention to psychological health.

This is not a weakness of the work or of those who do it. It is simply the reality of engaging deeply with human suffering. The very qualities that make excellent mediators, empathy, presence, and emotional attunement, also create vulnerability. Acknowledging and managing this vulnerability is not separate from professional competence. It is integral to it.

The communities and companies that mediators serve deserve practitioners who are fully present, emotionally available, and professionally capable. Mediators who neglect their own well-being cannot consistently provide this quality of service. Self-care, therefore, is not selfish indulgence. It is professional responsibility.

The field of mediation benefits when practitioners model healthy boundaries, sustainable practices, and honest acknowledgment of difficulty. When mediators demonstrate that it is possible to do this demanding work while maintaining well-being, they give others permission to do the same. This collective shift toward sustainability strengthens the entire field.

Ultimately, the sustainable mediator is one who has learned to care for themselves with the same attention and skill they bring to caring for parties. They recognize warning signs and respond early. They build resilience practices into daily life. They step back when necessary without shame. They seek help when needed. And through this ongoing attention to their own well-being, they ensure that they can continue to offer their gifts to the communities and companies that need them.

This handbook has asked much of mediators: to develop skills, navigate complexity, hold space for pain, and maintain neutrality amid injustice. It is fitting that it also asks mediators to care for themselves. Without that care, all the other capacities eventually deplete. The mediator who tends their own well-being is not less dedicated but better able to sustain the work across a full career.

Chapter Summary: Self-Assessment Questions

Use these questions regularly to assess your psychological state:

Domain	Questions to Ask Yourself
Energy and Engagement	Am I looking forward to my work? Do I have energy for sessions? Am I dreading any cases?
Intrusive Thoughts	Are case details intruding into my personal time? Am I having dreams about cases? Am I ruminating?
Emotional State	Am I more irritable, anxious, or sad than usual? Am I feeling numb? Is my emotional range narrowing?
Worldview	Am I becoming more cynical? Is my trust in people changing? Do I feel hopeless about positive outcomes?
Physical Well-Being	How is my sleep? Am I exercising? Am I eating well? Am I using substances more than usual?
Relationships	Am I withdrawing from friends and family? Am I present in my relationships? Have others expressed concern?
Professional Functioning	Can I maintain neutrality? Am I listening fully? Am I making unusual errors? Am I avoiding tasks?

If your answers to these questions raise concerns, consider whether adjustments to your practice or professional support might be needed. Early attention to warning signs prevents more serious problems from developing.

Key Takeaways

- Vicarious trauma and burnout are distinct conditions with different causes. Vicarious trauma changes how you see the world; burnout depletes your capacity to engage.
- Warning signs often appear gradually: sleep disruption, emotional numbness, cynicism, difficulty maintaining boundaries, and withdrawal from personal relationships.

- Self-monitoring is a professional duty, not a sign of weakness. Mediators who ignore their own distress risk harming the parties they serve.
- Organizations bear responsibility for creating conditions that support mediator wellbeing, including manageable caseloads, clinical supervision, and peer support structures.
- Recovery is possible but rarely linear. Returning to practice after burnout or vicarious trauma requires honest self-assessment and, often, professional support.
- The field isolation common in extractive-sector mediation intensifies vulnerability. Proactive connection with peers and supervisors is essential, not optional.

Reflection Questions

- When did you last honestly assess your own emotional and psychological state in relation to your mediation work?
- What early warning signs of vicarious trauma or burnout would you recognize in yourself? What signs might you miss?
- Does your current work environment provide adequate support for mediator wellbeing? If not, what one change would make the biggest difference?
- How do you create boundaries between your mediation work and your personal life? Are those boundaries holding?
- If a colleague showed signs of burnout, how would you raise the concern with them?

12.

MANAGING POWER ASYMMETRIES AND RESTORING TRUST

Mediators who maintain their own health and clarity of mind are better positioned to address one of mediation's most persistent challenges: the power imbalances that nearly always characterize company-community disputes. The company typically has greater financial resources, legal expertise, and political influence, while the community may have strength in numbers, moral authority, or tactical options like protests. Unchecked power asymmetry derails mediation: weaker parties feel voiceless while stronger parties dominate. Prolonged conflict also severely damages trust. This chapter addresses how to manage power differences and rebuild trust as foundations for lasting resolution.

Addressing these dynamics determines whether any mediation process produces fair, durable outcomes. Unaddressed power imbalances produce agreements that rarely last. The weaker party feels coerced into acceptance (undermining the voluntariness principle discussed in Chapter 3), leading to resentment, non-compliance, or renewed conflict. Broken trust causes even well-crafted agreements to fail, since parties doubt each other's commitment.

Practical Tip: Power Inventory

Before mediation begins, create a power inventory for each party. List their resources, expertise, connections, alternatives, and leverage. This systematic assessment helps you anticipate dynamics and plan balancing interventions. Update the inventory as power shifts during the process.

Key Concept: Perceived vs. Actual Power

Power exists in perception as much as reality. A community may feel powerless while holding significant leverage through media attention or regulatory pressure. A company may appear all-powerful while facing vulnerabilities the community cannot see. Help parties accurately assess both their own and others' power.

12.1 Identifying Power Asymmetries

Power operates openly or covertly. It is not simply about money or legal resources. Power manifests in multiple dimensions, and skilled mediators recognize them all. The first step in managing power imbalances is accurately identifying where they exist.

Types of Power in Company-Community Disputes

Different parties bring different forms of power to the mediation table. Understanding these categories helps mediators anticipate dynamics and design appropriate interventions.

Type of Power	Company Advantages	Community Advantages
Resource Power	Financial resources, lawyers, consultants, technical expertise	Local knowledge, numbers, time flexibility, grassroots networks
Information Power	Technical data, legal knowledge, industry expertise, scientific reports	First-hand understanding of impacts, community history, lived experience

Type of Power	Company Advantages	Community Advantages
Political Power	Government connections, lobbying capacity, regulatory relationships	Voting bloc, moral authority, media sympathy, international NGO support
Social Power	Status, credentials, professional networks, corporate reputation	Community solidarity, cultural authority, traditional leaders, collective identity
Procedural Power	Sets meeting times and venues, controls information flow, shapes agenda	Can disrupt operations, refuse participation, mobilize public attention

Key Concept: The Multidimensionality of Power

Power is not a single attribute but a complex web of advantages and disadvantages. A company may have more money but less moral legitimacy. A community may lack technical expertise but possess irreplaceable local knowledge. Effective mediators map all dimensions of power, not just the obvious ones, to understand the full dynamics at play.

Understanding Resource Power

Resource power refers to the tangible assets parties can deploy. Companies typically have significant advantages here. They can hire specialized lawyers, commission technical studies, retain public relations firms, and sustain lengthy processes without financial strain. Communities often operate with volunteer labor, limited funds, and competing demands on their time.

However, resource power is not absolute. Communities possess resources that companies cannot easily acquire. They have intimate knowledge of local conditions, historical context, and social networks. They have greater flexibility in their time commitments than corporate representatives, who are bound by quarterly targets and operational deadlines. They also have access to pro bono support from NGOs, legal aid organizations, or academic institutions.

Case Example: In the Guinea mining dispute (2017-2024), the community initially felt overwhelmed by the company's technical and legal resources. The involvement of the CAO (Compliance Advisor Ombudsman) helped balance this by providing neutral technical expertise and process support. The community also received assistance from international and national NGOs, which helped them organize their concerns and present them effectively. This illustrates how external support can help bridge resource gaps.

Understanding Information Power

Information asymmetry ranks among the most common and impactful power imbalances in company-community disputes. Companies control vast amounts of technical data, such as environmental impact assessments, production plans, financial projections, and legal analyses. Community members often lack access to this information or, even when it is provided, lack the expertise to interpret it meaningfully.

This creates a significant disadvantage. How can community members negotiate effectively about water contamination if they cannot interpret water quality data? How can they assess whether a proposed compensation package is fair if they do not understand the economic value of their land or resources?

At the same time, communities possess information that companies need. They understand local social dynamics, know which concerns are most pressing, and can identify solutions that will actually work in their context. A company might propose building a school in location A, while community members know that location B would serve more children and face less resistance from local politics.

> **Practical Tip: Joint Fact-Finding**
>
> As we've discussed previously, proposing joint fact-finding can be helpful when information disputes block progress. This approach served well in the Stuttgart 21 mediation, where mediator Heiner Geißler insisted on an independent "stress test" to verify technical claims about the railway station's capacity. Joint fact-finding builds shared understanding and removes information as a weapon.

Understanding Political and Social Power

Political power involves the ability to influence government decisions, access to decision-makers, and the capacity to shape regulatory outcomes. Companies often have established relationships with government officials, membership in industry associations, and resources for lobbying. Communities may feel excluded from political processes that directly affect their lives.

However, communities also wield political power. They vote. They can mobilize public opinion. They can attract media attention to their cause. In democratic systems, politicians are sensitive to constituent concerns. International attention from human rights organizations or development institutions can create pressure that companies cannot ignore.

Social power relates to status, credibility, and relational networks. Corporate executives may be treated with deference simply because of their titles and professional presentation. Community members may feel their concerns are dismissed or not taken seriously. Conversely, traditional leaders, respected elders, and community activists often carry moral authority that resonates with the broader public and can shame companies into action.

Recognizing Subtle Power Dynamics

Beyond these categorical types of power, mediators must recognize subtle dynamics that unfold in mediation sessions. These micro-level manifestations of power can significantly influence outcomes. Common examples include:

- **Verbal dominance:** Who speaks more? Who interrupts? Whose statements are treated as authoritative and whose are questioned? In many mediations, company representatives, accustomed to professional settings and confident in their expertise, naturally dominate discussions. Community members may hesitate to speak, defer to others, or fail to complete their thoughts before being interrupted.
- **Language control:** Whose terminology frames the discussion? If the conversation uses technical jargon, corporate euphemisms, or legal language, parties unfamiliar with these terms are at a disadvantage.

When community members describe "our sacred land" and company representatives refer to the same land as "the project site," a subtle struggle over narrative control is underway.

- **Setting and logistics:** Who controls the meeting space? If meetings occur at the company headquarters, community members may feel uncomfortable and out of place. If meeting times conflict with agricultural schedules or work obligations, community participation may be limited. Even seating arrangements can signal hierarchy, especially when company executives are placed at the head of the table.
- **Confidence and presentation:** Who appears confident versus hesitant? Body language, eye contact, and presentation style all communicate power. A community member who has never participated in formal negotiations may appear uncertain, even when expressing deeply held convictions.
- **Documentation and preparation:** Who arrives with prepared materials, data, and written proposals? Who relies on oral accounts and memory? Written documentation often carries more weight, even when oral testimony is equally valid.

> **Caution: Invisible Power Dynamics**
>
> Some power dynamics are nearly invisible to outside observers. Community members may fear retaliation for speaking honestly. They may have been told by local leaders what to say. Company representatives may face pressure from headquarters to achieve certain outcomes. Watch for signs of constraint: hesitation, glances at others before speaking, vague or evasive answers, or sudden changes in position without explanation.

Questions for Assessing Power Dynamics

Before and during mediation, mediators should systematically assess power dynamics by considering questions such as:

1. Who has more information about the issues being discussed? Who controls access to technical data, historical records, or legal analysis?

2. Who has more experience with negotiation and formal dispute resolution processes? Who is comfortable in this setting?
3. Who has more at stake? What are the consequences for each party if negotiations fail?
4. Who can sustain a long negotiation process? Who faces time pressure or resource constraints?
5. Who has external allies and support? What sources of legitimacy or assistance does each party have?
6. Within each party, who makes decisions? Are the people at the table empowered to make agreements, or must they seek approval elsewhere?
7. What are each party's alternatives to reaching an agreement here? What happens if mediation fails?

12.2 Strategies for Balancing Power

Once power imbalances are identified, mediators must take active steps to create conditions for fair negotiation. This does not mean artificially advantaging the weaker party or penalizing the stronger one. It means ensuring that both parties can participate effectively, express their interests fully, and make informed decisions.

Empowering the Weaker Party

Empowerment strategies help less powerful parties participate effectively without compromising the mediator's neutrality. The goal is not to advocate for one side but to ensure both sides can engage meaningfully.

Pre-Mediation Coaching and Preparation

Before formal mediation sessions, meet separately with less experienced parties to explain the process, help them organize their thoughts, and prepare their presentation. This is not coaching them on positions but ensuring they understand how mediation works so they can participate effectively.

What this looks like in practice: A mediator might spend an afternoon with community representatives before the first joint session. The mediator explains the process, such as what to expect, how to request breaks, and when caucuses might be used. The mediator helps them identify their key concerns and organize them clearly. The mediator might even suggest practicing how they will present their main points.

> **Sample Dialogue:**
>
> Mediator (to community, pre-mediation): *"Before we meet with the company, let's talk through your key concerns and how you'd like to present them. What are the three most important things you want the company to understand? Would it help to practice how you'll explain the water issue? Remember, in the joint session, you'll have uninterrupted time to share your perspective."*

Access to Advisors and Technical Support

Allow and encourage less powerful parties to bring advisors, whether legal, technical, or advocacy support. If the company has lawyers and engineers at the table, the community needs access to equivalent expertise. Connect them with pro bono legal services, NGO technical advisors, or community paralegals.

Why this matters: In many company-community disputes, technical complexity creates barriers. Communities cannot negotiate effectively about environmental impacts if they cannot interpret environmental data. They cannot assess compensation proposals if they lack economic or legal expertise. Advisors help level this playing field.

Case Example: In the Guinea mining dispute, the community was supported by international and national NGOs during mediation. These organizations provided technical knowledge about mining impacts, helped organize community concerns, and ensured community members understood their rights under international standards. This support was crucial for meaningful participation.

Capacity Building

Time permitting, invest in building the negotiation capacity of less experienced parties. This might include brief training in negotiation basics, explanation of interest-based bargaining, or workshops on effective communication in formal settings.

Practical application: Before a multi-session mediation, a mediator might conduct a half-day workshop with community representatives covering topics like the difference between positions and interests, how to prepare for negotiation, and techniques for handling difficult moments. This investment pays dividends throughout the mediation process.

Information Sharing and Education

Ensure that less powerful parties have access to relevant information and can understand it. This might involve requiring the company to share documents in advance, providing summaries in accessible language, or arranging for technical explanations.

Example approach: If the company presents a technical report on water quality, the mediator might pause and ask for a plain-language summary. If terms are unclear, the mediator should ask for definitions. If the community needs time to consult their own expert about the data, the mediator should accommodate this need.

> **Practical Tip: The "Explain It Simply" Test**
>
> Technical information presented to the group should be explained in simple terms that anyone could understand. Ask the presenting party to translate jargon into everyday language. This serves two purposes: it ensures the less technical party genuinely understands, and it prevents the use of jargon as a power tactic. If someone cannot explain a concept simply, they may not understand it themselves, or they may be using complexity to obscure the facts.

Caution: Transparent Balancing

Power-balancing interventions should be transparent in their purpose, if not always in their methods. If you give the community extra time to consult, explain why: "Technical complexity requires adequate processing time." Hidden balancing that is discovered can destroy trust in your neutrality.

Procedural Safeguards

Beyond empowering individual parties, mediators can build balance into the process itself through procedural design.

Equal Speaking Time and Structured Turns

Establish clear norms for participation that ensure all voices are heard. This might include structured speaking turns, where each party has uninterrupted time to present. It might consist of round-robin formats where the mediator specifically invites each participant to contribute. In some cases, it might even involve timers to ensure balanced participation.

Why this works: Left to natural dynamics, more confident or experienced speakers tend to dominate. Community members may hesitate to interrupt or assert themselves. Explicit structure creates space for all participants without requiring them to fight for the floor.

Sample Dialogue:

Mediator: *"I'd like us to go around the table and hear from each person. You'll each have about five minutes without interruption to share your perspective on this issue. After everyone has spoken, we'll open up for dialogue."*

Ground Rule Enforcement

Establish and consistently enforce ground rules that promote respectful, balanced dialogue. These rules create a level playing field by constraining behaviors that would otherwise give an advantage to more powerful parties.

Essential ground rules include:

- One person speaks at a time, no interruptions
- Respectful language, no personal attacks
- Questions and statements should focus on issues, not individuals
- Technical terms should be explained when used
- Anyone can request a break or caucus
- No retaliation for statements made in mediation

The enforcement piece is critical. Rules without enforcement favor the powerful. Direct interruptions of community members by company representatives require immediate mediator intervention. Jargon that excludes community members from understanding demands mediator clarification. Consistent enforcement signals that the process is genuinely fair.

Neutral Venue Selection

Where mediation occurs matters. Holding sessions at the company headquarters subtly signals company control, while community members may feel like guests in someone else's space. As discussed in Chapter 6 (Designing Mediation Processes), venue selection is a key element of process design. In the context of power asymmetries, venue choice takes on additional significance.

Best practices for venue selection:

- Choose genuinely neutral spaces, such as community centers, hotels, or civic buildings
- Ensure the venue is accessible to all parties, considering transportation and mobility needs
- Arrange seating to promote equality, such as a circular arrangement rather than "us versus them" configurations
- Provide comfortable conditions for extended sessions, including breaks, refreshments, and adequate facilities
- Consider cultural appropriateness of the space

Accessible Scheduling

Meeting times work best when they accommodate all parties, not just those with professional flexibility. If community members are farmers, avoid scheduling during planting or harvest seasons. If they work during the day, consider evening or weekend sessions. Provide adequate notice so participants can arrange their affairs.

Example: A company might naturally suggest Tuesday at 10:00 a.m., their normal meeting time. But community representatives might need to travel several hours, arrange childcare, or take unpaid leave from work. A mediator sensitive to these constraints might propose Saturday sessions or split sessions into multiple shorter meetings to facilitate easier participation.

Language Accommodation

Language barriers require competent interpretation services. But language accommodation goes beyond translation. Monitoring for jargon, acronyms, and technical terms is essential, since these can effectively exclude participants even when everyone speaks the same language.

Sample Dialogue:
Mediator: *"I noticed some technical terms in that explanation. Before we continue, could you explain what "EIA" and "baseline assessment" mean for those who may not be familiar with these terms?"*

Active Mediator Intervention

Sometimes, procedural safeguards are not enough. Active intervention becomes necessary when power dynamics distort the mediation process.

Stopping Power Plays

Threats, intimidation, and manipulation represent serious power misuse that demands direct mediator intervention. This requires courage and defines process integrity.

Sample Dialogue:

Mediator: *"Let's pause here. That statement felt like a threat. We agreed at the outset to negotiate in good faith. If the company is genuinely saying it will pursue legal action regardless of what happens here, it helps to discuss what that means for this process. But if this is a negotiating tactic, I'd ask that we return to constructive dialogue."*

Rebalancing Attention

Drawing out less vocal parties through deliberate invitations and ensuring their concerns receive adequate attention strengthens the process. This is not favoritism but rather compensation for natural dynamics that would otherwise marginalize them.

Sample Dialogue:

Mediator: *"I notice the community members haven't said much during this discussion of technical options. I want to make sure we're not moving too quickly. Maria, what's your reaction to what you've heard? Does this align with your community's concerns?"*

Reality-Checking the Powerful

Sometimes, powerful parties need help understanding the consequences of their approach. If a company is steamrolling toward an agreement that the community cannot accept, the mediator might use a caucus to help them see the risks.

Sample Dialogue:

Mediator (in caucus with the company): *"I understand your position on the compensation amount. But I want to share my observation: the community members seem deeply dissatisfied with this offer. If you push this through, what do you expect will happen? Will they comply with an agreement they feel was coerced? What does your experience suggest about the durability of such agreements?"*

Naming the Dynamic

Sometimes the most powerful intervention is simply naming what is happening. This brings hidden dynamics into the open where they can be addressed.

> **Sample Dialogue:**
>
> Mediator: *"I want to acknowledge something I'm observing. We've been discussing this issue for an hour, and the company representatives have spoken for about 50 minutes of that time. Community members have had far fewer opportunities to share their perspectives. I'd like to adjust our approach to ensure everyone has equal opportunity to contribute."*

Using Caucuses Strategically

Private meetings with each party, known as caucuses, are powerful tools for managing power imbalances. They create a safe space for candid conversation away from the pressure of the joint session.

How caucuses help balance power:

- **Safe space for candor:** Community members may be reluctant to express concerns in front of company officials. In caucus, they can speak freely about fears, frustrations, and their true priorities.
- **Coaching opportunity:** Helping less experienced parties strategize about how to present their interests, frame proposals, and respond to offers improves their participation.
- **Reality testing:** Assessment of realistic expectations must happen privately, not in front of the other party.
- **Exploring flexibility:** Parties may reveal flexibility in private that they would not acknowledge in a joint session.
- **Emotional processing:** If emotions run high, a caucus provides space to process feelings before returning to productive dialogue.

Caution: Caucus Confidentiality

Maintain strict confidentiality of caucus discussions unless parties explicitly grant permission to share specific information. If one party suspects the mediator is sharing their confidential statements, trust in the mediator evaporates. At the same time, be careful not to become a messenger who is perceived as favoring one side. Balance is essential.

Connecting Parties with External Support

Accessing resources that strengthen participation is particularly important for less powerful parties. This is not advocacy but rather ensuring both parties can engage meaningfully.

Types of external support:

- **NGOs with relevant expertise:** Organizations focused on environmental justice, community rights, or corporate accountability often provide technical support and advocacy.
- **Legal aid organizations:** Pro bono legal support helps communities understand their rights and the implications of proposed agreements.
- **Technical experts:** Independent experts can help interpret company data, assess environmental impacts, or evaluate compensation proposals.
- **Community paralegals:** Local individuals trained in basic legal concepts can bridge the gap between formal legal systems and community understanding.
- **Academic institutions:** Universities sometimes provide research support or student volunteers to assist communities.

Caution: Funding and Independence

If the company funds logistics for community participation, such as transportation, accommodation, or advisor fees, ensure this does not create dependency or the appearance of them buying the community's agreement. Funding mechanisms work best when they enable participation without controlling outcomes. Consider whether a third party, such as an NGO or development institution, could provide funding to maintain independence.

12.3 Building and Restoring Trust

Trust is the glue that makes agreements hold. In company-community disputes, trust has often been eroded over years of broken promises, miscommunication, or outright harm. Rebuilding trust is both a process and an outcome of mediation. Without trust, even well-crafted agreements fail because parties do not believe the other will honor commitments.

Why Trust Matters

Trust affects every aspect of mediation and its aftermath. Yet demonstrating accountability without inadvertently creating legal liability is a delicate balance. The following framework shows how parties can take meaningful responsibility while managing that tension.

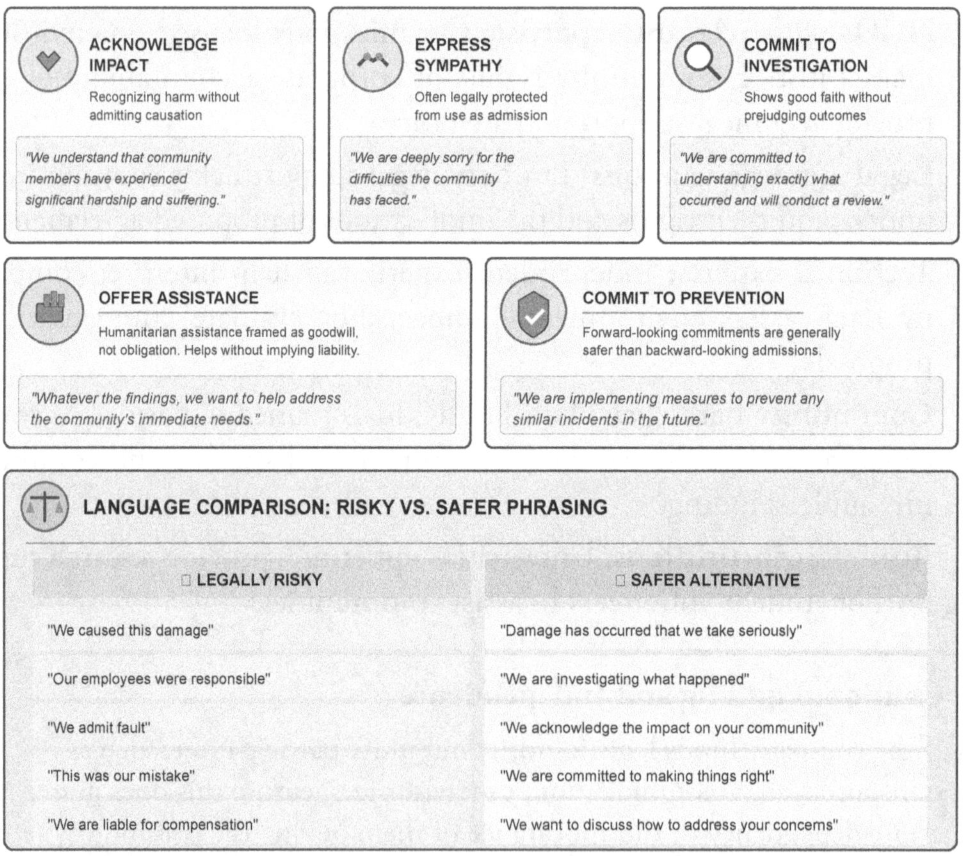

Figure 44: A framework for helping parties demonstrate accountability and responsibility without creating unintended legal liability exposure.

Demonstrating accountability without creating legal liability requires careful language and structure, and this framework helps you navigate the tension between genuine acknowledgment and overexposure to legal risk.

- **Information sharing:** Without trust, parties will not share their genuine concerns, constraints, and priorities. They withhold information, fearing it will be used against them. This makes it impossible to identify creative solutions that address everyone's real interests.
- **Agreement durability:** Agreements only hold if parties believe the other will comply. Low-trust parties hedge, demand excessive guarantees, or simply ignore agreements once signed. In the Guinea mining dispute, the long mediation process (2017-2024) included multiple interim agreements to gradually build trust before attempting a comprehensive settlement.
- **Interpretation of behavior:** Low trust causes parties to interpret everything negatively. A company's delay in implementing a promise is seen as bad faith, not a logistical challenge. A community protest is seen as unreasonable aggression rather than a legitimate expression of concern. This negative interpretation spiral escalates conflict (as discussed in Chapter 5 on conflict dynamics).
- **Creative problem-solving:** Trust enables risk-taking. Parties who trust each other are willing to try new approaches, make conditional offers, and explore creative solutions. Without trust, parties stick to defensive positions.

Key Concept: Trust as a Resource

Think of trust as a resource that can be accumulated or depleted. Every kept promise deposits trust. Every broken commitment withdraws it. An overdrawn trust account prevents any relationship from functioning. Mediation is often the process of rebuilding a trust balance sufficient for cooperation.

Trust-Building Principles

Certain principles consistently contribute to trust-building. Understanding and applying these principles strengthens both the process and the outcomes.

Principle	In Practice
Consistency	Do what you say you will do, every time. Keep small promises. If you say you will send a document by Wednesday, send it by Wednesday. Reliability builds trust incrementally.
Transparency	Share information openly. Explain constraints honestly. Withholding information requires explanation. Secrecy breeds suspicion.
Acknowledgment	Recognize past harms and their impact. Do not minimize or deny. Acknowledgment validates the other party's experience and creates space for moving forward.
Demonstrated Change	Show through actions, not just words. Words without action are empty. Early concrete actions build confidence that further commitments will be honored.
Verification	Build in monitoring so parties do not have to trust blindly. Joint oversight, independent verification, and regular reporting allow trust to develop gradually based on demonstrated compliance.

The Role of Acknowledgment and Apology

Genuine acknowledgment of past wrongs transforms mediation. For communities that have suffered harm, being heard and having their experience validated is as important as material compensation.

What Acknowledgment Accomplishes

Validation: Acknowledgment tells the community, "What happened to you was real, and it was wrong." This validation is psychologically powerful. Communities often feel that their suffering has been invisible or denied. Acknowledgment makes it visible.

Responsibility: Company acknowledgment of harm demonstrates responsibility rather than blame-shifting. This signals a fundamental shift in posture, from adversary to accountable partner.

An effective apology contains several key components that distinguish genuine acknowledgment from empty words.

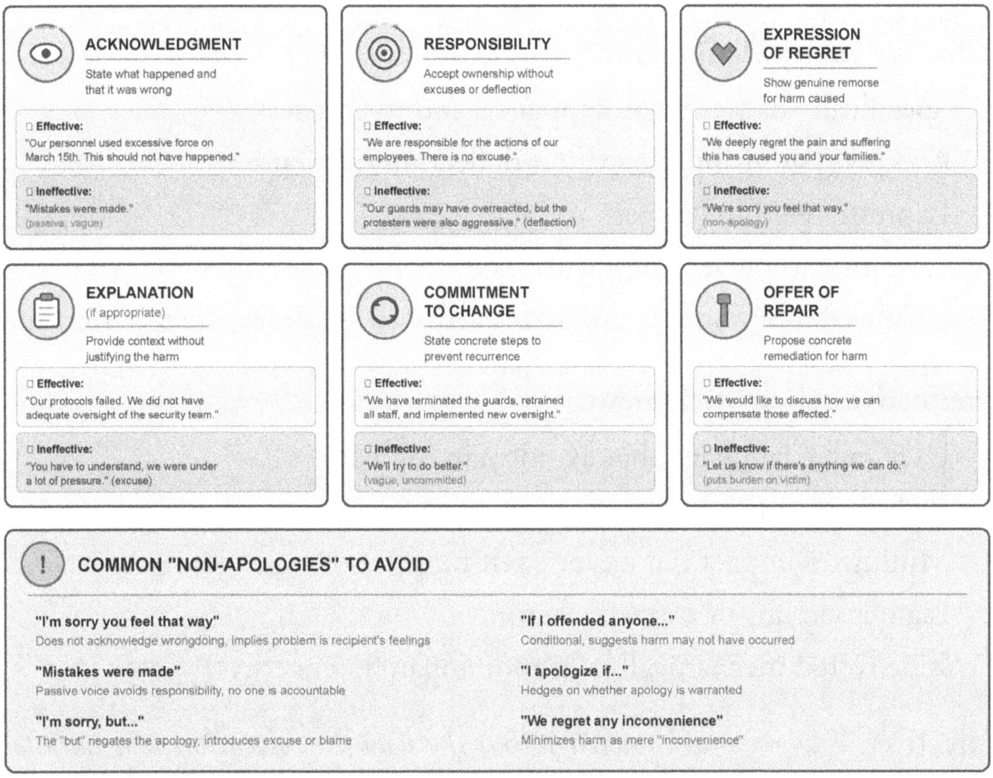

Figure 45: A breakdown of the key components that make an apology genuine and effective, including acknowledgement, responsibility, and commitment to change.

When guiding parties toward acknowledgment, focus on specificity over formulaic expressions. A meaningful apology names the harm, takes responsibility without qualifiers, and makes a concrete commitment to change.

Opening: Acknowledgment creates space for moving forward. It is difficult to work collaboratively with someone who denies your experience. Once harm is acknowledged, the focus can shift to remediation and prevention.

Respect: Acknowledgment demonstrates respect for the community's dignity. It says, "Your suffering matters to us."

Elements of Effective Acknowledgment

Not all acknowledgments are equally effective. A sincere, specific acknowledgment builds trust. A vague, defensive one worsens relations.

Effective acknowledgment:

- Specifically names what happened and its impact
- Accepts responsibility without deflection or excuse
- Expresses genuine regret
- Commits to preventing recurrence
- Is delivered by someone with authority to speak for the organization

Ineffective acknowledgment:

- Uses vague language that avoids naming harm
- Includes justifications or excuses
- Minimizes impact ("if anyone felt hurt")
- Blames victims or external factors
- Is delivered mechanically without apparent sincerity

Effective: *"I want to acknowledge that the way the relocation was handled three years ago caused real hardship. Families lost homes they had lived in for generations, and we did not provide adequate support. That should not have happened, and I am sorry for the pain it caused."*

Ineffective: *"We're sorry if anyone felt inconvenienced by the relocation process. We followed all legal requirements and did our best under difficult circumstances."*

> **Key Concept: Apology vs. Legal Liability**
>
> Companies often resist apologies due to legal concerns. Work with legal counsel to craft language that expresses genuine acknowledgment without creating legal liability. Many jurisdictions have "apology laws" that protect expressions of sympathy or regret from being used as evidence of liability. Focus on impact ("what you experienced was painful") rather than fault ("we were wrong to do X").

Early Wins and Confidence-Building Measures

Low-trust relationships do not permit jumping directly to comprehensive agreements. Instead, they need to build trust incrementally through small successes. Early wins demonstrate good faith and create positive momentum.

The Logic of Incremental Trust-Building

Consider the situation from a community's perspective. A company has broken promises before. Why would they readily believe new promises will be kept? The answer is that they typically do not believe immediately. Trust must be earned through demonstrated behavior.

Start with small, easily achievable commitments. Honoring these principles leads to success for both parties. This creates a foundation for larger commitments. Each kept promise deposits trust in the relational bank account.

Case Example: In the Guinea mining dispute, the parties did not immediately attempt a comprehensive settlement. Instead, they reached interim agreements over several years: improvements in water access (2019), rental allowances for interim housing and construction of a local market (2022), health center improvements (2023), and road maintenance (early 2024). Each agreement demonstrated that the mediation process could deliver real benefits. By the time they negotiated the final comprehensive agreement in September 2024, years of successful interim implementations had built sufficient trust for a larger commitment.

Examples of Early Wins

Depending on the context, early wins might include:

Company provides immediate relief: While permanent solutions are negotiated, the company provides water trucks, temporary shelter, or emergency assistance.

Community suspends hostile action: The community agrees to pause protests or blockades during mediation, demonstrating commitment to dialogue.

Information sharing: The company shares previously confidential environmental monitoring data, demonstrating transparency.

Joint activity: Both parties participate in a joint site visit or collaborative assessment, building familiarity and a working relationship.

Quick infrastructure fix: The company repairs a damaged road or provides equipment for a community need, showing practical goodwill.

Process agreements: Parties agree on ground rules, schedules, and communication protocols, demonstrating they can reach an agreement on something.

Practical Tip: Make Early Wins Visible

Early successes deserve visibility and celebration. Acknowledge them explicitly in mediation sessions. Summarize them in writing. Help parties see the pattern: "We've now successfully agreed on X, Y, and Z. This shows we can work together." Visibility reinforces positive momentum and builds confidence for tackling harder issues.

Key Concept: Trust Repair Sequence

Trust restoration typically follows a sequence: acknowledgment of harm, expression of genuine regret, commitment to change, demonstrated follow-through. Skipping steps rarely works. A company that jumps straight to solutions without acknowledgment often finds the community unmoved by even generous offers.

Practical Tip: Trust Temperature Check

Periodically assess trust levels explicitly: "On a scale of one to ten, how much do you currently trust that the company will follow through on commitments?" Track these ratings over time. They provide early warning of trust erosion and evidence of trust-building progress.

Caution: Premature Trust Demands

Parties sometimes demand that others trust them before they have earned it. "You just have to trust us" is not a trust-building strategy. Help parties understand that trust must be demonstrated through consistent behavior over time, not granted on request.

Building Personal Connections

Trust is built between people, not just institutions. Personal connections between company representatives and community members, beyond purely adversarial positions, significantly improve interaction quality.

Humanizing the Other Side

As explored in Chapter 10 (Trauma-Informed Approaches), conflict often creates dehumanization. Community members see "the company" as a faceless exploiter, while company representatives see "the community" as irrational protestors. In the context of trust restoration, breaking through these stereotypes requires deliberate personal connection.

Techniques for humanization:

- **Personal introductions:** At the start of mediation, have participants share something personal beyond their role. Where are they from? What do they care about? What do they hope for? Finding common ground, such as shared love of local sports teams or similar family situations, creates connection.
- **Shared meals:** Breaking bread together is powerful across cultures. Informal meals during breaks allow different kinds of conversation than formal sessions. People who have shared a meal find it harder to demonize each other.
- **Site visits:** Arrange for company representatives to visit the community, see homes, meet families, and experience daily life. Arrange for community members to tour the company's facilities, meet workers, and understand the company's operations. Direct experience builds understanding.

- **Names and relationships:** Use people's names. Remember personal details. Ask about family members mentioned in previous sessions. These small gestures signal that people matter as individuals.

> **Sample Dialogue**
>
> Mediator: *"Before we dive into the agenda, let's take a few minutes for everyone to share something about themselves beyond this dispute. Perhaps where you're from, or something you enjoy doing. Sometimes it helps to remember we're all people here."*

Creating Opportunities for Informal Interaction

Formal mediation sessions are crucial but limited. People maintain professional personas. They stick to prepared positions. Some of the most important relationship-building happens informally.

Practical approaches:

- Build generous break times into the schedule
- Arrange for shared transportation where appropriate
- Include social activities alongside work sessions
- Create opportunities for small group conversations rather than only plenary sessions

Structural Safeguards for Trust

Low-trust contexts require structural safeguards that allow parties to verify compliance rather than relying on blind faith. These mechanisms protect against the risk that commitments will not be honored.

Joint Monitoring Committees

Establish committees with representation from both parties to oversee the implementation of the agreement. Giving community members seats at the monitoring table allows them to verify progress directly rather than depending on company reports.

Design considerations:

- Balance representation, perhaps equal numbers from each party
- Clear mandate and authority
- Regular meeting schedule
- Access to relevant information
- Process for addressing non-compliance

Independent Third-Party Monitoring

In some cases, neither party fully trusts the other to monitor fairly. Independent monitoring by a trusted third party can provide credibility. This might be an NGO, an academic institution, a professional monitoring firm, or an international body.

Case Example: In the Guinea mining dispute, the final agreement included two years of CAO monitoring. This external oversight assures the community that commitments will be tracked by an impartial body, and provides the company with credible verification of their compliance.

Regular Progress Reports and Review Meetings

Build regular reporting and review into agreements. Quarterly progress reports, annual review meetings, and milestone checkpoints create ongoing accountability. They also provide opportunities to identify and address problems before they become crises.

Clear Escalation Procedures

Specify what happens if commitments are not met. Who needs to be contacted? What process works effectively? Having clear escalation procedures reassures parties that they have recourse if things go wrong.

Financial Safeguards

For financial commitments, consider mechanisms that protect against non-payment. Escrow accounts hold funds until conditions are met. Third-party administration ensures funds reach intended recipients. Payment schedules tied to milestones create accountability.

Key Concept: "Trust but Verify"

Verification mechanisms do not mean parties distrust each other. They mean parties are building trust carefully and responsibly. The phrase "trust but verify" captures this. We extend trust, but we also create systems that confirm trust is warranted. Over time, as compliance is demonstrated, verification can become less intensive. Trust grows through successful verification.

Gender and Power in Company-Community Disputes

Power asymmetries in mining disputes are not only between the company and the community. They exist within the community itself, and gender is among the most significant fault lines. Women may lack formal standing in traditional decision-making structures, meaning their interests are represented, if at all, by male leaders who may not share their priorities. Women who lose access to agricultural land or water sources may suffer greater economic impact than men who are offered employment at the mine, yet their losses may not feature in negotiations focused on jobs and cash compensation.

The mediator should recognize that a "community agreement" negotiated exclusively by male leaders may not serve the interests of women and children, and may in fact deepen existing inequalities.

Key Concept: Gendered Impacts of Mining

Research consistently shows that mining operations affect men and women differently. Men are more likely to benefit from direct employment, while women bear disproportionate costs through loss of agricultural land, increased water collection distances, disruption of market networks, and the social consequences of male labor migration (including increased rates of domestic violence and family breakdown in mining-affected communities). A power-aware mediator ensures that compensation and benefit-sharing agreements address these gendered impacts explicitly, rather than treating the community as a homogeneous unit with uniform interests.

Practical Strategies for Gender-Sensitive Mediation

Recognizing gendered power dynamics is necessary, but insufficient on its own. The mediator must translate awareness into concrete process design choices that give women meaningful voice and ensure their interests are reflected in outcomes. Party resistance triggered by power imbalances requires the strategies detailed in Chapter 14.

During the pre-mediation phase, hold separate consultations with women's groups within the community. These sessions serve a dual purpose: they help the mediator understand impacts that may not surface in male-dominated forums, and they give women space to articulate priorities without the social pressure of contradicting male leaders in public.

In many mining-affected communities, women's concerns center on water access, food security, children's health, and the preservation of social networks, priorities that may not align with the employment and cash compensation packages that dominate formal negotiations.

Inclusive process design requires examining whether the community delegation includes women. Raise this consideration with community leaders as a process design question rather than an accusation. Framing matters: "For the agreement to be durable, it needs to reflect the concerns of the whole community. Would it be helpful to include women's representatives in the delegation?" This approach respects community autonomy while signaling that exclusion carries practical risks for agreement durability.

Compensation frameworks deserve particular scrutiny through a gender lens. Cash payments directed to male household heads may not reach women or children. Land-for-land swaps that allocate replacement plots only to men named on title deeds may dispossess women who farmed common land without formal title. Livelihood restoration programs focused on construction or mining skills may exclude women who worked in agriculture or small-scale trade. The mediator could ask explicitly: "How will this compensation structure affect women in the community? Who will control the funds, and who will benefit from the livelihood programs?"

Practical Tip: The Gender Impact Check

Before finalizing any agreement, apply a gender impact check. For each major provision, ask: Who benefits from this? Who bears the cost? Are women's specific losses (agricultural land, water access, market networks, caregiving burdens) addressed, or only the losses that men have articulated? Does the implementation mechanism ensure that benefits reach women directly, or do they flow through intermediaries who may not distribute them equitably? If you cannot answer these questions with confidence, the agreement likely needs revision. This check takes less than an hour but can prevent years of resentment and non-compliance from community members whose needs were overlooked.

12.4 When Trust Has Been Severely Damaged

In some cases, serious harm destroys trust: violence, significant deception, major broken promises, or ongoing exploitation. Standard trust-building approaches may be insufficient. These situations require deeper intervention.

Recognizing Severe Trust Damage

Parties who refuse to be in the same room, who express that reconciliation is impossible, or who immediately reject any statement made by the other party likely have a history of trust damage. Several markers signal severe damage: past interactions that involved violence, harm, or other trauma; previous broken agreements; emotional intensity that persists despite time passing. Identifying these markers signals that severe trust damage is actively affecting mediation, requiring immediate remedial steps.

The following framework reveals the expectation-reality gap that often fuels trust damage, showing how divergent expectations create lasting resentment.

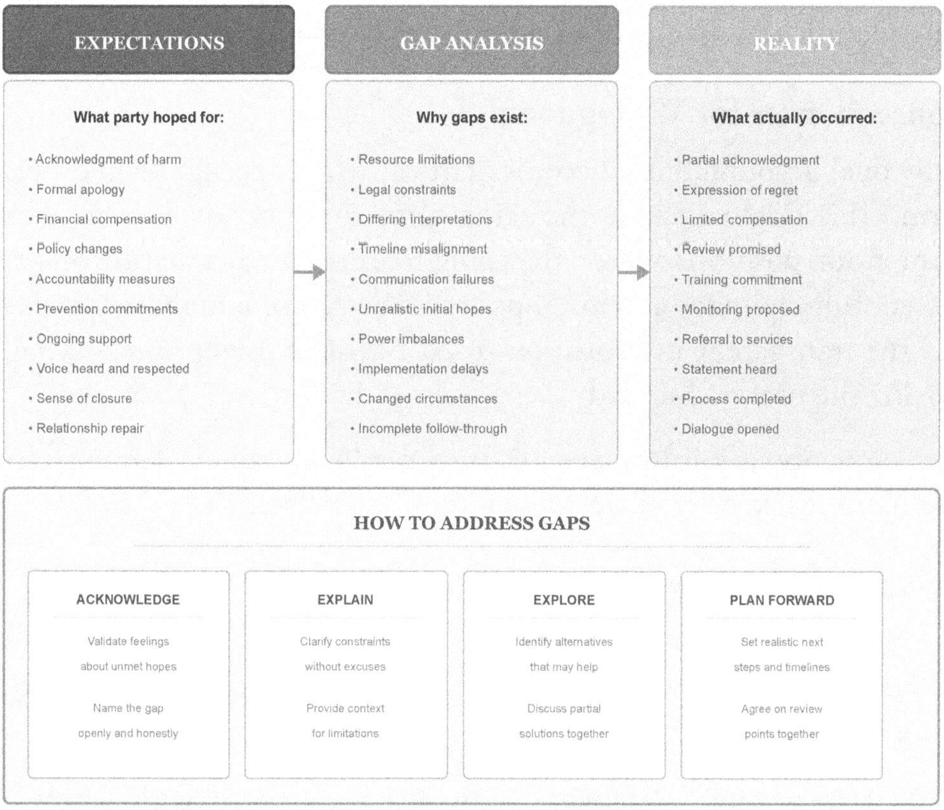

Figure 46: A visual tool showing the gap between community expectations and company commitments, helping parties identify and address perception mismatches.

The gap between expectations and reality is often the source of lasting resentment, which is why making this gap visible and addressable through honest dialogue is one of the most important services mediation provides.

Deeper Acknowledgment

Severe harm demands deeper acknowledgment than simple apologies. Generic expressions of regret will not suffice. Specific acknowledgment of specific harms, delivered with genuine emotion by someone with authority, is essential.

In cases involving violence or serious harm, acknowledgment might include a detailed accounting of what happened or public acceptance of responsibility. Direct apologies to affected individuals and a commitment to truth-telling about past events can also be effective, as can the construction of a memorial or other form of commemoration.

Consequences for Wrongdoers

Individual accountability becomes critical when specific people caused harm. This might include the removal of the individuals who caused harm from positions where they might cause further harm, or other forms of disciplinary action. Support for legal accountability processes and the transparent investigation of past actions might also be vital to moving the process forward.

This is not about punishment for its own sake but about demonstrating that harm is taken seriously and will not be tolerated.

Structural Changes

Severe trust damage often requires structural changes, not just individual accountability. If the problem is systemic, systemic changes are needed. These might include:

- **New personnel:** Removing individuals associated with past harm and bringing in fresh faces can signal a new chapter.
- **New policies:** Revising policies that enabled harm demonstrates commitment to preventing recurrence.
- **New structures:** Creating new oversight mechanisms, grievance procedures, or community engagement structures shows institutional change.
- **External oversight:** Inviting external monitoring or governance can provide assurance that internal changes are real.

Time for Healing

Severe trust damage cannot be repaired quickly. Communities that have experienced trauma need time to heal before they can engage in forward-looking negotiation. Rushing toward agreement before emotional wounds have begun to heal often produces agreements that do not last.

Practical implications:

- Allow time between acknowledgment and negotiation
- Provide access to psychological support
- Do not pressure parties to "move on" before they are ready
- Accept that healing timelines cannot be externally imposed

> **Sample Dialogue**
> Mediator: *"I understand the community's deep mistrust, given what happened. Rebuilding trust after such serious harm will take time and consistent action, not just words. What would help you begin to believe things could be different?"*

Independent Facilitation

Severe trust damage can render any facilitator suspect if they appear connected to either side. Independent, external facilitation becomes essential. This might mean bringing in mediators from outside the region or involving international bodies with credibility.

The CAO's involvement in the Guinea mining dispute exemplifies this. As an independent accountability mechanism associated with the World Bank Group, CAO brought credibility that neither the company nor the community could provide. Both parties trusted CAO to facilitate fairly, even when they did not trust each other.

When Mining Operations Have Destroyed Trust

Mining disputes present particular challenges for trust restoration because the harm is often ongoing, visible, and deeply personal. A community whose water source has been contaminated does not merely distrust the company in an abstract sense. They distrust the company every time they draw water, every time a child falls ill, every time they look at the river they once fished in. The environmental damage serves as a daily, tangible reminder that the company prioritized profit over their wellbeing.

In these circumstances, trust restoration cannot begin with words. Parties must begin with demonstrated action. This includes independent testing that confirms the contamination, a concrete remediation plan with timelines and penalties for delay, and interim measures such as clean water supply that show the company is willing to bear costs before any agreement is reached.

Broken resettlement promises are another common source of severe trust damage in mining contexts. Communities that agreed to relocate based on commitments about replacement housing, agricultural land, and livelihood support, only to find the reality far inferior to what was promised, carry a specific form of betrayal. They gave up something irreplaceable, their ancestral land, their community structure, their economic networks, based on promises that were not kept.

Rebuilding trust in these cases requires the company to first acknowledge the gap between what was promised and what was delivered, and to present a credible plan to close that gap, before any broader negotiation can proceed.

Practical Tip: Trust Restoration Sequencing in Mining Disputes

When trust has been severely damaged by mining operations, the mediator should structure the process in a deliberate sequence. First, facilitate the company acknowledging specific harms without qualifications or deflections. Second, establish independent verification of the current situation (water quality, housing conditions, livelihood impacts). Third, negotiate and implement immediate remedial actions with clear timelines. Fourth, create a monitoring mechanism that gives the community real-time visibility into compliance. Only after these confidence-building measures have been delivered, not merely promised, should the mediator move to broader negotiations about compensation, benefit-sharing, or future operations. Attempting to negotiate the big issues before trust has been partially restored through action will produce agreements that fail on implementation.

12.5 The Mediator as a Trust Bridge

Initially, parties may trust the mediator more than they trust each other. This creates both opportunity and responsibility. The mediator can serve as a bridge, enabling communication and agreement even when direct trust is absent.

Credible Information Conduit

When parties distrust each other's information, the mediator can serve as a credible conduit. Information verified or communicated by the mediator may be accepted when the same information from the other party would be rejected.

> **Sample Dialogue**
>
> Mediator: *"I've reviewed the company's budget documents. I can tell you that the financial constraints they described are real. They genuinely cannot offer more than X this year without risking operations. I know you believe you have been lied to before, but in this case, the numbers support what they're saying."*

Vouching for Sincerity

In caucus, parties often reveal genuine intentions they are reluctant to express in joint session. The mediator can, with permission, vouch for sincerity.

> **Sample Dialogue**
>
> Mediator: *"I've spent considerable time with both sides. I believe the company representative genuinely wants to find a solution that works for the community. Whether you agree with their constraints, I want you to know that I've seen no evidence of bad faith."*

Verifying Compliance

During implementation, the mediator can verify that commitments are being kept, providing assurance to both parties. This is particularly valuable for early commitments where parties are testing whether the other will follow through.

Practical Tip: Verification System Design

Help parties design verification systems that work for everyone involved. The community needs confidence that compliance is real. The company needs verification that is not unduly burdensome. Jointly designed monitoring processes build ownership and increase the likelihood that verification will actually occur.

Calling Out Trust-Breaking Behavior

If one party engages in behavior that undermines trust, such as leaking confidential information, making threats, or failing to honor commitments, the mediator must address it. This protects the process and signals that trust-breaking has consequences.

Sample Dialogue

Mediator (in caucus with the company): *"I need to raise something directly. Community members have reported that company security personnel have been photographing them as they arrive at mediation sessions. Whether intended or not, this feels like intimidation. If we want this process to succeed, this needs to stop immediately."*

Gradually Stepping Back

The goal is for parties to develop direct trust so they no longer need the mediator as an intermediary. As trust grows, the mediator should gradually step back, allowing the parties to communicate and cooperate directly. If the mediator remains central indefinitely, something has gone wrong.

Caution: Mediator Dependency

If parties become dependent on the mediator for all communication and cannot interact directly without mediation, this is a warning sign. The mediator should actively work to build direct communication channels between parties and test whether they can sustain dialogue independently. The goal is relationship repair, not permanent mediation.

12.6 Conclusion: Integration of Power and Trust

Managing power asymmetry and restoring trust are intertwined. Power imbalances undermine trust because they create conditions where exploitation is possible. Trust deficits exacerbate power imbalances because weaker parties cannot rely on stronger parties to act fairly.

Effective mediation addresses both simultaneously. By creating procedural fairness, mediators begin to restore trust. By building trust incrementally, mediators reduce the impact of power differences. The weaker party gains confidence. The stronger party learns that cooperation produces better outcomes than domination.

The ultimate goal: a mediation in which the weaker party feels empowered and the stronger party learns to listen, producing an agreement that sticks because both sides have a stake in its success. When parties have contributed to designing the solution, participated fairly in the process, and believe the other will honor commitments, they are invested in making the agreement work.

Skilled mediation can shift the dynamic from adversarial conflict to collaborative problem-solving, from mutual suspicion to working trust. It requires patience, skill, and persistent attention to both the procedural and relational dimensions of conflict. When achieved, it creates the conditions for durable agreements and genuine benefit-sharing between companies and communities.

Key Concept: Fairness and Trust

Managing power asymmetry is about ensuring fairness. Restoring trust is about rebuilding relationships. Both are essential for durable agreements. A process that achieves procedural fairness but leaves trust broken will produce agreements that are not honored. A process that builds trust without addressing power imbalances will produce agreements that favor the powerful. Skilled mediators attend to both dimensions, creating conditions where genuine collaboration becomes possible.

13.

NAVIGATING IMPASSES AND REBUILDING COOPERATION

Even when power dynamics are carefully managed and trust begins to rebuild, negotiations can still grind to a halt. An impasse occurs when parties stop moving toward resolution. Mishandled impasses can collapse talks, leaving both parties worse off.

This chapter focuses on recognizing an impasse, understanding its root causes, and implementing strategies to break through it. We also address how to rebuild cooperative momentum after a stalemate and how to design agreements that prevent future deadlocks. Mediators value these skills highly: the ability to navigate difficult moments determines whether mediation succeeds or fails.

> **Key Concept: The Nature of Impasses**
>
> An impasse signals that something important needs attention, whether that is unmet emotional needs, unclear communication, external pressures, or fundamental value differences, not failure. Experienced mediators view impasses as diagnostic information rather than defeat.

13.1 Recognizing an Impasse

The first step in addressing an impasse is recognizing when one has occurred. Develop sensitivity to the signs that discussions have moved from productive disagreement to genuine deadlock. This allows you to intervene early, before positions harden further.

Productive disagreement is healthy and expected in mediation. Parties naturally advocate for their interests and challenge each other's proposals. Impasses are different. They represent a qualitative shift in which forward movement has stopped and parties have become entrenched.Mediation process literature (Moore, 2014) distinguishes productive disagreement, where parties are still exploring options, from genuine impasse, where forward movement has stalled and process intervention is required.

Warning Signs of an Impasse

Warning Sign	What It Looks Like in Practice
Circular Arguments	The same points are repeated without new information, perspectives, or ideas emerging. Parties seem to be talking past each other, restating positions rather than exploring solutions. The conversation feels like it is going in circles.
Rigid Positions	Language becomes absolute: "non-negotiable," "final offer," "take it or leave it," "we will never agree to that." Parties stop qualifying their statements or acknowledging room for discussion.
Emotional Escalation	Rising frustration, anger, sarcasm, or complete withdrawal. Voices rise, body language closes off (crossed arms, avoiding eye contact), or parties become unnaturally quiet. Some participants may disengage entirely.
Communication Breakdown	Parties stop truly listening, talk past each other, or go silent. They respond to assumptions rather than actual statements. Questions go unanswered or are deflected.
Threats or Ultimatums	"If you don't, we will . . . " statements appear. Parties invoke their BATNA as a weapon rather than as information. References to litigation, media exposure, or escalation to higher authorities increase. (see Chapter 9 for detailed BATNA/WATNA analysis techniques)

Warning Sign	What It Looks Like in Practice
Focus on the Past	Conversation keeps returning to old grievances rather than discussing future solutions. Parties relitigate historical wrongs rather than explore what can be done now. Blame becomes more prominent than problem-solving.

Key Concept: Productive vs. Unproductive Struggle

Not all difficulties are impasses. Hard negotiation with gradual movement is a productive struggle. Circular arguments with no progress lead to an impasse. Learn to distinguish between them, noting that some deadlocks reflect resistance (Chapter 14) rather than true impasse. Productive struggle should be allowed to continue. Impasses require intervention.

Practical Tip: Impasse Early Warning

Watch for impasse precursors: parties repeating positions without variation, body language showing withdrawal or rigidity. Early intervention is easier than rescuing a full impasse. Act when you see warning signs rather than waiting for a complete breakdown.

Recognizing Impasse in Practice

Consider the following fictional scenario, inspired by common dynamics in mining mediations: Maria and Luisa, representing the community council, have been advocating for the company to hire fifty local residents within six months. Alex and Janis, representing the company, have offered twenty positions with gradual increases. After several rounds of discussion, the exchange sounds like this:

Maria: *"You promised fifty jobs. We need fifty jobs. Nothing less."*

Alex: *"We've explained our constraints. Twenty is what we can do right now."*

Maria: *"Then you're breaking another promise. Just like the school."*

Alex: *"We're trying to be realistic. Twenty positions is a significant commitment."*

Maria: *"Significant for you, maybe. For us, it means thirty families still without income."*

This exchange shows classic impasse indicators: circular arguments (both sides restating their positions), rigid language ("nothing less," "twenty is what we can do"), focus on the past ("just like the school"), and emotional undertones (frustration evident in both parties' statements).

> **Practical Tip: Tracking the Tone**
>
> Experienced mediators develop the habit of mentally tracking the "temperature" of the room. When you notice the conversation becoming repetitive, voices changing pitch, or body language closing off, these are early warning signs. Intervening early, before a full impasse develops, breaks through more easily than waiting for positions to harden completely.

13.2 Common Causes of Impasse

Understanding why parties are stuck is essential for choosing the right intervention. Different causes require different strategies. Skilled mediators develop diagnostic ability, reading beneath the surface of stated positions to identify the actual barriers to progress.

In extractive-industry disputes, impasses frequently stem from technical disagreements rather than pure negotiation failure. Competing assessments of water contamination levels, tailings dam stability, or acceptable residual environmental impacts can deadlock mediation because each party relies on different experts with different methodologies. These are genuine disputes about facts that affect long-term community health and company liability, not personality conflicts or positional bargaining.

Miscommunication

Parties genuinely misunderstand each other's proposals, intentions, or constraints. What appears to be disagreement may actually be confusion.

Words mean different things to different people, especially across cultural or professional divides.

These impasses are often the easiest to resolve. Once clarified, parties may discover they were closer to agreement than they realized. However, if left unaddressed, misunderstandings can escalate into genuine conflict.

Example: In another illustrative scenario, the community demanded "fair compensation" for displaced farmers. The company believed they had offered fair compensation based on market land values. The community, however, meant compensation that accounted for lost livelihoods, social networks, and ancestral connections to the land. The parties were using the same words with entirely different meanings.

Mediator approach: "I want to make sure we're all understanding the same thing. Company, can you explain specifically what your compensation offer includes? Community, what elements would need to be covered for compensation to feel fair to you?"

Lack of Trust

Parties doubt each other's follow-through. Past broken promises create skepticism about new agreements. The question becomes: "Why should we compromise if they won't keep their word anyway?"

Yet trust is the foundation of any durable agreement. Without it, even attractive proposals are rejected because parties don't believe implementation will follow. Trust deficits reflect legitimate concerns based on historical experience.

Example: Maria and Luisa's community has experienced years of broken promises from Alpha Mining Co. The partially built school, sitting unfinished, is a daily reminder. When the company now proposes a "phased approach" to employment, the community hears: "We'll make promises and not keep them, just like before."

Mediator approach: Address trust deficits directly. Ask: "What would the company need to do differently this time for you to believe the commitments will be kept? Are there accountability mechanisms or verification processes that would help build confidence?"

Face-Saving and Pride

No one wants to appear weak or defeated. Public commitments and reputational concerns make flexibility difficult. Moving from a stated position feels like "losing."

Face-saving concerns are invisible but powerful. A negotiator may genuinely want to compromise while feeling trapped by previous statements. The actual barrier isn't substantive disagreement but the perception of backing down.

Example: Sascha Martinez, the landowner negotiating with Mark Thompson from the mining company, has told family members that they'll "never accept less than 2,500 $ per month." Even if Sascha recognizes that 2,000 $ with additional benefits might meet their underlying needs, accepting it feels like a public defeat.

Mediator approach: Create face-saving opportunities. Reframe compromises as gains rather than concessions. Use caucuses to explore flexibility privately. Introduce new elements that allow parties to accept different terms without appearing to have "lost" on their original position.

> **Key Concept: Face-Saving Solutions**
>
> Many impasses persist because parties cannot find a way to change position without appearing weak or inconsistent. Your job is to provide face-saving narratives: "New information has emerged," "Circumstances have changed," "A creative new option addresses concerns." Creating pathways for parties to move while maintaining dignity often unlocks flexibility.

Unrealistic Expectations

One or both parties have inflated expectations about what they can achieve. This may stem from overconfidence in their BATNA, misunderstanding of the other party's constraints, or simply wishful thinking about possible outcomes.

Unrealistic expectations prevent parties from recognizing when a reasonable deal is available. They hold out for terms that the other side cannot possibly accept, missing opportunities for mutually beneficial agreements.

Example: Blair and Ali, representing the rural community in negotiations with Beta Mining Co., demand that "significant infrastructure investment" be made within the first two years of operations. They envision new roads, schools, and healthcare facilities. The company knows that revenues won't support such an investment until year four at the earliest. Both sides are operating with different assumptions about what's financially possible.

Mediator approach: Facilitate reality testing. Bring in financial information or independent experts. Help parties understand the other side's genuine constraints. Ask: "What do you understand about the company's revenue timeline? Company, when will funds become available?"

External Pressures

Stakeholders behind the scenes, including shareholders, community factions, political leaders, and family members, push negotiators to hold firm. The person at the table may want to compromise but lacks the authorization or fears consequences from their constituents.

External pressures create invisible constraints on flexibility. The negotiator's real audience may not be the other party but the people they'll have to face when they return home. Understanding these dynamics is essential for finding workable solutions.

Example: Mark Thompson, representing the mining company, personally believes the landowner deserves higher compensation. However, his boss is "obsessed with cost control," and offering above-market rates would require justification that Mark fears he cannot provide. His rigid position reflects institutional constraints, not personal conviction.

Mediator approach: In caucus, explore what constraints the negotiator faces. Ask: "What would happen if you agreed to this? Who else needs to approve? What arguments would help you make the case internally?" Sometimes the mediator can help craft proposals that the negotiator can "sell" to their constituents.

Emotional Barriers

Unaddressed emotional needs, including feeling disrespected, unacknowledged, or threatened, block rational problem-solving. The substantive issues are solvable, but emotional wounds prevent progress. People need to feel heard before they can hear others.

Emotions are data. They signal what matters most deeply to people. Ignoring emotions doesn't make them go away; it drives them underground, where they continue to influence behavior. Addressing emotional needs often unlocks substantive flexibility.

Example: The community leader described in the role-play documents feels that the mining company has "prioritized profit over the well-being of the people and the environment." Beyond specific demands for jobs or infrastructure, there is a deeper need to feel that the company genuinely cares about the community. Until that emotional need is addressed, substantive proposals may be rejected regardless of their terms.

Mediator approach: Name the emotional dimension. "I sense that beyond the practical issues, there's something else going on. Community, do you feel the company truly understands the impact of what has happened? Sometimes acknowledgment matters as much as the remedy itself."

Power Dynamics

Power imbalances create their own impasse dynamics (as discussed in Chapter 12). The stronger party may be trying to force concessions, believing time is on their side. The weaker party may be stonewalling as the only power they have, refusing to accept terms that feel exploitative.

Power-based impasses are among the most difficult to resolve. The stronger party may not feel incentivized to compromise, while the weaker party may view resistance as a matter of dignity. Addressing power dynamics requires both structural interventions and reframing of the relationship.

Example: Alpha Mining Co. has financial resources, legal teams, and government connections. The community council has local knowledge, moral authority, and the ability to disrupt operations through protests. The company may believe they can "wait out" the community. The community may believe that refusing to settle is their only leverage. Both positions can lead to a prolonged stalemate.

Mediator approach: Help parties see interdependence. The company needs a social license to operate; the community needs economic opportunities that the company can provide. Reframe from adversarial to mutual interest: "Both of you need something from the other. Neither can fully achieve your goals without cooperation. What would a relationship look like where both sides benefit?"

Caution: Multiple Causes Often Overlap

Impasses rarely have a single cause. Miscommunication can compound trust deficits. Emotional barriers can amplify power dynamics. Face-saving concerns can mask unrealistic expectations. Effective diagnosis requires looking at the whole picture, not just the most obvious symptom.

How Resistance to Change Creates and Sustains Impasse

The causes of impasse discussed above, from miscommunication and trust deficits to emotional barriers and power dynamics, share a common underlying thread: resistance to change. Before a mediator can select the right strategy for breaking through a deadlock, it is essential to understand why parties resist movement even when continuing the dispute carries real costs. Resistance to change is not simply stubbornness. It is a deeply rooted psychological response that, left unaddressed, transforms what might be a temporary disagreement into a hardened impasse.

At its core, resistance to change is a protective response. Human beings are wired to prefer predictability, because in evolutionary terms the familiar was safer than the unknown. This bias operates powerfully in conflict settings where uncertainty is already high and trust is already low. When a proposed resolution asks parties to accept new arrangements, relinquish established patterns, or trust commitments that have not yet been tested, the psychological cost of change can feel greater than the ongoing cost of the conflict itself. For the mediator, this explains why parties sometimes seem to prefer an unresolved dispute over a reasonable settlement: the impasse, however painful, is at least predictable.

Fear of the unknown is one of the most common reasons negotiations stall. Parties may understand intellectually that an agreement improves their situation, but they cannot know with certainty what life after the agreement will look like. For communities that have experienced broken promises before, this uncertainty is compounded by legitimate scepticism about whether commitments will be honored.

The result is a preference for the status quo, however unsatisfactory, over an uncertain future. Mediators who encounter an impasse rooted in this fear will often find that standard negotiation techniques fail because the barrier is not about the terms on the table but about the inability to trust what comes after signing.

Loss of control is closely related and amplifies resistance significantly. When people feel that change is being imposed upon them rather than chosen by them, their autonomy is threatened and resistance intensifies regardless of the merits of the proposal. This is particularly acute in company-community disputes where power asymmetries already leave communities feeling that decisions are made about them, not with them.

In such cases, an impasse may actually serve a psychological function: it is the one form of power available to the weaker party. Refusing to agree becomes a way of asserting agency. A mediation process that genuinely restores a sense of choice to all parties can reduce this form of resistance substantially.

Status quo comfort, sometimes called the endowment effect, means that people overvalue what they currently have simply because it is theirs. A community may resist a relocation package that is objectively superior to their current circumstances because the familiar landscape, the established social networks, and the known daily routines carry psychological weight that no compensation formula can fully capture. In impasse terms, this creates an asymmetry between what the proposing party considers a generous offer and what the receiving party experiences as an irreplaceable loss. Until the mediator surfaces this disconnect, the deadlock will persist.

Lack of trust sits at the heart of much resistance and, by extension, at the heart of many impasses. Where relationships have been damaged by past failures, broken agreements, or perceived disrespect, parties may resist change not because they oppose the substance of a proposal but because they do not believe the other side will follow through.

Each broken promise in the past raises the psychological cost of trusting again. For the mediator, this means that an impasse caused by trust deficits cannot be resolved through better terms alone. It requires building credibility through small, verifiable commitments before larger agreements become possible.

Lack of information drives resistance that leads to impasse. People naturally resist what they do not understand, and in many company-community disputes, technical complexity and information asymmetry leave communities feeling unable to evaluate proposals on their merits.

When a mining company presents a remediation plan full of technical specifications that community members cannot assess, resistance reflects not the plan itself but discomfort at being asked to accept something one cannot independently verify. The resulting impasse looks like substantive disagreement but reflects an information problem.

Community culture and collective identity add further layers. Some communities have a long history of resisting external pressures, and that resistance has become part of their identity and social cohesion. In these contexts, accepting an agreement can feel like a betrayal of collective values, even if the terms are favorable.

Emotional attachment to places, practices, and ways of life means that what appears on paper as a fair exchange may feel like an irreplaceable loss. When impasse is sustained by identity and culture, the mediator must work at a deeper level than interests and positions, acknowledging what is being asked of people and validating the weight of that ask.

Key Concept: Resistance as an Impasse Signal

When an impasse proves resistant to standard negotiation techniques, consider whether the real barrier is psychological resistance to change rather than a substantive disagreement. The diagnostic question is: “If the parties fully trusted that this agreement would be implemented as promised, would they accept it?" If the answer is yes, the impasse is not about terms. It is about fear, trust, control, or identity. Shift your intervention accordingly.

Resistance to Change in the Mining Sector

Resistance to change takes distinctive forms in mining-community disputes, where the stakes are high, the history is often painful, and the changes being proposed are frequently irreversible. Understanding how resistance manifests in this sector helps mediators anticipate the barriers they will face and design interventions that address the real sources of deadlock.

In resettlement disputes, resistance is rarely just about compensation figures. Communities facing relocation from ancestral lands experience a threat to their entire way of life. In many resettlement initiatives, communities resisted resettlement not because the compensation was inadequate in monetary terms, but because no financial package could replace sacred sites, burial grounds, and the social fabric woven into a specific landscape over generations. Negotiations stalled repeatedly until the mediators acknowledged that the resistance was rooted in identity and grief, not economics.

Environmental remediation proposals frequently trigger resistance born of past negative experience. When a mining company proposes a clean-up plan after contamination, communities that have watched previous remediation efforts fail, or that have seen monitoring reports quietly buried, will resist new proposals regardless of their technical merit.

In another case, decades of riverine tailings disposal created such deep community distrust that subsequent remediation commitments were met with scepticism that bordered on outright refusal to engage. The impasse was not about the science of remediation. It was about whether any promise from the company could be believed.

Mine closure and transition planning exposes resistance driven by fear of the unknown. Communities that have become economically dependent on mining operations may resist closure plans even when the environmental case for closure is strong, because the post-mining future is genuinely uncertain. Workers, local businesses, and municipal governments all face an unknown that no transition plan can fully resolve.

In coal mining regions undergoing transition, impasses in multi-stakeholder negotiations have often persisted not because parties disagreed about the need for change, but because the anxiety of an unfamiliar economic future was paralysing.

Benefit-sharing negotiations can stall when communities resist changes to existing arrangements, even flawed ones. A community receiving a modest but predictable royalty stream may resist renegotiation toward a potentially larger but more complex benefit-sharing structure because the familiar arrangement, however imperfect, is understood and trusted.

The endowment effect is powerful here: what parties have, they overvalue, and what they are offered, they discount. Mediators who push for objectively better terms without addressing this psychological dynamic will find themselves stuck in an impasse of their own making.

Caution: Do Not Pathologize Resistance

Resistance to change in mining-community disputes is often entirely rational. Communities that have been displaced, polluted, or deceived have legitimate reasons to resist new proposals. The mediator's role is not to overcome resistance but to understand it, validate what is legitimate, and create conditions in which parties can move when they are ready. Labeling resistance as irrational or obstructive will deepen the impasse, not resolve it.

13.3 Strategies to Break Impasse

Once the mediator has diagnosed the likely causes of the impasse, they can select appropriate intervention strategies. The following techniques constitute a comprehensive toolkit for breaking out of a deadlock. Skilled mediators often combine multiple strategies and adapt their approach based on how parties respond.

The following framework organizes the most effective impasse-breaking strategies by situation type, helping you choose the right intervention when dialogue stalls.

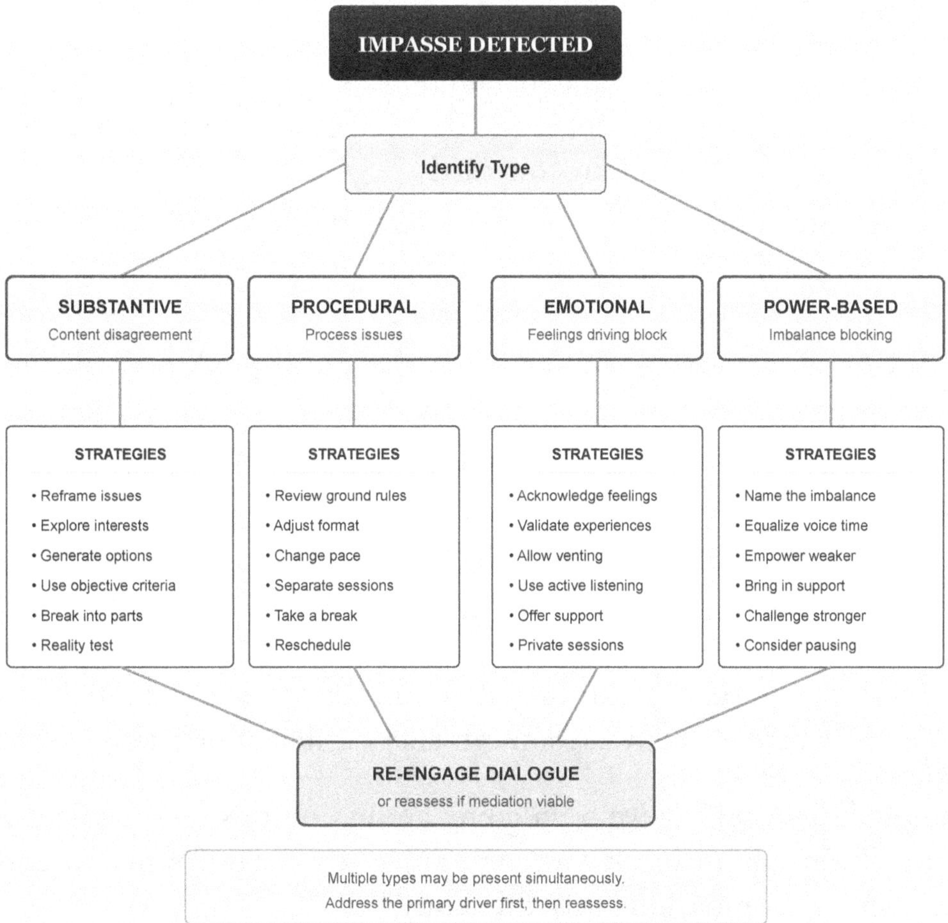

Figure 47: A toolkit of strategies for breaking through deadlocks when negotiations stall, including reframing, incremental steps, and creative problem-solving.

Impasses are often less about intractable positions and more about communication breakdown or inability to imagine alternatives, which is why these strategies focus on shifting the process and perspective rather than pressuring parties.

Take a Break

What it involves: Calling for a pause in the formal session. This break can range from fifteen minutes to several days, depending on the situation.

Why it works: Breaks serve multiple functions:

- **Emotional cooling:** Heated emotions subside when people step away from direct confrontation. The biological stress response calms, allowing rational thinking to return.
- **Reflection time:** Parties can reconsider positions without the pressure of immediate response. Ideas that seemed unacceptable in the moment may look different after reflection.
- **Informal conversation:** Some of the most productive dialogue happens during breaks. Without the formality of the session, people sometimes connect on a human level or share information they wouldn't state officially.
- **Consultation opportunity:** Negotiators can contact principals, advisors, or constituents to get guidance or authorization for new approaches.
- **Fresh perspective:** Returning after a break provides a natural "reset point" where the conversation can take a different direction.

Sample language: "We've been going around on this for a while. Let's take a fifteen-minute break. Get some air, have some tea. When we come back, let's try approaching this differently."

Timing considerations: Call breaks before the impasse hardens completely. If voices are rising or positions are becoming more rigid, intervene early. A well-timed break prevents escalation. A delayed break may allow damage that takes much longer to repair.

> **Practical Tip: Controlled Timeout**
> When calling a break during an impasse, be specific about the return to negotiation: "Let's take thirty minutes. During this time, I'll speak briefly with each party. When we return, I'd like us to try a different approach." Open-ended breaks can allow the impasse to harden. Structured breaks maintain engagement.

Caucus with Each Side

What it involves: Private meetings between the mediator and each party separately, away from the joint session.

Why it works: Caucuses create space for confidential exploration:Process interventions such as caucusing and shuttle mediation, well-established in mediation practice (Moore, 2014), allow mediators to explore each party's underlying concerns privately before reconvening joint sessions.

- **Hidden flexibility:** Parties often have more room to move than they'll admit in front of the other side. In private, they may reveal: "Well, we could probably accept X if they would give us Y."
- **Underlying concerns:** The real barriers to agreement may be things parties won't say publicly. In caucus, explore fear of appearing weak, internal disagreements, or concerns about precedent openly.
- **Idea generation:** Parties may have creative solutions they're hesitant to propose. The mediator can help develop and refine ideas before they're offered formally.
- **Reality testing:** The mediator can challenge unrealistic positions more directly in private than in the joint session.
- **Emotional venting:** Sometimes parties need to express frustration or anger in a safe space before they can return to productive dialogue.

Sample language (in caucus): "Help me understand what's really driving your position on this. Between us, what would you actually need to see to move forward? What's your biggest fear about compromising here?"

> **Practical Tip: Caucus Confidentiality**
>
> Before beginning caucuses, clarify with each party what information can be shared with the other side. Ask explicitly: "Is there anything you've told me that you want me to keep confidential?" and "Is there anything you'd like me to convey to the other party?" This maintains trust while allowing information to flow where appropriate.

Reframe the Issue

What it involves: Shifting the focus from fixed positions back to underlying interests, or presenting the problem in a new way that opens different solution paths.

Why it works: Impasses often occur when parties become locked into specific positions ("fifty jobs" vs. "twenty jobs"). Reframing helps them remember why they want those positions and consider whether other approaches might satisfy the same underlying needs. It's the difference between arguing over orange slices and discovering that one party wants the juice while the other wants the peel.The shift from positional bargaining to interest-based negotiation (Fisher and Ury, 1981) remains the most consistently effective approach to breaking impasses rooted in competing demands.

Sample language: "Let's step back from the specific numbers. Community, what will employment allow your people to achieve? Company, what's your main concern about hiring commitments? Maybe there's a way to address both."

Application example: In the Alpha Mining Co. negotiations, instead of "fifty jobs vs. twenty jobs," reframing (as discussed in Chapter 4 on communication skills) might reveal that the community's underlying interest is economic security and opportunity for local families, while the company's concern is skill availability and financial feasibility. This opens possibilities like training programs, contractor preferences for local businesses, or phased hiring with guarantees, none of which were visible when the parties were focused on specific numbers.

Change the Focus

What it involves: When stuck on one issue, setting it aside temporarily and working on something else.

Why it works:

- **Momentum building:** Success on easier issues creates positive energy and demonstrates that agreement is possible.

- **Relationship strengthening:** Working together on any issue builds collaborative habits and interpersonal connections.
- **Context clarification:** Sometimes, stuck issues become clearer once other elements are resolved. The hard issue may look different in light of the overall package.
- **Investment creation:** After investing time and achieving partial agreement, parties become more motivated to resolve remaining issues rather than lose what they've gained.

Sample language: "We're stuck on compensation. Let's set that aside for now and discuss the employment commitments. Sometimes making progress elsewhere helps us see the bigger picture."

Introduce Hypotheticals

What it involves: Exploring "what-if" scenarios that allow parties to consider options without committing to them.

Why it works: Hypotheticals reduce the risk of proposal. Parties can react to ideas without the other side claiming they've "agreed" to something. This creates psychological safety for exploration. Ideas that would be rejected as formal proposals can be considered when framed hypothetically.

Sample language: "Just hypothetically, if the company were to offer X amount spread over three years instead of a lump sum, how would that work for the community? I'm not saying anyone's proposing this; I'm just curious what you'd think."

Application example: In the landowner-mining company negotiation, the mediator might ask: "Hypothetically, what if the lease renewal included both a rent increase and a scholarship fund? Not as separate negotiations, but as a package? Would that change how either of you thinks about the overall value?"

Use a Mediator's Proposal

What it involves: When truly deadlocked, the mediator suggests a specific compromise as their own idea.

Why it works:

- **Neutral attribution:** Neither party has to "own" the proposal, reducing face-saving concerns.
- **External legitimacy:** A proposal from the mediator may carry weight as a professional judgment about what's reasonable.
- **Concrete focus:** A specific proposal gives parties something concrete to react to, which can be more productive than abstract discussion.
- **Starting point:** Even if rejected, the proposal provides a baseline for further negotiation.

Sample language: "Based on everything I've heard, let me suggest a possibility for you both to consider. This is my idea, not either of yours. What if we structured it this way . . . ?"

> **Caution: Mediator Proposal Risks**
>
> Use mediator proposals sparingly. If the proposal is rejected, it may compromise the mediator's perceived neutrality. If it's too close to one party's position, the other may feel the mediator has taken sides. Reserve this technique for true deadlocks after other approaches have failed.

Reality-Test Alternatives (BATNA Analysis)

What it involves: Helping parties honestly assess what happens if they don't reach an agreement by examining their BATNA and WATNA.

Why it works: Parties in impasse sometimes overestimate their alternatives. They imagine winning in court, gaining through protest, or finding better partners. Reality testing brings them back to earth. When both sides realize their alternatives are costly and uncertain, compromise becomes more attractive.

Sample language (in caucus): "If we don't reach an agreement, what will you do? How long will that take? What will it cost? What's the risk it doesn't work out? Sometimes looking honestly at alternatives helps clarify whether the deal on the table is worth taking."

Application example: The community's BATNA might be continued protests, media campaigns, and potential litigation. But reality testing reveals that protests are exhausting and risk alienating moderate community members, media attention is unpredictable, and litigation is expensive and takes years. The company's BATNA might be proceeding despite opposition, but this risks operational disruption, reputational damage, and regulatory scrutiny. Both alternatives look less attractive upon honest examination.

> **Key Concept: BATNA Reality Testing**
>
> BATNA reality testing is not a threat. It is helping parties make informed decisions. The mediator's tone should be curious and supportive, not adversarial. The goal is to help parties see clearly, not to pressure them into agreement. A party who understands their alternatives and still chooses to walk away has made an informed decision.

Break the Issue Apart

What it involves: Taking a single contentious issue and disaggregating it into parts.

Why it works: A considerable disagreement may contain within it several smaller questions. Parties might agree on some components while disagreeing on others. Partial agreement reduces the scope of the remaining dispute and creates momentum.

Application example: "Compensation" might be broken into: amount, form (cash vs. in-kind), timing (lump sum vs. installments), eligibility criteria (who qualifies), and administration (who manages distribution). Perhaps parties can agree on form, timing, and administration even while disagreeing on the amount. Those agreements narrow the dispute and provide a framework for the remaining negotiation.

Sample language: "Let's break this down. On compensation, there are several questions: how much, what form, when, and who decides. Can we start by agreeing on the form? Would direct payments or community projects be preferable? Let's see where we agree before tackling the harder questions."

Practical Tip: The Adjacent Possible

When parties cannot agree on the main issue, explore adjacent possibilities. "We cannot agree on the compensation amount, but can we agree on the process for determining fair compensation?" Moving forward on something, anything, maintains momentum and may unlock the core issue.

Bring in New Perspectives

What it involves: Introducing new voices or information that can shift the dynamics.

Options include:

- **Technical experts:** An independent environmental scientist, economist, or engineer can provide neutral data that resolves factual disputes.
- **Senior leaders:** Decision-makers with more authority may have flexibility that front-line negotiators lack.
- **Respected third parties:** A community elder, religious leader, or former official trusted by both sides may carry moral authority that helps unlock the impasse.
- **Site visits:** Seeing issues firsthand, whether environmental damage, community conditions, or operational constraints, can shift perspectives in ways that words cannot.

Application example: In the Beta Mining Co. negotiations, an impasse over environmental impact might be broken by jointly commissioning an independent Environmental Impact Assessment (EIA). With both parties involved in selecting the assessor and agreeing on the methodology, the results carry legitimacy that neither party's own data would.

Address Emotional Needs

What it involves: Explicitly acknowledging the emotional dimensions of the conflict and creating space for them to be addressed.

Why it works: Many impasses are maintained by unmet emotional needs rather than substantive disagreements. Parties may be holding out for acknowledgment, an apology, or simply the feeling of being heard. Addressing these needs can unlock the flexibility that emotional barriers have blocked.

Sample language: "I sense that beyond the practical issues, there's something else going on. Community, do you feel the company truly understands the impact of what happened? Sometimes acknowledgment matters as much as the remedy itself."

Application example: In the Alpha Mining Co. case, the community's insistence on "immediate" action may be driven less by timing than by the need to feel that their concerns are taken seriously. If the company can demonstrate genuine understanding and commitment, even if with a reasonable timeline, the urgency may diminish. The mediator might facilitate a moment where the company representative says, "I hear that you've been waiting for years and feel let down. That's understandable. We want to do better, and we want you to be confident that we mean it."

13.4 When Impasse Persists

Despite best efforts, sometimes an impasse does not resolve immediately. This doesn't necessarily mean failure. Skilled mediators have strategies for managing persistent deadlocks while keeping the door open for eventual resolution.

Adjourn with Purpose

What it involves: Ending the session in a structured way that maintains momentum and sets up a productive return.

Key elements:

- **Clear next steps:** Assign "homework" for each party. This might be gathering specific information, consulting with constituents, or developing proposals on particular issues.
- **Scheduled return:** Set a specific date and time to reconvene. Open-ended adjournment often allows mediation to die.

- **Maintained communication:** Establish how parties will stay in touch between sessions. This might include mediator check-ins with each side.
- **Positive framing:** End on a note that acknowledges the difficulties while expressing confidence that resolution is possible.

Sample language: "We've made progress today, even if we haven't resolved everything. I'd like to suggest we adjourn for two weeks. In that time, community, could you consult with your members about priorities? Company, could you explore what additional resources might be available? We'll meet again on the 15th with fresh perspectives. I'll check in with each of you next week to see how preparation is going."

Partial Agreements

What it involves: Documenting and potentially implementing agreed items even when some issues remain unresolved.

Why it works:

- **Preserves progress:** Agreements reached should not be lost just because other issues remain contentious.
- **Builds trust:** Implementing partial agreements demonstrates good faith and begins rebuilding trust.
- **Creates investment:** Once parties have implemented some agreements, they become more motivated to resolve remaining issues.
- **Reduces scope:** Taking resolved issues off the table narrows the dispute and makes the remaining issues more manageable.

Sample language: "We haven't resolved everything, but we've made real progress on three of five issues. Let's document those agreements. On the remaining two, let's agree to meet again in two weeks after you've each had time to think and consult."

Application example: In the case discussed in Chapter 17, the parties reached multiple interim agreements over several years before achieving a final settlement, with each interim agreement building trust and demonstrating that cooperation was possible.

Know When to Step Back

What it involves: Recognizing when mediation is not the right tool at this moment and being willing to pause the process.

Signs that stepping back may be appropriate:

- **Bad faith negotiation:** One party is clearly not negotiating genuinely, using mediation to delay or gather information rather than to resolve.
- **Severe power imbalance:** The imbalance is so great that meaningful negotiation is impossible. The weaker party may need to build leverage through other means before mediation can work.
- **External factors:** Outside circumstances need to change before resolution is possible. A pending election, regulatory decision, or market shift may be determinative.
- **Need to experience alternatives:** Sometimes parties need to try their BATNA and experience its costs before they're truly ready to settle.

How to step back constructively: Even when pausing mediation, the mediator can leave the door open: "It seems like the conditions for successful mediation aren't quite right at this moment. I'd like to suggest we pause for now, but I'm available if circumstances change and you'd like to try again. What I've learned about both of your perspectives may still be helpful when the time is right."

13.5 Rebuilding Cooperation After an Impasse

After breaking through an impasse, the atmosphere may be fragile. Parties have been in conflict mode, and the habits of adversarial interaction don't disappear immediately. The mediator must actively work to rebuild cooperative momentum and solidify the breakthrough.

Acknowledge the Breakthrough

Parties need to recognize that something significant has happened. They have demonstrated flexibility and problem-solving skills. This is evidence that cooperation is possible and should be explicitly noted.

Sample language: "That was difficult, and you both showed real flexibility. Thank you for hanging in there. What just happened shows you can work through tough issues together."

Impact: Acknowledgment reinforces the behavior you want to see more of. It also helps parties reframe their self-image from adversaries to collaborators who can solve problems together.

Solidify Progress Immediately

Verbal agreements can evaporate. What seems agreed in the moment may be remembered differently later, especially if parties return to constituents who weren't in the room. Documentation prevents backsliding.

> **Caution: Post-Impasse Fragility**
>
> After breaking through the impasse, the agreement is fragile. Parties may experience buyer's remorse, face constituent criticism, or encounter implementation challenges. Maintain close contact in the period immediately following the breakthrough. Address early problems before they destroy the agreement.

Actions to take:

- Write down what was agreed before anything changes.
- Get explicit verbal confirmation from both sides: "So we're agreed on X, correct?"
- Celebrate the progress, even if work remains.
- If appropriate, have parties initial the written agreement on that specific point.

Reflect on Success

Understanding what made the breakthrough possible helps parties replicate that success. It also reinforces the skills and attitudes that enabled resolution.

Sample language: "What helped us get past that impasse? Understanding that can help if we hit another hard spot."

Typical insights: Parties often identify things like: "We really listened to each other," "We focused on what we both needed rather than our positions," or "The company acknowledged how we felt." These insights become resources for future difficulties.

> **Practical Tip: Celebrating Progress**
> After impasse resolution, explicitly acknowledge the achievement: "You faced a very difficult moment and found a way through. That took courage from both sides." Celebration reinforces cooperative behavior and builds confidence for facing future challenges.

Build on Momentum

Positive energy from resolving a tough issue should be channeled into continued progress. The collaborative mindset that emerged during the breakthrough can carry forward.

How to build momentum:

- Move to another issue while energy is positive.
- Reference the breakthrough when approaching new challenges: "We solved that tough one; we can solve this too."
- Reinforce collaborative identity: "You've shown you can work together effectively."
- Use inclusive language: "*our* progress," "what *we've* accomplished," "*our* agreement."

13.6 Preventing Future Impasses

The best approach to impasse is prevention. Well-designed agreements include mechanisms that reduce the likelihood of future deadlocks by ensuring ongoing communication, early warning systems, and clear dispute-resolution procedures.

Elements to Build into Agreements

Regular communication channels: Scheduled meetings (such as monthly or quarterly) that keep parties in dialogue even when no crisis exists. Regular contact prevents the buildup of grievances and maintains the relationship.

Early warning systems: Designated contacts on each side who can raise concerns before they escalate. A commitment to flag potential issues early, with a norm that raising concerns is welcome rather than threatening.

Agreed dispute resolution procedures: A straightforward process for addressing disagreements: first direct discussion, then escalation to senior leaders, then return to mediation if needed. Knowing the pathway reduces anxiety and prevents escalation.

Periodic review meetings: Scheduled sessions specifically to review implementation, address emerging issues, and adjust agreements if circumstances have changed. This builds in adaptability.

Designated contacts for quick consultation: Named individuals on each side with authority to address day-to-day issues quickly, without requiring a full formal process.

> **Practical Tip: Sample Agreement Language**
>
> Include in your agreement: "If any dispute arises regarding implementation, the parties agree to first attempt to resolve it through direct discussion between the designated contacts. If unresolved within thirty days, either party may request mediation. The parties agree to participate in good faith in any such mediation before pursuing other remedies." This ensures future problems have a pathway to resolution.

Gender Dimensions of Impasse

Impasses often have gendered roots that go unrecognized. When a community delegation reaches deadlock with a company over compensation, the visible issue may be the monetary figure, but the underlying barrier may be that the compensation framework fails to address losses that women experience disproportionately: disrupted water sources, destroyed agricultural plots, fractured social networks.

If these losses are not on the table, the community may resist settlement without being able to articulate why, because the members most affected (often women) were not involved in defining priorities. The mediator who encounters an impasse that seems irrational or disproportionate to the stated issues should consider whether unrepresented voices hold the key to resolution.

Similarly, gendered communication norms can create impasses. In some cultural contexts, women may signal disagreement indirectly, through silence, withdrawal, or deference to male speakers, rather than through open opposition.

A mediator who reads only the explicit statements at the table may miss the fact that half the community has not consented. When an agreement that appeared settled unravels during implementation, the explanation often lies in voices that were present but unheard.

Building gender-sensitive communication practices into the process, including separate consultations, inclusive delegation structures, and explicit invitations for diverse perspectives, reduces the risk of impasses rooted in exclusion rather than genuine substantive disagreement.

13.7 Case Examples: Impasse Navigation in Practice

The following theoretical examples illustrate how the principles and techniques discussed in this chapter play out in real mediation scenarios.

Case Example 1: Employment Impasse (Fictional Scenario)

Situation: Maria and Luisa (community) demanded fifty local hires within six months. Alex and Janis (company) offered twenty with gradual increases. Discussions had become circular.

Diagnosis: Multiple factors were at play: trust deficit (past broken promises), emotional barriers (community feeling disrespected), and possible miscommunication about what "phased approach" meant.

Intervention sequence:

1. **Break:** Mediator called a break when voices began rising.
2. **Caucus with community:** Revealed that fifty was less important than "genuine commitment" and "accountability."
3. **Caucus with company:** Revealed willingness to go to thirty if the community would accept a training program for additional workers.
4. **Reframing:** In a joint session, discussions shifted from "numbers" to "economic security for families."
5. **Mediator proposal:** Suggested thirty immediate hires, a guaranteed training program, plus quarterly reporting to the community on progress.
6. **Addressing emotional needs:** Facilitated company acknowledgment of past shortfalls and commitment to do better.

Outcome: Agreement reached on thirty hires within six months, training program for additional community members, and quarterly progress reports to the community council.

Case Example 2: Environmental Assessment Impasse (Fictional Scenario)

Situation: Blair and Ali (community) demanded an independent Environmental Impact Assessment (EIA). Jordan and Patty (company) proposed an EIA with internal oversight. Discussions stalled over who would control the assessment process.

Diagnosis: The core issue was trust and control. The community didn't believe a company-controlled assessment would be honest. The company worried about costs and delays from a fully independent process.

Intervention:

The mediator broke the issue apart: "Let's separate the questions. Who selects the assessor? Who reviews methodology? Who receives results? How are concerns addressed?"

This revealed that the community's core concern was not controlling the entire process but ensuring they had input into the methodology and direct access to the results. The company's concern was not avoiding independence but managing costs and timeline.

Outcome: Agreement on independent EIA with community representatives involved in assessor selection and methodology review, as well as regular public updates on monitoring. The company retained budget management, but with agreed cost parameters.

Case Example 3: Lease Renewal (Fictional Scenario)

Situation: Sascha Martinez (landowner) wanted either a sale at 250,000 $ or a lease renewal at 2,500 $ per month. Mark Thompson (company) could justify only 1,750 $ per month or a market-value purchase at 200,000 $. The gap seemed unbridgeable.

Diagnosis: Sascha's underlying interest was funding his son Mateo's education. Mark's constraint was institutional approval for above-market costs. Both were stuck on specific numbers without exploring alternatives.

Intervention:

The mediator used a hypothetical: "What if the lease renewal included the company's Future Leaders scholarship program for Mateo? The scholarship has educational value separate from the rent amount."

Reality testing in caucus with Sascha: "The developer's offer is attractive but uncertain, since he's still seeking investors. The company can provide guaranteed income now."

Reality testing with Mark: "If Sascha sells to the developer, you'll need the alternate site at 250,000 $ additional annual cost. A creative package might be cheaper."

Outcome: The lease was renewed at 1,850 $ per month (within Mark's justifiable range), plus a scholarship nomination for Mateo (addressing Sascha's core interest), plus an option clause giving the company the first right of refusal if Sascha later decides to sell.

Cross-Cultural Considerations in Impasse Navigation

The impasse-breaking strategies outlined in this chapter are not culturally neutral. What constitutes an effective intervention in one cultural context may be ineffective or even counterproductive in another. Mediators working across cultural boundaries, as is common in extractive-industry disputes involving multinational companies and Indigenous or traditional communities, must adapt their approach to local norms around communication, authority, and conflict resolution.

Consider how cultural context shapes each element of impasse navigation. What counts as "trust" varies: in some communities, trust is built through personal relationships cultivated over months, not through contractual assurances offered in a single session. What constitutes an appropriate "acknowledgment" differs: a formal corporate apology may satisfy one community while another requires a ceremonial act witnessed by elders. The concept of "saving face" governs impasse dynamics in many Asian and Middle Eastern contexts, where direct confrontation of a party's position can harden resistance rather than open pathways to compromise. In many African contexts, impasse resolution may require engaging community elders or traditional leaders whose authority operates outside the formal mediation structure but whose endorsement is essential for any agreement to hold.

Practical implications follow from these observations. The caucus technique, while standard in Western mediation practice, may be viewed with suspicion in cultures that value collective transparency. Reality testing, which relies on direct questioning of a party's position, can feel disrespectful in high-context cultures where indirect communication is the norm. Even the mediator's proposal, discussed in Section 13.3, requires cultural calibration: in some settings, a mediator who offers a concrete proposal gains credibility as an engaged facilitator, while in others, the same action may be perceived as overstepping or imposing an outside solution. Mediators should invest time before and during the process to understand the cultural norms that will shape how impasse-breaking strategies are received, and should be prepared to adapt their toolkit accordingly (see also Chapter 10 for broader guidance on culturally sensitive mediation practice).

13.8 Conclusion

Impasses are not failures. They are challenging turning points that test both the parties and the mediator. With patience, creativity, and tactical intervention, most impasses can be transformed from roadblocks into stepping stones.

Successfully navigating an impasse together can actually strengthen the parties' relationship and confidence in each other. Like a team that has overcome a crisis, parties who have worked through a deadlock often emerge with improved mutual respect and greater trust in each other's good faith.

The mediator's role during impasse is to remain calm, diagnostic, and creative. When emotions run high, a steady presence matters more than clever technique. When options seem exhausted, fresh perspectives can reopen the path to agreement.

Key Takeaway

Every impasse contains the seeds of a breakthrough. The intensity that creates deadlock often reflects how much the issues matter to both parties, and that intensity, properly channeled, becomes the energy that drives resolution. The mediator's task is not to eliminate the difficulty but to transform it into motivation for finding solutions that work for everyone.

14. RESISTANCE SCENARIOS

Chapter 13 examined impasse, a situation in which both parties genuinely seek resolution but cannot bridge the gap between their positions. This chapter addresses a fundamentally different challenge: active resistance. An impasse reflects a failure of imagination or compromise, while resistance reflects a failure of willingness. Parties may obstruct the process, attempt to intimidate opponents, breach confidentiality, or reverse commitments already made. These situations test the mediator's ability to maintain process integrity when parties or circumstances threaten derailment. They also demand a different toolkit from the one used to navigate impasse.

Recognize resistance early. The strategies that resolve impasses, such as reframing, brainstorming options, and reality testing, are largely ineffective against a party that does not want resolution at all. Resistance manifests as silence, intimidation, external interference, or bad faith. These situations require mediators to make difficult judgment calls about whether to continue, suspend, or terminate mediation, often with incomplete information and under significant pressure.

This chapter provides practical guidance for navigating seven common resistance scenarios. For each, we examine the dynamics at play, present realistic response options with their trade-offs, and offer concrete tools mediators can use. The guidance here acknowledges that not every situation can be salvaged and that, at times, the ethical response is to recognize when mediation is no longer viable (as discussed in Chapter 8).

14.1 Silent Participation: When a Party Refuses to Speak

One of the most frustrating resistance scenarios occurs when a party physically attends mediation but refuses to engage verbally. Passive resistance manifests in multiple ways: complete silence, monosyllabic responses, deference to others who then also remain silent, or repetitive statements that add nothing new. Silent participation creates uncertainty about the party's intentions, placing the mediator in a difficult position.

Absence would be unambiguous, but this is not. In extractive-industry disputes, silence often reflects deep distrust rooted in years of broken promises about employment, environmental remediation, or benefit-sharing, making silence as much a statement about history as it is about the current process.

Research on communication in high-stakes conflicts (Stone, Patton, and Heen, 1999) demonstrates that silence often reflects not defiance but vulnerability and fear of consequences, particularly when power imbalances make honest expression feel dangerous.

Understanding the Dynamics

Silent participation typically stems from one of several underlying causes, each requiring a different response. Identify the correct cause before choosing an intervention.

When a party responds only in monosyllables, the mediator can use open-ended prompts that invite narrative rather than yes-or-no answers. Consider this exchange:

Mediator: *"I'd like to understand how the water situation has affected daily life in your village. Can you walk me through what a typical day looks like now compared to before the project began?"*

Community member: *"It's different."*

Mediator: *"Different in what way? I'm trying to picture what your mornings look like, where the water comes from now, how far people walk. Take your time."*

This kind of patient, specific questioning sometimes unlocks participation by signalling genuine interest rather than procedural obligation. If it does not, consider moving to a caucus, where one-on-one conversation may feel less exposed.

Strategic silence occurs when a party deliberately withholds engagement to signal displeasure, exert pressure, or wait for the other side to make concessions first. This is common when one party believes they hold leverage and that time is on their side. A company facing community protests might attend mediation to appear cooperative while waiting for legal proceedings to resolve in their favor.

By contrast, fear-based silence emerges when participants feel unsafe speaking openly. Community members may fear retaliation from powerful company interests. They may have experienced negative consequences from previous attempts to voice concerns. In trauma-affected communities, silence can be a protective response, particularly if past experiences taught them that speaking up leads to harm.

Cultural silence reflects communication norms in which direct confrontation or speaking before elders is inappropriate. In hierarchical cultures, junior members of a delegation may remain silent until explicitly invited to speak by their superiors. Similarly, indirect communication styles may mean that silence itself is communicating something significant.

Finally, confusion-based silence occurs when participants do not understand the process, the issues being discussed, or what is expected of them. Technical jargon, unfamiliar procedures, or language barriers can all contribute to withdrawal rather than engagement.

Key Concept: Reading Silence

Silence is, in itself, a form of communication. The mediator's task is to interpret what it communicates in context. Body language, eye contact, physical positioning, and responses to direct questions all provide clues. A participant who makes eye contact, nods occasionally, and leans forward is communicating differently than one who crosses their arms, looks away, and physically withdraws.

Response Options and Their Trade-offs

Option 1: Direct acknowledgment in joint session. Naming the silence directly but non-accusatorially can open the door: "I notice that we haven't heard from several members of your delegation today. Before we continue, I want to make sure everyone feels able to participate." This approach signals that the mediator is paying attention and creates space for explanation. However, it risks putting the silent party on the spot, which may intensify their withdrawal if fear or cultural factors underlie their silence.

Option 2: Request a caucus. A private session with the silent party's delegation offers opportunity for exploration. In caucus, this allows the mediator to understand what is happening without the other party present: "I wanted to check in with you privately. Is there something about today's session that is making participation difficult?" This approach provides safety for disclosure but takes time and may frustrate the engaged party, who might view it as accommodating obstruction.

Option 3: Process adjustment. Modifying the format can reduce barriers to participation. Such adjustments might include using written submissions, smaller breakout groups, or allowing the silent party to designate a spokesperson. For cultural silence, explicit invitations to specific individuals or permission to hear different voices may help. This approach addresses practical barriers but may not overcome strategic or fear-based silence.

Option 4: Recess and reality test. A longer break allows both parties to consult internally. During such recesses, it may help to separately remind the silent party of the consequences of non-engagement: "Without your active participation, the mediation cannot produce an outcome that reflects your interests. The other party may conclude that you are not genuinely committed to this process." This approach creates accountability but risks being perceived as pressure.

Option 5: Proceed with documentation. If silence persists despite interventions, one option is to continue with whatever participation is offered, carefully documenting the silent party's non-engagement. At the session's end, the record would reflect that one party did not substantively participate. This protects the record but does not resolve the underlying issue and may produce an agreement that lacks genuine buy-in.

Sample Mediator Dialogue

Mediator: *"I appreciate everyone being here today. Before we dive into the agenda, I want to take a moment to acknowledge something: Effective mediation depends on hearing from everyone. I've noticed that several of you haven't had the opportunity to share your perspectives yet. I want to make sure this space feels safe for open dialogue."*

and

Mediator: *"Let me suggest we take a short break. During this time, I'd like to speak with each delegation separately to ensure we're all prepared to engage productively. This isn't about pointing fingers. It's about making sure this process works for everyone."*

Practical Tip: The Private Check-In

Before attributing silence to bad faith, always conduct a private check-in. Ask open questions: "How are you experiencing this process?" "Is there something that would make participation easier?" "What would you need to feel comfortable sharing your perspective?" These questions often reveal practical issues, such as language barriers, cultural protocols, or legitimate safety concerns, that can be addressed. Transformative mediation theory (Bush and Folger, 2005) frames resistance not as obstruction but as an opportunity for recognition and empowerment, where mediators support parties in finding their own voice rather than pressuring them toward agreement.

When Silence Indicates Fundamental Problems

Sometimes silence signals that mediation is not appropriate or that prerequisites for productive dialogue are missing. If a party's silence stems from genuine fear of retaliation, the mediator must determine whether safety guarantees can be credibly established before continuing. If silence reflects strategic delay, the mediator must assess whether the party is engaging in bad faith and whether continuing serves any purpose.

The decision to suspend or terminate mediation due to non-participation warrants careful consideration. However, proceeding with silent parties often yields agreements that will not be honored, or, worse, create a false impression that community consent was obtained when genuine dialogue never occurred.

> **Caution: The Risks of Proceeding**
>
> An agreement signed by parties who never genuinely engaged creates significant risks. The community may later repudiate the agreement, claiming coercion or inadequate representation. The company may rely on a document with no actual buy-in. The mediator's credibility suffers if observers discover the process was one-sided. Sometimes the responsible choice is to suspend mediation until genuine participation is possible.

Silent participation is a form of passive resistance: the party is present but withholds engagement. The next scenario involves resistance that is overtly aggressive. When a party deploys armed security, occupies the venue with supporters, or uses physical displays of power, the dynamic shifts from withdrawal to confrontation, and the mediator's safety assessment becomes central to the facilitation strategy.

14.2 Intimidation Tactics: Armed Security and Power Displays

The mediator arrived at the mediation venue on a Tuesday morning, a rented community center near an active copper mining operation. As she pulled into the parking lot, she noticed two armed security personnel stationed near the entrance, identifying badges clipped to their vests. Inside, the community delegation sat rigidly in their chairs, eyes tracking the security officers' movements. When the mining company representative entered the room, accompanied by his own private security escort, the community members exchanged glances of visible unease. None of them had expected armed presence at a mediation session, and the mediator realized immediately that the event had fundamentally shifted. The community felt besieged in their own dispute, and no ground rule or facilitator statement could dispel the message that armed force backed one party's position.

Few situations threaten mediation's integrity more directly than when one party resorts to intimidation. The arrival of armed security personnel, whether uniformed guards, police escorts, or private security contractors, fundamentally alters the dynamics of voluntary participation. Even if no explicit threats are made, the presence of armed individuals communicates a message about power that can silence opposition and coerce compliance.

Recognizing Intimidation

Intimidation in mediation contexts takes various forms, some obvious and others subtle. Obvious intimidation includes bringing armed guards to the venue, having security personnel visibly present during sessions, or arriving with a large entourage designed to overwhelm the other party with numbers. Subtle intimidation might include choosing a venue associated with power, such as a company headquarters, arriving in official vehicles with government markings, or referring to authority figures who support one party's position.

The effect of intimidation is to undermine the voluntariness that defines legitimate mediation. When community members feel physically threatened or believe that refusing to agree will have consequences for their safety or that of their families, any resulting agreement is tainted. Moreover, the presence of security forces often triggers trauma responses in communities with histories of conflict, making meaningful dialogue impossible regardless of whether current threats are intended.

Key Concept: Asymmetric Power Display

Intimidation is inherently asymmetric. A company that brings security guards to a mediation venue is displaying resources that the community cannot match. This asymmetry communicates that one party operates under different rules and faces different consequences. Even if the company views security as routine or necessary, the community experiences it as a reminder of power imbalances that the mediation process is supposed to address.Cross-cultural conflict research (LeBaron, 2002) demonstrates that power asymmetries frequently manifest as behavioral resistance, and that mediators must address structural conditions rather than treating resistance as individual defiance.

Immediate Response Protocol

When a mediator arrives at a venue to find armed security present, or when security arrives with one of the parties, immediate action is required. Delaying action risks normalizing the intimidation and signals to the threatened party that the mediator will not protect the process.

Step 1: Do not begin the session. Opening formal proceedings while intimidation factors are present compromises the process from the start. Beginning the session implicitly accepts the conditions that undermine voluntariness.

Step 2: Speak privately with the party responsible. Request an immediate private meeting with the party that brought security. This conversation benefits from directness: "I need to discuss the presence of armed personnel before we can proceed."

Step 3: Explain the incompatibility. Articulate why armed presence is incompatible with voluntary mediation: "Mediation requires that all parties participate freely, without fear of consequences for what they say. Armed security presence, regardless of intent, creates conditions that undermine this fundamental requirement. We cannot proceed with mediation under these circumstances."

Step 4: Request removal or relocation. Require that security personnel leave the venue entirely or relocate to an invisible position. This must be an explicit requirement, not a suggestion: "For this mediation to proceed, security personnel need to be positioned entirely outside the venue, out of sight of participants."

Step 5: Check in with the affected party. After the intimidating presence has been addressed, a private conversation with the affected party helps assess their state. Even if security has been removed, the impact may linger: "I want to check in with you before we proceed. Are you comfortable continuing today, or would you prefer to reschedule?"

Sample Dialogue

Mediator: *"Before we begin, I need to address something directly. The presence of uniformed security at this venue is not compatible with the mediation process we agreed to undertake."*

Company Rep: *"They're just here for our protection. Standard procedure."*

Mediator: *"I understand your perspective, but mediation depends on all parties feeling safe to speak freely. Security presence, regardless of intent, fundamentally changes the dynamics. This is a neutral process in which power displays of any kind are inappropriate. I'm asking that security personnel wait at a location where they are not visible to any participants."*

Company Rep: *"What if we need them?"*

Mediator: *"If you have genuine safety concerns, let's discuss them now and find solutions that don't compromise the mediation. I can assure you that if any situation arises requiring security intervention, we will address it immediately. But having armed guards present during our discussions is something I cannot accept."*

If the Party Refuses to Comply

Some parties may refuse to remove security, citing genuine or pretextual safety concerns. The mediator then faces a critical decision point. Several factors can inform this decision. Asking the following questions can help determine what action needs to be taken:

- **Is the party's claim about safety concerns credible?** If the venue or situation genuinely poses risks, alternative arrangements merit exploration.
- **Is this a pattern of behavior or a one-time occurrence?** First-time issues may reflect a misunderstanding; repeated intimidation reflects intent.

- **What is the effect on the other party?** If community representatives indicate they cannot participate under these conditions, their assessment carries significant weight.
- **Are there alternative arrangements that address all concerns?** Perhaps the mediation could be relocated to a different venue, held at a different time, or conducted with additional neutral observers present.

If no acceptable resolution can be found, suspending the session protects the integrity of the process. The mediator might state: "I'm not able to facilitate this mediation under current conditions. I'm suspending today's session and will be in contact with both parties about whether and how we might reschedule under appropriate conditions."

Caution: Documentation Is Essential

Any incident involving intimidation must be thoroughly documented. Record what occurred, when, who was involved, what was said, and how the situation was resolved or left unresolved. This documentation protects the mediator, informs any future proceedings, and provides evidence if the mediation is later challenged or if the intimidation pattern continues.

Preventing Intimidation Through Process Design

Prevention is preferable to response. Addressing potential intimidation issues during the pre-mediation phase proves more effective than responding after problems arise.

Ground rules that explicitly prohibit armed personnel, security escorts, and power displays at the mediation venue, while the venue selection should prioritize truly neutral locations that are not associated with either party.

Transportation arrangements that ensure parties arrive and depart safely without intimidating displays. Including acknowledgment in the mediation agreement that any party creating conditions of intimidation forfeits the right to continue.

> **Practical Tip: The Pre-Session Walkthrough**
>
> Arrive at the venue before the parties are scheduled to arrive. Walk through the space. Note who is present, what vehicles are in the area, and what the environment communicates. If you observe concerning conditions, address them before participants arrive. It is far easier to prevent intimidation than to address it after parties are already in the room.

Intimidation operates through visible displays of force. The next form of resistance is more insidious: interference by external actors who hold institutional power over one or both parties. When government officials intervene to steer outcomes, the mediator faces a challenge that no amount of room arrangement or ground-rule setting can resolve, because the pressure originates outside the mediation itself.

14.3 External Override: Government Interference with Community Consent

A particularly challenging resistance scenario occurs when government officials attempt to override or replace community consent in the mediation process. This can take various forms, including officials claiming to speak for the community, pressuring community representatives to accept specific terms, threatening consequences if mediation does not yield "acceptable" outcomes, or directly intervening in sessions to advance state or corporate interests aligned with government priorities.

Understanding Government Intervention Patterns

Government interference typically manifests in specific patterns, each requiring a different response. These include:

- **Direct substitution** occurs when government officials claim authority to consent on behalf of the community or designate "official" community representatives who serve government interests rather than community interests. This is particularly common when the disputed project has government backing or when officials have financial stakes in the outcome.

- **Pressure and threats** involve government actors communicating to community representatives that they must reach an agreement or face consequences. These consequences might include loss of services, withdrawal of permits or licenses, or even physical threats. Such pressure fundamentally compromises the voluntary nature of mediation.
- **Session interference** occurs when government officials attend mediation sessions and attempt to direct outcomes, making statements about what the government will or will not accept, or implying that certain positions are non-negotiable regardless of what the community wants.
- **Parallel processes** involve the government initiating separate proceedings that undermine or supersede the mediation, such as announcing that land will be expropriated regardless of mediation outcomes or that permits have been granted irrespective of community concerns.

Key Concept: The Legitimacy Question

When government officials claim authority over community consent, the mediator must carefully assess the legitimacy of their claims. Does the official genuinely represent community interests? Did the community select this representative, or was the representative imposed? Are there other community voices that contradict the official position? Answering these questions may require research beyond the mediation room.

Response Strategies

Strategy 1: Clarify roles at the outset. Before mediation begins, clearly establish who speaks for whom. If government officials wish to participate, their role must be defined. Are they observers? Advisors? Parties to the dispute? If they claim to represent community interests, what is the basis for this claim? Documentation of community selection processes helps establish legitimate representation.

Strategy 2: Create protected space for community voices. Ensure that community representatives have opportunities to speak without government officials present. This might involve structuring separate sessions, using caucuses, or explicitly establishing that government observers will not speak during community presentations. The goal is to determine what the community actually wants, independent of government pressure.

Strategy 3: Document any interference. If government actors make threats, apply pressure, or attempt to override community positions, document these interventions carefully. This documentation serves multiple purposes: it protects the mediator, provides evidence for potential challenges to the process, and creates accountability for inappropriate behavior.

Strategy 4: Invoke mediation principles explicitly. When government officials attempt to direct outcomes, clearly articulate mediation principles: "I want to be clear about how this process works. The parties to this mediation are the community and the company. Any agreement must reflect what these parties genuinely accept, free from external pressure. My role is to facilitate that dialogue, not to achieve any particular outcome."

Strategy 5: Consult with parties about continuation. If government interference is persistent and cannot be managed, consulting with both parties, particularly the community, about whether continuing serves their interests. An agreement reached under government coercion may not be honored and may expose the community to claims that they consented when they did not.

Sample Dialogue

Government Official: *"I've spoken with the village headman. The community is prepared to accept the company's offer. Let's finalize this today."*

Mediator: *"Thank you for that perspective. In this mediation, my role is to hear directly from the designated community representatives about their position. Community representatives, can you share your views on the proposal we've been discussing?"*

Government Official: *"I'm telling you what they think. This is the government's position."*

Mediator: *"I appreciate that you have a perspective on this matter. However, the mediation process requires that I hear directly from the parties themselves. This is fundamental to how mediation works. The community representatives are here to speak on behalf of their communities. If your role is advisory, I welcome you to share your advice with them in their internal discussions. But in this session, I need to hear from them directly."*

The Limits of Mediation Under State Pressure

When the mediator successfully creates space for community voices, the response can be revealing:

Community representative: *"We appreciate the official's interest, but we have not agreed to accept the offer. There are conditions that matter to us that have not been discussed yet."*

Mediator: *"Thank you for sharing that. This is exactly why we need to hear from you directly. Can you tell us which conditions are most important to your community?"*

This exchange illustrates a critical moment: by protecting the community's voice, the mediator may uncover substantive issues that government intervention was obscuring. The community representative's willingness to speak after the official has been redirected often signals that the mediation can proceed productively.

Mediators must honestly assess when government interference renders mediation ineffective or even harmful. If the government has predetermined the outcome, mediation may serve only to legitimize that predetermined result while creating the false appearance of community consent. In such cases, participating in the process may cause more harm than refusing to proceed.

Indicators that mediation may not be appropriate include government announcements of decisions regardless of mediation outcomes, credible reports of threats against community members who do not cooperate, absence of any realistic possibility that community preferences will influence the result, and government rejection of fundamental mediation principles such as voluntariness and self-determination.

Caution: Complicity Risks

A mediator who proceeds despite clear government coercion risks becoming complicit in that coercion. The resulting "agreement" may be used to demonstrate community consent that never genuinely existed. Mediators have an ethical obligation to protect the integrity of the process, which sometimes means acknowledging that the process cannot proceed under current conditions.

Compound Pressure: When Government and Company Interests Align

The most challenging variant of government interference occurs when government officials and company representatives share aligned interests, whether through formal partnerships, revenue-sharing arrangements, or political alliances. In these situations, the community faces pressure from two powerful institutions simultaneously, and the mediator may find that both the company and the government resist the process protections that communities need most.

When compound pressure is present, standard mediation tools such as invoking process principles or clarifying roles may be insufficient. Engaging international observation mechanisms, involving independent legal advisors for the community, or seeking support from international development institutions may become necessary. In extreme cases, publicly stating that the process cannot continue under current conditions may be required, understanding that this statement itself may carry political consequences.

The Mediator's Own Safety

In politically charged environments, the mediator's personal safety deserves frank assessment. Mediators who challenge government interference may face retaliation ranging from professional exclusion to physical threat. Before accepting a mandate involving known government sensitivity, mediators should evaluate their own exposure, establish communication protocols with trusted colleagues outside the jurisdiction, and maintain clear documentation of all interactions. No mediation outcome justifies placing the mediator in danger, and acknowledging this reality is not a sign of weakness but of professional maturity.

Practical Tip: Building External Documentation

When government interference is a concern, consider engaging external observers from credible independent organizations. Their presence and documentation can protect community voices and hold the government accountable for inappropriate behavior. Discuss this possibility with all parties during the process design.

Government interference targets the process from outside the room. The next scenario targets it from within: when a participant, advisor, or observer breaches confidentiality by disclosing session content to the media or other external audiences. Confidentiality breaches erode the safe space that mediation depends on, and they can transform a private negotiation into a public spectacle overnight.

14.4 Confidentiality Breaches: Media Leaks and Information Disclosure

The morning of the fourth mediation session, the community delegation arrived with copies of the local newspaper. A headline read "Mining Company Offers Water Monitoring Concessions, Sources Say." The article cited "sources close to the negotiations" and detailed positions that the company representative had disclosed in confidence during a private caucus. The community delegation's first reaction was fury. Someone in the mediation had betrayed their conversation. Their second reaction was to threaten withdrawal. "How can we say anything here," the community leader asked the mediator, "if the next morning it's in the newspaper?" The company representative denied responsibility, but trust had shattered. The mediator now faced not only a practical problem of identifying the leak but a deeper crisis: neither party believed the process was safe anymore.

Confidentiality is foundational to effective mediation. When parties fear public disclosure of their words, they become guarded, positional, and reluctant to explore creative solutions or acknowledge position weaknesses. Media leaks during mediation poison the atmosphere, destroy trust between parties, and make continued negotiation impossible. Yet leaks happen, sometimes deliberately and sometimes accidentally. Mediators must be prepared to respond.

Understanding Why Leaks Occur

Leaks serve various purposes, and understanding the motivation helps determine the appropriate response.

Strategic leaks occur when a party deliberately releases information to gain an advantage. A company might leak information to demonstrate reasonableness to shareholders or regulators. A community might leak to generate public pressure on the company. Either party might leak to preempt the other's narrative or to lock in a position publicly before it can be modified in negotiation.

Accidental disclosures happen when participants share information with those outside the mediation without intending for it to spread further. A community member might tell family members, who then speak to journalists. A company employee might mention mediation developments to colleagues whose conversations are overheard.

Third-party breaches involve individuals who are not direct participants but who have access to information. Support persons, translators, advisors, or even venue staff might be sources of leaks, whether intentionally or inadvertently.

External investigation can result in disclosure when journalists, activists, or other parties actively seek information about the mediation. Even without deliberate leaks, determined investigators may piece together information from public records, social media, or multiple casual conversations.

> **Key Concept: The Trust Cascade**
>
> A single leak can trigger a cascade of trust breakdown. The party that did not leak feels betrayed and questions whether the process is safe. They may become defensive or retaliatory. The party that leaked (or

is blamed for leaking) faces accusations and loses credibility. The mediator's ability to promise confidentiality is undermined. Each subsequent session operates under a cloud of suspicion.

Immediate Response to a Leak

Step 1: Acknowledge and assess. When information from mediation appears in the media or circulates publicly, address the breach promptly. Contact both parties immediately to assess its scope. Determine what information was disclosed, how it was disclosed, and, if possible, from what source.

Step 2: Suspend sessions if necessary. Depending on the severity of the breach and the parties' reactions, it may be necessary to temporarily suspend mediation. Continuing under an atmosphere of accusation and mistrust is often counterproductive.

Step 3: Address the breach directly. In a session or in separate communications with each party, address the breach openly. Avoid accusatory tone, but be clear about the impact: "Confidentiality sustains this process. The disclosure of information from our sessions has damaged trust. Before we can productively continue, we need to address what happened and how we prevent it from happening again."

Step 4: Hear from both parties. Allow each party to respond to the breach. The accused party may have an explanation or may deny responsibility. The affected party needs to express how the breach has impacted their confidence in the process. Listen carefully to both.

Step 5: Reinforce confidentiality commitments. Recommitting to confidentiality strengthens the foundation for continuing mediation. This might involve reviewing the confidentiality agreement, identifying how the breach occurred and implementing safeguards, or limiting who has access to information going forward. Explicitly stating commitment expectations: "If we're going to continue, I need clear commitments from everyone about confidentiality. What happened cannot be undone, but we can prevent it from happening again."

Sample Dialogue

Mediator: *"I need to address something directly before we continue. I'm aware that information from our previous session has appeared in a news article. I want to hear from both of you about this."*

Company Rep: *"We didn't leak anything. This is exactly what we were worried about when we agreed to mediation."*

Community Rep: *"We didn't leak either. Maybe it was someone from their side trying to make us look bad."*

Mediator: *"I understand emotions are running high. I'm not here to assign blame today. What I need to know is whether both parties remain committed to this process and to confidentiality going forward. If we continue, we need to rebuild trust and ensure this doesn't happen again. Let's discuss what each of you needs to feel confident that the process remains protected."*

Once both parties confirm their commitment to continue, the mediator can re-establish confidentiality ground rules with renewed specificity:

Mediator: *"I appreciate that commitment. Going forward, let me be specific about what confidentiality means in this process. Nothing said in these sessions will be shared with anyone outside this room, including staff, media, or advisors who are not present, unless all parties agree otherwise. If either of you has concerns about specific information, raise them here and we will address them together. Can we both agree to those terms?"*

Company representative: *"Agreed. But we need assurance that community advisors outside this room will also respect those terms."*

Mediator: *"That is a fair point. Let us discuss how each party will manage information within their own teams. It may be helpful to identify, by name, who on each side will be informed and what they will be told."*

When the Leaker Is Identified

If an investigation clearly identifies the source of the leak, the mediator faces additional decisions. Was the leak deliberate or accidental? Does the responsible party acknowledge their role and express a genuine commitment to confidentiality in the future? Is the non-leaking party willing to continue despite the breach?

In cases of deliberate strategic leaking, the mediator may need to consider whether the responsible party can continue in the process. A deliberate breach of a fundamental mediation agreement suggests bad faith and may undermine the entire process. The mediator might state: "Deliberate violation of our confidentiality agreement raises serious questions about whether this process can continue productively. I need both parties to help me understand whether there's a basis for continuing."

Practical Tip: Confidentiality Protocols

Prevent leaks through robust confidentiality protocols established during process design. Clearly identify who may be informed about mediation and what they may be told. Consider whether support persons, advisors, and others with access should each sign a separate confidentiality agreement. Remind participants at each session about confidentiality obligations. Create clear rules about what, if anything, can be communicated externally.

Managing Media Interest

In high-profile disputes, the media may actively seek information regardless of confidentiality commitments. Anticipating media interest and working with parties to manage it constructively proves valuable.

Mining disputes attract specialized media attention focused on environmental justice and human rights. International coverage of water contamination, indigenous land rights violations, or tailings dam failures can shift power dynamics overnight. Mediators should anticipate that in some extractive-industry contexts, media attention is the only enforcement mechanism for environmental compliance, which complicates any request to limit media engagement.

Have both parties agree on joint public statements, if any, that acknowledge mediation is occurring without disclosing the substance. It also helps to designate spokespersons for each party who understand confidentiality boundaries.

When needed, prepare responses to media inquiries that protect confidentiality without appearing secretive or defensive. You may also want to consider whether limited transparency, such as announcing that mediation has reached certain milestones, might reduce pressure for unauthorized disclosures.

> **Caution: The Digital Footprint**
> In the age of social media, participants may inadvertently disclose information through posts, photos, or check-ins that reveal mediation is occurring, who is participating, or even where sessions are being held. Remind participants that confidentiality extends to all forms of communication, including digital platforms. Even seemingly innocuous posts can be pieced together by determined observers.

Where a confidentiality breach damages trust gradually, a walkout damages it dramatically. When a party stands up and leaves mid-session, it creates an immediate crisis that forces the mediator to decide, in real time, whether to pursue, pause, or proceed without them. Unlike the impasse-driven adjournment discussed in Chapter 13, a resistance walkout is a statement, not a negotiating tactic, and it requires a distinct response.

14.5 The Walkout: Managing Mid-Session Departures

Few moments in mediation are as dramatic or potentially destructive as when a party walks out mid-session. Whether preceded by an angry outburst or executed in cold silence, a walkout represents a direct challenge to the process and forces the mediator to make rapid decisions with significant consequences. Mediators must prepare response strategies before walkouts occur. This differs from the structured adjournment discussed in Chapter 13, where both parties agree to pause and return. A resistance walkout is unilateral, often emotional, and carries an implicit message that the process has failed. In extractive-industry disputes, walkouts frequently coincide with external events such as a new environmental incident, a leaked internal company memo, or the arrival of NGO observers who shift the community's strategic calculus.

Experienced mediators learn to read the warning signs, the chair pushed back, the papers gathered, the whispered consultation within a delegation, and intervene before the departure becomes final:

Mediator: *"I can see this discussion has become very difficult. Before anyone makes a decision about continuing, I want to suggest a fifteen-minute break so everyone can regroup. Sometimes the most productive conversations happen after we step away for a moment."*

Community leader: *"We are not sure there is any point in continuing. They are not listening."*

Mediator: *"I hear your frustration, and I take it seriously. During the break, I would like to speak with each delegation separately. If after that conversation you still feel this process is not serving your interests, that is your right. But I would ask for fifteen minutes before making that decision."*

This pre-emptive intervention succeeds more often than post-walkout recovery. By naming what is happening without judgment and offering a face-saving pause, the mediator gives the party room to reconsider without appearing to capitulate.

Why Parties Walk Out

Emotional overload occurs when the intensity of the discussion exceeds a participant's capacity to remain engaged. Hearing details of how one's actions harmed others, or listening to what feels like unfair accusations, can trigger fight-or-flight responses. The walkout becomes an escape from unbearable emotional pressure.

Strategic positioning involves walkouts calculated to demonstrate seriousness, create pressure on the other party, or test how much the mediator and other party will concede to bring them back. These walkouts are often accompanied by stated conditions for return.

Constituent pressure occurs when a representative feels they cannot continue without losing credibility with their constituents. Community leaders may walk out to demonstrate to their communities that they are not "selling out." Company representatives may walk out when discussions venture into territory they are not authorized to explore.

Fundamental breakdown represents a genuine assessment that the process cannot succeed. When a party concludes that the other is negotiating in bad faith, that essential issues are being ignored, or that continuing wastes time better spent on alternatives, the walkout reflects genuine abandonment rather than tactical maneuvering.

> **Key Concept: The Meaning of the Walk**
>
> Assess quickly what a walkout means. Is this a temporary break that the party needs to collect themselves? A negotiating tactic expecting pursuit? A signal of genuine deal-breakers that must be addressed? Or final abandonment of the process? The appropriate response differs dramatically depending on this assessment.

Immediate Response Protocol

At the moment of departure: As a party begins to leave, acknowledging the departure calmly, without physically stopping anyone or escalating the emotional intensity. A simple statement such as "I see you're leaving. I'd like to continue this conversation when you're ready" communicates openness to continuation without desperation or judgment.

With the remaining party: Once one party has departed, the mediator must manage the remaining party's response. They may feel triumphant, victimized, anxious, or relieved. Acknowledging what happened without assigning blame helps the remaining party: "This is clearly a difficult moment. Before we decide how to proceed, let me check in with you. How are you feeling about this?"

Immediate assessment: Determining whether pursuing the departing party immediately is worthwhile. In cases of emotional overload, a short cooling-off period is usually beneficial before any contact. In strategic walkouts, immediate pursuit may reward the tactic and encourage additional walkouts. Allowing some time to pass often proves more effective than immediate pursuit.

Communication within hours: Contacting the departing party within a reasonable time, typically the same day or the next morning. Non-judgmental contact and focused on understanding: "I wanted to reach out after you left the session today. I'm interested in understanding your perspective on what happened and whether there's a path forward."

> **Sample Dialogue**
>
> ***Community Leader:*** *Stands up and says, "This is pointless. They're not serious about addressing our concerns. I'm done." They walk toward the door.*
>
> ***Mediator:*** *"I hear that you're frustrated and that something is not working for you in this process. If you need to step out, that's your choice. I hope we can continue this conversation, whether that's in a few minutes or at another time."*
>
> ***Community Leader:*** *Pauses at the door and says, "They've had three opportunities to address the water issue. They keep changing the subject."*
>
> ***Mediator:*** "The water issue is clearly central for you. Would you be willing to sit back down so we can focus specifically on that? I'll make sure we address it directly."

Preventing Recurrence

After addressing an immediate walkout, reflecting on what contributed to a walkout and implementing preventive measures for future sessions. Ask questions such as:

- Were warning signs visible before the walkout that could have prompted earlier intervention?
- Did the session structure fail to address an issue the departing party considered essential?
- Were power dynamics allowing one party to dominate in ways that provoked the other?
- Did the emotional intensity of the discussion escalate without appropriate breaks or intervention?
- Was the departing party adequately prepared for what they might hear in the session?

Based on this reflection, useful modifications for future sessions might include building in more frequent breaks, restructuring the agenda to address priority issues earlier, implementing stronger process interventions when discussions become unproductive, or having preliminary discussions about difficult topics before raising them in joint sessions.

Practical Tip: The Pre-Commitment Strategy

At the beginning of each session, ask parties to commit to remaining for the full scheduled time and, if they need to leave, to first request a break or caucus rather than departing unilaterally. This pre-commitment creates a psychological barrier to impulsive walkouts and establishes an expectation that difficulties will be addressed within the process rather than by abandoning it.

Even with pre-commitment strategies in place, walkouts may still occur. The matrix below provides a quick reference for identifying patterns and responding in the moment.

TYPE	SIGNS	IMMEDIATE RESPONSE	RE-ENTRY LANGUAGE
EMOTIONAL OVERWHELM	Crying, shaking, sudden silence before leaving	Give space. Check on welfare after a few minutes. Do not pressure to return.	*"Take all the time you need. When you're ready, we can continue or reschedule."*
TACTICAL / STRATEGIC	Calm exit, announcement, ultimatum delivered	Note the stated reason. Do not chase. Work with remaining party briefly.	*"The door remains open. If [party] is willing to return, we can continue."*
ANGER ESCALATION	Raised voice, flushed face, aggressive body language before exit	Do not follow immediately. Ensure safety of remaining party. Wait for cooling.	*"I understand you were upset. What would need to change to feel safe continuing?"*
SAFETY CONCERN	Fear visible, party feels threatened or intimidated	Prioritize safety. Check if party needs escort or separate exit. Do not minimize.	*"Your safety matters most. We can explore shuttle mediation or other options."*
FUNDAMENTAL DISAGREEMENT	"This is pointless" or "We will never agree"	Acknowledge frustration. Explore if there is any path forward.	*"It sounds like you've lost hope in this process. What would make it worth trying?"*

Figure 48: Summary of signs and responses to a stakeholder walkout.

Understanding walkout patterns helps you respond in the moment without losing your center, and recognizing that walkouts are often signals of distress rather than permanent exits allows you to design re-engagement strategies.

When Walkouts Cannot Be Reversed

Sometimes a walkout signals genuine termination of the mediation relationship. The departing party may refuse further contact, communicate that the process has failed, or take actions inconsistent with continued mediation, such as filing a lawsuit or initiating a public campaign.

In these cases, documenting the termination clearly, including what led to the walkout, efforts made to continue, and the departing party's stated reasons for abandonment. Counseling the remaining party about their options, which may include waiting for circumstances to change, seeking alternative dispute resolution mechanisms, or pursuing their own alternatives to mediation.

> **Caution: The Manipulation Risk**
>
> Be alert to patterns of walkouts used as a manipulation tactic. If a party repeatedly walks out and returns after extracting concessions, they are training the other party that walkouts produce rewards. In such cases, address the pattern directly and consider whether structural changes, such as holding progress contingent on completed sessions, might address the manipulation.

The scenarios examined so far involve resistance directed at the other party or the process. The next scenario is different: it involves resistance that originates within one of the parties themselves. When a community delegation arrives at the table fractured by internal disagreement, the mediator cannot simply facilitate between two sides. The mediator must also help one side find its own voice before meaningful negotiation can begin.

14.6 Internal Division: When Community Factions Disagree

Mediation often assumes that each "party" has coherent interests and unified positions. In practice, particularly on the community side, this assumption is frequently false. Communities are not monolithic. They contain factions with different interests, leaders with competing claims to authority, and members who disagree about strategy, priorities, and acceptable outcomes. When these internal divisions surface during mediation, they can paralyze progress, expose the community to exploitation, and force mediators to navigate complex questions of legitimacy.

In mining-affected communities, internal divisions often reflect competing economic survival strategies rather than simple disagreement. Youth dependent on mining employment may support company operations while elders work to protect ancestral lands. Artisanal miners whose livelihoods are threatened by industrial-scale concessions form yet another faction. Mediators must legitimize that community members can simultaneously benefit from and oppose the same extractive project.

Common Sources of Community Division

Generational differences often pit elders invested in traditional ways against younger members seeking economic opportunity. A mining project might be welcomed by unemployed youth and opposed by elders who prioritize land and cultural preservation.

Economic stratification creates different interests within the community. Those who might gain employment with the company have different stakes than those who would lose land. Business owners may see opportunities that subsistence farmers fear.

Historical rivalries between families, clans, or ethnic groups within the community may be amplified by the dispute. Competition for who will represent the community or receive benefits can reactivate dormant conflicts.

Political alignment varies within communities. Some community members may be allied with government actors supporting the company, while others oppose both the company and the government. These alignments affect trust in the mediation process.

Strategy disagreements emerge when community members agree on goals but disagree on how to achieve them. Some may favor aggressive confrontation while others prefer dialogue. Some may want to settle quickly, while others want to hold out for better terms.

> **Key Concept: Representation Legitimacy**
> When community factions disagree, the mediator must assess who legitimately speaks for the community. This is not always the person with an official title or government recognition. Legitimate representation typically derives from genuine selection by community members, accountability to constituents, and the ability to deliver compliance with any agreement reached. A leader who cannot bring their community along with an agreement provides limited value as a negotiating partner.

Response Strategies for Internal Division

Strategy 1: Facilitate internal dialogue. Before continuing mediation with the company, the mediator may need to help the community work through its internal disagreements. This might involve separate sessions with community representatives only, during which different perspectives are heard and, ideally, reconciled. The mediator's role here is to help the community identify its common interests and develop unified positions, or at least understand where internal disagreement exists.

Strategy 2: Expand participation. If certain community voices are not represented at the table, consider expanding participation to include them. This may make sessions more complex, but it ensures that agreements reflect broader community input. A faction that feels excluded from mediation is more likely to reject or undermine any resulting agreement.

Strategy 3: Address division explicitly. Acknowledge to all parties, including the company, that the community is working through internal disagreements. Transparency about this reality can set appropriate expectations and may actually build the company's confidence that resulting agreements will have genuine community buy-in.

When Separate Mediation Tracks Are Needed

In some cases, internal division runs so deep that a single mediation process cannot accommodate all factions. Generational rifts, competing claims to land title, or fundamental disagreements about whether to engage with the company at all may require the mediator to facilitate parallel processes before attempting a unified negotiation. This approach is resource-intensive and time-consuming, but it respects the reality that community consent cannot be manufactured by selecting the most cooperative faction and calling its agreement representative.

Parallel tracks work best when each faction understands that its track is one input into a broader process, not a standalone negotiation. Transparency about the existence of multiple tracks (while respecting confidentiality within each) and a clear timeline for bringing the tracks together are essential. Without a convergence mechanism, parallel processes risk producing competing agreements that leave the company facing contradictory demands.

The Obligation Not to Paper Over Disagreement

Mediators sometimes feel pressure, from companies, from deadlines, from their own desire for resolution, to minimize internal community disagreement and push toward a unified position. This impulse is understandable but dangerous. An agreement that papers over genuine disagreement is an agreement waiting to collapse. The mediator's obligation is to ensure that any agreement reflects actual consensus, not the appearance of consensus. If genuine consensus is not achievable, the mediator serves the process better by acknowledging this honestly than by producing an agreement that one faction will repudiate the moment the mediator leaves.

Strategy 4: Focus on common ground. Identify issues on which community factions agree and prioritize those in negotiations. Contentious internal issues might be addressed later or through internal community processes outside of mediation. Building momentum through areas of consensus can sometimes help resolve more divisive questions.

Strategy 5: Consider multiple agreements. In some cases, a single community-wide agreement may not be achievable. The mediator might explore whether different arrangements for different community groups could work, though this approach carries risks of divide-and-conquer dynamics and must be handled very carefully.

Sample Dialogue

Community Rep A: *"We've decided to accept the company's offer on compensation. It's a fair deal."*

Community Rep B: *"You don't speak for everyone. The women's group wasn't consulted. We think the terms are inadequate."*

Mediator: *"I'm hearing that there are different perspectives within the community delegation on the current proposal. Before we proceed, I need to ensure that all community voices have been heard. Would it be helpful to take a break so your delegation can discuss internally? Or would you like to continue with the company hearing these different perspectives?"*

Community Rep A: *"We've discussed this already."*

Community Rep B: *"Not with everyone."*

Mediator: *"Reaching an agreement that the entire community supports is in everyone's interest, including the company's. An agreement that one faction rejects is unlikely to hold. I'm going to suggest we pause the joint session so the community can continue internal discussions. Company representatives, are you comfortable with this approach?"*

Protecting Against Divide-and-Conquer

Internal community division creates opportunities for companies to exploit disagreements, whether intentionally or inadvertently. The mediator must be alert to dynamics in which the company might leverage divisions to extract favorable terms from a minority faction, or in which internal competition for benefits might drive factions to undercut each other.

Watch for company communications with individual factions outside of mediation sessions, and be alert to proposals that benefit some community members at the expense of others. You should also ensure that any agreement addresses the interests of the community broadly, not just those at the table, and encourage community representatives to consult everyone before committing to positions.

Caution: The Weakest Link Problem

In divided communities, companies may be tempted to deal with the faction most willing to agree, regardless of whether that faction can deliver genuine community consent. Counseling companies that agreements with unrepresentative factions are unstable and may lead to renewed conflict, legal challenges, and reputational damage. Short-term convenience rarely justifies long-term risk.

Practical Tip: Mapping Internal Dynamics

During the pre-mediation phase, take time to understand community structure and dynamics. Who are the formal and informal leaders? What factions exist and what are their interests? How are decisions typically made within the community? This mapping helps you anticipate potential divisions and structure the process to address them constructively.

Facilitating Internal Community Dialogue

When a mediator facilitates internal community sessions to address divisions, the dynamics differ fundamentally from the joint mediation. The mediator is no longer balancing two parties but helping one party find coherence within itself. This requires a different posture: less referee, more process architect. The mediator's task is to create conditions in which factions can hear each other, identify shared interests beneath competing positions, and develop a mandate that their representatives can carry into the joint sessions with credibility.

Begin by meeting each faction separately to understand their priorities and red lines. Frame these conversations around interests rather than positions: "What outcomes matter most to your group? What would an acceptable agreement need to include?"

Often, factions that appear irreconcilable when stating positions discover significant overlap when articulating underlying interests. Youth demanding employment and elders defending ancestral land may share a common interest in long-term community prosperity, even though they disagree about how to achieve it.

Then convene a joint internal session where factions present their priorities to each other, not to the mediator. The mediator structures this exchange to prevent it from becoming a power struggle for control of the delegation.

Ground rules help: each group speaks without interruption, questions are for clarification before debate, and the goal is a shared understanding of the community's range of interests, not immediate agreement on a single position. The mediator might summarize what has been heard: "It sounds like there is strong agreement on the need for environmental remediation and community health services. There is genuine disagreement about whether employment at the mine is desirable. Can we proceed with the areas of agreement while continuing to discuss employment?"

Help the community establish decision-making rules for the mediation early. How will the delegation report back? Who has authority to accept or reject proposals? What happens when the delegation cannot reach internal consensus on a company offer? These procedural questions must be resolved before they arise in the heat of negotiation. A community that enters joint sessions with clear internal protocols projects confidence and coherence, which strengthens its bargaining position considerably.

Gender is frequently at the heart of internal community divisions, though it is rarely named as such. When women's groups within a community resist an agreement that male leaders have negotiated, the resistance is often framed as obstructionism or ignorance rather than as legitimate dissent reflecting different impacts. Recognize this dynamic:

If a community faction opposes a proposed agreement and that faction is predominantly female, the opposition likely reflects substantive concerns about how the agreement will affect women's livelihoods, safety, or social standing. Treating this resistance as a process problem to be managed rather than a substantive concern to be addressed will produce agreements that lack genuine community consent.

As discussed in Chapter 12, gendered impacts of mining operations are real and measurable. Internal resistance that reflects these impacts deserves the same careful attention as any other form of substantive disagreement.

Internal division threatens progress before an agreement is reached. The next scenario is arguably more damaging: it threatens progress after an agreement has already been concluded. When a party reverses commitments it made in good faith, or claims never to have had authority to make them, the mediator confronts the possibility that the entire process was built on a false foundation.

14.7 Bad-Faith Reversal: When Parties Change Position After Agreement

Three weeks after the mediation concluded and both parties signed a comprehensive water monitoring agreement, the community coordinator received a formal letter from the mining company. The letter stated that due to "changed economic conditions" and "revised financial projections," the company could no longer commit to the independent water testing regime that had been the centerpiece of the agreement. The company claimed the agreed provisions were "no longer commercially viable" and proposed a significantly reduced monitoring schedule. The community felt betrayed. They had held a community celebration, distributed the agreement to households, and told residents their water concerns would finally be addressed. Now the company was unilaterally rewriting the terms. The mediator, who had believed the agreement was durable, found herself dealing with a situation worse than the original impasse: an agreement had been made and broken.

Among the most damaging resistance scenarios is when a party reverses its position after an agreement has been reached. The community may have celebrated the resolution. The company may have announced the agreement to stakeholders. Then one party, usually the company, given its access to legal and strategic advice, declares that the agreement cannot be honored as written, that circumstances have changed, or that internal approval was not actually obtained. This bad-faith reversal can devastate trust and make future negotiations extremely difficult. Reversals are often driven by commodity price volatility and political transitions, with companies exploiting downturns to renegotiate agreements reached during favorable market conditions.

A typical reversal unfolds in a way that leaves the other party feeling betrayed and the mediator questioning whether the original commitment was ever genuine:

Company representative: *"Our legal team has reviewed the terms we discussed last month, and unfortunately they have identified several provisions that we cannot honor as drafted. We need to revisit the compensation timeline and the environmental monitoring commitments."*

Community leader: *"You agreed to those terms. We shook hands. Our people have already been told."*

Mediator: *"I want to make sure I understand what has changed. During our last session, we confirmed that your representative had the authority to commit to these terms, and we specifically reviewed each provision for feasibility. Can you identify which specific elements your legal team has flagged, and explain why these concerns were not raised during our discussions?"*

This response avoids either accepting the reversal or escalating the confrontation. Instead, it places the burden on the reversing party to justify the change with specifics, which often reveals whether the reversal is a genuine legal concern or a renegotiation tactic.

Understanding Why Reversals Occur

Authority gaps occur when the person negotiating did not actually have the authority to commit the organization to the agreed terms. Upon returning to headquarters, the representative is overruled by superiors, legal counsel, or board members who reject the agreed-upon terms.

Buyer's remorse involves second-guessing after the emotional intensity of negotiations has passed. What seemed acceptable in the moment may appear too generous when viewed dispassionately. The party begins looking for ways to reduce their commitments.

Changed circumstances can genuinely alter the feasibility of agreed terms. Market conditions, regulatory changes, or new information might make commitments impossible or significantly more costly than anticipated.

Strategic repositioning involves deliberately using the negotiation process to extract information or test positions, with no genuine intention to honor the resulting agreements. The party agrees, observes the other's reaction, and then seeks better terms.

Internal opposition surfaces when stakeholders within the organization who were not part of negotiations object to the agreement and mobilize to overturn it. This is particularly common when representatives exceed their mandate or when internal communication during negotiations was poor.

> **Key Concept: Agreement Fragility**
>
> Mediated agreements are inherently fragile. Unlike court judgments, they lack automatic enforcement mechanisms. Their strength derives from genuine party commitment and the belief that honoring the agreement serves everyone's long-term interests. When that belief wavers, the agreement's foundation crumbles. This fragility underscores the importance of ensuring genuine consent throughout the process, not just at the signing moment.

Responding to Position Reversal

Step 1: Verify and document the reversal. When a party signals that it will not honor an agreement, document precisely what they are saying, when, and in what form. Request written confirmation of their position.

Distinguish between complete repudiation and requests for modification.

Step 2: Understand the stated reasons. Meet with the reversing party to understand their explanation. Are they claiming the agreement was never valid? That circumstances have changed? That they misunderstood terms? Their explanation affects your response options.

Step 3: Assess good faith. Evaluate whether the reversal reflects legitimate concerns or bad-faith maneuvering. Legitimate concerns might include genuine authority gaps or changed circumstances that the agreement should address. Bad-faith indicators include vague explanations, new demands unrelated to the stated concerns, or patterns of commitment followed by reversal.

Step 4: Communicate with the affected party. Inform the non-reversing party promptly and honestly about what has occurred. They deserve accurate information about their situation. Discuss options and get their input on how to respond.

Step 5: Explore salvage options. Depending on the nature of the reversal, it may be possible to modify the agreement to address the reversing party's concerns while preserving core commitments. This requires careful judgment about which modifications are acceptable and which constitute capitulation to bad faith.

Sample Dialogue

Mediator to the company representative: *"I received your communication indicating that the company is unable to proceed with the terms we agreed to last month. Can you help me understand what has changed?"*

Company rep: *"After our legal team reviewed the agreement, they identified several concerns. They believe some commitments exceed what we can operationally deliver."*

Mediator: *"I appreciate you explaining that. However, I need to be direct. We spent considerable time ensuring that your representative had the authority to make these commitments. We specifically discussed* *implementation feasibility before finalizing terms. What specifically has your legal team identified that was not apparent during our negotiations?"*

Company rep: *"The timeline for the community development fund is problematic."*

Mediator: *"If the issue is timeline, let's discuss that specific element. But I want to be clear: the community entered this agreement in good faith based on your commitments. Wholesale reversal would severely damage trust and make future resolution much more difficult. If there are specific practical concerns, let's address them. But the core commitments need to stand."*

Prevention Through Process Design

The best response to bad faith reversal is prevention. Several process design elements reduce the risk of a reversal, many of which we have discussed previously.

Authority confirmation: Before substantive negotiations begin, require each party to confirm in writing that their representatives have the authority to bind the organization. Specify limits on that authority. If approval from higher authorities is required, build review periods into the process before finalizing agreements.

Incremental commitment: Rather than negotiating a comprehensive agreement all at once, build toward final terms through smaller commitments that are implemented and proven reliable before expanding. This creates track records and makes reversal more costly.

Implementation specificity: Agreements that specify who does what, when, and with what resources. Vague commitments are easier to reinterpret or deny. Specific commitments are harder to walk away from.

Verification mechanisms: Build verification and monitoring into agreements. When parties know their compliance will be observed and documented, they are less likely to reverse or evade commitments.

Consequences for breach: Agreements that address what happens if a party fails to honor its commitments. This might include a return to mediation, a referral to a third-party review, or predetermined remedies. Knowing that a breach has consequences encourages compliance.

Practical Tip: The Reality Test

Before finalizing any agreement, conduct a reality test with each party separately. Ask them to walk through exactly how they will implement each commitment. Who will approve expenditures? Who will communicate with stakeholders? What obstacles might arise? This exercise often surfaces authority gaps or feasibility concerns before they become justifications for reversal.

When Reversal Cannot Be Resolved

Some reversals represent fundamental bad faith that cannot be remedied. When a party has demonstrated unwillingness to honor commitments, the mediator and the non-reversing party must assess whether continuing serves any purpose.

Options in this situation include documenting the bad faith for potential legal or reputational consequences, seeking alternative dispute resolution mechanisms with binding authority, pursuing the non-reversing party's BATNA, and reserving the possibility of future mediation if circumstances change.

Being honest with all parties about the situation: "When agreements are not honored, it fundamentally undermines the mediation process. I'm not able to facilitate further negotiations until there is a basis for believing that commitments made will be kept."

Caution: The Precedent Problem

How a mediator responds to a bad-faith reversal sets a precedent. If reversal is accommodated without consequence, it signals that commitments are merely opening positions subject to renegotiation. Future mediations, both in this dispute and others, will be affected. Sometimes the most critical response to bad faith is to clearly name it and refuse to enable it.

The seven scenarios above have been presented individually, but in practice they rarely appear in isolation. A confidentiality breach may trigger a walkout. Government interference may deepen internal community divisions. Mediators must understand how these dynamics interact to build a coherent response when multiple forms of resistance surface in the same process.

14.8 Integrating Resistance Management into Practice

The resistance scenarios examined in this chapter share common threads that inform broader mediation practice. Understanding these patterns helps mediators prepare for challenges before they arise and respond effectively when they do.

Common Principles Across Resistance Scenarios

Resistance in extractive-industry disputes rarely announces itself clearly.

The first sign of silent participation, the subtle shift in a company representative's tone, the unexplained absence of a key community leader, or a casual mention of "competing priorities" can all signal emerging resistance. In these high-stakes, high-emotion contexts, the cost of misreading or ignoring these signals is considerable. Early recognition and swift, calibrated response before positions harden is typically more effective than attempting to recover trust and momentum after resistance has fully materialized and damaged the process.

Understanding motivation precedes effective response. The appropriate response to any resistance scenario depends on understanding why it is occurring. Strategic silence requires different handling than fear-based silence. Deliberate bad faith requires different handling than genuine authority gaps. Take time to assess motivation before selecting a response.

When Resistance Compounds. In practice, resistance scenarios frequently overlap and reinforce one another. A confidentiality breach may trigger a walkout. Government interference may deepen internal community divisions by emboldening one faction and alienating another. A bad-faith reversal by the company may prompt the community to pursue media disclosure as a pressure tactic, creating a new confidentiality crisis. Mediators who understand these cascading dynamics can choose responses that address root causes rather than surface symptoms.

When multiple forms of resistance surface simultaneously, prioritize responses in the following order. First, address any immediate safety concern, whether physical intimidation or credible threats. Second, stabilize the process by calling a recess and meeting with each party separately. Third, identify which form of resistance is primary and which are secondary effects. A walkout that follows a confidentiality breach, for example, is best addressed by resolving the breach rather than by persuading the departing party to return to a process they no longer trust.

Self-Assessment After Resistance Episodes

After any session involving significant resistance, engage in structured reflection, ideally with a co-mediator, supervisor, or trusted colleague. Key questions include: Did I identify the resistance early enough, or did I miss warning signs? Did my intervention address the root cause or only the surface behavior? Did I maintain impartiality, or did the resistance push me toward one party? Am I still the right person to continue this mediation, or has the episode compromised my standing with one or both parties? Honest answers to these questions, even uncomfortable ones, strengthen the mediator's practice over time and reduce the likelihood of repeated missteps.

Process integrity must be protected. Mediators serve the process, not just the parties. When resistance threatens the integrity of mediation, through intimidation, coercion, or systematic bad faith, protecting the process may require suspending or terminating it. A compromised process does more harm than no process at all.

Documentation creates accountability. Throughout resistance scenarios, careful documentation serves multiple purposes. It protects the mediator, creates records for potential future proceedings, and establishes accountability for inappropriate behavior. Make documentation a consistent practice.

Transparency builds trust. When challenges arise, being open about what is happening and why certain responses are needed builds trust with parties. Hidden concerns and unaddressed problems fester. Direct, honest communication about difficulties models the behavior mediators want from parties.

Key Concept: The Limits of Mediation

As we know by now, not every dispute can be mediated. Resistance scenarios sometimes reveal that the prerequisites for productive mediation are absent. Perhaps one party is negotiating in bad faith. Perhaps power imbalances cannot be adequately addressed. Perhaps external pressures make voluntary agreement impossible. Recognizing these limits is not failure. It is professional judgment about when a tool is appropriate for a situation.

Adapting Resistance Management Across Cultures

The resistance scenarios in this chapter are described in terms that apply broadly, but how resistance manifests and how mediators should respond varies significantly across cultural contexts. A mediator working in Latin America, Sub-Saharan Africa, Southeast Asia, or a Pacific Island community will encounter different norms around silence, authority, collective decision-making, and confrontation, and these differences shape both the form resistance takes and the interventions that will be effective.

Silent participation (Section 14.1), for example, carries different meanings across cultures. In many Indigenous communities, silence during a meeting signals careful deliberation and respect, not resistance. Pressuring a silent party to speak may itself constitute a form of cultural imposition. Similarly, what appears to be a "walkout" (Section 14.5) may in some contexts reflect a culturally appropriate withdrawal to consult with community members or elders before continuing, not an act of protest. The mediator who misreads these cues risks escalating a situation that does not require intervention.

Internal division (Section 14.6) also takes culturally specific forms. In communities with consensus-based governance, disagreement may remain hidden until a proposed agreement is brought to the full community for endorsement, at which point it surfaces as collective rejection. In hierarchical communities, faction leaders may publicly defer to a chief or elder while privately working to undermine positions they oppose. Understand local governance structures and decision-making traditions to anticipate where internal divisions will appear and how they can be addressed constructively. The general principle is that mediators should not assume that the resistance patterns described in this chapter will look the same everywhere. Before beginning any mediation, invest time in understanding the cultural norms of the communities involved, consult with local advisors or cultural liaisons, and remain open to revising your interpretation of what you observe (see Chapter 10 for a broader discussion of culturally sensitive mediation practice).

Building Resistance Resilience

Mediators can build resilience against resistance scenarios through preparation, self-awareness, and ongoing learning.

Preparation: Before each mediation, consider potential resistance scenarios based on the specific parties, context, and history. Prepare response strategies in advance. Discuss potential challenges with co-mediators or mentors. Having thought through possibilities reduces the chance of being caught off guard.

Self-awareness: Resistance scenarios often trigger emotional responses in mediators themselves. Being challenged, facing intimidation, or dealing with bad faith can provoke frustration, anxiety, or defensiveness. Recognizing your own emotional responses helps you manage them rather than having them drive your reactions.

Ongoing learning: Each resistance experience offers learning opportunities. After challenging situations, reflect on what worked, what did not, and what you might do differently. Seek feedback from colleagues. Build your repertoire of response strategies over time.

Practical Tip: The Debrief Habit

After any session involving resistance, take time to debrief, either with a co-mediator, a mentor, or through structured self-reflection. Ask yourself: What signs did I see? How did I respond? What was the effect? What would I do differently? This debrief habit converts challenging experiences into professional growth.

14.9 Conclusion: The Mediator's Judgment

Resistance scenarios test the mediator's judgment more than any other aspect of practice. There are no algorithmic solutions, no guaranteed responses that work in every situation. Each scenario requires reading context, assessing motivation, weighing trade-offs, and making decisions with imperfect information.

This chapter has provided frameworks and options, not formulas. The goal is to expand the mediator's repertoire of responses and deepen understanding of the dynamics at play. With this foundation, mediators can exercise judgment more confidently and effectively when facing resistance.

Resistance in extractive-industry mediation is not a failure of the mediator or a sign that settlement is impossible. Rather, it reflects the profound stakes involved: companies face regulatory, financial, and reputational consequences; communities face environmental legacies and broken trust spanning decades. When parties resist, it is often because what they fear losing matters more than what they might gain by agreement. Skilled mediators recognize resistance not as a barrier to be overcome by technique alone but as diagnostic information about underlying interests and power asymmetries that any sustainable agreement must address. The ability to acknowledge resistance, understand its sources, respond strategically without surrendering ethical commitments, and make clear-eyed judgments about when mediation remains viable and when it does not, is what separates mediators who merely facilitate conversations from those who genuinely advance the possibility of durable resolution in the world's most challenging disputes.

Key Takeaway

Resistance scenarios are not evidence that mediation has failed. They are inherent in the challenging contexts where mediation is most needed. The mediator's task is not to prevent resistance, which is often impossible, but to respond to it in ways that preserve the possibility of productive dialogue and genuine resolution. This requires preparation, skill, judgment, and the willingness to make difficult decisions when the integrity of the process is at stake.

Key Takeaways

- Resistance in mediation is often a signal, not an obstacle. Silence, walkouts, and procedural challenges frequently reflect legitimate fear, distrust, or past harm rather than bad faith.
- Seven common resistance patterns require distinct responses: silent participation, organized boycotts, procedural challenges, walkouts, external interference, media escalation, and intimidation or coercion.
- The private check-in is among the most effective tools for understanding resistance. What parties will not say in open session they may share in a safe, confidential conversation.
- Mediators must distinguish between resistance that can be addressed through process adjustments and resistance that signals the mediation should be suspended or terminated.
- Power dynamics shape resistance. A community that refuses to participate may be exercising the only form of agency available to it.
- When intimidation or coercion is present, the mediator's first obligation is to the safety of all participants, not to the continuation of the process.

Reflection Questions

- Which of the seven resistance scenarios feels most challenging to you personally? What makes it difficult?
- How do you currently distinguish between resistance rooted in fear and resistance driven by strategic bad faith?

- Think of a mediation where a party was silent or disengaged. Looking back, what might that silence have been communicating?
- What is your threshold for suspending a mediation due to resistance? How would you communicate that decision to the parties?
- How do you manage your own frustration or sense of helplessness when facing sustained resistance?

15.

LEARNING FROM MEDIATOR MISTAKES

This chapter shifts from managing party resistance to examining the mediator's own contributions to process breakdown. Mediation literature celebrates success stories: the breakthrough moment when adversaries shake hands, the creative solution that satisfied everyone, the trust rebuilt after years of conflict. Experienced mediators know that failure teaches more than success. This chapter examines the common mistakes mediators make, not to discourage, but to provide a roadmap of pitfalls that even skilled practitioners fall into. Studying these errors helps mediators recognize warning signs and develop safeguards.

These cases derive from real mediations across Africa, Europe, and Latin America. Details have been anonymized and, when necessary, combined to protect confidentiality while preserving the essential lessons. What emerges is a taxonomy of mediator mistakes, organized into distinct categories: ego traps, cognitive biases, cultural blind spots, capacity limitations, ethical compromises, and process errors. Each section explores not just what went wrong, but why, and how the consequences rippled through the mediation and beyond.

Key Concept: The Learning Mindset

Professional mediators treat every case as a learning opportunity. They conduct post-mediation reviews, seek feedback from parties when appropriate, and maintain reflective journals. This chapter is an extension of that practice, sharing lessons learned from the field to benefit the broader mediation community.

15.1 The "Hero Mediator" Trap

Perhaps no mistake is more seductive or more damaging than the Hero Mediator syndrome. This occurs when a mediator, consciously or unconsciously, begins to believe that they are essential to resolving the conflict. They shift from facilitating the parties' own resolution to driving toward an outcome they have determined is best. The shift is subtle, beginning with good intentions but ending in overreach that undermines the very foundations of voluntary mediation.

The Psychology Behind the Trap

The Hero Mediator trap stems from several psychological sources. First, mediators who have successfully resolved difficult conflicts develop an inflated sense of their own capabilities. Each success reinforces the belief that they possess special skills that others lack. Second, the emotional intensity of company and community disputes can trigger a rescuer mentality, particularly when mediators witness suffering or injustice. Third, external pressure from funders, employers, or the parties themselves to "get a deal" pushes mediators toward taking control rather than trusting the process.Research on reflective practice (Schön, 1983) identifies this pattern as a predictable stage in professional development, where practitioners must learn to balance confidence in their skills with humility about the limits of their role.

This trap is particularly dangerous because it masquerades as competence and dedication. A mediator pushing hard for a resolution might appear to observers (and to themselves) as simply being thorough and committed. The distinction between facilitation and manipulation can blur, especially when the mediator genuinely believes they know what is best for the parties.

Case Study: The Savior Complex in the Delta Region

A highly experienced international mediator was brought in to address a long-standing dispute between an oil company and fishing communities in a West African delta region. The mediator had an impressive track record and arrived confident that the same techniques that had worked elsewhere would succeed here. Within two weeks, she had drafted a comprehensive agreement that she believed addressed all the key issues: compensation for past environmental damage, employment quotas, and a community development fund. She presented this to both parties as "the solution," framing it as a fair compromise based on her expertise. The community leaders felt pressured to accept what the company had already approved. They signed, but with reservations they did not voice. Within six months, the agreement collapsed. Community members who had not been adequately consulted rejected the terms. Protests resumed, and the company accused the mediator of having misrepresented community support. The mediator's reputation suffered, but more importantly, the conflict intensified. The community now distrusted not just the company but the entire concept of mediation, having experienced it as another form of external imposition.

Warning Signs of the Hero Trap

Mediators benefit from watching for these indicators in their own behavior:

- Finding yourself mentally drafting solutions before fully understanding the parties' interests
- Feeling frustrated when parties don't accept your suggestions
- Speaking more than the parties during sessions
- Telling parties what they "need" rather than asking what they want
- Taking personal credit (or feeling personally responsible) for mediation outcomes
- Resisting when parties want to take the process in a different direction

> **Caution: The Expertise Paradox**
>
> Ironically, the more expertise a mediator develops, the greater the risk of falling into the Hero Mediator trap. Experience brings knowledge of what has worked before, but this knowledge can blind mediators to the unique aspects of each new situation. The most skilled mediators combine deep expertise with genuine humility about their role.

Dialogue Example: Crossing the Line

The following exchange illustrates how a mediator's language can shift from facilitation to direction:

Mediator (appropriate):	"What would a fair compensation arrangement look like from your perspective?"
Mediator (borderline):	"Based on similar cases, compensation of around $500 per household seems reasonable. What do you think?"
Mediator (problematic):	"I really think you should accept the $500 per household. It's a fair offer, and you're unlikely to get more."

Notice how the shift occurs gradually. The first statement invites the party to define their own interests. The second introduces external benchmarks that subtly anchor expectations. The third abandons facilitation entirely, substituting the mediator's judgment for the party's self-determination.

> **Practical Tip: The 80/20 Rule**
>
> In healthy mediation sessions, parties speak about 80 percent of the time, with the mediator contributing about 20 percent. When you find yourself talking more than the parties, ask more open-ended questions. Creating space for their dialogue, rather than filling that space yourself, strengthens mediation.

Long-Term Consequences

The Hero Mediator trap produces agreements that lack genuine ownership. Because the parties did not truly create the solution, they feel less committed to implementing it. When challenges arise during implementation, as they inevitably do, parties lack the collaborative relationship and mutual understanding needed to adapt. The mediator may have left, but the conflict has not been transformed. It has merely been suppressed temporarily, to resurface with greater intensity.

Beyond the immediate case, Hero Mediators can damage the broader reputation of mediation. Communities that have experienced pushy, directive mediation become skeptical of future mediation offers. They may view subsequent mediators with suspicion, assuming that mediation is just another mechanism for powerful actors to impose their will. This poisoning of the well affects not just the individual mediator but the entire field.

15.2 The False Balance Fallacy

Neutrality is a foundational principle of mediation ethics. However, some mediators misinterpret neutrality as requiring them to treat all positions as equally valid, regardless of evidence or moral weight. This false balance fallacy can lead to outcomes that entrench injustice rather than resolve conflict. It is a mistake born from a rigid, almost mechanical understanding of impartiality that fails to account for the realities of power, truth, and harm.

Understanding True Neutrality

Authentic mediator neutrality means neither favoring one party over another nor having a personal stake in specific outcomes. It does not mean pretending that documented facts are merely opinions, or that harmful conduct is simply a matter of perspective. A mediator can acknowledge that a company violated environmental regulations while remaining neutral about how that violation could be remedied. The neutrality pertains to the outcome, not to the underlying facts.

The false balance fallacy manifests when mediators are uncomfortable with conflict or when they fear being accused of bias. Rather than doing the difficult work of facilitating honest dialogue about disputed facts, they retreat to a position of artificial equivalence. "Both sides have their perspective" becomes a way of avoiding uncomfortable truths.

Case Study: When Balance Became Complicity

In a Central American mining dispute, community members presented extensive documentation of water contamination, including government agency reports, medical records showing elevated rates of kidney disease, and water-quality tests conducted by an independent laboratory. The mining company disputed these findings, citing their own internal monitoring data that showed compliance with standards. The mediator, committed to appearing neutral, treated both sets of data as equally credible. He refused to engage with the substance of the evidence, repeatedly stating, "It's not my role to determine who is right." The result was a mediation that never addressed the core issue. The community felt that their documented harm was being dismissed. The company felt validated in its denial of responsibility. After months of circular discussions, the mediation collapsed. The community pursued litigation, eventually winning a court judgment that referenced many of the same documents the mediator had refused to engage with. The delay caused by the failed mediation allowed contamination to continue, resulting in additional harm that might have been prevented.

Key Concept: Process Neutrality vs. Factual Engagement

Mediators can remain neutral about outcomes while still engaging with the facts. Process neutrality means treating parties fairly and not advocating for particular solutions. It does not require pretending that verifiable facts are unknowable or that all claims are equally credible. When clear evidence exists, acknowledging it while facilitating discussion about what could be done in response.

The Moral Dimensions

The false balance fallacy becomes particularly problematic when the dispute involves serious harm, such as violence, environmental destruction, or rights violations. In these cases, treating the perpetrator's denials as equivalent to the victim's documented experiences can retraumatize survivors and perpetuate injustice. This does not mean the mediator should become an advocate or judge. It means recognizing that facilitated dialogue must occur within a framework that acknowledges basic facts and moral realities.

Consider a mediation involving sexual assault allegations against company security personnel. A mediator who treats the survivor's detailed account and medical documentation as equivalent to a blanket denial from the company is not being neutral. They are actively undermining the survivor's credibility and creating conditions where accountability becomes impossible. True neutrality involves facilitating a process where facts can be established and responsibility appropriately assigned, while remaining neutral about the specific remedies.

Practical Approaches

Mediators can avoid the false balance fallacy through several approaches:

1. **Establish fact-finding mechanisms:** When parties dispute facts, suggest joint fact-finding with agreed-upon experts rather than simply accepting that facts are unknowable.
2. **Acknowledge documented evidence:** When clear documentation exists (such as government reports, court findings, and scientific studies), acknowledge its existence while remaining open to discussion of its implications.
3. **Separate factual from evaluative questions:** You can facilitate discussion about what happened (factual) while remaining neutral about what should be done (evaluative).
4. **Name the dynamic:** If one party is denying documented harm, gently name this as an obstacle to progress without taking sides on the remediation.

> **Caution: The Cost of False Equivalence**
>
> When mediators create false equivalence between documented harm and denial, they often think they are protecting their neutrality. In reality, they are taking a side. They are siding with the party that

benefits from ambiguity and delay. They are choosing to privilege denial over documentation. This is not neutrality; it is complicity disguised as procedure.

15.3 Cultural Erasure: Imposing Foreign Solutions

International mediators, particularly those trained in Western dispute resolution traditions, often arrive with a toolkit of techniques that have proven effective in their home contexts. Cultural erasure occurs when mediators impose these approaches without adequate adaptation to local cultural contexts, effectively erasing indigenous conflict-resolution traditions, communication norms, and value systems. What works in a London boardroom may fail disastrously in a rural African village, not because the techniques are wrong, but because they are being applied in a context where they do not fit.

Forms of Cultural Erasure

Cultural erasure in mediation can take multiple forms:

- **Communication style imposition:** Expecting direct, confrontational dialogue in cultures where indirect communication and face-saving are paramount. Pressuring parties to "say what they really mean" when their culture values circumlocution and metaphor.
- **Decision-making process imposition:** Expecting individual representatives to make binding commitments when the culture requires collective decision-making or elder approval. Setting artificial deadlines that conflict with consensus-building traditions.
- **Value hierarchy imposition:** Prioritizing financial compensation when the community values apology, relationship restoration, or spiritual remediation. Assuming that "rational" economic interests should override cultural or spiritual concerns.
- **Gender role imposition:** Either ignoring traditional gender roles in ways that alienate participants, or reinforcing oppressive gender dynamics without critical reflection. Neither extreme serves the parties well.

Case Study: The Spirit of the Ancestors

A European mediation team was engaged to resolve a land dispute between a mining company and indigenous communities in Southern Africa. The team arrived with a standard interest-based negotiation framework, ready to identify underlying interests and generate options for mutual gain. What they failed to understand was that for the community, the disputed land was not simply an economic asset. It contained ancestral burial sites and was central to spiritual practices. The community's "interest" was not in compensation or alternative land. Their interest was in maintaining their relationship with ancestors who resided in that specific place. The mediators kept trying to reframe spiritual concerns as "cultural heritage" that could be preserved through documentation and memorials elsewhere. They proposed generous compensation packages and offered to fund cultural centers on alternative land. Each proposal missed the point entirely. The community leaders eventually stopped attending sessions, concluding that the mediators were incapable of understanding what was at stake. The mediation failed, and the company ultimately proceeded through legal channels, winning a court case that technically granted them access but created lasting resentment that manifested in ongoing operational disruptions for years afterward.

The Colonialism Parallel

Cultural erasure in mediation echoes historical patterns of colonialism, where Western institutions and values were imposed on colonized peoples as "civilizing" forces. Contemporary mediators often replicate these dynamics when they assume that their frameworks are universal and that local practices are obstacles to overcome rather than resources to integrate.

This becomes especially damaging in company-community disputes, where the company holds global economic interests and the community comprises local, indigenous tribes with long-standing, important traditions. When mediators align their process with corporate communication styles and Western legal concepts, they unintentionally tilt the playing field toward the company even while believing they are being neutral.

Practical Tip: Cultural Mapping Before Mediation

Before beginning any community mediation, invest time in understanding local conflict resolution traditions. Who resolves disputes in this community? What processes do they use? What values guide resolution? Are there ritual or ceremonial elements? This mapping should inform your process design, even if you cannot fully replicate traditional approaches. At a minimum, understanding what you are departing from and why strengthens your approach.

Avoiding Cultural Erasure

Mediators can guard against cultural erasure through deliberate practices (for a broader discussion of cultural competence, see Chapter 9: Tools and Competencies in the Mediator's Toolbox):

- **Engage local cultural advisors:** Work with community members or anthropologists who can explain cultural nuances and alert you to potential missteps.
- **Consider co-mediation:** Partner with a mediator from the local culture who can create a bridge between your techniques and local expectations.
- **Invite cultural guidance:** Ask community elders or leaders how they would typically address such conflicts. Integrate their suggestions into your process where possible.
- **Be explicit about your framework:** Rather than assuming your approach is universal, explain that you are offering one approach among many and invite feedback on how to adapt it.
- **Allow time for cultural processes:** If the community needs to consult elders, perform ceremonies, or reach consensus through traditional means, build this into your timeline.

Key Concept: Cultural Humility

Cultural competence suggests mastery of another culture. Cultural humility is more realistic and more useful. It involves recognizing that you cannot fully understand another culture from the outside, remaining curious rather than assuming, and being willing to adapt based on feedback. Cultural humility is a stance of learning rather than expertise.

15.4 Burnout Blindness: Mediating While Depleted

Mediating company and community disputes is emotionally demanding work. Mediators hear stories of suffering, witness raw conflict, and carry the weight of parties' hopes for resolution. Over time, without adequate self-care, mediators can become depleted, burned out, and blind to their own diminished capacity. Burnout blindness occurs when exhausted mediators continue to practice without recognizing how their depletion is affecting their work.

How Burnout Affects Mediation

Burnout does not simply make mediators tired. It fundamentally alters their capacity to perform essential mediation functions. Research on burnout in helping professions identifies three core dimensions that directly impact mediation effectiveness:

- **Emotional exhaustion** reduces a mediator's capacity for empathy and active listening (discussed in Chapter 4). The burned-out mediator may go through the motions of reflective listening without actually connecting with the speaker. They may miss emotional cues, fail to validate important feelings, or become impatient with parties who need time to process their experiences.
- **Depersonalization** leads mediators to view parties as problems to be managed rather than humans to be respected. The burned-out mediator becomes cynical, treating community grievances as predictable complaints or company positions as corporate stonewalling. This cynicism, even when hidden, communicates itself to parties and undermines trust.
- **Reduced personal accomplishment** can push mediators toward the Hero Mediator trap, overcompensating for feelings of inadequacy by becoming more directive. Alternatively, it can lead to passivity, where the mediator fails to intervene when intervention is needed because they doubt their ability to help.

Case Study: The Marathon Mediator

A mediator with an excellent reputation was engaged in a complex dispute involving a cement factory and surrounding communities. The case required travel to a remote area, long sessions, and emotional discussions about the impacts of respiratory health on children. The mediator was already fatigued from a previous demanding case but felt obligated to accept the assignment because of the urgency. During the third session, while a community member was describing her daughter's hospitalization, the mediator's attention visibly wandered. He checked his phone, shuffled papers, and offered only a perfunctory acknowledgment of her story. The community members noticed. They interpreted his disengagement as disrespect, as evidence that their suffering did not matter to outsiders. The community subsequently withdrew from the mediation. In the debrief, the mediator acknowledged that he had been operating on autopilot, that he simply did not have the emotional capacity to fully engage. He had known he was depleted but had convinced himself he could push through. The consequences extended beyond the failed mediation: his reputation in the region was damaged, and the community became hostile to subsequent mediation attempts by other practitioners.

Warning Signs of Mediator Burnout

As discussed in detail in Chapter 11 (Mediator Health and Well-Being), monitoring yourself for these indicators helps identify potential challenges.

- Dreading upcoming sessions or feeling relieved when they are canceled
- Difficulty remembering details from recent sessions or confusing cases
- Irritability with parties, colleagues, or family members
- Physical symptoms: persistent fatigue, sleep disturbances, headaches, or illness
- Emotional numbing or difficulty feeling empathy for parties
- Cynicism about mediation, about the parties, or about the possibility of resolution
- Increased use of alcohol or other substances to cope
- Intrusive thoughts or dreams about cases

Prevention and Recovery

Sustainable mediation practice requires proactive attention to well-being:

1. Build recovery time into your schedule. Do not schedule demanding cases back-to-back. Allow time between cases to process and restore.
2. Establish regular supervision or peer consultation. Having colleagues who can notice your depletion when you cannot is invaluable.
3. Develop rituals for leaving work at work. Physical transitions, debriefing practices, or mindfulness exercises can help prevent cases from following you home.
4. Know your limits and honor them. If you are depleted, decline new cases or bring in a co-mediator. The parties deserve a mediator who is fully present.
5. Seek professional help when needed. Therapists who specialize in working with helping professionals can provide valuable support.

Practical Tip: The Honest Assessment

Before accepting any case, ask yourself honestly: Do I have the emotional capacity to be fully present for these parties? If the answer is no, it is more ethical to decline or delay than to proceed while depleted. Your obligation to the parties includes being in condition to serve them well.

15.5 Co-Optation Risk: Becoming a Tool of Power

In disputes between companies and communities, significant power asymmetries exist. Companies typically have more resources, more sophisticated legal support, and often greater political connections. One of the most insidious mistakes a mediator can make is becoming an unwitting instrument of this power imbalance, lending legitimacy to a process that serves the stronger party while appearing neutral. This co-optation can occur without the mediator's conscious awareness, making it particularly dangerous.

Mechanisms of Co-Optation

Co-optation is closely related to the concept of "mediator capture" discussed in Chapter 8 (When Mediation Should Not Proceed). While Chapter 8 focuses on recognizing capture and deciding whether to continue, here we examine the specific mechanisms through which co-optation occurs and how it constitutes a professional failure:

- **Financial dependence:** When the company pays for the mediation, mediators may unconsciously favor the entity that controls their compensation. This does not require overt corruption. Subtle biases emerge: being slightly more patient with company representatives, giving their arguments more weight, or hesitating to challenge company positions for fear of losing the assignment.
- **Social affinity:** Professional mediators often share educational backgrounds, communication styles, and cultural frameworks with corporate representatives. This affinity can lead to implicit alignment: the mediator may find company arguments more "reasonable" simply because they are expressed in familiar terms, while community grievances seem emotional or unsophisticated.
- **Procedural capture:** The company shapes the mediation framework before the mediator arrives, selecting convenient venues, setting favorable timelines, or limiting the scope of issues to be discussed. A mediator who accepts these constraints without question has already been co-opted, regardless of their conduct within those constraints.
- **Information asymmetry:** Companies control information critical to the dispute. If the mediator relies primarily on company-provided information without independent verification, they operate within a constructed reality that serves company interests.

Case Study: The "Neutral" Venue

A mediation was organized to address community grievances about a large agricultural project in Southeast Asia. The company offered to fund the mediation, including providing a "neutral" venue at a resort. The mediator accepted, reasoning that the comfortable setting would facilitate dialogue. What he did not fully appreciate was that the venue was a three-hour drive from the community, requiring overnight stays that were uncomfortable for community members accustomed to sleeping at home. Community representatives felt out of place in the resort setting, while company representatives were entirely at ease. Meeting schedules were set to accommodate corporate work patterns rather than agricultural rhythms. The mediator conducted the sessions with technical proficiency but never questioned whether the structural choices were affecting the process. The community felt disadvantaged throughout, but their complaints were framed as logistical rather than substantive. The resulting agreement heavily favored the company. It was only during implementation, when the community rejected terms they felt they had been pressured into accepting, that the mediator began to question whether the process had been compromised from the start.

Recognizing Co-Optation Dynamics

Asking yourself these questions helps assess co-optation risk.

- Who is paying for this mediation, and does that create any pressure on me?
- Who designed the mediation framework, and does it advantage either party?
- Am I more comfortable with one party than the other, and if so, why?
- Whose language am I using when I frame issues? Corporate jargon or community terms?
- Have I independently verified the facts, or am I relying on one party's information?
- If the community withdraws, will it damage my relationship with the company? How does that affect my conduct?
- Would I conduct this mediation differently if roles were reversed and the community were the more powerful party?

Key Concept: Structural Neutrality

True neutrality requires attention to structural factors, not just interpersonal conduct. A mediator can behave with perfect impartiality during sessions while presiding over a structurally biased process. Structural neutrality means examining venue, timing, language, information access, and process design to ensure that the framework itself does not favor either party.

Safeguards Against Co-Optation

Mediators can implement several safeguards against this issue, including:

1. **Independent funding:** Where possible, arrange for mediation costs to be shared equally or funded by a neutral third party. If the company must fund the process, ensure that payment is not contingent on outcomes.
2. **Community-accessible process design:** Consult with the community about the venue, timing, and procedures. Ensure that logistical arrangements do not systematically disadvantage them.
3. **Independent information:** Do not rely solely on company-provided information. Seek independent sources, and facilitate community access to technical advisors who can evaluate company claims.
4. **Power-balancing interventions:** Actively work to equalize capacity. This might include ensuring the community has legal or technical advisors, providing more support for community preparation, or slowing the process to allow community consultation.
5. **External accountability:** Arrange for oversight by a neutral party (perhaps an ombudsman or advisory board) who can monitor for co-optation dynamics.

Caution: The Legitimacy Trap

Companies sometimes engage mediators primarily to create the appearance of a fair process rather than to achieve a genuine resolution. The mediator's presence lends legitimacy to outcomes that might otherwise be seen as imposed. Before accepting any engagement, assess whether the company is seeking a genuine resolution or merely procedural cover. If the latter, your participation makes you complicit in injustice.

15.6 Premature Closure: Pushing for Agreement Before Healing

Mediation is framed as a problem-solving process aimed at reaching an agreement. This framing, while accurate, can lead mediators to prioritize closure over the deeper work of relationship repair, healing, and genuine understanding. Premature closure occurs when mediators push toward agreement before parties are psychologically ready, before underlying issues have been adequately addressed, or before trust has been sufficiently rebuilt to sustain implementation.

Sources of Pressure for Closure

Premature closure pressures come from multiple directions, including:

- **External stakeholders:** Funders, employers, or sponsors may expect results within specific timeframes. Project delays cost money, and there is often pressure to resolve disputes quickly so operations can proceed.
- **Mediator ego:** A signed agreement is tangible evidence of success. Mediators may unconsciously prioritize outcomes that validate their skills, pushing toward closure even when the process is incomplete.
- **Party fatigue:** Prolonged mediation is exhausting. Parties signal willingness to sign simply to end the process when they harbor unresolved concerns.
- **False momentum:** When progress is made on some issues, there is pressure to capitalize on momentum by pushing through the remaining issues. This can result in superficial agreement on complex matters.

Case Study: The Agreement That Unraveled

After six months of mediation between a mining company and affected communities in East Africa, an agreement was reached. The mediator was proud of the comprehensive document, which covered compensation, environmental monitoring, and community development. All parties signed, photographs were taken, and the mediator submitted a final report. Within three months, community members were protesting again. Investigation revealed that many signatories had not fully understood what they were agreeing to. Translation had been rushed. Influential community members who had concerns did not speak up because the atmosphere in the final session emphasized celebrating the agreement rather than careful review. The company had made commitments that their local management did not support and would not implement. Most fundamentally, the deep resentment over past harms had never been adequately addressed. The community had signed because they felt they had no better option and were tired of the process, not because they believed the agreement was just. The mediator had noticed some of these warning signs but had convinced herself that signing the agreement was the first step toward healing rather than its culmination. She had interpreted silence as consent, fatigue as satisfaction, and procedural completion as substantive resolution.

Signs That Closure Is Premature

Watching for these indicators helps identify when parties are not ready to conclude.

- **Passive agreement:** Parties say yes without enthusiasm, engagement, or questions
- **Rushed final sessions:** A sudden push to conclude after slow progress may indicate pressure rather than genuine readiness
- **Unaddressed emotions:** If parties still express anger, grief, or resentment about underlying events, emotional processing is incomplete
- **Outstanding information needs:** If either party is still seeking information or clarification, they cannot give truly informed consent
- **Power-driven acquiescence:** When the weaker party agrees primarily because they feel they have no choice, the agreement lacks genuine consent
- **Consultation gaps:** If community representatives have not had adequate time to consult with their constituents, they may be agreeing beyond their mandate

Practical Tip: The 24-Hour Review

Before final signing, build in a mandatory review period of at least 24 hours. Ask parties to take the draft agreement home, review it carefully, and return with any concerns. This simple pause can surface issues that were suppressed in the momentum of the final session. It also ensures that parties make deliberate choices rather than being swept along.

What Readiness Looks Like

Genuine readiness for closure involves more than agreement on terms. It includes:

- **Emotional shift:** The tone of the room has changed from adversarial to collaborative. Parties are able to acknowledge each other's perspectives and express hope for the future.
- **Active ownership:** Parties are enthusiastically explaining and defending the agreement, not passively accepting it.
- **Implementation planning:** Parties are spontaneously discussing how they will implement terms, identifying potential challenges, and proposing solutions.
- **Relationship repair:** Beyond the transactional elements, there are signs of restored trust, respect, and a willingness to work together.
- **Confidence in sustainability:** Both parties express belief that the agreement will hold and that future disagreements can be managed constructively.

Key Concept: Agreement vs. Resolution

An agreement is a document. A resolution is a transformed relationship. Sustainable outcomes require both, but the document is meaningless without the underlying transformation. Mediators who focus solely on reaching an agreement may achieve signatures but not resolution. The goal is not closure but genuine settlement, both legally and emotionally.

How can a mediator tell the difference between premature closure and genuine readiness? The following diagnostic comparison offers concrete indicators for each, helping mediators assess whether the parties have truly reached resolution or are simply eager to end the process.

PREMATURE CLOSURE vs. GENUINE READINESS

WARNING SIGNS OF PREMATURE CLOSURE	INDICATORS OF GENUINE READINESS
Passive Agreement Parties say yes without enthusiasm, engagement, or questions. Silence is mistaken for consent.	**Emotional Shift** Tone has changed from adversarial to collaborative. Parties acknowledge each other's perspectives and express hope.
Rushed Final Sessions Sudden push to conclude after slow progress. Momentum driven by fatigue or external pressure rather than genuine resolution.	**Active Ownership** Parties enthusiastically explain and defend the agreement. They are driving the process, not passively accepting it.
Unaddressed Emotions Parties still express anger, grief, or resentment about underlying events. Emotional processing is incomplete.	**Implementation Planning** Parties spontaneously discuss how to implement terms, identify challenges, and propose solutions.
Power-Driven Acquiescence Weaker party agrees because they feel they have no choice. Agreement lacks genuine consent or ownership.	**Relationship Repair** Signs of restored trust, respect, and willingness to work together beyond the transactional elements.
Consultation Gaps Representatives have not consulted with their constituents. They may be agreeing beyond their mandate.	**Confidence in Sustainability** Both parties express belief the agreement will hold and future disagreements can be managed constructively.

If most indicators fall on the left, closure is premature. If most fall on the right, parties may be ready.

Figure 49: Premature Closure vs. Genuine Readiness: A Diagnostic Comparison

The left column shows warning signs that the process needs more time, while the right column confirms genuine readiness for agreement. Use this tool proactively in final-stage sessions to avoid the costly mistake of terminating prematurely.

15.7 Additional Mediator Traps

Beyond the major mistakes discussed above, experienced mediators have identified numerous other traps that can undermine the effectiveness of mediation. This section briefly surveys additional pitfalls that merit attention.

Confirmation Bias in Assessment

Once mediators form an initial understanding of a conflict, they may unconsciously filter subsequent information to confirm that understanding. This confirmation bias leads to selective listening: information that fits the mediator's mental model is noted, while contradictory information is dismissed or minimized.Behavioral research on judgment under uncertainty (Kahneman, 2011) demonstrates that confirmation bias and related heuristics affect professionals across all fields, and that mediators are not immune to systematic errors in how they interpret party behavior and assess outcomes.

Those who initially conclude that a community's grievances are primarily economic may miss evidence of deeper cultural or spiritual concerns. Similarly, a mediator viewing the company as acting in bad faith may discount genuine efforts at accommodation. The assessment formed in pre-mediation research or early sessions becomes a lens that distorts all subsequent observations.

Key Concept: Reframing the mindset

Internal thought: *"I knew this company was just trying to buy off the community. This offer of a community center is just another bribe."*
Alternative: *"This offer could be genuine engagement or strategic maneuvering. Let me explore how the community perceives it before forming a judgment."*

Practical Tip: The Devil's Advocate Review

Periodically ask yourself: "What evidence would contradict my current understanding of this conflict?" Then actively look for that evidence. This practice helps counteract confirmation bias by deliberately seeking disconfirming information.

Process Rigidity

Mediators trained in specific methodologies become rigidly attached to those processes, applying them regardless of whether they fit the particular conflict or the parties. Those committed to interest-based negotiation may force parties to engage in interest identification exercises even when the conflict is fundamentally about values or relationships that do not reduce to interests. Transformative-minded practitioners, by contrast, may resist providing structure even when parties are lost and need guidance.

Process rigidity reflects insecurity: the mediator clings to familiar techniques because they are uncertain about improvising. It can also reflect overconfidence: the belief that one's preferred methodology is superior to alternatives. Either way, the parties suffer when the process does not adapt to their needs.

Case Study: The Textbook Approach

A newly trained mediator was assigned to facilitate discussions between a palm oil company and indigenous communities in Indonesia. He had recently completed an intensive training program that emphasized a structured nine-stage mediation model. Determined to apply his training correctly, he insisted on moving through each stage sequentially, even when the parties wanted to jump ahead to specific issues. Community elders, accustomed to more fluid deliberation styles, became frustrated by what felt like arbitrary constraints. The company representatives, eager to address urgent operational issues, chafed at being required to complete "interest identification exercises" before discussing practical solutions. The mediation eventually succeeded, but it took twice as long as necessary because the mediator prioritized adherence to his model over responsiveness to the parties' actual needs. In his supervision session afterward, he reflected that he had been mediating for his training rather than for the parties.

Emotional Contagion

Mediators are human beings who absorb the emotional atmosphere of the room. In high-conflict mediations, this emotional contagion compromises their effectiveness. Absorbing the community's anger can lead a mediator to become unconsciously adversarial toward the company. Likewise, feeling the company's frustration with unrealistic demands may make mediators impatient with community participants.

Emotional contagion is particularly dangerous because it operates below conscious awareness. The mediator may genuinely believe they are being neutral while their tone, body language, and word choices are transmitting absorbed emotions. Parties pick up on these signals, which can inflame the very dynamics the mediator is trying to manage.

Caution: The Mirror Effect

Research on emotional contagion shows that emotions spread primarily through nonverbal cues within groups. A mediator who is unconsciously mirroring one party's distress or frustration is broadcasting that emotion to everyone in the room. Regular self-monitoring for physical tension, facial expressions, and posture can help identify when contagion is occurring.

Documentation Failures

Inadequate documentation creates multiple problems. During lengthy mediations, poor note-taking leads to forgotten details, unresolved issues that were set aside, and disagreements about what was previously discussed. At the conclusion, vague or ambiguous agreement language produces implementation disputes.

Documentation failures often occur because mediators are so focused on managing the live interaction that they neglect record-keeping. They may also hesitate to take notes in front of parties, fearing it would disrupt rapport. In some cases, mediators simply underestimate the importance of detailed records, trusting that everyone will remember what was agreed.

Common documentation failures include:

- Failing to document interim agreements or tentative understandings
- Using vague language in final agreements ("appropriate compensation" rather than specific amounts)
- Omitting implementation details, timelines, or verification mechanisms
- Not specifying what happens if commitments are not fulfilled
- Failing to ensure documents are translated and understood by all parties

Scope Creep and Mission Drift

As mediation proceeds, parties may introduce new issues beyond the original scope. While flexibility is valuable, unconstrained scope creep can make resolution impossible. A mediation that began focused on compensation for a specific incident may expand to encompass decades of grievances, structural injustices, and issues beyond either party's capacity to address. The mediator who allows unlimited expansion may find themselves presiding over a forum for airing grievances rather than a process for achieving resolution.

Related to scope creep is mission drift, where the mediator's role expands beyond facilitation. Mediators may find themselves becoming investigators, advocates, therapists, or advisors. Each expansion compromises their primary function and can create ethical conflicts.

> **Practical Tip: The Parking Lot**
>
> When important issues arise that are outside the agreed scope, acknowledge their importance and "park" them on a visible list for potential future discussion. This validates the issue without derailing current progress. Periodically review the parking lot with parties to determine whether parked issues should be integrated, addressed separately, or set aside.

Confidentiality Breaches

As discussed in Chapter 3 (Core Principles and Ethics of Mediation), confidentiality is foundational to mediation trust. Here we focus specifically on how breaches occur as mediator errors, through carelessness, misjudgment, or external pressure.

Even minor confidentiality breaches can have serious consequences. Once parties learn that information shared in confidence was disclosed, they will withhold sensitive information in future sessions. The atmosphere of trust that enables honest dialogue is difficult to restore once compromised. In some cases, confidentiality breaches have led to retaliation against community members who revealed information in mediation that the company or government did not want disclosed.

Case Study: The Overheard Conversation

A mediator was working on a sensitive dispute involving allegations of sexual harassment by company security personnel. During a lunch break, she took a phone call in the hotel lobby, not realizing that a company employee was seated nearby. In the conversation with a colleague, she mentioned specific details about a complainant's testimony and her assessment of its credibility. The company employee reported this to management, who used the information to prepare their response. The complainant, learning that her confidential testimony had been overheard, withdrew from the process and spread word in the community that the mediation was not safe. The mediator's moment of carelessness destroyed not just this mediation but also the possibility of future engagement.

Power Blindness

Distinct from co-optation, power blindness occurs when mediators fail to perceive the power dynamics at play in the mediation. They may not recognize subtle intimidation, understand the pressures community members face, or appreciate how educational differences affect a person's capacity to participate. A mediator who treats all parties as if they come to the table with equal power is not being neutral; they are being naive in ways that advantage the more powerful party.

Power blindness often stems from the mediator's own position of relative privilege. Mediators who have never experienced structural powerlessness may struggle to recognize its manifestations. They may interpret community members' reluctance to speak as a lack of interest rather than a fear of consequences. They may see company confidence as reasonableness rather than privilege.

Key Concept: Visible and Invisible Power

Power in mediation operates at multiple levels. Visible power includes formal authority, resources, and expertise. Invisible power includes agenda-setting capacity, framing control, and the ability to define what counts as legitimate concerns. Mediators must attend to both, recognizing that invisible power can shape outcomes even when visible power appears balanced.

Solution Fixation

Related to the Hero Mediator trap but distinct from it, solution fixation occurs when a mediator becomes attached to a particular solution and subtly steers the discussion toward it. This can happen even when the mediator has no ego investment in the outcome. Perhaps they have seen a similar solution work elsewhere and believe it is optimal. Perhaps one party mentioned it early, and it lodged in the mediator's mind as "the answer."

The danger of solution fixation is that it narrows the exploration of alternatives. The mediator, consciously or unconsciously, gives more attention to the favored solution and less to alternatives. The mediator frames questions to highlight the advantages of the favored solution. The mediator addresses concerns about it more thoroughly than concerns about alternatives. The result is a mediation process that appears open but is actually channeled toward a predetermined outcome.

Sample Dialogue: Subtle Steering

Mediator: *"So we have several options on the table: a compensation fund, direct payments, or a community development project. The community development project seems to offer long-term benefits. What do you think about that approach?"*

Analysis: *The mediator has subtly elevated one option by characterizing it positively ("long-term benefits") while presenting the others neutrally. A more balanced approach would present all options equally and allow the parties themselves to identify their advantages and disadvantages.*

15.8 Building a Practice of Learning from Mistakes

The mistakes catalogued in this chapter are not signs of mediator failure; they are features of the terrain that every mediator must navigate. The difference between competent and incompetent practice lies not in whether mistakes occur but in whether mediators recognize them, address them, and learn from them. This final section offers a framework for building ongoing learning from mistakes into mediation practice. Such learning is essential when mistakes occur during impasses (Chapter 13) or resistance situations (Chapter 14).

Post-Mediation Reflection Protocol

After each mediation, set aside time for structured reflection on these questions:

1. What moments made me uncomfortable during this mediation? What might that discomfort signal?
2. Were there times when I talked more than I should have? Or times when I offered solutions rather than facilitating the parties to find their own?
3. Did I feel more aligned with one party than the other? If so, how might that have affected my conduct?
4. Were there cultural dimensions I may have missed or mishandled?
5. What did I assume that I did not verify? Were any of my assumptions wrong?
6. If I could do this mediation again, what would I do differently?

Peer Consultation and Supervision

Individual reflection has limits. We all have blind spots that only outside perspectives can reveal. Regular consultation with colleagues provides crucial feedback. Consider establishing a peer consultation group that meets regularly to discuss challenging cases, or engage a supervisor who can review your practice over time and identify patterns you might miss. Research on mediator development (Kolb and Associates, 1994) confirms that structured reflection, peer supervision, and honest self-assessment distinguish effective practitioners from those who repeat the same mistakes across cases.

When presenting cases for consultation, resist the temptation to frame yourself in a favorable light. Share your uncertainties, your uncomfortable moments, your possible mistakes. The value of consultation depends on honest disclosure. A presentation that highlights your successes while minimizing your struggles will generate reassurance rather than growth.

> **Practical Tip: The Failure File**
>
> Keep a confidential record of your mediation mistakes and near-misses. Review it periodically to identify patterns. Are you consistently vulnerable to certain traps? Do mistakes cluster around certain types of cases, parties, or conditions? This systematic tracking transforms isolated errors into learning opportunities.

Party Feedback

Where appropriate and ethical, seek feedback from mediation participants. This might be through post-mediation surveys, follow-up conversations, or structured debriefs. Parties often have insights into mediator conduct that the mediator cannot see. They may have felt pressured, unheard, or confused at moments when the mediator believed everything was proceeding well.

Party feedback requires a high degree of humility to receive. Hearing that you failed to make someone feel heard, that you seemed biased, or that your process felt confusing can be painful. But this feedback is a gift. Parties who take the time to share their experience are helping you become a better mediator.

Creating a Learning Culture

Organizations that engage mediators should foster cultures where mistake discussion is normal rather than shameful. When mistakes are hidden to protect reputations, learning becomes impossible. When they are openly examined, they become collective resources. Senior practitioners should model vulnerability by sharing their own mistakes and how they learned from them. Formal case reviews should examine failures as carefully as successes.

The mediation field as a whole benefits when practitioners share mistakes publicly, as this chapter has attempted to do with anonymized cases. Published analyses of mediation failures create shared learning that improves practice across the profession. While confidentiality must be protected, the lessons extracted from failures are too valuable to remain locked in individual memories.

Key Concept: The Growth Mindset in Mediation

Carol Dweck's research on mindsets distinguishes between a fixed mindset (the belief that abilities are static) and a growth mindset (the belief that abilities can develop through effort and learning). Mediators with a growth mindset treat mistakes as learning opportunities rather than evidence of inadequacy. This stance enables honest self-examination, which professional development requires.

15.9 Conclusion: Embracing Imperfection

This chapter has surveyed the range of mediator mistakes, not to discourage but to equip. Every mediator will encounter these traps. Many will fall into them, some repeatedly. What distinguishes skilled practitioners is not immunity to error but the capacity to recognize, recover from, and learn from mistakes.

The Hero Mediator trap reminds us that our role is facilitation, not rescue. The false balance fallacy teaches that neutrality does not mean moral or factual blindness. Cultural erasure warns against assuming our frameworks are universal. Burnout blindness demands that we care for ourselves so we can care for others. Co-optation risk requires vigilance about structural dynamics. Premature closure insists that genuine resolution takes time. And the additional traps surveyed remind us that mediation is endlessly complex, with pitfalls at every turn.

The cases presented here represent real suffering, real failure, and real consequences. They also represent real learning. The mediators who made these mistakes, in many cases, went on to do better work, informed by painful experience. Their failures informed better practice, both for themselves and for colleagues who learned from their experience.

The awareness this chapter offers is the first tool for avoiding, or recovering from, the mistakes it describes.

Perfect mediation does not exist, but honest reckoning with where things went wrong is how expertise develops.

> **Practical Tip: Final Reflection**
>
> After reading this chapter, identify the two or three traps to which you may be most vulnerable, based on your personality, training, or circumstances. Write these down and post them somewhere you will see them before mediations. Self-awareness of your particular vulnerabilities is the best protection against them.

Quick Reference: Mediator Traps Summary

The following reference maps each of the ten major mediator traps to their root causes and recommended safeguards, helping you build self-awareness around your particular vulnerabilities.

COMMON MEDIATOR TRAPS: ROOT CAUSES AND SAFEGUARDS

TRAP	CORE ERROR	KEY SAFEGUARD
Hero Mediator	Believing you are the essential ingredient in resolving the conflict	Trust the process and the parties. Apply the 80/20 speaking rule.
False Balance	Treating all positions as equally valid regardless of evidence	Engage with facts while remaining neutral on remedies.
Cultural Erasure	Imposing your cultural frameworks as universal solutions	Cultural mapping before mediation. Practise cultural humility.
Burnout Blindness	Mediating while depleted without recognising diminished capacity	Proactive self-care and honest self-assessment before each case.
Co-Optation	Becoming an unwitting tool of the more powerful party	Structural neutrality checks. Independent funding where possible.
Premature Closure	Pushing for agreement before parties are psychologically ready	Assess readiness indicators. Mandatory 24-hour review period.
Confirmation Bias	Filtering information to confirm your initial understanding	Devil's advocate review. Actively seek disconfirming evidence.
Emotional Contagion	Absorbing parties' emotions and unconsciously mirroring them	Self-monitoring for physical tension. Grounding practices between sessions.
Power Blindness	Failing to perceive visible and invisible power dynamics	Active power analysis at every stage. Capacity building for weaker parties.
Solution Fixation	Steering discussion toward a predetermined preferred outcome	Present all options neutrally. Let parties evaluate trade-offs.

Self-awareness of your particular vulnerabilities is the best protection against these traps.

Figure 50: Common Mediator Traps: Root Causes and Safeguards

Keep this reference visible during complex mediations. When you notice yourself falling into a familiar pattern, the corresponding safeguard gives you an immediate course correction.

16.

DIGITAL MEDIATION

Whether mediators work to avoid the pitfalls described in Chapter 15 or encounter them firsthand, their practice must also adapt to a practical reality: mediation increasingly occurs in digital spaces. Mediation practice has changed considerably since 2020. Online platforms, once considered emergency alternatives, have become integral tools in the mediator's practice. For company-community disputes, where stakeholders are scattered across continents, remote mediation offers unprecedented opportunities for connection. Yet it also introduces challenges that can undermine the trust and safety that mediation requires. This chapter provides practical guidance for mediators working in this space, recognizing that these tools are neither universal solutions nor insurmountable barriers, but rather instruments requiring careful, culturally sensitive deployment.

> **Key Concept: Digital Mediation Defined**
>
> Digital mediation encompasses any mediation process that uses electronic communication technologies, including fully virtual sessions (all parties join remotely via video or audio), hybrid sessions (some participants in-person, others remote), and technology-assisted in-person mediation (using digital tools for translation, data visualization, or documentation while meeting face-to-face). The choice of format should flow from process design principles discussed in Chapter 6, driving the selection by the parties' needs, not by the mediator's convenience.

A note on technology references: Digital tools and platforms evolve rapidly. The specific features, security capabilities, and platform names referenced in this chapter reflect the state of technology at the time of writing. Mediators should verify current capabilities, pricing, and availability before selecting tools for their practice, and should build relationships with technology advisors who can provide current guidance.

16.1 Virtual Session Protocols: When It Works and When It Fails

Remote mediation is not simply in-person mediation conducted through a screen. It requires distinct protocols, careful preparation, and honest assessment of whether the format serves the parties' interests. Discerning when online mediation can succeed and when it will likely fail is central to ethical practice.

Online dispute resolution research (Ebner and Zeleznikow, 2015) confirms that virtual mediation requires distinct competencies and protocols, as the digital environment fundamentally alters communication dynamics, power perceptions, and trust-building processes.

Conditions Favoring Virtual Mediation

Mediation works well in virtual formats under specific conditions.

Studies on mediation format effectiveness suggest that virtual mediation is most suitable when parties have established baseline trust and when disputes center on technical or procedural issues rather than deep relational or identity-based conflicts.

Online formats also work when parties have established a baseline level of trust through prior in-person contact. If the community and company representatives have met face-to-face during initial consultations or earlier mediation phases, subsequent online sessions can build on that foundation. The screen becomes less of a barrier when faces are already familiar.

Technical and procedural issues translate well to virtual settings. Discussions about implementation timelines, monitoring mechanisms, fund disbursement schedules, or clarification of agreement terms can proceed effectively online. These conversations require less emotional processing and benefit from the focused, time-bounded structure of remote meetings.

Finally, remote mediation succeeds when all parties have adequate technological access and comfort with online tools. This includes reliable internet access, appropriate devices, quiet, private spaces to participate, and familiarity with the chosen platform.

Virtual mediation serves extractive-industry disputes well when stakeholders are geographically dispersed, with company headquarters in a capital city, mining operations in a remote region, and affected communities scattered across a watershed. The format also facilitates sharing technical data such as contamination maps, water test results, and remediation plans. However, virtual formats are inappropriate when they prevent site visits needed to verify environmental claims on the ground.

Conditions Where Virtual Mediation Often Fails

Recognizing situations in which remote mediation is likely to fail. These red flags warrant reconsidering the format.

Trauma-centered disputes require careful attention in virtual settings. When trauma is central to the dispute (Chapter 10 provides trauma-informed guidance), screen-based m

Caution: Trauma Survivors and Virtual Settings

Never assume that virtual mediation is appropriate for cases involving violence, sexual assault, or severe harm. Trauma responses can be triggered unexpectedly, and through a screen, the mediator has a limited ability to provide immediate support. A participant experiencing a trauma response may freeze, disconnect, or leave the call abruptly, leaving them without support. If virtual mediation is unavoidable in such cases, ensure professional psychosocial support is physically present with the survivor, not merely available by phone.

High-distrust situations also translate poorly to virtual formats. When communities suspect that companies are acting in bad faith or have a history of broken promises, the physical absence of company representatives can reinforce the perception that they are not truly committed. The ability to look someone in the eye, to share a meal, to see them travel to your community, all carry symbolic weight that cannot be replicated digitally.

Initial relationship-building phases typically require in-person contact. The opening stages of mediation, where parties are first establishing whether they can work together, benefit enormously from face-to-face interaction. Resisting pressure to conduct initial sessions virtually unless circumstances absolutely require it.

Significant power imbalances amplify in online settings. A company representative joining from a well-equipped office, with a professional background and stable internet, projects a different image than a community member joining from a shared device in a noisy environment. These visual disparities reinforce the power dynamics that mediation seeks to balance.

Mining-affected regions, particularly in developing countries where extraction commonly occurs, often have poor telecommunications infrastructure. Remote extraction sites may lack reliable internet for sustained video conferencing. Mediators must verify that virtual formats do not exclude the very communities most affected by mining operations, and consider hybrid approaches where regional in-person meetings complement virtual sessions for central negotiations.

Essential Protocols for Virtual Sessions

Appropriate virtual mediation demands careful protocols to maximize effectiveness.

Pre-Session Technical Testing

Never begin a mediation session cold. Schedule technical tests with each party at least 24 to 48 hours in advance. Test video and audio quality, screen sharing capabilities, and breakout room functionality. Identify backup communication methods (phone numbers, WhatsApp contacts) in case of technical failures. These tests also serve as brief opportunities to build relationships with participants.

Practical Tip: The 90-Minute Rule

Research on video conferencing fatigue, including studies from Stanford University (Bailenson, 2021) and Microsoft Human Factors Lab (2020), suggests that cognitive and emotional fatigue typically sets in after approximately 90 minutes of continuous video interaction. Structure virtual mediation sessions with this in mind: 60 to 90 minutes of substantive discussion, followed by a 15 to 20-minute break. For complex discussions, consider scheduling two shorter sessions on different days rather than one marathon session.

Modified Ground Rules

Standard mediation ground rules need adaptation for virtual contexts. Add explicit agreements about cameras (do they stay on?), muting protocols, chat function usage, and what to do if someone disconnects unexpectedly. Establish that technical difficulties are not interpreted as disrespect or disengagement. Create clear signals for when someone wants to speak, since the natural flow of turn-taking is disrupted online.

Virtual Caucuses

Breakout rooms enable private caucuses, but they require more explicit management than simply stepping into another room. Announce clearly when you are moving parties to breakout rooms, how long the caucus will last, and what will happen when it ends. Test breakout room functionality before the session to ensure smooth transitions.

Sample Mediator Dialogue:

Mediator: *"We're going to take a short pause now. I'll move each group into a private virtual room for about fifteen minutes. During this time, please discuss among yourselves what would be most important for you in any agreement about water monitoring. I'll join each group briefly. When the fifteen minutes are up, you'll see a message on screen, and then we'll all return to the main room. Is everyone comfortable with this plan?"*

Documentation and Recording

Recording on virtual platforms is technically easy, but it can undermine the psychological saf

16.2 Hybrid Mediation: Bridging Physical and Virtual Worlds

Hybrid mediation, where some parties participate in person while others join remotely, presents unique challenges exceeding those of fully remote or fully in-person formats. The asymmetry between participants creates dynamics that mediators must actively manage.

When Hybrid Formats Are Appropriate

Use hybrid mediation when key local stakeholders cannot travel, but their participation is necessary. A community elder who cannot make the journey to a regional center, or a company executive who cannot travel from headquarters on short notice, can join virtually while others meet in person.

It also works for bringing in expert advisors or observers who provide technical input but are not primary negotiators. An environmental consultant reviewing monitoring data, or a legal advisor clarifying regulatory requirements, might join virtually for specific portions of the session.

Hybrid formats can accommodate phased transitions, where parties begin virtually and move toward in-person sessions as trust develops, with some hybrid sessions in between.

Managing Asymmetry

The core challenge of hybrid mediation is that participants experience the process in fundamentally different ways. Those in the room can read body language, whisper to colleagues, and feel the energy of the space. Those joining remotely see only what the camera shows, hear only what microphones pick up, and may feel excluded from the real conversation.

Caution: The "Second-Class Participant" Problem

Remote participants in hybrid settings often feel like second-class citizens. They may miss side conversations, struggle to interject, and feel that those in the room are really making decisions. If remote participants represent the less powerful party (for example, community members joining from a village while company representatives meet in a city office), this asymmetry compounds existing power imbalances. Consider whether the hybrid format is truly serving all parties or inadvertently privileging some.

Managing this asymmetry involves implementing several practices. First, ensure high-quality audio-visual equipment in the physical room. A single laptop camera at the end of a conference table is inadequate. Invest in wide-angle cameras that capture all in-person participants, high-quality microphones that pick up voices throughout the room, and screens large enough for remote participants' faces to be clearly visible to those present.

Second, actively equalize participation. Check in with remote participants more frequently. Explicitly invite their input before moving to new topics. Pause periodically to ask whether they have questions or observations.

Sample Mediator Dialogue:

Mediator: *"Before we continue, I want to check in with Maria and the other community representatives joining us online. Maria, I can see you've been listening carefully. Do you have any reactions to what's been said, or anything you'd like to add before we move forward?"*
Maria (remote): *"Thank you for asking. I did want to clarify one point about the water testing schedule that I'm not sure came through clearly . . . "*

Third, consider having a dedicated moderator or co-mediator focused on the virtual participants. This person monitors the chat, watches for raised hands or other signals, and alerts the lead mediator when remote participants want to contribute.

Fourth, during breaks, ensure remote participants also take genuine breaks rather than sitting alone at their screens. Announce breaks clearly and confirm that remote participants know when to return.

Technical Setup for Hybrid Sessions

The technical requirements for effective hybrid mediation exceed those for either fully virtual or in-person sessions.

Equipment	Purpose and Recommendations
Camera	Wide-angle camera showing all in-room participants, or multiple cameras with switching capability. Remote participants should see faces clearly.
Microphones	Conference microphones that capture voices from anywhere in the room. Test for echo and feedback before sessions begin.
Display Screens	Large screens positioned so that all in-room participants can see remote participants' faces clearly. Consider multiple screens if the room is large.
Internet Connection	Stable, high-bandwidth connection in the physical room. Have backup options (mobile hotspots, alternative venue) identified in advance.
Document Sharing	Screen sharing capability plus physical copies for in-room participants. Ensure remote and in-person participants view the same documents simultaneously.

Practical Tip: Site Visit for Hybrid Setup

If conducting hybrid mediation from a location you have not used before, visit the physical space in advance. Check internet connectivity, acoustics, lighting, and power outlet locations. Identify where cameras and screens will be positioned. A brief site visit can prevent major technical failures during the actual session.

Getting the physical and technical setup right is just as important as the procedural design. The following figure provides a practical reference for room layout, camera positioning, screen placement, and remote participant management in hybrid mediation sessions.

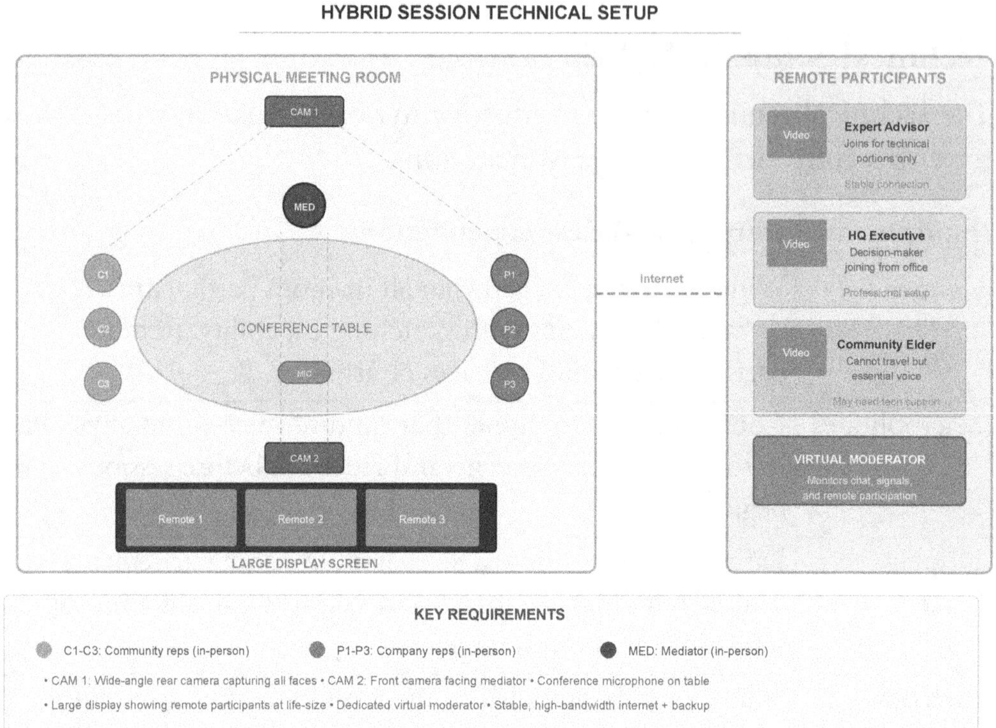

Figure 51: Hybrid Session Technical Setup: Room Layout and Remote Participant Management

Effective hybrid mediation requires careful technical setup to prevent remote participants from feeling like second-class citizens. A dedicated virtual moderator, high-quality audio-visual equipment, and life-size display of remote participants are necessary.

16.3 Digital Tools for Enhanced Mediation

Beyond basic video conferencing, various digital tools can enhance the effectiveness of mediation. Selecting tools based on the parties' needs and technological capacity, not the mediator's preferences.

Real-Time Translation Tools

Language barriers are common in company-community disputes, particularly when multinational corporations operate in regions with local languages distinct from corporate working languages. Digital translation tools can supplement (though rarely replace) human interpreters.

AI-powered translation services have advanced considerably as of 2024, with several platforms offering real-time captioning in multiple languages during video calls. Platforms like Zoom, Microsoft Teams, and Google Meet offer live captioning features (features available as of early 2025; mediators should verify current capabilities, as platform features change frequently) that, while imperfect, can help participants follow discussions in languages they partially understand.

Caution: Limits of Automated Translation

Automated translation tools make errors, particularly with nuance, idiom, and emotional content. In mediation, precise understanding of concerns and proposals requires human interpreters to supplement automated translation. Avoid sole reliance on automated translation for discussions involving commitments, agreements, or emotionally charged content. Use professional human translation when agreements are drafted.

For professional translators in virtual settings, several approaches work. Simultaneous translations can be enabled via separate audio channels, where interpreters listen to the original language and speak the translation in real time to participants who have selected their language channel. Consecutive translations, where speakers pause after each statement to allow translation, work well for smaller meetings and enable participants to observe both the original speaker and the translation process.

Working with interpreters in virtual settings requires thorough briefing on the dispute context and

Environmental Monitoring Data Sharing

Mining-specific applications of digital environmental monitoring are particularly powerful. Real-time water quality sensors downstream from tailings storage facilities can provide shared, objective data that replaces contested claims. Satellite imagery and GIS mapping tools can visualize the mine's expanding footprint relative to community land, water sources, and sacred sites, making abstract concerns concrete. Air quality monitors near processing facilities can track dust and particulate levels, with data shared on dashboards accessible to both company and community representatives. When both parties view the same data in real time, disputes over "whether" harm is occurring shift to productive discussions about "how much" and "what to do about it."

Many company-community disputes involve environmental concerns where data is central to the discussion. Digital tools can make environmental monitoring data more accessible and comprehensible to all parties.

Dashboard platforms can display real-time or regularly updated monitoring data in accessible formats. Rather than presenting dense technical reports, mediators can facilitate sessions in which parties jointly view data, such as graphical displays of water quality readings, air monitoring data, and noise level measurements. This shared visual reference can depersonalize technical disputes and focus discussion on the data itself.

Using monitoring data in mediation requires careful consideration of several factors:

Key Concept: Digital Joint Fact-Finding

Digital tools can support joint fact-finding by enabling shared access to information previously controlled by a single party. When environmental monitoring data, project documents, or impact assessments are made available through shared platforms, it can reduce information asymmetry and build trust. The key is ensuring that all parties have equal access to and understanding of the information, which may require training or technical support for less digitally equipped participants.

Visual Presentation of Impact Zones

Geographic Information System (GIS) tools and mapping applications can powerfully illustrate the spatial dimensions of disputes. Overlaying project boundaries, community land use areas, environmental impact zones, and proposed mitigation measures on interactive maps helps parties understand spatial relationships and identify potential solutions.

In virtual mediation, screen sharing these maps allows all parties to view the same visualization simultaneously. The mediator or a technical facilitator can zoom into specific areas, toggle different data layers on and off, and annotate the map with proposed changes or boundaries.

Satellite imagery and time-lapse visualizations can document changes over time, which may be relevant in disputes about historical land use, environmental degradation, or project expansion. These tools can provide visual evidence that, while powerful, requires careful interpretation, as satellite imagery resolution, timing, and analysis methods can be contested by parties with different interests that supplements party testimonies.

Practical Tip: Inclusive Map Presentations

Digital maps and GIS tools require consideration of participant familiarity. Not all participants may be familiar with readi

Digital Agreement Drafting and Signing

Reaching an agreement in mediation is only meaningful if that agreement is properly documented and authenticated. Digital tools can streamline this process while maintaining appropriate formality and legal validity.

Collaborative document editing platforms allow parties to work on agreement text in real time, with all participants seeing proposed language and modifications as they occur. This can be more efficient than exchanging drafts by email and prevents version confusion.

Electronic signature platforms provide legally valid signatures in many jurisdictions. Platforms such as DocuSign, Adobe Sign, and similar services create audit trails that show who signed, when, and from where. Before using electronic signatures, confirm that they are legally recognized in all relevant jurisdictions for the type of agreement being signed.

Caution: Electronic Signatures and Community Agreements

While electronic signatures are convenient, consider their appropriateness for Company-Community agreements. Community members may be unfamiliar with electronic signature processes and may not trust that clicking a button carries the same weight as a physical signature. In some cultural contexts, the act of signing together in person, perhaps with a ceremony or witnesses, carries crucial symbolic weight that electronic processes cannot replicate. Consider whether a hybrid approach, with electronic signatures for some parties and physical signatures for others, might be appropriate.

Drafting agreements digitally during virtual sessions requires projecting the document so all parties can

16.4 Managing Confidentiality in Virtual Spaces

Confidentiality, central to mediation, faces distinct challenges in virtual environments. Mediators must actively address these challenges rather than assuming that virtual confidentiality mirrors in-person confidentiality.

Physical Environment Risks

Parties joining from their own locations remove the mediator's control over who else might be prese

At the beginning of each virtual session, explicitly ask each participant to confirm they are in a private space where they cannot be overheard. Ask them to identify anyone else present in their location. Make clear that the confidentiality commitment extends to ensuring that no unauthorized listeners are present.

Sample Dialogue

Mediator: *"Before we begin today's session, I need to confirm that everyone is in a private space. Please look around and confirm that no one else can hear our conversation. If anyone else is present with you, please let us know who they are. This is important for maintaining the confidentiality we all agreed to."*

Community Representative: *"I'm in a private room at the community center. The door is closed, and no one else is here."*
Company Representative: *"I'm in a meeting room at our office. Our legal advisor, Ms. Chen, is here with me, as we discussed beforehand."*
Mediator: *"Thank you both for confirming. Let's proceed."*

Digital Security Risks

Digital records and transmission streams created by virtual sessions can potentially be intercepted

Basic security measures include using platform features such as waiting rooms and meeting passwords. More sensitive sessions might require end-to-end encryption, though these platforms often have fewer features. Sharing documents through secure platforms rather than as email attachments.

Key Concept: Layers of Virtual Security

Security in virtual mediation operates in layers: platform security (is the video platform itself secure?), acces

Recording and Screenshot Risks

While mediators may disable recording functions on the platform, they cannot prevent participants from using external devices to record screens or take screenshots. This technical reality warrants consideration in confidentiality discussions.

Include explicit provisions in virtual mediation confidentiality agreements prohibiting screenshots, external recordings, or any capture of the session content. While enforcement is difficult, explicitly naming these behaviors as violations sets clear expectations and provides grounds for consequences if they are breached.

Consider the practical implications of these risks. In particularly sensitive discussions, participants might be more candid speaking without visual display, using audio-only connections for certain conversations.

Documents containing sensitive information might need to be described verbally rather than shared via screen.

Modified Confidentiality Agreements

Standard mediation confidentiality agreements benefit from supplementation for virtual contexts. Consider adding clauses addressing the following.

1. Participant commitment to join from private spaces and disclose all persons present.
2. Prohibition on external recording, screenshots, or any capture of session content.
3. Agreement about chat log retention and deletion.
4. Commitment to secure storage and eventual deletion of any electronic documents exchanged during mediation.
5. Acknowledgment of the technical limitations of virtual confidentiality.

> **Practical Tip: Chat Function Management**
>
> The chat function in video platforms can be useful, but it creates a written record of the session. At the start of each session, decide whether to use the chat and for what purposes. If you enable the chat, remind participants that platform messages may be logged. At the end of each session, explicitly save or delete chat logs as agreed by the parties. Do not assume that closing the meeting automatically deletes the chat history.

16.5 When Virtual Mediation Saves the Process

Despite its challenges, virtual mediation can be transformative in the right circumstances. Understanding when technology genuinely serves the process helps mediators advocate appropriately for virtual options.

Geographic Dispersion

Stakeholder geographic dispersion across multiple locations or continents makes virtual mediation an option that

Remote technology collapses geographical distances instantly.

Maintaining Momentum

Complex disputes require ongoing engagement. Scheduling in-person sessions only when all parties can travel may result in meetings months apart, during which momentum fades, circumstances change, and frustration builds. Virtual sessions can fill these gaps, maintaining connection and progress between more substantial in-person meetings.

A protracted multi-year mediation (such as the Kintinian community and Siguiri gold mine case described in Chapter 17) could have been accelerated by strategically using virtual sessions for routine check-ins and technical discussions, while reserving in-person sessions for relationship-building and major negotiations.

Crisis Response

Crisis situations demand immediate responses, and virtual platforms enable rapid convening.

> **Example: Digital Mediation After an Environmental Incident**
>
> Tailings dam breaches or chemical spills demand rapid communication between the co

Involving Specialists

Technical experts, legal specialists, or other advisors may be essential for specific discussions but not needed throughout the entire mediation. Virtual participation allows these specialists to join for relevant portions without the expense and time commitment of physical travel. For example, an environmental scientist can present water quality analysis, answer questions, and then leave the call while parties continue their negotiation.

Key Concept: Strategic Virtual Integration

The most effective approach often strategically combines in-person and virtual elements. Initial relationship-building and trust-establishing sessions might occur in person. Technical discussions, progress updates, and clarification meetings might occur virtually. Final agreement negotiations and signing ceremonies might return to in-person sessions. This blended approach captures the strengths of each format while minimizing their weaknesses.

16.6 When Virtual Mediation Destroys the Process

Equally important is recognizing when virtual mediation will undermine rather than support resolution. Mediators must be willing to advocate against virtual formats when circumstances warrant it, even when clients or parties push for the convenience of virtual sessions.

Trauma-Centered Disputes

As discussed earlier, disputes involving violence, sexual assault, displacement, or other trauma require particular care. Virtual mediation can fail in these situations in multiple ways.

Trauma survivors may need to feel physical safety and containment, which screens cannot provide. They may also need a support person physically present who can read their body language and intervene if they become distressed. Additionally, they may need the option to step outside, take a walk, or otherwise physically remove themselves from the conversation while remaining connected to support.

Through a screen, mediators cannot fully observe distress signals. They cannot offer a glass of water, a tissue, or a reassuring physical presence. If a survivor disconnects in distress, they may be left alone with their trauma while the mediator frantically tries to re-establish contact.

Caution: The Virtual Disconnect

Participant distress during in-person sessions allows mediators to pause, offer support,

High-Distrust Situations

High-distrust situations present particular challenges: virtual mediation can reinforce rather than address them.

The symbolic weight of physical presence matters. A company executive who travels to a rural community demonstrates commitment in a way that joining a video call cannot replicate. The shared experience of being in the same room, of breaking bread together, of looking each other in the eyes without screens between, builds a connection that virtual interaction struggles to match.

In high-distrust situations, reserving virtual meetings for subsequent technical discussions after in-person sessions have established a relationship foundation. Starting with virtual in these circumstances often means starting at a disadvantage.

Cultural Contexts Requiring Physical Presence

In many cultures, important agreements require physical presence, ritual, and ceremony. The formal handshake, the shared meal, the presence of witnesses, the blessing of elders, and the exchange of symbolic gifts cannot be replicated virtually.

Investigating whether the community has expectations about how agreements should be concluded. Imposing virtual processes on communities for whom physical presence carries deep cultural significance can undermine the very agreements being reached, even if technically valid documents are signed.

Significant Power Imbalances

Power imbalances amplify in virtual mediation in ways that undermine fair process.

The party with better technology also has practical advantages: clearer audio makes their voice more present, better video makes their expressions more visible, and stable connections mean fewer interruptions. These technical advantages can translate into negotiation advantages in subtle but real ways.

Significant power imbalances warrant reconsideration of virtual formats.

The following decision framework helps you navigate format selection by weighing power dynamics, relationship stage, and technical access against the demands of each mediation phase.

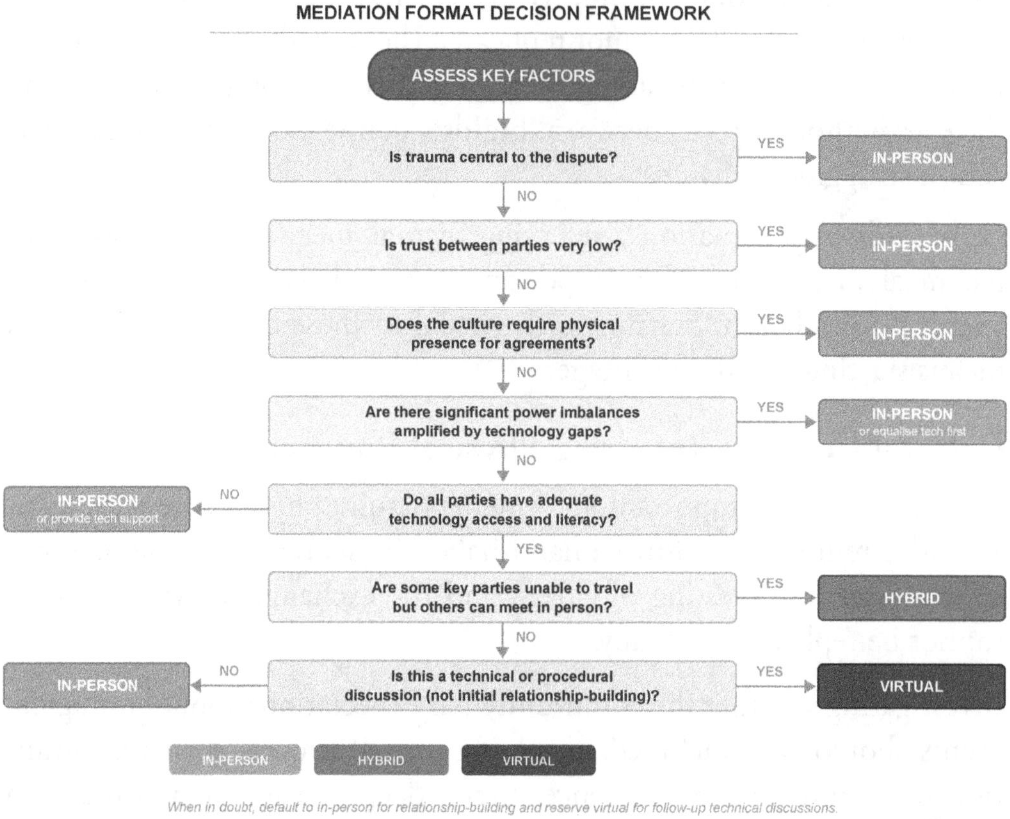

Figure 52: Mediation Format Decision Framework: Virtual, Hybrid, or In-Person

This decision framework guides mediators through the key factors that determine whether virtual, hybrid, or in-person mediation is appropriate. When in doubt, default to in-person for relationship-building sessions.

16.7 Technology Access and the Digital Divide

Any discussion of digital mediation must confront the reality of unequal access to technology. The digital divide extends beyond device ownership to include connectivity, tech literacy, and the infrastructure supporting technology use.

Understanding the Digital Divide

In many regions where company-community disputes occur, reliable internet access is unavailable or unaffordable. Rural communities in Sub-Saharan Africa, remote areas of Southeast Asia, indigenous territories in the Amazon, and mining regions in Central Asia may have limited or no cellular coverage, irregular electricity, and limited experience with online communication tools.

Even where technology exists, it may be distributed unequally. Men may have greater access to smartphones than women. Younger people may be more digitally literate than elders who hold traditional authority. Wealthier community members may have personal devices, while others share limited community resources.

> **Key Concept: Multi-Dimensional Digital Divide**
>
> The digital divide has multiple dimensions, including access (physical availability of devices and connectivity), affordability (ability to pay for data and equipment), literacy (ability to use digital tools effectively), quality (speed and reliability of connections), and agency (ability to choose when and how to use technology). A mediation process that assumes all parties have equal capacity across all these dimensions risks excluding or disadvantaging those who do not.

Assessing Technological Capacity

Before proposing remote or hybrid mediation, conduct an honest assessment of all parties' technological capacity. This assessment should cover several dimensions, including:

- **Connectivity:** What internet access is available at proposed participation locations? Is it reliable? What bandwidth is available? Can it support video calls, or only audio?
- **Devices:** What devices do participants have access to? Do they have personal smartphones, shared community computers, or

company-provided equipment? Can they access devices in private spaces?

- **Skills:** Are participants comfortable using video platforms? Have they used them before? Do they know how to mute, use chat functions, and join breakout rooms?
- **Environment:** Can participants access private spaces for confidential conversations? Are those spaces quiet enough for clear audio? Is electricity reliable?
- **Cost:** Who bears the cost of data usage, equipment, or travel to connectivity hubs? Does virtual participation impose financial burdens on some parties that should be addressed?

Addressing Technological Inequity

Technological inequity revealed through assessment offers several response options:

- **Choose in-person instead:** If technology barriers are significant and the dispute's importance warrants it, advocate for in-person mediation. The improved quality of participation may justify the added travel cost.
- **Provide technology support:** If the company has resources and the community lacks them, consider whether the company can fund technology provision for community participants, such as devices, data plans, or access to equipped facilities. This must be done carefully to avoid creating dependency or the appearance of improper influence.
- **Use hub locations:** If individual connectivity is poor but a central location has better infrastructure, community participants could gather at that location while company participants join remotely. This creates a partial hybrid in which the community is together in person.
- **Reduce technology requirements:** Audio-only calls require less bandwidth than video. Simple platforms require less learning than feature-rich ones. Consider whether minimal technology approaches might enable participation where sophisticated solutions cannot.

Practical Tip: Low-Bandwidth Alternatives

Limited connectivity requires consideration of lower-bandwidth alternatives: audio-only conference calls,

Caution: Technology Provision and Neutrality

If one party provides technology to enable another party's participation, consider the implications for the mediator's neutrality and the parties' perceptions. A community using devices or data paid for by the company might feel obligated to reciprocate in a certain way or might be accused of being bought. If technology support is necessary, consider whether it should come from a neutral third party or an NGO partner, and whether costs should be shared in ways that minimize perceived influence.

The digital divide in mining contexts is particularly acute. Many mining operations are located in remote regions of sub-Saharan Africa, Southeast Asia, or Latin America where mobile network coverage is unreliable and electricity supply is intermittent. Community representatives may have limited experience with video conferencing technology, and the stress of navigating unfamiliar platforms can compound the power asymmetry that already exists.

When a company executive joins from a high-definition conference room in London while a community leader connects from a shared phone in a village with inconsistent signal, the medium itself becomes a source of inequality. Mediators must honestly assess whether digital formats serve all parties equitably or whether they inadvertently reinforce existing power imbalances. (see Chapter 12 for broader strategies on managing power asymmetries)

Digital Mediation in Extractive-Industry Disputes

Extractive-industry disputes present a distinctive combination of challenges for digital mediation that merit specific attention. These disputes typically involve multinational corporations headquartered in one country, operating through subsidiaries in another, and affecting communities in remote locations with limited infrastructure. The geographic spread makes digital tools attractive, but the trust dynamics and power asymmetries that characterize these disputes demand careful calibration of how those tools are deployed.

Security concerns are particularly salient. In regions where extractive operations generate social conflict, community leaders who participate in mediation may face retaliation from local authorities, company-aligned actors, or rival community factions. Digital communication creates records that can be intercepted or subpoenaed. Video recordings, chat logs, and even metadata showing that a community leader was in a virtual meeting with a company can carry risks in volatile environments.

Mediators should use end-to-end encrypted platforms. In contexts with limited internet infrastructure, mediators should verify that encrypted platforms function reliably on available bandwidth and consider whether the security benefits justify potential connectivity challenges. Avoid cloud storage of session recordings, and discuss with participants whether any digital footprint from their participation could expose them to harm. In some cases, the safest option may be low-technology alternatives: encrypted voice calls rather than video, or even in-person meetings with no digital record at all.

The multi-stakeholder nature of extractive disputes also complicates digital formats. A mining mediation may involve the operating company, its parent corporation, government regulators, affected communities (potentially several with different interests), environmental organizations, and traditional authorities.

Managing a virtual session with eight or ten parties, each with different levels of technological capacity and different languages, requires a degree of facilitation skill and technical support that exceeds ordinary virtual mediation. Consider appointing a dedicated technical facilitator alongside the mediator, and design the session architecture to use breakout rooms or sequential bilateral conversations rather than attempting full plenary sessions with all parties on screen simultaneously.

Finally, the long time horizons of extractive-industry disputes, which may span years or even decades, make the strategic integration of digital tools especially valuable. A mining community mediation might progress through phases where digital tools play different roles: encrypted messaging for initial trust-building contacts, video calls for routine technical discussions about environmental monitoring data, in-person sessions for the emotionally charged negotiations over compensation or resettlement, and shared online platforms for long-term agreement monitoring.

The mediator who understands these phases and matches the communication format to the needs of each stage will serve the parties far more effectively than one who defaults to a single format throughout.

16.8 Preparing Participants for Digital Mediation

Successful digital mediation requires preparation beyond what in-person mediation demands. Participants who are uncomfortable with technology or unclear about how virtual sessions will work cannot engage effectively.

Technical Orientation

Before the first substantive virtual session, provide technical orientation to participants who need it. This might involve practice sessions where participants learn to join calls, use basic features, and troubleshoot common problems.

Create simple guides in appropriate languages explaining how to join the platform, what participants will see, and what to do if problems arise. Include screenshots and step-by-step instructions. For participants with limited literacy, video tutorials or phone-based walkthrough calls may be more effective.

Identify a technical support person who can be available during sessions to help participants experiencing difficulties. This might be an NGO partner, a local community member with technical skills, or a dedicated support line.

Process Adaptation Explanation

Explain how virtual mediation will differ from in-person processes. Cover session structure (shorter, with more breaks), turn-taking protocols (how to signal wanting to speak), caucus procedures (breakout rooms), and document sharing (screen sharing or pre-distributed materials).

Discuss confidentiality adaptations. Explain the additional commitments regarding private spaces, no recording, and secure document handling. Ensure participants understand both their obligations and the limitations of virtual confidentiality.

Address what happens if technology fails. Explain backup plans, how participants should respond to disconnections, and how the session will be resumed or rescheduled if needed.

Psychological Preparation

Beyond technical preparation, help participants psychologically prepare for digital interaction. Some people find video calls more stressful than in-person meetings. Others feel less connected or less able to express themselves.

Encourage participants to set up their space thoughtfully. Good lighting, a neutral background, and a comfortable chair all contribute to better engagement. Suggest they minimize distractions by closing other applications and silencing their phones.

Normalize the awkwardness that often accompanies video interaction. Explain that turn-taking is harder, that silences may feel longer, and that technical glitches happen. Reassure participants that these challenges will be managed together.

Sample Dialogue

Mediator (in pre-session call): *"I know some of you have not participated in a video mediation before. It can feel a bit strange at first. There's often a slight delay in audio, so it's harder to know when it's your turn to speak. Sometimes people talk over each other by accident. Don't worry about that. We'll work together to make sure everyone gets heard. If you want to speak, you can raise your hand on screen or simply say, "I'd* *like to add something." Does anyone have questions or concerns about the process before we begin next week?"*

16.9 Ethical Considerations in Digital Mediation

The shift to digital mediation raises ethical questions that mediators must thoughtfully navigate. The core ethical principles of mediation remain constant, but their application requires adaptation.

Voluntariness in Digital Contexts

Voluntariness means parties choose to participate freely. In digital contexts, this includes the format choice. Avoiding pressure on parties to use virtual mediation if they are uncomfortable with it or lack adequate access to technology.

Ensuring that format decisions genuinely reflect the parties' preferences rather than the mediator's convenience or cost considerations. If one party prefers in-person mediation and it is feasible, giving their preference serious weight, particularly if they represent the less powerful party.

Self-Determination and Technology

Self-determination means parties control outcomes. Technology can either support or undermine this principle depending on how mediators deploy it.

Digital tools that make information more accessible, such as shared dashboards showing monitoring data, can enhance self-determination by ensuring both parties have equal access to facts. Digital tools that advantage one party's communication, such as sophisticated presentation software that a company deploys when the community lacks similar capabilities, can undermine it.

Evaluating whether technology choices support or impede genuine party control over outcomes.

Do No Harm in Digital Spaces

The ethical principle of "do no harm" requires particular attention in digital mediation. Harm can occur through inappropriate exposure, such as conducting sensitive discussions over insecure platforms. It can happen through exclusion, such as proceeding with virtual formats that some participants cannot effectively access. And it can occur through retraumatization, such as conducting trauma-related discussions without adequate support structures.

Mediators must honestly assess whether virtual formats in particular contexts might cause harm that in-person formats would avoid. When potential harm is identified, the mediator has an ethical obligation to address it, whether by adapting the process, providing additional support, or advocating for a format change.

16.10 The Future of Digital Mediation

Technology continues evolving rapidly. Staying informed about emerging tools while maintaining focus on the fundamentally human nature of conflict resolution.

Emerging technologies may offer new possibilities. Virtual reality environments could provide more immersive experiences than current video platforms. AI-powered translation may improve to the point of near-real-time, accurate interpretation. Blockchain-based agreement systems could provide tamper-proof documentation.

Yet technology cannot replace the essential human work of mediation: building trust, acknowledging suffering, facilitating understanding, and guiding parties toward agreements they can live with. Whatever tools emerge, the mediator's core competencies remain central, including the communication skills discussed in Chapter 4 that must be adapted for digital contexts.

The most effective mediators will be those who can thoughtfully integrate technology where it helps while recognizing and respecting its limitations. They will advocate for in-person connection when technology falls short. They will ensure that digital tools serve the parties rather than substituting for the hard work of human relationship-building.

Practical Tip: Continuous Learning

Technology changes faster than handbooks can be updated. Stay current by participating in mediator networks that share experiences with digital tools, attending training on new platforms, and experimenting with new technologies in low-stakes settings before deploying them in important mediations. Approach new technology with curious skepticism. Be interested in its possibilities but alert to its limitations.

16.11 Conclusion

Digital mediation is neither a panacea nor a threat. It is a set of tools that, when used thoughtfully, can expand access to resolution processes and maintain engagement across distances. When used carelessly, it can exclude participants, amplify power imbalances, and undermine the trust-building that mediation requires.

The mediator's task is discernment: understanding when remote formats serve the parties, when hybrid approaches bridge gaps, when in-person presence is essential, and how to adapt protocols to electronically mediated contexts while preserving mediation's core values. This discernment requires honest assessment of parties' needs and capacities, willingness to advocate against convenient but inappropriate format choices, and continuous learning as technology evolves.

Ultimately, mediation remains a human endeavor. Technology can support it, but cannot replace the mediator's skill, presence, and judgment. In company-community disputes, where trust is fragile, power is imbalanced, and stakes are high, that human element remains indispensable, whether delivered in person or through a screen.

Chapter Summary: Digital Mediation Decision Framework

Consider Virtual/Hybrid When:	Prioritize In-Person When:
Geographic dispersion makes travel impractical	Trauma is central to the dispute
Some baseline trust already exists	Distrust is high and unaddressed
Discussions are technical or procedural	Initial relationship-building is needed
All parties have adequate technology access	Significant power imbalances exist
Momentum needs to be maintained between in-person sessions	Cultural context requires physical presence for agreements
Specialists need to join for specific portions	Technology access is limited or unequal
A rapid response to a crisis is needed	Final agreement signing and ceremonial closure

Key Takeaways

1. Digital mediation is not simply in-person mediation conducted online. It requires distinct protocols for trust-building, confidentiality, and emotional safety.
2. The decision between virtual, hybrid, and in-person formats should be driven by context, not convenience. Factors include participant safety, technological capacity, geographic dispersion, and the emotional intensity of the issues.
3. The digital divide is a real barrier in extractive-industry disputes. Mediators must assess and address disparities in internet access, device availability, and digital literacy before proposing virtual formats.
4. Hybrid mediation creates inherent asymmetries between in-person and remote participants. Without deliberate design, remote participants become second-class voices in the process.
5. Confidentiality in virtual settings requires additional safeguards: private physical spaces for all participants, prohibitions on recording, and clear protocols for chat and document sharing.

6. The 90-minute rule reflects research on attention and engagement. Virtual sessions should be shorter and more structured than their in-person equivalents.

Reflection Questions

- What is the technological capacity of the communities you work with? How would you assess readiness for virtual mediation?
- Have you facilitated a virtual or hybrid session where remote participants seemed disengaged? What might you do differently?
- How would you ensure confidentiality when a participant is joining from a shared household or a community center?
- What is your decision framework for choosing between in-person, virtual, and hybrid formats? What factors weigh most heavily?
- How comfortable are you with the technical demands of digital mediation? What skills would you need to develop?

17.

CASE STUDIES

The preceding chapters established principles, skills, and techniques across diverse mediation contexts. This chapter brings those elements together through two detailed case studies that illustrate the principles, challenges, and techniques discussed throughout this handbook. Rather than offering brief summaries of many cases, we examine two mediations in depth, following them from initial conflict through process design, key turning points, impasses, and ultimate outcomes. This approach allows practitioners to see how multiple principles interact in practice and to learn from both successes and difficulties.

The cases were selected to provide complementary perspectives:

- **Case Study A: The Guinea Mining Mediation (2017-2024)** represents a protracted, multi-year process involving a multinational mining company and an affected community in West Africa. It demonstrates phased agreement-building, trust restoration over time, and addressing legacy grievances.
- **Case Study B: The Stuttgart 21 Mediation (2010)** represents a compressed, high-profile public dialogue on a major infrastructure project in Germany. It demonstrates stakeholder engagement under intense media scrutiny, technical fact-finding, and the limits of mediation in politically charged contexts.

These cases span different continents, sectors, timelines, and power configurations, offering transferable lessons for mediators working in diverse company-community contexts.

17.1 Case Study A: The Kintinian Community and Siguiri Gold Mine, Guinea

A Seven-Year Journey from Complaint to Comprehensive Agreement (2017-2024)

Background and Conflict History

The Setting

The Siguiri Gold Mine, operated by Société AngloGold Ashanti de Guinée (SAG), a subsidiary of the multinational AngloGold Ashanti, has operated in the Siguiri Prefecture of northeastern Guinea since the late 1990s. The mine is one of the largest gold operations in West Africa and a significant contributor to Guinea's economy. It operates in a region characterized by artisanal and small-scale mining traditions, agricultural livelihoods, and communities whose relationship with industrial mining has been shaped by decades of promises, disappointments, and power asymmetries.

The Area One community (Kintinian and surrounding villages) was directly affected by the mine's expansion. Community members depended on subsistence farming, small-scale gold panning, and local trade. The land held not only economic importance but also cultural and ancestral significance. When mine expansion required community resettlement, the seeds of a protracted conflict were planted.

The Conflict Emerges

The grievances that eventually led to formal mediation had accumulated over years. Community members alleged:

- **Inadequate consultation:** Decisions about resettlement were made without meaningful community participation. Information was provided late or not at all, and community members felt excluded from choices that would fundamentally alter their lives.

- **Insufficient compensation:** Compensation for lost land, homes, and livelihoods was perceived as inadequate. Valuation methods were opaque, and many families felt they received far less than the actual value of what they lost.
- **Broken promises:** Commitments regarding alternative housing, water access, schools, and healthcare facilities were not fully honored. Promised infrastructure was delayed, incomplete, or of poor quality.
- **Livelihood destruction:** Families lost access to farmland and artisanal mining sites without receiving adequate support for alternative livelihoods. Economic security that had existed for generations was disrupted.
- **Human rights concerns:** Allegations of intimidation, heavy-handed security responses to community protests, and disregard for community rights under international standards added a human rights dimension to the economic grievances.

Confidence between the community and the company had deteriorated to the point where direct dialogue was ineffective. Community members viewed company representatives with suspicion, believing that any engagement was designed to delay or deflect rather than genuinely address their concerns. The company, for its part, faced operational pressures, viewed some community demands as excessive, and struggled to navigate the complexity of local politics and expectations.

Escalation and the Decision to Seek External Mediation

By 2017, the conflict had escalated significantly. Community protests disrupted operations. Relationships were characterized by mutual accusations and hostility. NGO partners working with the community encouraged them to explore accountability mechanisms beyond direct negotiation with the company.

The community, with support from international and national NGOs, filed a complaint with the Compliance Advisor Ombudsman (CAO), the independent accountability mechanism for the International Finance

Corporation (IFC) and the Multilateral Investment Guarantee Agency (MIGA). Because the mining project had received IFC financing, the CAO had jurisdiction to facilitate dispute resolution.

> **Key Concept: Accountability Mechanisms**
>
> The CAO represents a category of independent accountability mechanisms associated with development finance institutions. These mechanisms can provide communities with access to dispute resolution processes that would otherwise be unavailable, addressing the power imbalance that often prevents affected communities from engaging effectively with multinational corporations. For mediators, understanding when and how to involve such mechanisms can be crucial in complex disputes.

Stakeholder Mapping and Power Analysis

Effective mediation requires understanding not just the primary parties but the entire ecosystem of stakeholders and power relationships. In this case, the stakeholder landscape, which included primary and secondary parties, was complex.

Primary Parties

- **The Area One Community:** Not a monolithic entity, but a collection of villages with internal dynamics, traditional leadership structures, and varying degrees of impact from the mine. Some families were directly displaced; others were indirectly affected. Youth, women, and elders had different priorities. Identifying legitimate representatives who could speak for the community while ensuring inclusive input was itself a challenge.
- **Société AngloGold Ashanti de Guinée (SAG):** The operating company, a subsidiary of a global mining corporation. Decision-making involved both local management and corporate headquarters. The company faced multiple pressures: operational efficiency, investor expectations, reputational concerns, regulatory requirements, and the practical challenges of operating in a complex environment.

Secondary Stakeholders

- **NGO partners:** National and international NGOs provided the community with technical support, documentation assistance, and advocacy capacity. Their involvement helped balance power but also introduced additional perspectives and expectations.
- **Local and national government:** Guinean authorities had interests in both community welfare and continued mining revenue. Their role was somewhat peripheral to the mediation but relevant to implementation.
- **IFC:** As a financier, IFC had leverage over the company and requirements regarding environmental and social standards. The IFC's Performance Standards provided normative benchmarks for the mediation.
- **CAO:** As the independent mechanism facilitating dispute resolution, CAO mediators brought neutrality, process expertise, and institutional credibility. Their involvement was essential to creating a space where the community felt safe engaging in the process.

Power Analysis

The power asymmetry in this mediation was severe and spanned multiple dimensions, including:

Dimension	Company	Community
Financial resources	Substantial corporate budget, legal and technical experts on retainer	Limited, dependent on NGO support for travel and participation
Technical expertise	Access to engineers, lawyers, environmental specialists	Limited formal education, reliant on NGO expertise
Political access	Direct relationships with government officials	Peripheral, mediated through local leaders
Alternatives (BATNA)	Continue operations, manage reputational risk, litigate if necessary	Protest (with risk of repression), international advocacy, uncertain legal options
Moral authority	Weakened by a history of broken promises	Strong claim as the affected population with legitimate grievances

The CAO's involvement was crucial precisely because it helped level this playing field. The presence of a neutral, credible institution meant the community could engage without fear that the process would simply be another venue for company dominance.

Why Mediation Was Chosen

Several factors made mediation the appropriate intervention, including:

1. **Willingness to engage:** Despite the hostility, both parties recognized that continued conflict was costly. The company faced operational disruptions, reputational damage, and pressure from the IFC to resolve grievances. The community wanted tangible improvements in their lives, not perpetual protest.
2. **Negotiable issues:** The core grievances, while significant, involved matters that could be addressed through negotiation: compensation amounts, infrastructure commitments, livelihood support, and improved consultation processes.
3. **Availability of neutral facilitation:** The CAO provided experienced mediators who were acceptable to both parties. Without this option, the parties had no trusted venue for dialogue.
4. **Opportunity for ongoing relationships:** Unlike a one-time commercial dispute, the community and company would continue to be neighbors for decades. A mediated solution that rebuilt the relationship had value beyond any specific agreement terms.

Alternatives Considered

Before formal mediation, the community and its advocates considered several alternatives. These included:

- **Continued direct negotiation:** This had repeatedly failed due to credibility deficits and power imbalances.
- **Litigation:** Legal options in Guinea were limited by weak judicial capacity. International litigation was theoretically possible but would be slow, expensive, and uncertain.

- **International advocacy campaigns:** Naming and shaming could pressure the company, but would not directly produce remedies for affected families.
- **Escalated protest:** Blockades and disruption could force the company's attention but carried risks of violence, arrest, and further harm to community members.

CAO-facilitated mediation offered a path that could produce concrete outcomes while preserving the possibility of other options if mediation failed.

Process Design Decisions

The process design reflected the specific challenges of this dispute. Key design decisions included:

Phased Approach

Rather than attempting to resolve all issues in a single comprehensive negotiation, the mediators designed a phased process. This decision was crucial because trust was too low for the parties to negotiate a comprehensive package at the outset. Additionally, some urgent issues, such as water access and interim housing, required immediate attention and could not wait for the resolution of more complex matters.

Mediators knew that early agreements on minor issues could demonstrate good faith and build momentum for harder negotiations. A phased approach allowed for learning and adjustment as the process evolved.

Community Preparation and Representation

The mediators invested significant time in pre-mediation community engagement to ensure genuine representation and informed participation. This included:

- Multiple community meetings to identify priorities and concerns.
- Support from NGO partners to help the community understand the mediation process and their rights within it.

- Careful attention to ensuring that community representatives genuinely reflected the views of affected households, including women, youth, and elders.
- Capacity building to enable community members to articulate their interests effectively.

Neutral Venue and Logistics

Sessions were held in locations acceptable to both parties, neither on company premises nor in community spaces that might intimidate company representatives. Logistical support ensured community members could participate without financial hardship.

Documentation and Transparency

Agreements were documented in writing, translated into local languages, and explained to community members who could not read. This documentation served multiple purposes, including ensuring clarity about commitments, creating a record for accountability, and enabling community members to verify that their representatives had secured appropriate terms.

> **Practical Tip: Building Trust Through Small Wins**
>
> In protracted, low-trust disputes, early agreements on urgent but manageable issues can demonstrate that mediation works. In the Guinea case, addressing water access early provided immediate benefits to the community while showing the company that making commitments in mediation reduced conflict. Each kept promise became evidence that the process was worth continuing.

Key Turning Points and Impasse Moments

Over seven years, the mediation navigated numerous challenges, with several moments standing out as particularly significant.

The First Interim Agreement (2019)

After extensive initial discussions, the parties reached their first interim agreement, which addressed water access, schooling, consultation mechanisms, human rights protocols, and livelihood restoration programs. This agreement was a turning point because it demonstrated that agreement was possible after years of failed direct negotiation.

It also validated community engagement by requiring the company to make concrete commitments, not just expressions of goodwill.

Finally, it set precedents for structuring and monitoring subsequent agreements.

Impasse Over Compensation Methodology

One of the most difficult impasses arose over how to calculate compensation for lost land and livelihoods. The community believed past compensation was grossly inadequate; the company pointed to its compliance with legal requirements and budget constraints.

The mediators navigated this impasse by:

1. **Separating the discussion of methodology from the debate on amounts.** Before negotiating numbers, the parties agreed on principles: what should compensation cover, what standards should apply, and how should different types of loss be valued?
2. **Introducing external benchmarks.** The IFC Performance Standards on Land Acquisition and Involuntary Resettlement provided normative criteria that both parties could reference. This shifted the discussion from adversarial bargaining to joint application of recognized standards.
3. **Caucusing extensively.** Private sessions allowed each party to express concerns and explore flexibility that they could not reveal in joint sessions.
4. **Reframing the question.** Rather than asking, "How much is owed?" the mediators reframed the discussion around "What do families need to restore their livelihoods and achieve security comparable to what they had before displacement?"

Momentum Through Infrastructure Delivery

Between 2019 and 2024, the parties reached additional interim agreements on specific issues: rental allowances for interim housing (2022), construction of a local market (2022), health center improvements (2023), and road maintenance (2024). Each agreement followed the same pattern: identification of a specific need, negotiation of terms, documentation, implementation, and monitoring.

This accumulation of implemented agreements proved crucial. Each improvement demonstrated tangible results for community members. The company saw that meeting commitments led to reduced conflict and improved relations. Both parties developed working relationships with each other and with the mediators, making subsequent negotiations easier.

> **Caution: Implementation as Test of Good Faith**
>
> Agreements on paper mean nothing without implementation. In protracted mediations, the period between interim agreements becomes a critical test. If the company fails to deliver, community skepticism proves justified, and the process may collapse. The Guinea mediation succeeded partly because the company honored its commitments, and because monitoring mechanisms allowed problems to be identified and addressed before they derailed the process.

What Worked, What Didn't, and Why

Factors Contributing to Success

1. **Credible neutral facilitation:** CAO's independence and experience provided a process both parties found credible. Without this, the community would not have engaged, and the company would have faced continued confrontation.
2. **Phased approach:** Building rapport incrementally through smaller agreements before tackling the most contentious issues allowed the relationship to develop alongside the substantive work.

3. **NGO support for community capacity:** Technical and advocacy support helped the community participate more effectively, reducing the power asymmetry.
4. **Company willingness to commit resources:** The company's agreement to fund infrastructure improvements and compensation required corporate authorization and budget allocation. Their willingness to do so signaled genuine commitment.
5. **External normative framework:** IFC Performance Standards provided shared reference points that helped depoliticize some disputes.
6. **Patience:** Seven years is a long time. Both parties, and the mediators, demonstrated sustained commitment even when progress was slow.

Challenges and Limitations

1. **Time required:** Seven years is a long time for families waiting for compensation and reconciliation. While the phased approach delivered incremental benefits, many community members had to wait years for their claims to be fully resolved.
2. **Internal community dynamics:** Ensuring that agreements reflected the views of all affected households, not just the most vocal leaders, required ongoing attention. There were tensions about representation and distribution of benefits.
3. **Corporate decision-making constraints:** Company negotiators sometimes lacked authority to make commitments, causing delays while they obtained corporate approval.
4. **Ongoing operational tensions:** Even during mediation, new incidents arose that threatened to derail the process. Managing these required vigilance and flexibility.

Outcome and Implementation

In September 2024, the parties reached a final comprehensive agreement. The key elements included:

- Individual Compensation. Families affected by resettlement received individual compensation, provided directly by the company. The amounts **were determined using** the methodology developed during mediation, **which addressed** previous shortfalls.

- Sustainable Development Fund. A portion of the resources was allocated to establish a Sustainable Development Fund for the community. This fund would finance projects to improve livelihoods and living standards, and was managed with community involvement. IFC agreed to provide technical support for project identification and assessment. This structure was significant because it provided ongoing benefits rather than a one-time payment, gave the community a role in determining how resources were used, and created a framework for continued collaboration.
- Commitment to Ongoing Relationships. Both parties committed to continued collaboration. The agreement included mechanisms for addressing future concerns, reducing the likelihood that new grievances would escalate into the kind of protracted conflict that had characterized the previous decade.
- Monitoring. CAO will monitor implementation for two years. This external oversight provides assurance to the community that commitments will be honored and gives the company a structured framework for demonstrating compliance.

Transferable Lessons

The Guinea case offers several lessons applicable to other company-community mediations, including:

1. **Time investment is often necessary.** Complex disputes with deep credibility deficits resist quick resolution. Mediators and parties should set realistic expectations about timelines.
2. **Phased approaches can manage complexity.** Breaking a large dispute into smaller agreements makes the task manageable and builds momentum.
3. **Power balancing requires deliberate intervention.** Without NGO support and neutral facilitation, the community could not have participated effectively.

4. **Implementation matters more than agreements.** Each delivered commitment built credibility for subsequent negotiations.
5. **External normative frameworks help.** International standards can provide shared reference points that depoliticize disputes.
6. **Long-term relationships matter.** The final agreement created structures for ongoing collaboration, not just one-time remedies.
7. **Accountability mechanisms enable access.** CAO's role was essential. Mediators should understand available mechanisms and help communities access them.

17.2 Case Study B: Stuttgart 21 Infrastructure Mediation, Germany

High-Profile Public Dialogue Under Crisis Conditions (2010)

Background and Conflict History

The Project

Stuttgart 21 (S21) is one of Europe's largest and most controversial infrastructure projects: a comprehensive redevelopment of Stuttgart's main railway station from an above-ground terminus into an underground through-station, linked to new high-speed rail connections. The project involved demolishing large portions of the historic station, excavating vast underground spaces, and removing trees from the adjacent Schlossgarten park.

Sponsors conceived the project in the 1990s and secured approval through standard German planning processes. Project sponsors included Deutsche Bahn (German Rail), the federal government, the state of Baden-Württemberg, and the city of Stuttgart. The projected cost at the time of the 2010 conflict was approximately €4.5 billion, though this would later increase significantly.

The Opposition

Opposition to Stuttgart 21 grew over many years but intensified dramatically in 2010. A broad coalition of citizens, environmental groups, heritage preservation advocates, urban planners, and local politicians argued that the project was:

- **Economically unjustified:** Critics questioned whether the benefits justified the enormous costs, especially given ongoing cost escalations.
- **Environmentally damaging:** The removal of old trees from the park and potential impacts on local water systems raised environmental concerns.
- **Architecturally misguided:** The historic station, designed by architect Paul Bonatz, was considered a cultural landmark. Opponents argued for preserving and renovating rather than demolishing.
- **Democratically illegitimate:** Despite formal approvals, many citizens felt decisions had been made without genuine public input. The process was perceived as a technocratic imposition rather than a democratic deliberation.
- **Technically flawed:** Alternative proposals, particularly "Kopfbahnhof 21" (K21), which would modernize the existing terminus station, were claimed to offer comparable benefits at lower cost and with less disruption.

Escalation and Crisis

Throughout 2010, protests grew. Tens of thousands of citizens participated in weekly demonstrations. The movement drew support across political lines, attracting conservatives concerned about fiscal prudence alongside environmentalists and leftists.

The crisis peaked on September 30, 2010, "Black Thursday," when police used water cannons and pepper spray against protesters attempting to prevent tree removal in the park. Over 100 people were injured, including elderly participants and children. The images of police violence against nonviolent protesters shocked Germany and transformed what had been a local planning dispute into a national scandal.

Black Thursday fundamentally changed the situation. The state government faced a legitimacy crisis. Project opponents were radicalized and energized. International media coverage damaged Germany's reputation.

It was clear that simply proceeding with the project by force was no longer politically viable.

> **Key Concept: Crisis as Catalyst**
>
> The Stuttgart case illustrates how a crisis can create openings for dialogue that were previously impossible. Before Black Thursday, project sponsors saw no need for additional public engagement; formal approvals were complete. After Black Thursday, the political costs of continuing without dialogue exceeded the costs of opening a potentially challenging public process. Mediators should understand that timing matters; sometimes intervention is only possible when all parties experience the unacceptability of continued conflict.

Stakeholder Mapping and Power Analysis

Primary Parties

- **Project supporters:** Deutsche Bahn, the state government of Baden-Württemberg (led by Minister-President Stefan Mappus of the CDU), the city of Stuttgart, and the federal government. These parties had legal authority, committed funding, and institutional power.
- **Project opponents:** A coalition including organized citizen groups (notably the umbrella organization "Aktionsbündnis gegen Stuttgart 21"), environmental organizations, heritage groups, opposition politicians, and prominent individuals. While lacking formal authority, they had mobilization capacity, moral authority (especially after Black Thursday), and electoral influence.

Power Dynamics

This was not a typical company-community dispute with severe power asymmetry. Rather, it featured organized, educated, politically sophisticated opponents facing governmental and corporate institutions in a democracy with a functioning rule of law. Both sides had resources and leverage:

- **Supporters** held legal authority, budget control, and institutional inertia in their favor.
- **Opponents** held moral authority, mobilization capacity, and, crucially, electoral pressure on an unpopular government facing elections in 2011.

The relative balance of power made dialogue politically necessary. The government could not simply ignore opponents without facing electoral consequences. Opponents could not simply block the project because they lacked the legal authority.

Why Mediation Was Chosen

After Black Thursday, the state government proposed a public "conciliation process" (*Schlichtungsverfahren*). This was an unusual format: not private mediation but a series of public sessions broadcast live on television and the internet.

The choice of this format reflected specific circumstances, including:

- **Public legitimacy deficit:** The core complaint was that decisions had been made without genuine public input. A behind-closed-doors mediation would not address this concern. Only a fully transparent process could restore public confidence.
- **Technical complexity:** The dispute involved complex claims about costs, engineering, and alternatives. A fact-based public examination could potentially clarify which claims were valid.
- **Political calculation:** The government likely hoped that public examination would validate the project and undermine opposition. Opponents hoped it would expose flaws. Both accepted the process because each believed the facts would favor them.
- **Cooling function:** The process provided a structured alternative to street confrontation, allowing tempers to cool while substantive issues were examined.

The Mediator: Heiner Geißler

The choice of mediator was crucial. Dr. Heiner Geißler was a former federal minister and longtime CDU politician, but also a maverick with a reputation for independence. At eighty years old, he had nothing to prove politically. He was respected across political lines and had the stature to confront powerful interests.

Geißler brought several qualities to the role, including:

- **Authority:** His political seniority meant he could challenge both Deutsche Bahn executives and citizen activists when necessary.
- **Credibility with both sides:** As a CDU figure, he was acceptable to the government. His independence and reputation for fairness made him acceptable to opponents.
- **Communication skills:** He was experienced in public discourse and comfortable in the spotlight.
- **Willingness to render judgment:** Unlike a traditional mediator who only facilitates, Geißler was empowered to issue recommendations at the end of the process.

> **Caution: Mediator as Arbiter**
>
> The Geißler role blended facilitation with quasi-arbitration. He was not simply helping parties reach their own agreement; he was empowered to evaluate evidence and make recommendations. This hybrid role suited the specific context (a public dispute requiring authoritative fact-checking) but is not appropriate in all mediations. The voluntary, self-determination principle of pure mediation was partially compromised. Practitioners should be clear about what role they are playing.

Process Design

The conciliation process consisted of eight public sessions held at Stuttgart City Hall between October 22 and November 27, 2010. Each session lasted approximately eight hours and was broadcast live.

Session Structure

Each session focused on a specific theme:

- Session 1: Procedural matters and opening statements
- Session 2: Traffic and transport benefits
- Session 3: Alternative proposal (K21)
- Session 4: Costs and financing
- Session 5: Geological and hydrogeological issues
- Session 6: Fire safety and emergency evacuation
- Session 7: Ecology and urban development
- Session 8: Closing arguments and mediator's statement

Participation and Format

Top representatives from both sides participated, including the Minister-President, Deutsche Bahn executives, Stuttgart's mayor, and leaders of the citizen opposition. Technical experts presented evidence and answered questions. The format allowed for presentation, cross-examination, and mediator questioning.

Transparency

The live broadcast was unprecedented. Tens of thousands watched sessions in real time. This radical transparency served multiple purposes, including preventing either side from misrepresenting what was said and educating the broader public on the substantive issues. It also pressured the participants to behave responsibly and addressed the core legitimacy complaint by demonstrating openness.

Mediator's Role

Geißler was not a passive facilitator. He actively questioned presenters, demanded clarity when jargon obscured substance, and pushed back when claims seemed unsupported. He famously "relentlessly demanded comprehensibility from the experts," ensuring that technical arguments were accessible to the viewing public.

Key Moments and Challenges

The "Stress Test" Proposal

A central dispute was whether the new underground station could handle the same train volume as the existing terminus. Project supporters claimed it could handle more; opponents claimed the opposite. Rather than resolve this himself, Geißler proposed an independent "stress test": a computer simulation by a neutral third party to determine the actual capacity of the proposed station.

This was a classic mediator move: when parties dispute facts, introduce objective fact-finding rather than trying to determine who is right. Both sides accepted the proposal, which was later conducted (though its results remained disputed).

Emotional Testimony

While the process was technically focused, Geißler also allowed space for emotional expression. Citizens spoke about their attachment to the old station, their memories, and their sense of loss. This acknowledgment of emotional dimensions, even in a fact-based process, was important for opponents who felt their concerns had been dismissed as irrational.

Cost Escalation Revelations

During the sessions, it emerged that internal Deutsche Bahn documents projected significantly higher costs than publicly acknowledged. This revelation, obtained through a transparent process, validated opponents' skepticism and damaged the credibility of project supporters.

Outcome

Geißler's Recommendations

On November 30, 2010, Geißler presented his conclusions. He recommended that the project proceed, but with significant modifications, which included an independent "stress test" to verify capacity claims, retention of some surface tracks as a contingency (a sort of "Stuttgart 21 Plus"), and additional ecological and architectural improvements. Additionally, he called for a cost cap, with regional elections allowing democratic reassessment if exceeded.

Importantly, Geißler framed his recommendation not as a vindication of either side but as a pragmatic compromise: cancellation would be too costly and disruptive, but the project needed improvement.

Aftermath and Referendum

The conciliation process did not end the conflict, but it did transform it. Street protests subsided. In 2011, the CDU lost power in Baden-Württemberg, partly due to fallout from Stuttgart 21. The new Green-led government held a statewide referendum on the project in November 2011. Despite the Greens' opposition to the project, 58 percent of voters chose to continue (partly because cancellation costs had become prohibitive).

The project continued, with ongoing cost overruns and delays. As of 2024, it remains under construction with costs exceeding €10 billion.

What Worked, What Didn't, and Why

Factors Contributing to Success

- **Violence prevention:** The process provided an alternative to street confrontation. After Black Thursday, further escalation could have caused serious harm.
- **Public education:** Citizens gained a substantive understanding of the issues. The quality of public discourse improved.
- **Transparency modeling:** The process demonstrated that complex infrastructure decisions could be publicly examined, setting a precedent.
- **Emotional acknowledgment:** Opponents felt their concerns were finally heard, even if not entirely accepted.
- **Mediator authority:** Geißler's stature enabled him to hold powerful institutions accountable.

Challenges and Limitations

- **No consensus:** The process did not produce agreement. Opponents remained opposed; supporters continued supporting. The outcome was a recommendation, not a negotiated settlement.
- **Timing:** The process came after formal approvals and substantial investment, limiting options. Earlier engagement might have produced different outcomes.
- **Structural constraints:** The mediator could only recommend; he could not bind the parties. Actual decision-making remained with formal institutions.
- **Ongoing conflict:** While transformed, the conflict continued. Protests resumed periodically. Trust was not fully restored.

> **Practical Tip: Mediation as Conflict Transformation**
>
> The Stuttgart case illustrates that mediation success should not be measured solely by agreement. Sometimes the most realistic goal is conflict transformation: shifting from violence to dialogue, improving mutual understanding, creating frameworks for ongoing engagement, or providing democratic legitimacy even in the absence of consensus. A process that prevents harm and improves discourse may be a success even if parties remain in disagreement.

Transferable Lessons

- **Public transparency can address legitimacy deficits.** When the core complaint is a lack of public input, private mediation may be insufficient. Radical transparency can rebuild trust, though it requires parties to accept scrutiny.
- **Mediator authority matters.** In high-profile disputes, mediators need sufficient stature to challenge powerful institutions and be taken seriously by all parties.
- **Fact-finding can depoliticize.** When disputes involve empirical claims, joint fact-finding or independent expert analysis can shift the debate from advocacy to evidence.

- **Crisis creates opportunity.** Dialogue that was impossible before Black Thursday became possible after. Mediators should understand that intervention timing often depends on when parties experience the costs of conflict.
- **Mediation has limits.** Not all disputes can be fully resolved through dialogue. Democratic processes, legal mechanisms, or time may be necessary complements to mediation.
- **Early engagement is better.** Stuttgart 21's mediation came after billions of euros had been committed to the project. Earlier, more genuine public participation might have prevented or transformed the conflict before escalation.

17.3 Comparative Reflections

These two cases differ dramatically in context, timeline, and outcome, yet they share many common threads, including:

- **Trust as foundation:** Both cases involved severe trust deficits that had to be addressed before substantive progress was possible. Trust-building was not a preliminary step but an ongoing requirement throughout.
- **Neutral facilitation:** Both required mediators perceived as credible by all parties. The CAO's institutional independence and Geißler's personal authority served parallel functions.
- **Power dynamics:** Both involved significant power asymmetries that had to be actively managed through process design.
- **Limits of mediation:** Neither produced perfect outcomes. Guinea's resolution took seven years and left some grievances unaddressed. Stuttgart's "conciliation" did not yield consensus, and the project continues to face cost overruns and lingering opposition.
- **Context-specific design:** Each process was designed for its specific circumstances. Approaches that worked in one would not necessarily work in the other.

Practitioners can draw lessons from both cases, but the most important lesson may be that mediation is not a formula to be applied but a practice to be adapted. Understanding principles and techniques provides a foundation; applying them wisely requires attention to the unique features of each dispute.

Key Concept: Learning from Imperfection

These cases were selected not because they represent flawless successes but because they illustrate real mediation in all its messiness.
The Guinea process took seven years and required extraordinary patience. The Stuttgart process failed to achieve consensus, and the project remains controversial. Yet both cases represent meaningful improvements over the alternatives: continued violent conflict, community suffering without remediation, and political crisis without resolution. Practitioners should study not only what worked but also what remained difficult, developing realistic expectations about what mediation can achieve.

18.

SIMULATION EXERCISES AND ROLE-PLAY SCENARIOS

Case studies offer lessons from real experience. Simulation exercises build on that foundation, giving mediators the opportunity to apply principles, test techniques, and learn from mistakes in a safe environment. This chapter provides a comprehensive collection of simulation exercises and practical training activities designed to develop the competencies explored throughout this handbook. Each exercise reflects real-world complexities, offering practice in active listening, strategic questioning, reframing, managing power imbalances, and navigating impasses.

Research on expertise development (Ericsson, Krampe, and Tesch-Römer, 1993) demonstrates that deliberate practice, characterized by structured repetition with immediate feedback, is the primary mechanism through which professionals develop complex skills.

These scenarios draw from patterns in mining, infrastructure, and extractive industry conflicts across Africa and Europe. They incorporate trust breakdown, cultural factors, economic pressures, environmental concerns, and psychological dynamics. By engaging with these simulations, mediators, NGO workers, and company representatives will build the "muscle memory" needed to respond effectively when facing similar challenges in actual mediation settings. The case studies in Chapter 17 provide real examples demonstrating similar themes and challenges.

Adult learning theory (Knowles, 1984) establishes that experienced professionals learn most effectively through problem-centered activities that connect directly to their practice contexts, which is why these simulations draw from actual extractive-industry dispute patterns.

> **Key Concept**
> Simulations bridge theory and practice. They allow participants to experiment with different approaches, observe their impact, and refine their techniques without the high stakes of real disputes.

18.1 Foundational Communication Skills Exercises

Before engaging in complex multi-party simulations, mediators benefit from building foundational communication competencies. The following exercises focus on building core skills that underpin effective mediation: active listening, empathetic responding, strategic questioning, and reframing. These exercises can be conducted in pairs or small groups and typically require 15 to 30 minutes each.

> **Practical Tip: Realistic Complexity**
> Effective simulations balance complexity with manageability. Too simple, and they fail to develop real skills. Too complex and learners become overwhelmed. Start with simpler scenarios for novices and increase complexity as skills develop. Adjust based on participant feedback.

For maximum realism in extractive-industry simulations, assign participants roles that involve technical expertise disagreements, such as a community health officer reporting elevated cancer rates versus a company environmental consultant citing inconclusive epidemiological data. Include at least one participant playing a regulatory official with conflicting mandates, balancing economic development goals against environmental protection obligations.

> **Caution: Emotional Safety in Role-Play**
>
> Role-plays involving trauma, violence, or intense conflict can be emotionally triggering for participants with relevant personal history. Provide content warnings, offer alternative roles, and create clear mechanisms for stepping out of a role if needed. Training should develop skills without causing harm.

Exercise 1: Active Listening and Empathetic Paraphrasing

Purpose and Learning Objectives

Active listening is at the core of mediation practice. This exercise develops the capacity to listen not just to words but also to the emotions, values, and underlying concerns embedded in a speaker's message. As discussed in Chapter 4, active listening involves giving the speaker your full attention, observing body language and tone, and responding in ways that demonstrate genuine understanding. This skill is vital in company-community disputes where participants feel unheard or dismissed by the other party.

Active listening is consistently identified in mediation research (Kolb and Associates, 1994; Moore, 2014) as the foundational competency that distinguishes effective mediators, yet it requires sustained practice to move from intellectual understanding to reliable performance under pressure.

Learning Objectives:

- Develop the ability to accurately capture both content and emotional dimensions of spoken messages
- Practice paraphrasing techniques that validate speakers without agreeing or disagreeing
- Build awareness of nonverbal cues and their significance in communication
- Cultivate the capacity to separate the content from the delivery style

Scenario Context

Participants work in pairs. One person plays a community member expressing a grievance, while the other practices mediator responses. The community member should deliver statements that contain factual claims, emotional content, and, occasionally, accusatory language. These statements reflect the kind of charged communication mediators frequently encounter when communities feel wronged by company actions.

Sample Grievance Statements:

1. *"Your company's trucks have been destroying our roads for three years now. Every day, dust covers our homes, our crops are ruined, and you people don't care at all about what happens to us. My children can't breathe properly anymore!"*

This statement contains multiple layers: factual claims (truck traffic, dust, three-year duration), health concerns (children's breathing), property damage (crops), and emotional content (feeling uncared for, frustration, and fear). An effective mediator response must acknowledge both the factual substance and the emotional weight.

2. *"We were promised jobs when the mine opened. They said our sons and daughters would work there. But look around! All the skilled positions go to people from the city. We get nothing but broken promises and polluted water."*

Here, the statement reflects a history of unmet expectations (a common escalation factor discussed in Chapter 5), disappointment, and a sense of being deliberately excluded. The mediator must acknowledge the breach of trust while creating space for dialogue.

3. *"My grandmother is buried on that land. Her grandmother before her. Seven generations of my family have lived and died there. And now you want us to move because you found minerals underground? This is not about money. This is about who we are."*

This statement involves deep cultural and identity issues, ancestral connections to land, and resistance to relocation. It explicitly states that the dispute transcends economic considerations, highlighting the value-based conflicts discussed in Chapter 5.

Exercise Instructions

Step 1: Listening Phase (2-3 minutes)

The "community member" delivers their statement. The mediator listens without interrupting, maintains appropriate eye contact, and uses encouraging nonverbal cues (such as nodding and showing attentiveness through body posture). The mediator should observe not just the words but the speaker's tone, pace, volume changes, and body language.

Step 2: Paraphrasing Response (1-2 minutes)

The mediator responds with a paraphrase that captures both the content and emotion. The structure should follow this pattern: "What I'm hearing is that [content summary]. It sounds like this has left you feeling [emotional acknowledgment]."

Example Response to Statement 1:

"What I'm hearing is that for three years, truck traffic from the company has created dust that's affecting your home, damaging your crops, and most concerning of all, impacting your children's health. It sounds like you feel that your community's well-being has been overlooked, and that's deeply frustrating and worrying for you as a parent."

> **Practical Tip:**
>
> When paraphrasing, avoid beginning with "I understand" as this can seem presumptuous. Instead, use phrases like "What I'm hearing is . . . " or "It sounds like . . . " which acknowledge what was said without claiming complete understanding.

Step 3: Verification (30 seconds)

After paraphrasing, the mediator asks: "Have I understood you correctly?" or "Have I missed anything?" This step demonstrates respect for the speaker's authority over their own experience and creates an opportunity for correction.

Step 4: Role Reversal

Partners switch roles and repeat the exercise with a different grievance statement.

Debrief Questions

- How did it feel to be genuinely heard and have your statement reflected back accurately?
- What was most challenging about capturing both the content and emotion?
- Did you notice yourself wanting to respond, explain, or defend before fully listening?
- How might accurate paraphrasing help de-escalate tension in actual disputes?

Application to Real Mediation

This exercise directly applies to Phase 1 (Opening Session) and Phase 3 (Exploring Interests) of the mediation process outlined in Chapter 6. When community members make opening statements, they typically include years of accumulated frustration. A mediator who accurately captures and reflects this content demonstrates impartiality and creates psychological safety. As noted in Chapter 6, people calm down when they feel genuinely heard, which makes subsequent dialogue more productive.

> **Caution: Paraphrasing vs. Parroting**
>
> Translating messages into your own words while preserving meaning works better than verbatim repetition, which can feel hollow. True paraphrasing requires preserving the emotional weight while avoiding the hollow or mocking feel of parroting.

Exercise 2: Strategic Questioning to Uncover Interests

Purpose and Learning Objectives

As discussed in Chapter 4, questions are among the mediator's most powerful tools. This exercise develops proficiency in using different question types, particularly open-ended, probing, and clarifying questions, to move beyond stated positions and uncover underlying interests. The distinction between positions and interests (explained in Chapter 6) is fundamental to the success of mediation: positions are what parties say they want, while interests are why they want it.

Learning Objectives:

- Distinguish between open-ended, closed, probing, and clarifying questions
- Practice using questions to move from positions to interests
- Develop comfort with exploratory questioning that doesn't feel like interrogation
- Learn to sequence questions strategically to build understanding

Scenario Context

Groups of three participants take on the roles of mediator, company representative, and community representative. The scenario involves a dispute over compensation for agricultural land affected by mining operations.

Background:

The Mwenzi Community in a rural African region has been farming the land around the Gamma Mining Co. operation for generations. The recent expansion of tailings storage has contaminated groundwater used for irrigation. The community is demanding 500,000 $ in compensation. The company has offered 50,000 $, citing its environmental impact assessment, which showed "manageable" contamination levels.

Community Position:

"We demand 500,000 $. Our crops have failed, our cattle are sick, and our children cannot drink the water. This is the minimum we need to recover from what you have done to us."

Company Position:

"Our experts confirm the contamination is within acceptable limits. We've already offered 50,000 $ as a goodwill gesture, which is more than generous given our data. We cannot set a precedent by paying exorbitant claims based on unsubstantiated fears."

> **Key Concept: Positions vs. Shared Interests**
> Positions are frequently incompatible (500,000 vs. 50,000), but interests can be compatible or shared. Both parties likely share interests in community health, stable operations, and avoiding prolonged conflict.

Question Types and Examples

Open-Ended Questions: These invite detailed responses and exploration. They typically begin with "What," "How," "Tell me about," or "Describe."

1. "Can you help me understand what life was like for your community before the contamination occurred?"
2. "What would your community's future look like if this situation were resolved in a way that felt fair?"
3. "How has this situation affected your relationship with your neighbors and the broader community?"

Probing Questions: These dig deeper into specific aspects of what has been shared.

- "You mentioned your cattle are sick. Can you tell me more about when you first noticed this?"

- "When you say the compensation would help you 'recover,' what specific recovery does your community envision?"
- "You mentioned setting a precedent. What concerns does the company have about how this resolution might affect other situations?"

Clarifying Questions: These ensure an accurate understanding and eliminate assumptions.

- "When you say 'acceptable limits,' what standard or measurement are you referring to?"
- "You mentioned the children cannot drink the water. Are they currently getting water from another source, and if so, what is that arrangement?"
- "To make sure I understand, is the 500,000 figure based on a specific calculation, or is it an estimate of total damages?"

Hypothetical Questions: These encourage parties to consider alternatives and can reveal flexibility.

- "If the company could guarantee clean water for the community going forward, how would that affect your view of the situation?"
- "What if compensation included both immediate support and a long-term investment in the community's agricultural recovery?"

Exercise Instructions

Round 1 (10 minutes): The mediator engages with the community representative using only open-ended questions. The goal is to explore what lies beneath the 500,000 $ demand.

Round 2 (10 minutes): The mediator shifts to the company representative, using probing and clarifying questions to understand the resistance to higher compensation and the concern about setting a precedent.

Round 3 (5 minutes): The mediator uses hypothetical questions with both parties to explore potential areas of flexibility.

Practical Tip: Prepare a few Questions

Write down at least five questions before each round. This helps prevent reliance on closed questions under pressure and ensures a variety of question types are used.

Discovering Hidden Interests

Through skillful questioning, the following interests might emerge:

Community Interests:

- Health security for children and elders
- Restoration of agricultural livelihood
- Recognition that their concerns are legitimate and taken seriously
- Assurance that contamination won't worsen in the future
- Dignity and respect in how they are treated

Company Interests:

- Operational continuity without disruption from protests
- Protection of reputation (both locally and with international investors)
- Financial predictability and avoiding open-ended liability
- Not setting precedents that encourage other claims
- Demonstrating corporate social responsibility

Notice that several interests are potentially compatible: both parties want the health situation resolved, both want to avoid prolonged conflict, and both have concerns about the future. These shared or compatible interests become the foundation for generating options (Phase 4 in Chapter 6).

Debrief Questions

- Which question types yielded the most insightful responses?
- Were there questions that seemed to make either party defensive? Why might that be?

- What interests did you discover that weren't apparent from the initial positions?
- How might knowing these interests change the approach to generating solutions?

> **Caution: Avoid Accusatory Questions**
>
> Avoid questions that sound like cross-examination or that carry implicit judgments. "Why did you wait so long to complain?" implies blame. A better alternative would be: "Help me understand the timeline of events from your perspective."

Exercise 3: Reframing Charged Statements

Purpose and Learning Objectives

Reframing is the art of taking negative, accusatory, or positional statements and restating them in more constructive, neutral terms that preserve the core meaning while opening space for dialogue. As explained in Chapter 4, reframing removes inflammatory language and refocuses attention on underlying concerns and potential solutions. This skill enables productive dialogue when emotions run high.

Learning Objectives:

- Develop the ability to quickly identify the underlying concern within charged statements
- Practice converting accusations into expressions of need or concern
- Learn to preserve meaning while neutralizing inflammatory language
- Build confidence in real-time reframing under pressure

Exercise Format

This exercise can be conducted individually, in pairs, or as a group activity. Participants are presented with charged statements and must generate reframed versions of them. The exercise progresses from written practice to real-time verbal reframing.

Charged Statements and Model Reframes

Statement 1:

"The company is full of liars. They promised us jobs and clean water, and they have delivered nothing but poison and broken dreams."

Analysis: This statement contains accusations ("liars"), specific claims (broken promises about jobs and water), and emotional content ("poison," "broken dreams"). The underlying concerns are unmet commitments, health impacts, and lost opportunities.

Reframe: "It sounds like there were specific commitments made about employment and water quality that haven't materialized as expected. The gap between what was promised and what has happened has deeply affected your community's trust and well-being."

Statement 2:

"These people are unreasonable. No matter what we offer, they demand more. They think we're made of money and they're trying to bleed us dry."

Analysis: This company statement labels the community ("unreasonable"), expresses frustration with negotiations ("demand more"), and implies bad faith ("bleed us dry"). The underlying concerns are financial sustainability, feeling unappreciated for efforts made, and uncertainty about when demands will end.

Reframe: "The company has made several offers and feels uncertain about how to reach an agreement that works within its constraints. There's concern about finding a sustainable resolution that addresses community needs while remaining financially viable."

Statement 3:

"The government is in the company's pocket. They're supposed to protect us, but they've been bought off. There's no one fighting for the ordinary people anymore."

Analysis: This statement expresses distrust of institutions and feelings of abandonment and powerlessness. The underlying concerns are a lack of protection, feeling marginalized, and a desire for allies.

Reframe: "There's a sense that the community doesn't have the institutional support it needs. You feel that there should be someone advocating for community interests in this process, and that protection has been inadequate."

Statement 4:

"They just want to shut us up with a check. They don't actually care about what happens to us after they've extracted everything they want from our land."

Reframe: "The community is concerned that any resolution be genuine and lasting, not just a quick fix. There's a desire for the company to demonstrate real commitment to the community's long-term well-being, not just to resolve the immediate dispute."

> **Key Concept: The Power of Reframing**
> Effective reframing transforms positions into interests, accusations into concerns, and attacks into opportunities for understanding. The goal is not to sanitize or dismiss emotions, but to redirect energy toward problem-solving.

Practice Activity: Rapid Reframing

In pairs, one person reads charged statements aloud (one every 30 seconds) while the other practices immediate verbal reframing. This builds the quick-thinking capacity needed in actual mediation sessions.

Additional Statements for Practice:

1. *"The mining company has shown time and again that they have absolutely no respect for our traditions or our sacred sites."*
2. *"These protesters are just anti-development extremists who want to keep everyone poor."*

3. *"The company's environmental reports are nothing but lies designed to cover up their crimes."*
4. *"Our security personnel have been patient beyond belief, but these villagers keep provoking incidents."*
5. *"The company is committing slow genocide against our people through their pollution."*

With foundational communication skills practiced, mediators are ready to tackle the full complexity of multi-party disputes.

> **Practical Tip: Opportunity for Correction**
>
> When reframing in mediation, checking with the speaker shows respect: "Have I captured what you're saying?" This allows correction if the reframe missed something important.

> **Facilitator Notes:**
>
> Allow 25-30 minutes total. Begin with the moderator demonstrating one reframe before participants attempt their own (5 minutes). Common pitfall: participants minimize emotions rather than reframing them. Watch for reframes that dismiss the speaker's concern rather than redirecting it. Progression signal: participants can reframe without losing the emotional core of the original statement.

18.2 Multi-Party Mediation Simulations

The following simulations provide comprehensive scenarios for practicing the full mediation process. Each simulation includes detailed background information, role assignments, and facilitator guidance. Facilitators can use these exercises with groups of four to eight participants. They typically require 60 to 90 minutes to complete, plus 20 to 30 minutes for debriefing.

Participants in extractive-industry simulations should specifically practice: questioning conflicting environmental data without alienating either party, managing power imbalances when company representatives outnumber or outrank community participants, and mediating between a community's short-term survival needs and its long-term environmental protection interests. They should also practice navigating situations where external actors, including NGOs, government inspectors, or media, pressure one party to abandon the mediation process.

Key Concept: Deliberate Practice

Skill development requires deliberate practice: focused repetition with feedback on specific aspects of performance. Simply running through scenarios does not build skill unless followed by targeted feedback and repeated attempts to improve. Structure practice sessions to include observation, feedback, and retry opportunities.

Practical Tip: Video Review

With participants' permission, video practice sessions. Self-observation reveals habits invisible in the moment, including verbal tics, body language patterns, and timing issues. Video review dramatically accelerates skill development by making behavior visible for analysis.

Simulation 1: The Alpha Mining Co. Dispute

Scenario Overview

This simulation addresses a common pattern in company-community conflicts: the accumulation of unmet promises leading to trust breakdown and escalating demands. It provides practice in rebuilding trust, managing power imbalances, and finding creative solutions under resource constraints. The scenario reflects protracted disputes where years of unfulfilled commitments erode community trust (see Case Study A in Chapter 17).

Detailed Background

The Company: Alpha Mining Co. has operated a rare-earth elements extraction facility in the Kamwala Valley for eight years. The company extracts minerals required for electronics and renewable energy technology. During the initial community engagement in 2016, company representatives made several commitments:

- **Employment:** Hire at least 60 percent of the workforce from local communities within five years
- **Infrastructure:** Construct a new secondary school and health clinic by 2019
- **Environment:** Implement best-practice environmental management and provide quarterly public reports
- **Community Development Fund:** Establish a fund receiving 2 percent of annual profits

What Actually Happened:

- Local employment peaked at 35 percent, with most positions being unskilled labor. A global commodity price crash in 2019 led to workforce reductions that disproportionately affected local workers.
- The school foundation was laid in 2018, but construction halted due to budget constraints. The partially built structure now stands as a visible symbol of broken promises.
- Environmental reports were produced but not made accessible to the community. Recent water quality concerns have emerged, with villagers reporting sick livestock and skin irritation.
- The Community Development Fund was established but has received inconsistent contributions, and community members report they have no clarity on how funds have been used.

Current Situation: After a road blockade in March that halted operations for three days, the company agreed to participate in voluntary mediation. The community has presented three core demands, while the company faces genuine financial constraints but is motivated to restore operational stability and reputation.

> **Key Concept: Accumulated Grievances Behind the Impasse**
> This scenario illustrates the concept of "accumulated grievances" from Chapter 5. The current impasse isn't really about the three specific demands but about years of trust erosion. Effective mediation must address both the substantive issues and the underlying relationship breakdown.

Role Cards

Roles and Character Briefings

ROLE: Community Representatives, Maria and Luisa

Leaders of the Kamwala Valley Community Council

Your Background:

You have been advocating for your community for over a decade. You remember the excitement when Alpha Mining Co. first arrived. They made many promises, and you helped convince skeptical community members to support the project. Now you feel personally responsible for the disappointment your community has experienced. Community members are angry, and some are calling for more aggressive action. Your authority as community leaders depends on achieving tangible results from this mediation.

Your Community's Situation:

- Unemployment among youth exceeds 50 percent. Many young people have left to seek work in distant cities.
- Children currently walk 8 kilometers to the nearest secondary school. The unfinished school building is a daily reminder of broken promises.
- Three families have reported livestock deaths they attribute to water contamination. Two elders have complained of skin problems.

- There is a faction in the community that wants to involve national NGOs and media. You have held them off by promising that mediation will produce results.

Your Opening Position:

1. **Employment:** Hire fifty local residents within six months, as initially promised
2. **Infrastructure:** Complete the school by year's end
3. **Environment:** Implement all environmental protection measures immediately

Your Underlying Interests (consider but don't openly state):

- Your personal credibility depends on achieving something concrete
- Youth employment is the community's most urgent concern
- You need something visible that demonstrates progress
- Long-term sustainability matters more than short-term gains
- You want a genuine partnership, not charity

Your Flexibility (do not reveal unless negotiation requires):

You could accept thirty local hires within six months if paired with a meaningful training program for additional community members. You could accept school completion by the end of the next fiscal year if there are quarterly progress reports and community involvement in construction oversight. You could accept phased environmental measures if the most critical issues are addressed immediately and a joint task force is established.

ROLE: Company Representatives, Alex and Janis

Co-Directors of Community Relations, Alpha Mining Co.

Your Background:

You joined the company five years ago, after many of the original promises were made by a previous management team. You've inherited a difficult situation. You genuinely believe in corporate social responsibility, and you're frustrated that the company's financial troubles have prevented it from fulfilling its commitments. Your CEO has authorized you to negotiate, but has made clear that the company cannot afford solutions that threaten its financial stability. Your job security depends on resolving this dispute without excessive concessions.

Company's Current Situation:

- The global rare earth market collapsed in 2019 and has only partially recovered. Profit margins remain thin.
- The three-day road blockade cost the company approximately 2 million $ and damaged relationships with buyers.
- International investors are increasingly concerned about ESG (Environmental, Social, Governance) performance. Continued conflict threatens financing for a planned expansion.
- Several skilled local workers were laid off during the downturn. Rehiring them would be relatively easy.
- The company has a budget allocated for CSR activities, but cannot exceed it without board approval.

Your Opening Position:

1. **Employment:** Hire twenty local residents in the next six months, increasing gradually over two years
2. **Infrastructure:** Allocate next year's budget to complete the school
3. **Environment:** Implement some measures immediately, phase in the rest over three years

Your Underlying Interests (consider but don't openly state):

- You need operational stability to secure the expansion investment
- You want to demonstrate ESG progress to investors
- You need to manage expectations without making promises you can't keep
- You genuinely want better community relations
- You're worried about setting precedents that other communities might demand

Your Flexibility (do not reveal unless negotiation requires):

You could agree to hire thirty local residents within six months if paired with realistic job categories. You could commit to completing the school by the end of the next fiscal year through quarterly progress reports. You could implement critical environmental measures immediately and create a joint task force to implement the remaining measures in phases. You have some discretion to offer a training program partnership with the local vocational college.

> **Practical Tip:**
> Notice that both role cards include a "bottom line" that overlaps. This reflects real mediation situations where parties have more flexibility than their opening positions suggest. The mediator's skill lies in uncovering this hidden space for agreement.

Mediator Guidance Notes

Facilitation Phases

This simulation provides opportunities to practice several key mediation competencies.

Phase 1: Opening Session:

Begin by establishing ground rules (Chapter 6). Given the history of broken promises, trust is low. Consider explicitly acknowledging this:

"I understand there's a history here that has affected trust between you. This mediation is an opportunity to begin rebuilding that trust, and everything we do here will be transparent and fair to both sides."

Phase 2: Exploration:

Use open-ended questions (Exercise 10.1.2) to move beyond stated positions. For the community: "Help me understand what it's been like for your community over these eight years." For the company: "Tell me about the pressures the company has faced in trying to meet its commitments." Look for shared interests such as stability, youth opportunities, and future partnership.

Phase 3: Option Generation:

Brainstorm creatively. The gap between twenty and fifty jobs seems large, but what if training programs bridged it? What if school construction involved community labor that counted toward employment? What if environmental monitoring included community members as paid monitors?

Power Dynamics:

The company has financial resources and legal expertise. The community has moral authority and the ability to disrupt operations. Ensure both parties have an equal voice. If the company representatives use technical language, ask them to explain in accessible terms. If community representatives seem intimidated, invite them to share their perspective specifically.

Potential Agreement Framework

A successful mediation might produce an agreement including:

- **Employment:** Thirty direct hires within six months, plus a training partnership with the regional vocational college for fifty additional community members, with a commitment to priority hiring as positions open

- **Infrastructure:** School completion by the end of the next fiscal year, with quarterly community progress meetings and employment of local labor in construction
- **Environment:** Immediate independent water quality assessment, immediate remediation of any acute issues found, creation of a joint Environment Committee with community representatives receiving training as monitors, phased implementation of remaining measures with public quarterly reports
- **Governance:** Establishment of a quarterly Company-Community Liaison Committee to address ongoing concerns and prevent the future accumulation of grievances

Facilitator Notes:

Phase 1 (Opening and Ground Rules): 10-15 minutes. Phase 2 (Hearing Grievances): 20-25 minutes, allowing each party uninterrupted time. Phase 3 (Interest Exploration): 15-20 minutes, using caucuses if needed. Phase 4 (Option Generation): 15-20 minutes. Phase 5 (Agreement Framework): 10-15 minutes. Common breakdown: the accumulated grievances often surface in Phase 2 and threaten to derail the process. Mediators should acknowledge the weight of past harms before moving to future-focused discussion.

Debrief Questions

1. What communication techniques were most effective in moving from positions to interests?
2. How did the mediator handle the power dynamics between a multinational company and rural community leaders?
3. What role did acknowledging the history of broken promises play in building trust?
4. Were there creative options generated that neither party had initially considered?
5. If an impasse occurred, what techniques were used to overcome it?

6. How does this scenario reflect the principles discussed in Chapter 12 on managing power asymmetries and restoring trust?

Simulation 2: The Beta Mining Co. New Development Dispute

Scenario Overview

Simulation 2 introduces a different layer of complexity. Where Simulation 1 focused on rebuilding trust after broken commitments, this scenario addresses deeper cultural and identity conflicts surrounding large-scale relocation combined with environmental uncertainty. Participants will navigate competing claims rooted not only in economic interests but in ancestral connection to land.

This simulation addresses a different pattern: conflicts arising from new development rather than accumulated grievances. It provides practice in negotiating prospective agreements, addressing fears about future impacts, and balancing economic development with environmental and social concerns. Unlike Simulation 10.2.1, where trust was broken, here trust was never established, and the community is reacting to uncertainty and fear.

Detailed Background

The Discovery: Six months ago, Beta Mining Co. announced the discovery of significant copper and cobalt deposits beneath agricultural land in the Riverside Valley. The deposit is estimated to be worth billions of dollars and could make the region economically significant on a national scale. The government has granted preliminary exploration licenses, and Beta Mining Co. is now seeking community consent to proceed with full development.

The Community: Riverside Valley is home to approximately 5,000 people across seven villages. The economy is primarily agricultural, with families farming the same plots for generations. The valley is known for high-quality organic produce sold at premium prices in distant urban markets. Two villages would be directly affected by mining operations, while all seven rely on the river for irrigation.

Community Concerns:

1. **Environmental Fear:** Stories of mining disasters elsewhere have created anxiety. Residents have seen documentaries about toxic tailings and dead rivers.
2. **Land and Livelihood:** Twenty-three farming families would need to relocate. Their land has been in their families for generations.
3. **Identity and Culture:** The community's identity is tied to farming. "We are farmers," is how they describe themselves.
4. **Power Imbalance:** Previous experience with government and large companies has taught community members that their voices are disregarded.

Company Perspective: Beta Mining Co. has learned from other companies' failures. They want to do this project differently, but face significant pressure from investors to begin operations quickly. Copper and cobalt are required for electric vehicle batteries, positioning the project as a contributor to climate solutions.

Current Situation: Initial community meetings devolved into shouting matches. A local environmental group has begun organizing resistance. Beta Mining Co. has requested mediation to find a path forward. The community has agreed to participate but remains deeply skeptical.

> **Caution: Fear of Future Harm vs. Past Grievances**
>
> This scenario involves fear of future harm rather than a response to past harm. Different psychological dynamics are at play. People protecting themselves from anticipated loss often hold positions more rigidly than those responding to known grievances.

Role Cards

Roles and Character Briefings

ROLE: Community Representatives, Blair and Ali

Co-Chairpersons of the Riverside Valley Community Association

Your Background:

You are well-respected leaders who have successfully advocated for your community before. Blair led the campaign that stopped a garbage dump from being built upstream ten years ago. Ali organized the farmers' cooperative that now sells produce at premium prices. You've agreed to mediation because outright resistance might lead the government to override local concerns, but you're under enormous pressure from community members not to "sell out."

What You've Heard About Mining:

- A colleague visited a mining region in another country and described devastated landscapes and polluted rivers.
- Documentary films have shown community members sick from contamination.
- Stories circulate of mining companies making promises and then abandoning communities when minerals run out.

Your Demands:

1. **Environmental Impact Assessment:** An independent EIA conducted by experts chosen by the community, with complete transparency and regular community updates
2. **Land and Relocation:** Full fair-market compensation for all affected families, plus support for relocating their homes and establishing new farms of equivalent quality
3. **Community Benefits:** Significant investment in local infrastructure, including roads, schools, and healthcare facilities, within the first two years of operations

Your Underlying Interests:

- Protection for the river that is the lifeblood of the valley
- Security that if something goes wrong, there will be accountability and effective remediation
- Ensuring that families who relocate end up better off, not worse
- Wanting your community's children to have opportunities
- Being treated as partners, not obstacles

Your Flexibility:

You could accept an EIA conducted by mutually agreed experts (not solely community-chosen) if community representatives are involved in oversight. You could accept fair compensation determined by independent appraisal, plus a dedicated relocation fund and job training for those affected. You could accept some infrastructure investment being frontloaded with a detailed timeline for further investments.

ROLE: Company Representatives, Jordan and Patty

Co-Directors of Corporate Social Responsibility, Beta Mining Co.

Your Background:

You are experienced professionals who have managed community relations for multiple projects. You've seen both successful partnerships and disastrous conflicts. You believe this project can be different, but you're facing significant pressure from your CEO and investors to move quickly. The market for copper and cobalt is hot, and delays cost millions. You also know that projects that begin with community conflict rarely end well.

What You Know:

- Beta Mining Co. has an above-average environmental record compared to industry peers.
- Independent EIAs cost more but actually benefit the company by identifying issues early.

- The company has successfully relocated communities elsewhere, and those communities are now better off economically.
- Projects with strong community relations have fewer disruptions and better returns for investors.
- Your competitors have had projects blocked or delayed for years due to community opposition.

Your Opening Position:

1. **Environmental Impact Assessment:** The company will conduct an EIA with internal oversight
2. **Land and Relocation:** Compensation at government-set rates, with limited relocation support
3. **Community Benefits:** Phased investment over ten years

Your Underlying Interests:

- Getting to production quickly to capture market opportunity
- Avoiding the kind of conflict that has negatively affected competitors
- Building a positive reputation that helps with future projects
- Managing costs within approved budgets
- Demonstrating ESG credentials to investors

Your Flexibility:

You could agree to an independent EIA if the community is involved in oversight and there are reasonable timelines. You could offer fair-market compensation determined by independent appraisal, plus a dedicated fund for relocation support and job training. You could frontload some infrastructure investments, particularly healthcare and education, with a detailed timeline for the rest.

Mediator Guidance Notes

Facilitation Phases

Key Dynamics:

The community is operating out of fear of unknown future harm. The psychological literature on loss aversion (Chapter 5) is relevant: people weigh potential losses more heavily than equivalent gains. The mediator should acknowledge these fears while exploring what would make the community feel secure.

Opportunities for Common Ground:

- Both parties benefit from an independent, credible environmental assessment
- Both parties want to avoid prolonged conflict
- Both parties want relocated families to thrive, not just survive
- Both parties have interests in community development and opportunity

Potential Creative Solutions:

- Joint oversight committee for environmental monitoring, with community representatives receiving training and payment
- Relocation support that includes not just land and housing but also startup funds and technical support for new farming operations
- Community benefit agreement with specific milestones and consequences if milestones are missed
- Escrow account holding funds for closure and rehabilitation, demonstrating long-term commitment

Key Concept: Joint Fact-Finding to Break Impasses

This scenario illustrates the importance of "joint fact-finding" discussed in Chapter 6. When parties disagree about likely impacts, agreeing on a neutral assessment process can break the impasse and build shared understanding.

Debrief Questions

1. How did the mediator address the community's fear-based resistance (see Chapter 14 for resistance scenarios)?
2. What role did the concept of "independent verification" play in building trust?
3. How did the mediator balance the company's time pressures with the community's need for thorough consideration?
4. Were there moments when the mediator needed to reframe statements to keep dialogue productive?
5. How does this scenario differ from the Alpha Mining Co. scenario, and what different skills were required?

> **Facilitator Notes:**
>
> Allow 75-90 minutes. The fear-based resistance dynamic often causes mediators to rush toward reassurance rather than exploring what security means to the community. Common breakdown point: around 30 minutes in, when community representatives feel their fears have been heard but see no concrete response. At this point, guide mediators toward joint fact-finding proposals. Pitfall: introducing environmental assessment too early can feel dismissive of emotional concerns.

Simulation 3: The Landowner-Company Negotiation

Scenario Overview

This simulation focuses on a bilateral negotiation between a mining company and a private landowner, without the community dimension. It provides practice in interest-based negotiation, BATNA analysis, and creative option generation in a more controlled setting. This scenario is particularly useful for practicing the phase of negotiating and bargaining (Phase 5).

Detailed Background

The Situation:

Delta Mining Co. has been leasing a 10-hectare parcel from landowner Sascha Martinez for two years at 1,500 $ per month. The land, currently unused, will be needed for equipment storage as operations expand in the coming year. The lease expires in three months, and renewal negotiations have stalled.

External Factors:

- The property has zoning approval for commercial or residential development
- A real estate developer has expressed interest in purchasing the land for 300,000 $, although financing is uncertain
- Current market value of the land is approximately 200,000 $
- Local property values have fluctuated due to mining activity in the area

Role Cards

ROLE: Landowner, Sascha Martinez

Personal Background:

You purchased this land fifteen years ago as a security investment for your family. Your youngest child, Mateo, has just been accepted to an engineering program with an annual tuition of 25,000 $. You've remortgaged your home to cover the first semester, and your financial situation is precarious. The mining lease seemed like a good deal two years ago, but now you're wondering if you could do better.

Your Concerns:

- Funding your child's education is your top priority
- You're worried that mining operations might decrease your property's value

- The developer's offer is appealing but uncertain
- You've been losing sleep over financial stress
- Your spouse thinks the mining lease is a blessing; you're having arguments about what to do

Your Position:

- Sell the land to the mining company for 250,000 $, or
- Renew the lease at 2,500 $ per month

Your Underlying Interests:

- Secure funding for your child's four-year education (approximately 100,000 $ total)
- Financial security and reduced stress
- Protection of your asset's long-term value
- Avoiding the uncertainty of the developer's offer

BATNA (Best Alternative): Try to sell to the developer for 300,000 $, though timing and financing are uncertain.

WATNA (Worst Alternative): Developer deal falls through, mining company finds alternative land, property value drops due to nearby mining activity, you're stuck with a depreciating asset.

ROLE: Mining Company Representative, Mark Thompson

Land Acquisition Manager, Delta Mining Co.

Professional Background:

You've worked at Delta Mining Co. for nearly a decade and have negotiated many land deals. This particular parcel seemed straightforward when you first leased it. Now you face competing pressures: the operations team needs the land for expansion, your CEO demands cost control, and local activists are criticizing the company for "buying off" the community. You live in this community and want to be seen as fair.

Your Constraints:

- You could justify up to 1,750 $ monthly rent, but above 2,000 $ would require board approval
- Market value for the land is approximately 200,000 $; paying above that creates precedent concerns
- There is an alternative site 15 km away, but it lacks infrastructure and would increase operational costs by 250,000 $ annually
- The company has a "Future Leaders" scholarship program for STEM students in the region

Your Position:

- Renew the lease with a modest increase to 1,750 $ per month

Your Underlying Interests:

- Secure the land at a reasonable cost
- Maintain positive community image
- Avoid setting precedents for overpaying
- Minimize operational disruption

BATNA: Use the alternative site, accepting higher costs but avoiding potential criticism.

WATNA: Landowner sells to developer, alternative site costs spiral, the company delays operations, and it faces criticism for poor community relations.

Secret Information: You know the landowner's child might qualify for the company's scholarship program. This could be worth 20,000 to 30,000 $ over four years. This information could be introduced if negotiations seem stuck, offering a creative way to address the landowner's interests without a large cash payment.

Key Concept: BATNA and the Zone of Agreement

BATNA/WATNA analysis (Chapter 9) helps parties understand their alternatives to negotiated agreement. When both parties' alternatives are unattractive, there is usually a "zone of possible agreement" where negotiated solutions can benefit both sides.

Mediator Guidance Notes

This scenario is excellent for practicing interest-based negotiation because the parties' positions (250,000 $ sale vs. 1,750 $ rent) seem far apart, but their interests are potentially compatible.

Key Mediator Moves:

1. **Explore what's driving the landowner's numbers:** "Help me understand what the 250,000 $ would accomplish for you." This should reveal the child's education as the core interest.
2. **Explore the company's constraints:** "What concerns does the company have about the landowner's proposal?" This reveals concerns about precedent and budgetary limits.
3. **Reality-test both BATNAs:** "What happens if you can't reach an agreement here?" Both alternatives have significant downsides, which should motivate flexibility.
4. **Facilitate creative options:** Are there ways to meet the landowner's education funding interest without the company paying above-market rates? Perhaps a combination of increased rent, extended lease term with guaranteed renewal, and the scholarship program?

Potential Creative Solutions:

- Five-year lease at 1,900 $/month with built-in increases, providing predictable income
- Scholarship support for the landowner's child, addressing the core financial concern
- Option-to-purchase clause at fair market value determined by independent appraisal, providing future flexibility

- Guarantee that if the property value declines due to mining, the company will compensate for the difference

Debrief Questions

1. How did understanding each party's BATNA influence the negotiation?
2. What questions helped uncover the underlying interests behind the stated positions?
3. Were there creative options that addressed both parties' core interests?
4. How did the mediator handle the significant gap between opening positions?

> **Facilitator Notes:**
> Allow 60-75 minutes. The "secret information" (scholarship program) should not be revealed until at least 20 minutes into negotiation, after both parties have established their core interests. Common pitfall: mediators focus on the financial package without exploring non-monetary interests (legacy, community standing, future relationship). Progression signal: parties begin asking questions about each other's constraints rather than repeating demands.

18.3 Specialized Exercises for Challenging Situations

The following exercises address specific challenging situations that mediators commonly face: managing impasse, handling emotional escalation, and dealing with sensitive topics.

Exercise 4: Breaking Impasse Through Creative Options

This exercise provides intensive practice in overcoming deadlocks, using the strategies described in Chapter 13. Participants experience the frustration of impasse and develop tools for breaking through.

Exercise Setup

Two participants take positions that seem irreconcilable. A third serves as mediator. The exercise begins mid-negotiation, at the point where dialogue has stalled.

Scenario: The community demands that the company pay 500,000 $ for environmental damage. The company insists its maximum liability is 100,000 $. Both sides have rejected the other's number, and negotiations have ground to a halt. The mediator has called a brief recess and will now attempt to restart the dialogue.

Instructions for Community Role: You believe strongly that 500,000 $ is fair. You've done calculations based on crop losses, health costs, and water treatment needs. You feel the company is trying to escape responsibility with a lowball offer. You're willing to consider creative solutions, but you need to feel your concerns are taken seriously first.

Instructions for Company Role: You believe 100,000 $ is generous, given that your experts say the damage is limited. You're concerned about setting precedents. However, you know prolonged conflict is costing money and reputation. You're willing to consider creative solutions if they provide certainty and don't establish dangerous precedents.

Impasse-Breaking Techniques to Practice

1. **Reframe from Positions to Interests:** "Let's step back from the numbers for a moment. Help me understand what the compensation needs to accomplish for the community. And what constraints is the company facing?"
2. **Introduce Hypotheticals:** "What if the payment weren't purely cash? What if some portion were invested in infrastructure that addresses the underlying damage?"
3. **Use Joint Fact-Finding:** "You clearly disagree about the extent of damage. Would it help to have a neutral expert assess the situation? Could we agree on who would do that assessment?"

4. **Explore BATNAs:** "If we can't reach an agreement here, what will each of you do? Let's think through what that would actually look like."
5. **Break the Issue Apart:** "Can we separate this into components? Perhaps immediate remediation costs, ongoing monitoring, and compensation for affected families are different questions with different answers?"
6. **Mediator's Proposal:** "Based on what I've heard from both of you, let me suggest a framework that might address your concerns. This is just a starting point for discussion . . . "

Begin with reframing and open-ended hypothetical questions, which carry the lowest risk of appearing partial. If these do not shift positions, move to reality testing and BATNA analysis, which apply gentle pressure. Issue separation should be used when parties conflate multiple concerns. Reserve the mediator's proposal for situations where parties have exhausted their own creativity but appear genuinely willing to accept outside suggestions.

Facilitator Notes:

Allow 40-50 minutes. The most common mistake is jumping to a mediator's proposal before exploring other techniques. Start with reframing and hypothetical questions (10 minutes each), then progress to reality testing and issue separation. Reserve mediator's proposal as a last resort. Pitfall: participants may confuse brainstorming with evaluating. Remind them to generate options before assessing feasibility.

Practical Tip: Breaking Impasses Through Change

When an impasse occurs, don't push harder on the same issue. Instead, change something: the framing, the venue (call a break), the participants (caucus), or the topic (move to a different issue and return to this one later).

Exercise 5: Managing Emotional Escalation

This exercise develops skill in handling moments when emotions flare and threaten to derail dialogue. These moments are inevitable in disputes involving loss, injustice, or trauma.

Exercise Setup

The exercise simulates a moment when a community member becomes visibly upset during mediation. The mediator must respond in a way that acknowledges the emotion, maintains the process, and creates conditions for productive dialogue to resume.

Trigger Scenario: The company representative has just said, "Our environmental studies show the contamination levels are within acceptable limits. We don't understand why the community keeps making these exaggerated claims."

Community Member Response (to be acted out): [Standing up, voice raised] "Acceptable limits?! My daughter has been sick for six months. My neighbors have lost their livestock. And you sit there with your reports telling us nothing is wrong? You call our suffering 'exaggerated'?" [Voice breaking] "Do you even see us as human beings?"

Mediator Response Practice

Immediate Response:

- Remain calm and present
- Acknowledge the emotion directly: "I can see and hear how much pain you're carrying. This matters deeply to you, and it should."
- Offer choice and control: "Would you like to take a brief break, or would you prefer to continue?"

After Initial Response:

- Address the company representative: "The word 'exaggerated' landed hard. Can you help us understand what you were trying to communicate?"

- Reframe the underlying issue: "There's clearly a disconnect between what the technical studies show and what community members are experiencing. Perhaps we need to explore that gap rather than argue about whose perception is correct."
- Reset ground rules if needed: "I'd like to remind us all that we committed to approaching this with open minds. That means not dismissing each other's experiences, even when we see things differently."

> **Caution: Never Tell Someone to Calm Down**
> Never tell an upset person to "calm down." This typically has the opposite effect. Instead, validate the emotion ("Anyone would feel that way given what you've experienced") and offer support ("What would be helpful right now?").

Practice Variations

Run the exercise multiple times with different triggers and emotional responses:

- **Anger:** A participant becomes confrontational and accuses the other side of lying
- **Tears:** A participant begins crying while describing the impact on their family
- **Withdrawal:** A participant becomes silent and refuses to engage
- **Threat:** A participant threatens to walk out or escalate to legal action

The following facilitation guide helps trainers implement all exercises effectively in workshop settings.

> **Facilitator Notes:**
> Allow 30-40 minutes for the core exercise plus 15 minutes for practice variations. Assign the "Accusation of Corruption" variation to more experienced participants, as it requires balancing validation with neutrality. Common pitfall: mediators attempt to reason with the escalated party before acknowledging their emotion. Progression signal: the mediator can de-escalate without dismissing the underlying concern.

18.4 Facilitation Guide for Trainers

This section provides guidance for trainers and facilitators using these exercises in workshop settings.

Setting Up Effective Simulations

Physical Environment:

- Arrange seating to simulate real mediation settings (parties facing each other, mediator between)
- Have separate spaces available for caucus practice
- Provide flipcharts or whiteboards for agenda setting and option generation
- Ensure the space allows observers to watch without disrupting

Time Management:

- Communication skills exercises: 15 to 30 minutes each, plus 10 to 15 minutes debrief
- Full simulations: 60 to 90 minutes, plus 20 to 30 minutes debrief
- Always allow more time for debrief than you think you'll need

Role Assignment:

- Rotate roles so everyone can practice being the mediator
- Consider having company employees play community roles and vice versa to build empathy
- Use observers who take notes on specific skills, such as questioning and reframing.

Conducting Effective Debriefs

The debrief is where learning is consolidated. Structure debriefs using these questions:

For the Mediator:

- What were you trying to accomplish at each stage?
- What techniques did you use, and what effect did they have?
- Where did you feel most challenged?
- What would you do differently next time?

For Role Players:

- What did the mediator do that was helpful?
- What made you feel heard or understood?
- What might have made you more willing to be flexible?
- Were there moments when you felt dismissed or frustrated with the process?

For Observers:

- What techniques did you observe the mediator using?
- What turning points did you notice in the dialogue?
- Were there missed opportunities you noticed?
- How did the mediator handle power dynamics?

Practical Tip: Structured Debrief

Use a consistent debrief structure: What happened? How did participants feel? What worked well? What would you do differently? What principles apply? This sequence moves from description through reflection to generalization, maximizing learning extraction from each exercise.

Caution: Debrief Time

Allowing substantial debrief time helps insights crystallize. Rushed debriefs forfeit most learning value. If time is limited, shorten the exercise rather than the debrief. The conversation afterward is where insights crystallize and transfer to future practice.

Adapting Exercises to Your Context

These scenarios can be modified to reflect local realities:

- **Industry Context:** Change "mining" to oil and gas, infrastructure, renewable energy, or other relevant industries
- **Cultural Context:** Adapt names, locations, and cultural practices to match participants' experience
- **Language:** Translate materials and consider language dynamics in multilingual settings
- **Specific Issues:** Modify the central issues to reflect common disputes in your region

Practical Tip: Use Real-World Scenarios

Have participants generate scenarios from their own experience. Real cases (appropriately anonymized) create more powerful learning than hypothetical situations.

Key Concept: The Transfer Gap

Skills practiced in training do not automatically transfer to real situations. Stress, complexity, and stakes interfere with recall and application. Bridge the gap through increasingly realistic practice, reflection on real experiences, and a conscious effort to apply specific techniques in actual mediations.

18.5 Conclusion: From Practice to Proficiency

Mediation skills develop through structured practice and reflection. The exercises in this chapter provide structured opportunities to apply the principles and techniques described throughout this handbook. Each simulation addresses core concepts. These include active listening (Chapter 4), understanding conflict dynamics (Chapter 5), managing the mediation process (Chapter 6), using the mediator's toolbox (Chapter 9), trauma-informed and culturally sensitive approaches (Chapter 10), managing power asymmetries (Chapter 12), and navigating impasses (Chapter 13).

As participants repeatedly engage with these scenarios, their responses become more natural and intuitive. What initially feels awkward, like paraphrasing emotions and reframing accusations, becomes automatic. This "muscle memory" enables effective mediation because real disputes don't pause to allow mediators time to consult their notes.

Most importantly, these exercises help mediators develop genuine empathy for all parties in company-community disputes. By playing different roles, such as the frustrated community member and the constrained company representative, participants begin to understand that both sides typically have legitimate concerns, real constraints, and genuine humanity. This understanding is the foundation of effective mediation.

Key Concept: Proficiency Over Perfection

The goal of practice is not perfection but proficiency. Even experienced mediators continue learning from every case. What matters is developing a solid foundation of skills and the reflective capacity to keep improving.

Mediators who invest in developing these skills through simulation and practice will be better equipped to serve parties in conflict, guiding them from grievance toward resolution, from mistrust toward partnership, and from confrontation toward collaboration.

19. CONCLUSION

19.1 The Journey from Conflict to Collaboration

This handbook has examined the difficult, rewarding work of mediating disputes between companies and communities. From the foundational principles of voluntary mediation to the intricate skills of communication and facilitation, from understanding conflict dynamics to navigating impasses and resistance, we have assembled a comprehensive framework for practitioners committed to transforming adversarial relationships into collaborative partnerships.

Eighteen chapters, three appendices, and a glossary provide both theoretical grounding and practical tools. The case studies from Guinea and Stuttgart (Chapter 17) have demonstrated that these principles work in practice, though never without difficulty. They also show what happens without mediation: protracted conflict, damaged relationships, lost opportunities, and sometimes violence. The high stakes in company-community disputes are precisely why skilled mediation matters. The simulation exercises in Chapter 18 offer opportunities to practice these principles in realistic scenarios.

As you close this handbook and prepare to apply its teachings, let us revisit the core themes that bind these chapters together, offering both a summary and a call to action for mediators entering this field.

19.2 Foundations: The Bedrock of Ethical Mediation

Chapter 1 (Introduction) established the purpose, audience, and philosophy of this handbook, clarifying who should use it and how. It introduced the guiding philosophy that conflict is natural, but violence is not inevitable, that all parties have legitimate interests, and that processes matter as much as outcomes.

Chapter 2 (Executive Overview) provided a concise summary of what company-community mediation is and is not, when it is appropriate, and the mediator's role and ethical posture. This executive-level overview is a quick reference for experienced practitioners and an orientation for newcomers.

Chapter 3 (Core Principles and Ethics) established that voluntary mediation rests on non-negotiable ethical principles: voluntariness, self-determination, neutrality, confidentiality, informed consent, safety, honesty, and the commitment to do no harm. These are not merely theoretical ideals. They are the practical foundation upon which all successful mediation is built.

When community members sit across from company representatives, they carry the weight of historical grievances, power imbalances, and deep skepticism. Creating space for genuine dialogue requires demonstrating, through consistent action, that the process itself is trustworthy. This means the mediator must be visibly neutral, protective of confidentiality, and committed to letting parties control their own outcome.

19.3 The Art and Science of Communication

Chapter 4 (Key Communication and Facilitation Skills) equipped mediators with the essential tools of their trade: active listening, empathy, effective questioning, reframing, summarizing, and facilitation techniques. These skills are the mediator's primary instruments for transforming conflict.

Active listening goes far beyond hearing words. It requires full presence, attentiveness to body language and tone, and the ability to make speakers feel genuinely understood. When a farmer whose land was contaminated by mine runoff feels truly heard, perhaps for the first time, something shifts. Defensive walls begin to lower. The possibility of dialogue opens.

Reframing is perhaps the mediator's most powerful transformative tool. When a community member declares, "The company is poisoning our children, and they don't care," the mediator must acknowledge the pain. Then she redirects toward problem-solving: "You're expressing deep concern about your children's health and safety, and you need assurance that the company takes this seriously." This approach defuses inflammatory language without dismissing the legitimate underlying concern, keeping the door to dialogue open.

Effective questioning moves parties from positions to interests. "We want 5 million dollars" is a position. "Why is this amount important to you?" reveals interests: healthcare for sick community members, educational opportunities for youth, and economic security for families. When interests are exposed, creative solutions become possible that might satisfy those interests in ways neither party initially imagined.

19.4 Understanding the Nature of Conflict

Chapter 5 (Understanding Conflict Dynamics and Escalation) explored the anatomy of conflict, examining its three dimensions: facts, feelings, and processes. Effective mediation addresses all three. Focusing solely on facts while ignoring emotions guarantees failure. Similarly, acknowledging feelings without addressing substantive issues leaves the underlying conflict unresolved.

The Triangle of Satisfaction provides a useful framework: sustainable agreements must meet procedural needs (was the process fair?), emotional needs (do I feel heard and respected?), and substantive needs (does the outcome address my real interests?). An agreement that scores high on substance but low on procedure and emotion will likely collapse under implementation stress.

Understanding conflict escalation, including Friedrich Glasl's nine-stage model, helps mediators diagnose where a dispute stands and what interventions are appropriate. Early-stage conflicts characterized by tension and debate may respond well to straightforward dialogue facilitation.

Late-stage conflicts marked by dehumanization and crisis require more intensive trust-building and possibly cooling-off periods before substantive negotiation can begin.

19.5 Designing Processes That Work

Chapter 6 (Designing Mediation Processes) provided the architectural framework for mediation: the phases from preparation through agreement, and the flexibility required to adapt structure to circumstances.

Preparation is everything. The mediator who thoroughly understands the conflict history, the stakeholders, the power dynamics, and the cultural context before convening the parties is vastly more likely to succeed than one who arrives unprepared. This means conducting pre-mediation interviews, reviewing documentation, understanding technical issues (even if only at a basic level), and thinking through potential obstacles.

Ground rules create safety. Agreeing at the outset that one person speaks at a time, that personal attacks are forbidden, that confidentiality will be maintained, and that anyone can call a break when needed establishes the psychological container within which difficult conversations can occur.

Flexibility within structure remains essential. The phases of mediation provide guidance, not rigid prescription. A skilled mediator knows when to deviate from the agenda. If an emotional issue demands immediate attention, she addresses it. If tensions are rising, she calls an unscheduled break. If the parties have not yet revealed their true concerns, she spends extra sessions on interest exploration.

19.6 From Agreement to Lasting Change

Chapter 7 (Post-Agreement Implementation) addressed a critical reality: the signed agreement is a milestone, not a destination. Many mediated agreements fail not because they were poorly designed but because implementation was neglected.

The chapter provided frameworks for designing agreements that can actually be implemented, establishing monitoring systems, creating communication infrastructure, building early warning mechanisms, and managing the inevitable challenges that arise when commitments meet reality. The focus on sustainable long-term success reflects the understanding that company-community relationships must endure beyond any single agreement.

19.7 Knowing When Not to Proceed

Chapter 8 (When Mediation Should Not Proceed) addressed one of mediation's most important but often overlooked questions: when should mediation NOT continue? Not every conflict is suitable for mediation, and not every moment is right for dialogue. Recognizing these situations requires courage and discernment.

Mediation should not proceed in several critical situations. These include cases where safety cannot be guaranteed, where severe power imbalances combine with bad faith, where genocide or war crimes have occurred, where ongoing violence prevents meaningful dialogue, where the mediator has been captured by one party, or where hidden decision-makers render agreements meaningless. Proceeding in these circumstances does not merely risk failure. It can cause active harm, entrench power imbalances, retraumatize victims, or legitimize unjust outcomes.

In the extractive sector specifically, mediators should decline when a company is operating without a valid mining license or in violation of environmental standards, since mediation should not legitimize illegal operations. Mediation is also inappropriate when a community has no genuine alternative except accepting a project vital to company revenue, as coercive economic conditions undermine voluntariness. Similarly, when government actors use the mediation process to bypass indigenous peoples' right to free, prior, and informed consent, the process cannot serve justice.

19.8 The Mediator's Toolbox

Chapter 9 (Tools and Competencies in the Mediator's Toolbox) assembled the analytical tools, process management techniques, and personal competencies that distinguish effective mediators.

BATNA/WATNA analysis is not merely a negotiation concept but a practical tool for breaking impasses. When parties understand their alternatives to agreement, especially their worst alternatives, they often become more flexible. The community that realizes a court battle will take years and may fail becomes more willing to negotiate. The company that faces a potential operational shutdown recognizes that compromise is preferable to disruption.

Caucusing provides space for confidential exploration that joint sessions cannot. In private, parties may reveal flexibility they cannot show publicly, express fears they would not admit to their adversary, or brainstorm options they are not yet ready to propose. Joint fact-finding transforms disputes over data into a collaborative inquiry. These tools, combined with the personal competencies of patience, cultural fluency, and emotional resilience, form the mediator's professional toolkit.

19.9 Honoring the Human Dimension

Chapter 10 (Trauma-Informed and Culturally Sensitive Approaches) addressed perhaps the most sensitive aspects of mediation. Company-community disputes frequently involve real human suffering: families displaced from ancestral lands, workers injured or killed, communities poisoned by pollution, livelihoods destroyed. These are not abstract grievances. They are lived traumas that affect how participants engage with mediation.

A trauma-informed approach recognizes that safety must come first. Participants need to feel physically and emotionally secure before they can engage productively. They need choice and control over their participation. They need protection from retraumatization through invasive questioning or pressure to forgive before they are ready.

Cultural sensitivity requires humility and preparation. Communication styles, decision-making norms, concepts of time, gender roles, the importance of ritual, and countless other factors vary across cultures. The mediator who assumes that their own cultural framework is universal will fail. The mediator who takes time to learn, asks respectful questions when uncertain, and adapts processes to honor local practices demonstrates the respect that builds trust.

19.10 Caring for the Caregiver

Chapter 11 (Mediator Health) turned the lens inward, addressing mediator health and the impact of trauma work on those who facilitate it. This chapter acknowledged a truth too often ignored: mediators are not immune to the emotional weight of the conflicts they help resolve.

Vicarious trauma, compassion fatigue, and burnout are occupational hazards in this field. Mediators who work with survivors of violence, displacement, or environmental harm absorb some of that pain. Without conscious attention to self-care and professional support, this accumulated burden can compromise both personal well-being and professional effectiveness.

The chapter offered practical strategies for sustaining a mediation career. These include establishing boundaries between professional and personal life, developing peer support networks, seeking supervision or debriefing after difficult cases, and recognizing warning signs of burnout. Building sustainable practices allows for long careers in this demanding work. The ethical obligation to step back when depleted protects both mediators and the parties they serve.

19.11 Navigating Power and Rebuilding Trust

Chapter 12 (Managing Power Asymmetries and Restoring Trust) confronted the reality that company-community disputes are rarely between equals. The company typically commands greater financial resources, legal expertise, political connections, and informational advantages. The community may have moral authority, numbers, and tactical options like protests, but often lacks the capacity to engage effectively in formal processes.

The mediator's responsibility is to level the playing field without abandoning neutrality. This means ensuring the weaker party has access to information, supporting their preparation, enforcing ground rules that prevent domination, and perhaps connecting them with advisors who can strengthen their participation. It does not mean advocating for their position. It means ensuring they can advocate for themselves effectively.

Trust reconstruction is often the most critical work in company-community mediation. Years of broken promises, dismissive treatment, or outright harm frequently shatter any foundation for collaboration. Trust must be rebuilt deliberately, through consistent behavior, small kept commitments, transparent communication, meaningful acknowledgment of past wrongs, and structural safeguards that reduce dependence on good faith alone.

19.12 When Progress Stalls

Chapter 13 (Navigating Impasses and Rebuilding Cooperation) acknowledged that impasses are normal, not exceptional. Even the best-conducted mediations can reach a point where the parties cannot move forward. The key is recognizing impasses early and deploying appropriate strategies.

Sometimes a simple break is enough. Parties return with a fresh perspective. Sometimes a caucus reveals hidden flexibility or unspoken concerns. Sometimes reframing the issue transforms an impossible demand into a solvable problem. Sometimes introducing hypothetical scenarios allows parties to explore options without commitment. And sometimes a mediator's proposal provides a face-saving way to accept a compromise neither party could propose on their own.

When an impasse persists despite best efforts, partial agreements may preserve progress. Agreeing on three issues while leaving the fourth for future discussion is better than talks that collapse entirely. The mediator who successfully guides parties through an impasse has not merely resolved a procedural obstacle. They have demonstrated that collaborative problem-solving can work even when it seems impossible.

19.13 Understanding and Addressing Resistance

Chapter 14 (Resistance Scenarios) explored the various forms of resistance in mediation and strategies for addressing them constructively. From silent participants and intimidation tactics to walkouts, confidentiality breaches, internal community divisions, and bad-faith reversals, this chapter offers practical strategies for the challenging behaviors that can derail mediation.

Understanding the source of resistance is essential to addressing it. Fear of the unknown, loss of control, past negative experiences, lack of trust, and emotional attachment to positions all drive resistant behaviors. The skilled mediator neither dismisses resistance nor surrenders to it, but engages with it as valuable information about what parties need to feel safe enough to participate constructively.

19.14 Learning from Mistakes

Chapter 15 (Learning from Mediator Mistakes) offered something rarely found in professional handbooks: an honest examination of mediator mistakes and failures. Learning from failure is essential to professional growth, yet the field often focuses exclusively on success stories.

Common mediator mistakes include the Hero Mediator trap, false balance fallacy, cultural erasure, burnout blindness, co-optation risk, and premature closure. Each of these errors is understandable, often stemming from good intentions, yet each can derail a mediation or cause lasting harm.

The chapter emphasized that mistakes are inevitable but not irredeemable. What matters is how mediators respond: acknowledging errors, repairing relationships where possible, extracting lessons for future practice, and developing the resilience to continue despite setbacks. The best mediators are not those who never err, but those who learn and grow from every experience.

A critical lesson from extractive-industry mediation: communities under economic pressure sometimes agree to environmental compromises because they need immediate employment and have no other income sources. Mediators must distinguish between agreement and voluntary consent. Post-agreement monitoring often reveals that economic desperation led to commitments that communities later find unsustainable, restarting the very conflict mediation was meant to resolve.

19.15 Embracing the Digital Frontier

Chapter 16 (Digital Mediation) addressed the growing importance of digital mediation, covering virtual session protocols, hybrid approaches, and digital tools for enhanced practice. Virtual platforms offer new possibilities for dispute resolution but also present unique challenges.

Digital mediation can improve access for geographically dispersed parties, reduce costs, enable more flexible scheduling, and provide documentation capabilities unavailable in face-to-face settings. These advantages are particularly significant in company-community disputes where great distances separate parties.

However, virtual environments also lose important interpersonal dynamics. Reading body language becomes more difficult. Building rapport requires different techniques. Technical difficulties can disrupt emotional moments. Digital divides may disadvantage some participants. The chapter provides guidance on when virtual mediation helps and when it harms the process, and addresses ethical considerations specific to digital formats.

19.16 Lessons from the Field

Chapter 17 (Case Studies) illuminated both successes and instructive challenges. The Kintinian community and Siguiri Gold Mine mediation in Guinea demonstrated the power of patience and incremental progress, achieving over six years what could never have been accomplished in six months. The Stuttgart 21 infrastructure mediation showed how radical transparency can address public concerns, even when the outcome disappoints some participants.

Across both cases, specific themes recur: the centrality of trust, the importance of genuine engagement (not performative consultation), the need for patience, the value of independent mediation, the power of early wins, and the necessity of addressing both substance and relationship. These are not abstract principles but lived realities from practitioners who have navigated these waters.

19.17 From Theory to Practice

Chapter 18 (Simulation Exercises and Role-Play Scenarios) recognized that reading about mediation is not the same as doing it. The simulation exercises and role-play scenarios provide opportunities to develop skills in realistic contexts, to make mistakes in safe environments, and to build the muscle memory that effective mediation requires.

We encourage trainers and practitioners to use these exercises extensively. Debrief thoroughly after each simulation. Discuss what worked, what didn't, and why. Have participants rotate through the following roles: mediator, community representative, company representative, and observer. Each perspective teaches something different.

The Appendices provide additional practical resources. APPENDIX A offers comprehensive templates for every stage of mediation, from pre-mediation assessment to post-agreement monitoring. **The Glossary** provides quick reference for key terms, supporting consistent understanding of the vocabulary used throughout.

Beyond the information and exercises found in this book (particularly the case studies in Chapter 17 and simulation scenarios in Chapter 18), reflective habits support growth through practice. After each mediation session, ask yourself: "What did I handle well? What would I do differently? What surprised me? Where did I miss an opportunity?" Keep a journal. Discuss difficult cases with colleagues. Seek supervision or mentorship from experienced practitioners. The learning never ends.

19.18 Looking Forward: The Future of Company-Community Mediation

As we look to the future, several trends will shape company-community disputes and the mediation processes designed to address them.

The energy transition will create new categories of conflict. Lithium mines for electric vehicle batteries, wind farms, solar installations, transmission lines, and hydrogen facilities will all generate community impacts and potential disputes. Mediators understanding these new contexts and the passionate positions they evoke is essential.

International frameworks will continue to evolve. The UN Guiding Principles on Business and Human Rights have established expectations for access to remediation. Performance standards from international financial institutions increasingly require grievance mechanisms and meaningful stakeholder engagement. Familiarity with these frameworks and how to leverage them constructively is essential for mediators working in this space.

Technology will create both opportunities and challenges. Virtual mediation can improve access but may lose important interpersonal dynamics. Data and monitoring technologies can support joint fact-finding but also raise privacy concerns. Social media can empower communities but also spread misinformation and inflame conflict. Navigating this evolving landscape thoughtfully is essential for mediators.

Climate change will intensify resource conflicts. Competition over water, arable land, and stable environments will increase. Communities displaced by climate impacts will have complex grievances against both corporations and governments. Mediators will increasingly find themselves at the intersection of environmental justice and corporate responsibility.

Through all these developments, one constant remains: the work depends on dedicated individuals willing to step into difficult spaces and facilitate dialogue. With that in mind, this handbook closes with a reflection addressed directly to those practitioners.

19.19 Final Reflections

To those who will take up this work: understand that you are entering a field that matters. The disputes you will mediate are not abstract exercises. They affect real communities whose water, land, health, and livelihoods hang in the balance. They affect real workers whose jobs and safety depend on operational outcomes. They affect real ecosystems that future generations will inherit.

The work is challenging. You will face situations where parties seem intractably opposed, where power imbalances feel overwhelming, where trauma runs deep, where cultural barriers seem insurmountable, and where progress evaporates overnight. You will be criticized by both sides. You will question whether your efforts make any difference.

In those moments, remember why you entered this field. Remember that every conflict resolved through dialogue is a conflict not resolved through violence or litigation. Remember that sustainable agreements create lasting value for all parties. Remember that the alternative to skilled mediation is usually worse outcomes for everyone.

As Chapter 11 emphasized, the emotional demands of mediation are substantial, especially in trauma-affected contexts. Develop support systems. Practice self-care not as indulgence but as a professional necessity. Burned-out mediators serve no one well.

Every mediation and every failure teaches something valuable. Stay curious. Seek diverse perspectives. Question your assumptions. The best mediators are perpetual students of human nature and conflict dynamics.

Company-community mediation is both an art and a science. It requires technical skill and human sensitivity, structured process and adaptive flexibility, neutrality and passionate commitment to justice. It demands patience when resolution seems distant and urgency when opportunities arise. It calls for intellectual rigor and emotional intelligence, professional detachment, and deep caring.

The framework presented in this handbook, across eighteen content chapters, three appendices, and a detailed glossary, provides guidance, but you will ultimately develop your own style, your own approaches, your own wisdom through experience. The principles are foundational. The application is creative.

As you proceed to apply these insights, remember that your goal is not merely to resolve disputes but to transform relationships. A signed agreement is a milestone, not a destination. The true measure of success is whether former adversaries can work together constructively, whether communities feel heard and respected, and whether companies learn to operate as genuine partners rather than as imposed powers.

The journey from grievance to agreement is rarely easy or linear. It winds through setbacks and breakthroughs, through frustrations and surprises. But with skilled mediation, patience, and genuine commitment from all parties, parties can heal even deeply damaged relationships and direct them toward mutual benefit.

We close with wisdom that remains urgently relevant:

"Peace is not the absence of conflict, but the ability to cope with conflict by peaceful means.",
Ronald Reagan

This handbook has aimed to impart that ability. The rest is in your hands. Use these tools wisely. Adapt them thoughtfully. Keep the human element at the center of your work. And know that every conflict you help transform through dialogue contributes to a more peaceful, more just world.

APPENDIX A
RESOURCES

This appendix provides practical resources that complement the theoretical frameworks and principles discussed throughout the handbook. These templates, tools, and reference materials are designed to support mediators at every stage of the mediation process, from initial conflict assessment through implementation monitoring.

Each template connects directly to specific chapters and concepts covered in the main text. Cross-references are provided to help practitioners understand not only *how* to use each tool, but *why* it matters in the context of company-community disputes. The templates are designed to be adapted to local contexts, cultural requirements, and specific dispute characteristics.

Key Concept: Adapting Templates to Context

These templates serve as starting points rather than rigid frameworks. Effective mediators adapt tools to fit the specific cultural context, power dynamics, and nature of each dispute. As discussed in Chapter 10, cultural sensitivity requires flexibility in how processes are structured and documented.

Caution: Template Over-Reliance

Templates can constrain creative thinking. If you find yourself forcing a situation to fit a template rather than adapting the template to suit the situation, step back. Sometimes the best approach is to design something new rather than modify an existing solution.

The appendix is organized into seven major sections:

1. **Pre-Mediation Assessment Templates** for conflict analysis and stakeholder mapping
2. **Process Documents and Agreements** for establishing the mediation framework
3. **Communication Tools Quick Reference** for active listening, questioning, and reframing
4. **Interest Mapping and Analysis Tools** for uncovering underlying needs
5. **Agreement Documentation Templates** for formalizing settlements
6. **Post-Mediation and Implementation Tools** for monitoring and follow-up
7. **Cultural Sensitivity and Trauma-Informed Practice Guides** for specialized approaches

A.1 Pre-Mediation Assessment Templates

Thorough preparation is the foundation of successful mediation, as emphasized in Chapter 6 (Phase 0: Preparation). These assessment templates help mediators systematically gather information, understand conflict dynamics, and evaluate whether conditions are suitable for productive dialogue. The tools in this section directly support the conflict analysis approaches discussed in Chapter 5.

A.1.1 Conflict Assessment Form

This comprehensive form guides mediators through a structured assessment of the dispute. It incorporates the conflict dynamics framework from Chapter 5, including root cause analysis and escalation assessment based on Friedrich Glasl's conflict escalation model.

> **Practical Tip: Completing the Assessment**
>
> Complete this form through a combination of document review, stakeholder interviews, and direct observation. Schedule separate meetings with each party before joint sessions to gather information confidentially. This approach builds trust and provides richer data than relying solely on written submissions.

PART 1: Basic Information

Case Reference Number:	[To be assigned]
Date of Assessment:	
Assessor Name(s):	
Location/Region:	
Company Name:	
Company Sector:	☐ Mining ☐ Oil/Gas ☐ Infrastructure ☐ Agriculture ☐ Other: ________________
Community Name(s):	

Estimated Population Affected:	

PART 2: Conflict History and Context

When did the conflict begin?	
Triggering Event(s):	*Describe the specific incident(s) that initiated or escalated the conflict:*
Previous Resolution Attempts:	☐ None ☐ Direct negotiation ☐ Previous mediation ☐ Legal action ☐ Government intervention ☐ Other Describe outcomes:
Historical Context:	*Note any historical factors influencing current dynamics (colonial history, previous company operations, political context):*

PART 3: Root Cause Analysis

Rate each potential root cause on a scale of 0-3 (0=Not a factor, 1=Minor factor, 2=Significant factor, 3=Primary driver). Add notes to explain your rating.

Root Cause Category	**Rating (0-3)**	**Notes/Evidence**
Resource Competition (land, water, minerals)		
Unmet Expectations/Broken Promises		
Environmental Damage/ Concerns		
Inadequate Consultation/ Communication		

Employment/Economic Grievances		
Cultural/Sacred Site Impacts		
Health and Safety Concerns		
Displacement/Resettlement Issues		
Power Imbalance/Lack of Voice		
Human Rights Violations		
Other (specify):		

PART 4: Escalation Assessment (Based on Glasl's Model)

As discussed in Chapter 3, understanding the escalation stage of the conflict helps determine appropriate intervention strategies. Check for indicators present and determine the overall stage.

Stage	Indicators (check all that apply)	Present?
Stage 1: Tension/Hardening	☐ Discomfort but issues not openly confronted ☐ Parties still willing to talk directly ☐ Hope remains for amicable resolution ☐ Minor complaints being raised informally	☐ Yes ☐ No
Stage 2: Debate/Polarization	☐ Positions hardening, win-lose thinking ☐ Public statements and media involvement ☐ Stereotyping of the other party ☐ Communication becoming argumentative	☐ Yes ☐ No

Stage 3: Actions Replace Dialogue	☐ Protests, blockades, or demonstrations ☐ Legal actions initiated ☐ Security presence increased ☐ Communication breakdown; talking about not to	☐ Yes ☐ No
Stage 4: Crisis/Hostility	☐ Violence or threat of violence ☐ Dehumanization of the other party ☐ International attention/ campaigns ☐ Trust completely shattered	☐ Yes ☐ No

Overall Assessment: Current conflict stage is: ☐ Stage 1 ☐ Stage 2 ☐ Stage 3 ☐ Stage 4

Caution: High Escalation Stages

Conflicts at Stage 3 or 4 require careful trust-building measures before formal mediation can proceed. Consider confidence-building steps such as informal dialogue, cooling-off periods, or interim agreements (e.g., a community suspending protests while the company pauses disputed operations). As noted in Chapter 5, attempting formal mediation without addressing severe mistrust often backfires.

A.1.2 Stakeholder Mapping Template

Effective mediation requires identifying all relevant stakeholders, understanding their roles, and assessing their influence. This template helps mediators systematically map the stakeholder landscape. As discussed in Chapter 6, ensuring the right people are at the table is critical, particularly in community disputes where leadership structures may be complex or contested.

Primary Stakeholders (Direct Parties)

Stakeholder Group	Key Representatives	Interests	Power Level	Notes
Company Management			☐H ☐M ☐L	
Community Leaders			☐H ☐M ☐L	
Traditional Authorities			☐H ☐M ☐L	
Affected Households			☐H ☐M ☐L	
Women's Groups			☐H ☐M ☐L	
Youth Representatives			☐H ☐M ☐L	

Secondary Stakeholders (Influencers)

Stakeholder	Role/Interest	Influence Type	Engagement	Strategy
Local Government			☐Active ☐Passive	
National Government			☐Active ☐Passive	
NGOs/Civil Society			☐Active ☐Passive	
International Bodies			☐Active ☐Passive	
Media			☐Active ☐Passive	
Investors/ Lenders			☐Active ☐Passive	

Key Concept: Power-Interest Analysis

Chapter 12 emphasizes that power imbalances can derail mediation. Use this mapping to identify where power disparities exist. Stakeholders with high power but low direct interest may need to be consulted, but do not need a seat at the table. Those with high interest but low power (often community subgroups) require special attention to ensure their voices are heard.

A.1.3 Mediation Readiness Assessment Checklist

Before commencing formal mediation, assess whether conditions are conducive to productive dialogue. This checklist evaluates willingness, capability, and safety factors. A score below the threshold suggests that pre-mediation work is needed before convening joint sessions.

Score each item: 0 = Not met | 1 = Partially met | 2 = Fully met

Willingness Indicators	Score	Notes
All primary parties have expressed willingness to participate		
Parties understand the voluntary nature of mediation		
No party is participating solely under external pressure		
Parties are open to considering alternatives to their current positions		
Key decision-makers will be present or accessible		
Capability Indicators	**Score**	**Notes**
Representatives have authority to negotiate and commit		

Community has mechanisms to consult with constituents		
Company representatives can access necessary information		
Language/interpretation needs can be met		
Logistics (venue, transportation, scheduling) are feasible		
Safety and Trust Indicators	**Score**	**Notes**
No imminent threat of violence		
Neutral venue is available and acceptable to all parties		
Parties can commit to no retaliation during and after mediation		
Minimum level of trust exists or can be established through pre-mediation		
TOTAL SCORE (Maximum 30)		

Interpretation Guide:

- **Score 24-30:** Conditions favorable for mediation. Proceed with process design.
- **Score 16-23:** Some concerns. Address gaps through pre-mediation activities before convening.
- **Score below 16:** Significant barriers exist. Consider alternative approaches or an extended preparation phase.

A.2 Process Documents and Agreements

Formal process documents establish the framework for mediation, clarifying roles, expectations, and commitments. These templates support the Opening Session (Phase 1) described in Chapter 6 and reinforce the core principles of voluntariness, confidentiality, and self-determination discussed in Chapter 5.

A.2.1 Agreement to Mediate Template

This agreement formalizes the parties' commitment to the mediation process. It should be reviewed and signed at the outset of formal mediation, typically during the Opening Session. The agreement reinforces the ethical principles from Chapter 3 and establishes clear expectations.

AGREEMENT TO MEDIATE

This Agreement is entered into on [DATE] between:

Party A (Company): [Company Name], represented by [Name, Title]

Party B (Community): [Community Name], represented by [Names, Titles]

Mediator(s): [Name(s)], [Affiliation]

Article 1: Purpose

The parties agree to engage in mediation to address the following matters: [describe dispute areas, e.g., "environmental impacts, employment concerns, community development commitments, and communication protocols related to the [Project Name] operations"]. The parties commit to working collaboratively toward mutually acceptable solutions.

Article 2: Voluntary Participation

Participation in this mediation is entirely voluntary. Each party enters freely and may withdraw at any time without penalty. Any agreement reached will be by mutual consent only. No party shall be pressured, coerced, or compelled to accept any outcome.

Article 3: Confidentiality

3.1 All discussions, documents, and information shared during mediation sessions are confidential and shall not be disclosed to any third party without the written consent of all parties.

3.2 Statements made during mediation cannot be used as evidence in any legal, administrative, or arbitration proceeding, except as required by law.

3.3 The mediator shall not be called as a witness in any proceeding relating to this dispute.

3.4 Limited exceptions to confidentiality: Disclosure may occur where required by law, to prevent imminent harm, or where all parties provide written consent.

Article 4: Role of the Mediator

4.1 The mediator is a neutral facilitator who assists the parties in communicating and exploring solutions. The mediator does not act as a judge, arbitrator, or advocate for any party.

4.2 The mediator will not impose solutions or make binding decisions. All outcomes rest with the parties.

4.3 The mediator may conduct private sessions (caucuses) with individual parties. Information shared in caucus will remain confidential unless the party authorizes disclosure.

Article 5: Ground Rules

The parties agree to the following ground rules:

1. Treat all participants with respect and dignity
2. Allow each person to speak without interruption
3. Listen actively and seek to understand different perspectives
4. Focus on interests and solutions rather than blame
5. Participate in good faith with genuine intent to resolve issues
6. Refrain from any form of retaliation for statements made in mediation

7. Turn off mobile phones or set them to silent during sessions

Article 6: Interim Measures

During the mediation process, the parties agree to: [Customize as appropriate, e.g., "suspend legal proceedings", "maintain current operations without expansion", "refrain from public statements that could inflame the situation", "suspend protests/blockades"]

Article 7: Logistics

7.1 Sessions will be held at [neutral venue] unless otherwise agreed.

7.2 Language: Mediation will be conducted in [language(s)]. Interpretation services will be provided as needed.

7.3 Costs: [Specify cost-sharing arrangements for mediation fees, venue, travel, interpretation, etc.]

Article 8: Signatures

By signing below, the parties confirm they have read, understood, and agree to the terms of this Agreement to Mediate.

Party A (Company)	**Party B (Community)**
Name: ____________________ Title: ____________________ Signature: ________________ Date: ____________________	Name: ____________________ Title: ____________________ Signature: ________________ Date: ____________________
Mediator Name: ____________________ Signature: ________________ Date: ____________________	

A.2.2 Ground Rules Visual Reference Card

This visual reference can be displayed during mediation sessions to remind participants of shared commitments. Consider printing on a poster or distributing as a handout. Ground rules create the "safe container" for dialogue emphasized in Chapter 4.

<table>
<tr><td>RESPECT

Treat everyone with dignity.

No personal attacks.

Honor cultural differences.</td><td>LISTENING

One speaker at a time.

Listen to understand.

Ask before assuming.</td><td>HONESTY

Speak truthfully.

Share concerns openly.

Express real interests.</td></tr>
<tr><td>OPENNESS

Consider new ideas.

Be willing to learn.

Focus on the future.</td><td>CONFIDENTIALITY

What's said here stays here.

No media/social media.

Safe space for sharing.</td><td>SAFETY

No retaliation.

Breaks when needed.

Right to pause or stop.</td></tr>
</table>

A.3 Communication Tools Quick Reference

Chapter 4 detailed the key communication skills essential for effective mediation: active listening, questioning, reframing, and summarizing. These quick reference guides provide mediators with practical tools to use during sessions. They can be printed as desk references or laminated cards for easy access.

A.3.1 Active Listening Quick Reference

Active listening is the foundation of mediation communication. As noted in Chapter 4, it involves giving the speaker your full attention, observing body language and tone, and responding in ways that demonstrate understanding. This table provides techniques with sample phrases.

Technique	Purpose	Sample Phrases
Paraphrasing	Confirm understanding of content	*"So what I'm hearing is . . . "* *"Let me make sure I understand: you're saying that . . . "* *"In other words, your concern is . . . "*
Reflecting Emotions	Validate feelings and show empathy	*"It sounds like this has been very frustrating for you . . . "* *"I can see that this issue is painful for your community . . . "* *"You seem worried about what might happen next . . . "*
Clarifying	Ensure accuracy and fill gaps	*"When you say 'community,' who specifically do you mean?"* *"Can you help me understand what happened next?"* *"What do you mean by 'adequate compensation'?"*

Summarizing	Organize and confirm key points	*"Let me summarize what I've heard so far . . . "* *"The main points seem to be: first . . . second . . . third . . . "* *"Before we move on, let me check: we've covered X, Y, and Z. Is that right?"*
Encouraging	Invite continued sharing	*"Tell me more about that . . . "* *"What else is important for us to understand?"* *"Please continue . . . " [with attentive silence]*
Nonverbal Cues	Show attention and engagement	Maintain appropriate eye contact (cultural sensitivity applies). Nod occasionally to show understanding. Lean slightly forward; open posture. Avoid distracting movements or looking at your phone/watch.

A.3.2 Question Types and Applications

Effective questioning is one of the mediator's primary tools for uncovering interests and guiding productive dialogue. This reference covers six question types with guidance on when and how to use each. Chapter 4 emphasized utilizing a mix of question types and avoiding interrogation when seeking insight.

Type	When to Use	Examples	Avoid
Open-ended	To encourage explanation and storytelling	*"Can you tell us more about what happened when the mine opened?"* *"How has this affected your daily life?"* *"What would an ideal outcome look like?"*	Leading or loaded questions that suggest an answer
Probing	To dig deeper into underlying needs	*"Why is having a school built so important to the village?"* *"What's behind that concern?"* *"Help me understand what that would mean for you . . . "*	Aggressive "why" questions that feel like interrogation

Clarifying	To ensure understanding and avoid assumptions	*"When you say 'the community wasn't consulted,' who specifically are you referring to?"* *"What time period are we talking about?"*	Assumptions that you already understand
Hypothetical	To explore options without commitment	*"What if the company were to offer training programs instead of direct payments?"* *"Suppose we could address the water issue first. How would that change things?"*	Hypotheticals that seem to favor one side
Closed	To confirm facts or decisions	*"Do you have the authority to agree on this today?"* *"Is next Tuesday acceptable for the next session?"*	Overusing closed questions, which limits dialogue
Reflexive	To encourage self-reflection and perspective-taking	*"How do you think the other side sees this situation?"* *"What assumptions might you be making here?"*	Questions that might feel like accusations

A.3.3 Reframing Reference Guide

Reframing transforms negative or positional statements into neutral, constructive language that opens dialogue. As explained in Chapter 4, effective reframing removes accusatory language while preserving the core concern. This skill keeps discussions productive and prevents spiraling into personal attacks.

Original Statement	Reframed Version
"The company has zero respect for us and keeps lying!"	"It sounds like trust has been broken and you need assurances that promises will be kept."
"We refuse to relocate!"	"Staying on your ancestral land is very important to you. Can you help us understand what makes this so significant?"
"The mining company is destroying our environment and causing irreparable damage."	"There are serious concerns about environmental impacts that need to be addressed. What specific changes would help protect the environment while allowing operations to continue?"
"These villagers are anti-development and don't understand business."	"The community has concerns that haven't yet been addressed in a way that works for them. What information might help bridge this understanding gap?"
"They're just trying to extort money from us."	"There seem to be different views on what fair compensation looks like. What criteria might both sides consider reasonable?"
"The company poisoned our river!"	"There are significant water quality concerns that are affecting the community's health and livelihoods. This is clearly a priority issue to address."
"We won't pay a cent more than we've offered."	"The company has constraints on what's financially possible. Let's explore what flexibility might exist and what forms support could take."
"The government is on their side. We can't win."	"You're feeling like the power balance is unfair. What would help you feel that your voice is being heard equally in this process?"

Key Concept: The Essence of Reframing

Good reframing preserves the speaker's core concern while removing language that would provoke defensiveness. Notice how each reframe: (1) acknowledges the underlying feeling or need, (2) removes blame or accusation, (3) opens the door to discussion, and (4) often ends with a question or invitation to elaborate.

A.4 Interest Mapping and Analysis Tools

Chapter 6 (Phase 3: Exploring Interests) emphasized that understanding the interests behind positions is the heart of mediation. These tools help mediators and parties move beyond stated demands to uncover the underlying needs, values, and concerns that can form the basis for creative solutions.

A.4.1 Position-Interest Analysis Worksheet

This worksheet helps mediators and parties distinguish between positions (what people say they want) and interests (why they want it). Complete one worksheet for each major issue in the dispute. This framework is based on principled negotiation theory and is essential for finding win-win solutions.

Issue Being Analyzed:
[e.g., Compensation for displaced households]

Community Perspective	**Company Perspective**
STATED POSITION: *(What they say they want)*	**STATED POSITION:** *(What they say they want)*
UNDERLYING INTERESTS: *(Why they want it: needs, concerns, hopes)*	**UNDERLYING INTERESTS:** *(Why they want it: needs, concerns, hopes)*
DEEPER VALUES/NEEDS: *(Security, dignity, fairness, respect, autonomy, sustainability . . .)*	**DEEPER VALUES/NEEDS:** *(Predictability, viability, reputation, legal compliance . . .)*

SHARED INTERESTS (interests both parties have in common):
COMPATIBLE INTERESTS (different but not conflicting):
POTENTIAL OPTIONS (solutions that might address key interests):

EXAMPLE: Completed Position-Interest Analysis

Issue: Compensation for 50 households displaced by mine expansion

Community	Company
Position: "We demand $1 million in cash compensation."	**Position:** "We can only pay $300,000 maximum."
Interests: • Every family can rebuild a home • Children can continue schooling • Maintain farming livelihoods • Community stays together	**Interests:** • Stay within budget limits • Avoid setting expensive precedent • Ensure funds are used effectively • Maintain community relations
Values: Security, dignity, continuity, fairness	**Values:** Predictability, responsibility, sustainability

Shared Interests: Both want stable community relations; both want displaced families to have sustainable futures; both want the project to proceed without ongoing conflict
Potential Options: • Community Development Fund ($500k over 5 years) managed by a joint committee • Land-for-land swap with company developing new housing • Skills training + guaranteed employment for displaced youth • Combination: $200k cash + $300k development projects + employment program

A.4.2 BATNA/WATNA Analysis Tool

Understanding alternatives to negotiated agreement is crucial for realistic bargaining. As discussed in Chapter 9, clarifying each party's Best Alternative to a Negotiated Agreement (BATNA) and Worst Alternative to a Negotiated Agreement (WATNA) injects realism and can motivate flexibility when parties realize their alternatives are unattractive. Use this tool in caucus sessions.

COMMUNITY BATNA/WATNA WORKSHEET

BATNA: Best Alternative to Negotiated Agreement	**WATNA: Worst Alternative to Negotiated Agreement**
If mediation fails, our best realistic option is:	*If mediation fails, our worst realistic outcome is:*
Likelihood of achieving this: ☐ High ☐ Medium ☐ Low	Likelihood of this happening: ☐ High ☐ Medium ☐ Low
Time required: ______ months/years	What would trigger this outcome:
Costs involved (financial, social, emotional):	Consequences for community:

COMPANY BATNA/WATNA WORKSHEET

BATNA: Best Alternative to Negotiated Agreement	**WATNA: Worst Alternative to Negotiated Agreement**
If mediation fails, our best realistic option is:	*If mediation fails, our worst realistic outcome is:*
Likelihood of achieving this: ☐ High ☐ Medium ☐ Low	Likelihood of this happening: ☐ High ☐ Medium ☐ Low
Time required: ______ months/ years	Potential costs (financial, reputational, operational):
Costs involved:	Impact on operations and stakeholder relations:

A.5 Agreement Documentation Templates

Chapter 6 (Phase 5: Reaching Agreement) emphasized that written agreements must be clear, detailed, and practical. This section provides a comprehensive template for settlement agreements, incorporating all essential elements for enforceability and implementation. This template reflects best practices from successful mediations, including the Guinea case study (Chapter 17).

A.5.1 Mediation Settlement Agreement Template

This template provides a detailed structure for documenting mediated agreements. Adapt sections as needed for specific disputes. Legal review is recommended before finalization.

MEDIATION SETTLEMENT AGREEMENT

PREAMBLE

This Mediation Settlement Agreement ("Agreement") is made and entered into as of [DATE] ("Effective Date") by and between:

[COMPANY NAME], a company incorporated under the laws of [Jurisdiction], with registered offices at [Address] (hereinafter "the Company");

and

[COMMUNITY NAME], represented by its duly authorized representatives listed in Schedule A (hereinafter "the Community");

(The Company and the Community are collectively referred to as "the Parties.")

RECITALS

WHEREAS:

1. The Company operates [describe operations, e.g., "a gold mining operation"] in the [Region/District], in proximity to the Community's traditional lands and settlements;

2. A dispute arose between the Parties concerning [briefly describe nature of dispute, e.g., "environmental impacts, resettlement compensation, employment opportunities, and community development commitments"];
3. The Parties voluntarily engaged in mediation facilitated by [Mediator Name/Organization] from [start date] to [end date];
4. Through the mediation process, the Parties have reached a mutual understanding and wish to record their agreement to resolve the dispute and establish a framework for ongoing cooperation;

NOW, THEREFORE, in consideration of the mutual promises and covenants contained herein, the Parties agree as follows:

ARTICLE 1: DEFINITIONS

1.1 In this Agreement, unless the context requires otherwise:

"Affected Households" means the households identified in Schedule B who have been directly impacted by [specific impact, e.g., resettlement, land acquisition];

"Community Development Fund" means the fund established under Article 4 of this Agreement;

"Implementation Period" means [X] years from the Effective Date;

"Joint Committee" means the committee established under Article 7 to oversee implementation of this Agreement.

ARTICLE 2: ACKNOWLEDGMENTS

2.1 The Company acknowledges that its operations have affected the Community's [land/environment/livelihoods/other] and recognizes the Community's legitimate concerns.

2.2 The Community acknowledges the Company's commitment to addressing these impacts and its good faith participation in the mediation process.

2.3 Both Parties express their commitment to building a constructive relationship based on mutual respect, ongoing dialogue, and shared benefits.

ARTICLE 3: COMPENSATION AND RESTITUTION

3.1 Individual Compensation: The Company shall provide compensation to Affected Households as follows:

a. [Describe compensation formula or amounts per household/category]
b. Payment shall be made within [timeframe] of the Effective Date
c. Payment method: [Describe, e.g., bank transfer, mobile money, other]

3.2 The eligibility criteria and specific amounts for each Affected Household are detailed in Schedule B.

ARTICLE 4: COMMUNITY DEVELOPMENT FUND

4.1 Establishment: The Company shall establish a Community Development Fund with an initial contribution of [amount] within [timeframe] of the Effective Date.

4.2 Ongoing Contributions: The Company shall contribute [amount/percentage] annually for the duration of the Implementation Period.

4.3 Governance: The Fund shall be managed by a Board comprising [describe composition, e.g., "50% Community representatives, 50% Company representatives"].

4.4 Priority Areas: Fund resources shall prioritize: [List priority areas, e.g., education, healthcare, water infrastructure, livelihood programs].

ARTICLE 5: EMPLOYMENT AND ECONOMIC OPPORTUNITIES

5.1 Local Hiring: The Company commits to prioritizing local hiring, with a target of [percentage] of [unskilled/semi-skilled/all] positions filled by Community members.

5.2 Training Programs: The Company shall establish vocational training programs to prepare Community members for employment opportunities.

5.3 Local Procurement: The Company shall give preference to local suppliers and contractors where feasible.

ARTICLE 6: ENVIRONMENTAL COMMITMENTS

6.1 Environmental Standards: The Company commits to [describe specific environmental commitments, e.g., water quality standards, dust control, waste management].

6.2 Monitoring: Environmental monitoring shall be conducted [frequency] by [entity], with results shared with the Community.

6.3 Remediation: The Company shall address any environmental impacts identified through monitoring within [timeframe].

ARTICLE 7: CONSULTATION AND COMMUNICATION

7.1 Joint Committee: A Joint Committee shall be established comprising [number] representatives from each Party to oversee implementation of this Agreement.

7.2 Meetings: The Joint Committee shall meet [quarterly/monthly] or as needed.

7.3 Grievance Mechanism: A grievance mechanism shall be established for Community members to raise concerns, with a response within [timeframe].

7.4 Information Sharing: The Company shall provide regular updates to the Community on operations, environmental performance, and Agreement implementation.

ARTICLE 8: IMPLEMENTATION AND MONITORING

8.1 Implementation Timeline: A detailed implementation timeline is provided in Schedule C.

8.2 Progress Reports: The Company shall provide [quarterly/semi-annual] progress reports to the Community and any external monitor.

8.3 External Monitoring: [If applicable: Organization Name] shall monitor implementation for [period].

8.4 Review: This Agreement shall be reviewed [timeframe, e.g., annually] by the Parties and may be amended by mutual written consent.

ARTICLE 9: DISPUTE RESOLUTION

9.1 Any disputes arising under this Agreement shall first be addressed through the Joint Committee.

9.2 If unresolved within [timeframe], disputes may be referred to mediation.

9.3 The Parties agree to engage in good faith to resolve disputes before pursuing any legal action.

ARTICLE 10: GENERAL PROVISIONS

10.1 Entire Agreement: This Agreement constitutes the entire understanding between the Parties.

10.2 Amendment: Amendments require written consent of both Parties.

10.3 Governing Law: This Agreement shall be governed by the laws of [jurisdiction].

10.4 Language: This Agreement is executed in [language(s)]. In case of discrepancy, the [language] version shall prevail.

IN WITNESS WHEREOF, the Parties have executed this Agreement as of the date first written above.

SIGNATURES

Company	**Community**
Name: ____________________ Title: ____________________ Signature: ________________ Date: ____________________	Name: ____________________ Title: ____________________ Signature: ________________ Date: ____________________
Mediator Name: ____________________ Signature: ________________ Date: ____________________	

SCHEDULES:

Schedule A: Community Representatives

Schedule B: Affected Households and Compensation Details

Schedule C: Implementation Timeline

A.6 Post-Mediation and Implementation Tools

As emphasized throughout the handbook, a signed agreement is just the beginning. Sustainable resolution requires effective implementation and monitoring. Chapter 7 noted that voluntary mediation compliance relies on trust and goodwill, making follow-up mechanisms essential. These tools support the transition from agreement to action.

A.6.1 Implementation Monitoring Checklist

Beyond implementation monitoring, mediators should also build a habit of reflecting on each session itself. The following assessment tool captures what worked well, what could be improved, and what lessons apply to future sessions.

Figure 53: A structured assessment tool for evaluating the mediation session after it concludes, capturing outcomes, process quality, and areas for improvement.

Building this reflection habit into your routine after each session accelerates your growth as a mediator and helps you recognize patterns in your own practice that might otherwise go unnoticed.

A.6.2 Mediation Session Debrief Form

Complete this form after each mediation session to track progress, reflect on mediator performance, and prepare for subsequent sessions. As discussed in Chapter 9, reflective practice is essential for developing mediator competencies.

Session Information	
Date:	
Session Number:	
Participants Present:	
Duration:	
Progress Assessment	
Issues Discussed:	
Agreements Reached:	
Outstanding Issues:	
Impasses Encountered:	
Mediator Self-Reflection	
What worked well?	
What could I improve?	
Did I maintain impartiality?	☐ Yes ☐ Partially ☐ Concern area:
Emotional climate of session:	☐ Constructive ☐ Tense but manageable ☐ Difficult

Next Steps	
Actions before next session:	
Topics for next session:	
Date of next session:	

A.7 Cultural Sensitivity and Trauma-Informed Practice Guides

Chapter 10 explored the psychological dimensions of conflict, including trauma and cultural factors. These specialized guides provide quick reference tools for mediators working in contexts where trauma and cultural sensitivity are particularly important. The sexual assault mediation handbook included as a project resource provides additional depth on trauma-informed approaches.

A.7.1 Cultural Sensitivity Preparation Checklist

Use this checklist when preparing for mediation in cross-cultural contexts. Complete before the first session and review periodically throughout the process.

Cultural Research and Preparation	Done?	Notes
Researched community's cultural background, traditions, and values	☐	
Identified local leadership structures and decision-making norms	☐	
Understood gender roles and ensured appropriate representation	☐	
Learned appropriate greetings and protocols for addressing elders/leaders	☐	
Identified any religious observances or holidays to consider in scheduling	☐	
Communication Preparation	**Done?**	**Notes**
Arranged for qualified, neutral interpreters if needed	☐	
Prepared materials in appropriate language(s)	☐	
Understood communication norms (direct vs. indirect, eye contact, etc.)	☐	

Prepared to explain concepts in culturally appropriate terms	☐	
Logistical Adaptations	**Done?**	**Notes**
Selected venue acceptable to all parties (neutral, accessible, comfortable)	☐	
Scheduled at times that work for all parties (considering work patterns)	☐	
Arranged appropriate seating (considering hierarchy, comfort)	☐	
Planned for refreshments/meals if culturally appropriate	☐	
Incorporated opening ritual if desired (prayer, traditional greeting)	☐	

A.7.2 Trauma-Informed Practice Quick Reference

When mediating disputes involving trauma (violence, displacement, loss), apply these principles. Refer to Chapter 10 and the Sexual Assault Mediation Handbook for detailed guidance.

Principle	Application in Mediation
Safety	• Ensure physical and emotional safety of all participants • Use neutral venues away from sites of trauma • Allow support persons to accompany survivors • Make clear that participation is voluntary and withdrawal is permitted
Choice and Control	• Give trauma survivors choices whenever possible (seating, breaks, topics) • Do not pressure disclosure; let people share at their own pace • Empower survivors by involving them in shaping the process

Avoiding Retraumatization	• Do not probe for graphic details of traumatic events • Watch for signs of distress (freezing, agitation, withdrawal) • Take breaks when needed; do not push through distress • Use sensitive language; avoid blame or minimization
Support Resources	• Have psychosocial support available (counselor on standby) • Provide information about ongoing support services • Check in with participants after sessions
Patience and Trust	• Accept that trust-building takes time with trauma survivors • Be consistent and predictable in your approach • Do not rush toward forgiveness or "moving on"

Conclusion

The templates, tools, and reference materials in this appendix are designed to support mediators throughout the mediation process. They translate the principles and techniques discussed in the handbook's chapters into practical, actionable resources.

Remember that these are starting points, not rigid formulas. Effective mediation requires adapting tools to each unique situation, respecting cultural contexts, and maintaining the flexibility to respond to what emerges in dialogue. The best mediators use these resources as guides while remaining fully present with the parties and responsive to their needs.

As you gain experience, you will develop your own variations and additions to these tools. The goal is always the same: to facilitate voluntary, respectful dialogue that enables parties to find their own path from conflict to collaboration.

Final Thought

The journey from grievance to agreement is rarely easy, but with skilled mediation, even deeply strained relationships can be repaired. These tools exist to help you guide parties through that journey. Use them wisely, adapt them thoughtfully, and always keep the human element at the center of your work.

APPENDIX B GLOSSARY OF KEY TERMS

Accountability Mechanism: An independent system or institution designed to ensure that parties fulfill their commitments under a mediation agreement and provide remedies when obligations are violated. In mining contexts, these may include joint monitoring committees, ombudsman offices, or international mechanisms such as the CAO.

Acknowledgment: A statement or action by which a party recognizes and validates the experiences, suffering, or concerns of another party. In company-community mediation, acknowledgment often involves the company recognizing the impact of its operations on community members, which can be a crucial step in rebuilding trust and facilitating healing.

Active Listening: A communication technique that involves giving full attention to the speaker, observing body language and tone, and responding in ways that demonstrate understanding. Key components include paraphrasing, reflecting emotions, maintaining eye contact, avoiding interruptions, and picking up on unspoken concerns. Active listening builds rapport and creates a safe space for dialogue.

Agenda Setting: The phase in mediation where parties collaboratively identify and prioritize the issues to be discussed. Topics are listed in neutral language, clarified for shared understanding, and organized in a logical sequence. Effective agenda setting ensures no key grievance is overlooked and makes complex conflicts feel more manageable.

Anchoring Bias: A cognitive bias in negotiation where the first number or offer presented disproportionately influences subsequent discussions and perceptions of fairness. Mediators help parties focus on objective criteria and interests rather than arbitrary anchors to counteract this bias.

Apology: A formal expression of regret or remorse for harm caused. In mediation, sincere apologies can be powerful tools for healing and trust-building. Effective apologies acknowledge specific impacts, express genuine empathy, and may be accompanied by commitments to prevent future harm. Legal considerations may require careful wording.

Arbitration: A formal dispute resolution process in which a neutral third party (the arbitrator) hears evidence and arguments from both sides and renders a binding decision. Unlike mediation, the parties do not control the outcome. Arbitration may be voluntary or mandated by contract, and is sometimes used when mediation has been attempted but failed to produce agreement.

Artisanal and Small-Scale Mining (ASM): Labor-intensive mining operations conducted by individuals, families, or small groups using minimal mechanization and capital. ASM communities are often affected by the arrival of large-scale industrial mining operations, which may displace them from deposits they have worked for generations, creating a distinct category of stakeholder in company-community disputes.

BATNA (Best Alternative to a Negotiated Agreement): The most favorable outcome a party can achieve if negotiations fail and they pursue their next-best option outside of mediation. Understanding BATNAs helps parties assess whether proposed agreements are acceptable and provides a realistic baseline for evaluation. A weak BATNA often increases motivation to reach an agreement.

Benefit-Sharing Agreement: A formal arrangement in which a company commits to sharing benefits from its operations with affected communities. These may include financial compensation, community development funds, infrastructure projects, employment opportunities, or other tangible benefits designed to ensure communities receive fair value from resources extracted or operations conducted in their area.

Brainstorming: A creative problem-solving technique used in the option-generation phase of mediation, where parties generate multiple potential solutions without immediate evaluation or commitment. Ground rules typically include suspending criticism, welcoming all ideas, and building on suggestions. The goal is to expand possibilities before narrowing to preferred options.

Burnout: A state of chronic physical and emotional exhaustion resulting from prolonged occupational stress, characterized by three dimensions: emotional exhaustion, depersonalization (cynical detachment from work), and reduced sense of personal accomplishment. Mediators working in protracted, high-conflict mining disputes are particularly vulnerable.

CAO (Compliance Advisor Ombudsman): The independent accountability mechanism of the International Finance Corporation (IFC) and the Multilateral Investment Guarantee Agency (MIGA). The CAO addresses complaints from communities affected by IFC/MIGA-supported projects, offering dispute resolution services and compliance investigations. It is one of the few international mechanisms available to communities in disputes with mining companies financed by development institutions.

Capacity Building: The process of developing skills, knowledge, and resources within a group to enable more effective participation. In company-community mediation, capacity building may involve training community representatives in negotiation, providing technical advisors, or helping parties understand complex information to reduce power imbalances.

Caucus: A private meeting between the mediator and one party, conducted separately from joint sessions. Caucuses allow parties to express concerns confidentially, explore flexibility without losing face, reality-test positions, and receive coaching on presentation. Mediators must maintain the confidentiality of caucus discussions unless given permission to share them.

Closed Questions: Questions that elicit specific, brief responses, often yes or no answers. Examples include "Do you have authority to agree today?" and "Was the meeting held on March 15th?" Closed questions are useful for confirming facts, clarifying details, and establishing concrete information during mediation.

Co-Mediation: A mediation approach involving two or more mediators working together. Co-mediation can bring diverse expertise, help manage complex multi-party disputes, facilitate cultural bridging, balance gender representation, and enable mentoring of less experienced mediators. Roles and responsibilities should be clearly defined beforehand.

Co-optation: The process by which a mediator, community leader, or other actor becomes an unwitting instrument of a more powerful party, lending legitimacy to processes or outcomes that primarily serve that party's interests. In mining disputes, co-optation risks are heightened when one party funds the mediation process or provides logistical support.

Cognitive Bias: A systematic pattern of deviation from rational judgment in which individuals draw inferences about other people and situations in an illogical fashion. Common cognitive biases in mediation include anchoring bias, confirmation bias, loss aversion, reactive devaluation, and the endowment effect. Mediators must recognize these biases in themselves and in the parties.

Community Development Fund: A financial mechanism established to channel resources toward community improvement projects. Often included in company-community agreements, these funds may support infrastructure, education, healthcare, livelihood programs, or other priorities identified by the community. Governance structures typically include community representation in decision-making.

Compassion Fatigue: A specific form of burnout affecting professionals who work with traumatized populations, characterized by a diminished capacity for empathy and emotional engagement. Mediators who repeatedly hear accounts of community suffering, displacement, and environmental harm may develop compassion fatigue, reducing their effectiveness and personal wellbeing.

Concession (Mining): A specific tract of land or set of mineral rights granted by a government to a company for exploration and extraction over a defined period under specified conditions. Concession boundaries frequently overlap with community lands, creating the foundational land-use conflict that mediation seeks to address.

Confidentiality: A core principle of mediation ensuring that information shared during the process remains private and cannot be disclosed outside mediation or used in subsequent legal proceedings without consent. Confidentiality creates psychological safety for honest dialogue and candid exploration of interests and options.

Confirmation Bias: The tendency to notice, seek out, and remember information that confirms existing beliefs while ignoring or dismissing contradictory evidence. In conflict, parties often interpret the other side's actions through a negative lens. Mediators can counteract this bias by highlighting exceptions and encouraging perspective-taking.

Conflict Assessment: A systematic analysis of a dispute conducted before or during mediation to understand its dynamics, causes, parties, issues, history, and context. Assessment tools may include stakeholder mapping, conflict timelines, issue trees, and analysis of power dynamics. Thorough assessment informs process design and intervention strategies.

Conflict Escalation: The process by which conflicts intensify over time through cycles of action and reaction. Stages typically progress from initial tension and disagreement, through polarization and position-hardening, to actions replacing dialogue, and potentially culminating in a crisis marked by hostility or violence. Understanding escalation helps mediators tailor interventions appropriately.

Conflict Mapping: A visual or analytical tool used to diagram the parties, issues, relationships, alliances, and dynamics in a dispute. Conflict maps help mediators understand the conflict systemically, identify all stakeholders who should be involved, and reveal underlying factors that may not be immediately apparent.

Cultural Competence: The knowledge, skills, and attitudes required to work effectively across cultural differences. In mediation, cultural competence involves understanding local customs, communication styles, power structures, gender dynamics, and decision-making norms. It requires humility, curiosity, and willingness to adapt processes to cultural contexts.

De-escalation: The process of reducing tension and intensity in a conflict. De-escalation strategies include improving communication, building empathy, focusing on problem-solving rather than blame, making incremental agreements, and creating space for emotions to subside. Successful de-escalation often requires addressing both substantive issues and emotional needs.

Dehumanization: The psychological process in intense conflict in which parties view each other as less than human, resorting to extreme characterizations or stereotypes. Dehumanization enables hostile attitudes and actions. Mediators work to counteract this by using humanizing exercises, storytelling, and perspective-taking to reveal shared humanity.

Digital Divide: The inequality of access to technology, including reliable internet connectivity, devices, digital literacy, and supporting infrastructure. In mining contexts, the digital divide is particularly acute because many operations are located in remote regions where community representatives may lack the technological access that company personnel take for granted.

Digital Mediation: Mediation conducted through electronic communication platforms, including fully virtual sessions, hybrid formats where some participants are remote, and technology-assisted in-person processes. Digital mediation raises distinct challenges around power dynamics, nonverbal communication, confidentiality, and equitable access to technology.

Do No Harm: An ethical principle requiring mediators to ensure their interventions do not worsen the situation, exacerbate power imbalances, or cause psychological harm to participants. This principle is particularly important when working with trauma survivors or vulnerable populations and guides decisions about process design, questioning, and timing.

Domestic Violence: Patterns of abuse, including physical, emotional, psychological, or financial harm, occurring within intimate or family relationships. Domestic violence may affect participation and safety in mediation processes, requiring mediators to assess whether conditions are appropriate for mediation to proceed and to implement safety measures when necessary.

Duty of Care: The legal and ethical obligation of companies to take reasonable steps to prevent foreseeable harm to communities affected by their operations. In the mediation context, duty of care may extend to ensuring that the mediation process itself does not cause additional harm to vulnerable participants.

Emotional Intelligence: The ability to recognize, understand, and manage one's own emotions while also perceiving and responding appropriately to others' emotions. High emotional intelligence helps mediators remain calm under pressure, read the room accurately, respond to emotional cues, and navigate intense feelings constructively.

Empathy: The capacity to understand and share the feelings of another by imagining oneself in their position. In mediation, empathy involves acknowledging emotions, validating experiences, and demonstrating genuine concern for each party's perspective. Mediators model empathy to encourage parties to develop empathy for one another.

Endowment Effect: A cognitive bias causing people to overvalue what they already possess simply because they own it. In land disputes, for example, communities may value their current land far more than objectively equivalent alternatives. Mediators should respect these attachments and address them through symbolic recognition or transition rituals.

Environmental Impact Assessment (EIA): A formal study evaluating the likely environmental effects of a proposed project before it proceeds, including baseline conditions, predicted impacts, and proposed mitigation measures. EIAs are frequently contested in mining disputes, with communities challenging the adequacy of assessments or the independence of the consultants who prepared them.

Escrow: A financial arrangement in which funds are held by a neutral third party and released only when specified conditions are met. In mediation agreements, escrow accounts can build trust by ensuring that compensation payments or development contributions are actually available and will be disbursed as agreed.

Evaluative Mediation: A mediation approach in which the mediator actively assesses the strengths and weaknesses of each party's position and may suggest specific settlement terms. This contrasts with facilitative mediation, where the mediator refrains from offering opinions on the merits. Evaluative approaches carry greater risk of perceived bias but may be useful when parties are deeply entrenched.

Facilitation: The skill of guiding group discussions and processes in a neutral manner to help participants achieve their goals. Facilitation techniques include setting ground rules, managing participation, keeping discussions on track, summarizing progress, and ensuring all voices are heard. The facilitator focuses on the process, while the parties focus on the content.

Free, Prior and Informed Consent (FPIC): A principle recognized in international law requiring that indigenous peoples and local communities give their voluntary, informed agreement before projects that affect their lands, territories, or resources may proceed. FPIC requires that consent be sought sufficiently in advance, based on full and accessible information, and free from coercion, intimidation, or manipulation.

Gender-Based Violence: Violence directed at individuals because of their gender, including intimate partner violence, sexual assault, harassment, and exploitation. In extractive-industry contexts, gender-based violence may increase with the influx of workers or displacement of communities. Mediators must assess whether such violence is present, implement safety measures, and determine whether conditions are appropriate for mediation to proceed.

Grievance Mechanism: A formal process through which individuals or communities can raise complaints, concerns, or claims against a company or organization. Effective grievance mechanisms are accessible, predictable, equitable, transparent, and rights-compatible. They provide structured channels for addressing issues before they escalate into larger conflicts.

Ground Rules: Agreed-upon guidelines for conduct during mediation that establish expectations for respectful behavior. Common ground rules include: one person speaks at a time, no interruptions, attack the problem not the person, maintain confidentiality, and respect cultural norms. Ground rules create psychological safety and structure for productive dialogue.

Grounding Technique: A psychological technique used to redirect attention from traumatic memories or overwhelming emotions to immediate sensory experience in the present moment. Mediators working with traumatized communities may use grounding exercises (such as focusing on physical sensations or surroundings) to help participants manage distress during difficult sessions.

Group Polarization: The tendency for group deliberation to push members toward more extreme positions than they individually held before discussion. In community assemblies preparing for mediation, group polarization can harden negotiating positions and make compromise more difficult. Mediators should be aware of this dynamic when assessing the flexibility of group-designated representatives.

Hybrid Mediation: A mediation format in which some participants are physically present while others join remotely via technology. Hybrid formats create inherent asymmetries in participation quality, nonverbal communication, and relationship-building that mediators must actively manage to ensure procedural fairness.

IFC Performance Standards: The environmental and social standards established by the International Finance Corporation that companies receiving IFC financing must meet. The Performance Standards address issues central to mining disputes, including land acquisition, resettlement, indigenous peoples, biodiversity, and stakeholder engagement. They are frequently referenced as benchmarks in company-community mediation.

Impartiality: The mediator's commitment to treating all parties fairly and without favoritism. Unlike neutrality (which focuses on issues), impartiality focuses on equal respect and support for all parties in the process. Some describe this as "multi-partial" or "all-partial," meaning fully supportive of everyone reaching a fair outcome.

Impasse: A point in negotiation at which the parties are stuck and unable or unwilling to make further progress. Signs include circular arguments, rigid body language, breakdown in communication, and statements of incompatibility. Impasse-breaking strategies include caucusing, reframing, introducing new options, reality-testing BATNAs, and taking breaks.

Implementation Gap: The distance between what is written in a mediation agreement and what actually occurs in practice, resulting from unclear language, insufficient resources, changing circumstances, or lack of accountability mechanisms. Addressing the implementation gap is one of the most persistent challenges in company-community mediation.

Incremental Agreement: A strategy of building toward comprehensive resolution through smaller, achievable agreements on specific issues. Each successful agreement builds trust, demonstrates good faith, and creates momentum for addressing more difficult issues. This approach is particularly valuable in complex disputes where full resolution requires extended time.

Informed Consent: The principle that participants must understand and voluntarily agree to the mediation process with full knowledge of what it entails. Informed consent requires explaining the process, participants' rights, the limits on confidentiality, the mediator's role, and how outcomes may be used. Consent should be ongoing throughout the process.

Interest-Based Negotiation: An approach to negotiation that focuses on underlying interests, needs, and concerns rather than stated positions. By understanding what parties truly need (interests) rather than what they demand (positions), mediators can help identify creative solutions that satisfy multiple interests simultaneously, creating value for all parties.

Interests: The underlying needs, desires, concerns, and motivations that drive parties' stated positions in a dispute. While positions are specific demands ("We want $1 million"), interests explain why ("We need to rebuild homes and secure our children's future"). Understanding interests enables creative problem-solving and win-win outcomes.

Joint Fact-Finding: A collaborative process where disputing parties agree to work together to gather and analyze information relevant to their dispute. This may involve jointly hiring independent experts, conducting shared investigations, or forming technical committees. Joint fact-finding builds shared understanding and trust while removing factual disputes as barriers.

Loss Aversion: A cognitive bias whereby people feel the pain of losses more strongly than the pleasure of equivalent gains. In mediation, parties may fiercely resist changes perceived as losses even when potential gains outweigh them. Mediators can address this by reframing proposals in terms of gains or loss prevention.

Mediation: A voluntary, confidential process in which a neutral third party (the mediator) assists disputing parties in communicating, understanding each other's perspectives, and working toward mutually acceptable resolutions. Unlike arbitration or adjudication, the mediator does not impose decisions; parties retain control over outcomes.

Mediation Agreement: A document formalizing the outcomes of successful mediation. The agreement specifies commitments, responsibilities, timelines, monitoring mechanisms, and consequences for non-compliance. Effective agreements are specific, clear, realistic, and address all issues identified in the mediation. They may be legally binding or operate on good faith.

Mediator Capture: A situation in which a mediator loses their independence and becomes aligned with or controlled by one party, whether through financial dependence, social relationships, or gradual ideological alignment. In mining disputes, mediator capture most commonly occurs when the company funds the mediation and provides logistical support.

Mediator's Proposal: A settlement suggestion offered by the mediator when parties are deadlocked, typically presented as a middle-ground option based on the mediator's understanding of both sides' interests. This technique allows parties to save face by accepting "the mediator's idea" rather than appearing to concede to the other side.

Monitoring: The ongoing process of tracking the implementation of mediated agreements to ensure commitments are fulfilled. Monitoring mechanisms may include joint committees, periodic review meetings, third-party verification, progress reports, or independent oversight. Effective monitoring builds trust by providing accountability and early warnings of problems.

Moral Distress: The psychological experience of knowing what the ethically correct course of action is but feeling unable to pursue it due to institutional constraints, professional role limitations, or external pressures. Mediators experience moral distress when they observe injustice or harm but feel constrained by their neutral role from intervening directly.

Moral Injury: Deep psychological harm resulting from perpetrating, witnessing, or being unable to prevent acts that violate one's fundamental moral beliefs and expectations. Community members who have witnessed environmental destruction or violence may carry moral injury that shapes their capacity to engage in mediation.

Multipartiality: An active mediator stance that involves being equally committed to the legitimate interests of all parties, rather than maintaining passive neutrality. A multipartial mediator advocates for a fair process and outcome for everyone, which may require giving more support to less powerful parties to achieve genuine balance.

Neutrality: The mediator's stance of not taking sides on the substantive issues in dispute. A neutral mediator does not advocate for particular outcomes or express opinions about who is right or wrong. Neutrality is maintained by treating all positions as worthy of consideration and helping each party present their case effectively.

Opening Statement: The initial presentation by each party at the beginning of mediation, sharing their perspective on the dispute without interruption. Opening statements allow parties to feel heard, provide information to the mediator and other parties, and can serve as an opportunity for emotional expression. The mediator typically summarizes key themes afterward.

Option Generation: The phase in mediation where parties brainstorm potential solutions to address identified interests. Effective option generation separates invention from decision-making, encourages creativity, builds on others' ideas, and aims for multiple options for each issue. The goal is to expand possibilities before evaluating and selecting preferred solutions.

Package Deal: A negotiation approach in which multiple issues are bundled for agreement, allowing trade-offs across issues. One party may concede more on Issue A in exchange for gains on Issue B. Package deals can create value by accommodating different priorities and ensuring overall balance even when individual issues favor different sides.

Paraphrasing: A communication technique in which the listener restates what the speaker said in their own words to confirm understanding. Effective paraphrasing captures both content and emotion: "So you're saying the contamination has affected your health, and you feel the company hasn't taken your concerns seriously." Paraphrasing demonstrates active listening.

Perspective-Taking: The cognitive and emotional exercise of imagining oneself in another's situation to understand their viewpoint. In mediation, perspective-taking exercises help parties see beyond their own experience, recognize others' legitimate concerns, and develop empathy. This can transform adversarial dynamics into collaborative problem-solving.

Positions: The specific demands, solutions, or outcomes that parties state they want in a dispute. Positions are often presented as fixed requirements ("We demand $1 million compensation"). Effective mediation moves beyond positions to explore underlying interests, opening the door to creative solutions that satisfy both parties' true needs.

Power Asymmetry: An imbalance in power between parties, which can manifest in resources, information, status, expertise, or influence. In company-community disputes, companies typically have greater financial and legal resources. Mediators must recognize and address power imbalances to ensure fair processes and outcomes, potentially through capacity-building or process adaptations.

Premature Closure: The tendency to push toward agreement before parties are psychologically ready, before underlying issues are adequately addressed, or before sufficient trust has been rebuilt. Premature closure often results in agreements that fail during implementation because the parties never genuinely committed to the outcome.

Procedural Fairness: The perception that the process used to reach decisions was fair, regardless of the outcome itself. Elements of procedural fairness include voice (opportunity to be heard), consistency, impartiality, accuracy, and respect. When parties perceive the process as fair, they are more likely to accept and comply with outcomes.

Psychological Safety: An environment where participants feel safe to express themselves, share concerns, and take interpersonal risks without fear of negative consequences. Creating psychological safety is essential for honest dialogue and is established through confidentiality, ground rules, respectful communication, and trauma-informed practices.

Reactive Devaluation: A cognitive bias where proposals are valued less simply because they come from an adversary. Even if a proposal meets a party's interests, they may reject it because accepting it would feel like losing to the other side. Mediators can counteract this by reattributing ideas or framing proposals as joint solutions.

Reality Testing: A technique used to help parties evaluate the feasibility and consequences of their positions by asking probing questions about alternatives and outcomes. Reality testing often involves exploring BATNAs: "If you don't reach an agreement here, what will you do? What are the costs and risks of that path?" It injects realism without being coercive.

Reconciliation: The restoration of a relationship between parties after conflict, involving acknowledgment of harm, expression of remorse, rebuilding trust, and commitment to changed behavior. Reconciliation goes beyond settlement of immediate issues to address the relationship itself, often through symbolic acts, ceremonies, or ongoing collaboration.

Reframing: The technique of restating a negative, accusatory, or positional statement in more constructive, neutral terms. For example, transforming "The company lies and doesn't care about us" into "Trust has been broken, and you need assurances that commitments will be honored." Reframing de-escalates emotions and refocuses on interests.

Resettlement: The process of relocating individuals or communities from their original location, typically due to development projects or resource extraction. Resettlement raises significant concerns about compensation, livelihood restoration, cultural preservation, and consent. Poorly managed resettlement is a major source of company-community conflicts.

Retraumatization: The experience of having trauma symptoms triggered or worsened by subsequent events, discussions, or processes that recall the original traumatic experience. Trauma-informed mediation practices aim to minimize retraumatization by providing choice and control, avoiding invasive questioning, and creating supportive environments.

Secondary Traumatic Stress: Psychological symptoms, including intrusive thoughts, avoidance, and hyperarousal, that develop in professionals who are repeatedly exposed to the traumatic experiences of others through empathic engagement. Mediators working with communities that have experienced violence, displacement, or environmental harm are at risk.

Self-Determination: The fundamental mediation principle that parties retain control over the outcome and make their own decisions about whether to agree and on what terms. The mediator facilitates the process but does not impose solutions. Self-determination respects parties' autonomy and produces more durable agreements because parties own the outcome.

Shuttle Diplomacy: A mediation technique where the mediator moves between parties who are not meeting face-to-face, carrying messages, proposals, and information between them. Shuttle diplomacy is useful when direct interaction has broken down, emotions are too high for joint sessions, or parties need to consider proposals privately before committing.

Social License to Operate: The ongoing acceptance and approval of a company's activities by its stakeholders, particularly the local community. Unlike a legal or regulatory license, a social license is granted informally and can be withdrawn at any time. Its loss has been identified as one of the top business risks in the extractive sector, often motivating companies to engage in mediation.

Stakeholder: Any individual, group, or organization that has an interest in or is affected by the dispute and its resolution. In company-community mediation, stakeholders may include affected community members, company representatives, local government officials, traditional authorities, NGOs, and others with an interest in the outcome.

Structural Neutrality: Neutrality that extends beyond the mediator's personal conduct to encompass the design of the mediation process itself, including venue selection, timing, information access, language of proceedings, and funding arrangements. A process that is structurally biased toward one party undermines mediation regardless of the mediator's personal impartiality.

Substantive Needs: The tangible outcomes or concrete results that parties seek from negotiation, such as compensation, resources, policy changes, or specific actions. Substantive needs form one corner of the Triangle of Satisfaction, alongside procedural needs (fair process) and emotional needs (acknowledgment and respect).

Summarizing: The technique of concisely restating key points that have emerged in discussion to confirm understanding, organize the conversation, validate contributions, and create a shared narrative. Effective summaries capture both substance and emotion, highlight areas of agreement, and identify remaining differences.

Sustainable Development Fund: A long-term funding mechanism designed to provide ongoing benefits to a community, often established as part of company-community agreements. These funds typically support projects that promote sustainable livelihoods, infrastructure, education, or healthcare, and may involve community participation in governance and project selection.

Tailings: The waste material left after the target mineral has been extracted from mined ore. Tailings are typically stored in large engineered facilities (tailings dams or storage facilities) near the mine site. Community concerns about tailings storage, including risks of dam failure, water contamination, and dust, are among the most common triggers for mining disputes.

Three Dimensions of Needs: A framework identifying three types of needs that must be addressed for parties to feel satisfied with mediation outcomes: procedural needs (fair process, voice, inclusion), emotional needs (acknowledgment, respect, validation), and substantive needs (tangible outcomes). Lasting agreements address all three dimensions.

Transformative Mediation: A mediation approach that focuses on two key dynamics: empowerment (helping parties gain clarity about their own needs and options) and recognition (helping parties understand and acknowledge each other's perspectives). Transformative mediation prioritizes relationship transformation over settlement, which can be particularly valuable in long-term company-community relationships.

Trauma-Informed Approach: A framework for practice that recognizes the widespread impact of trauma, understands potential paths for recovery, recognizes trauma signs and symptoms, and responds by integrating knowledge about trauma into policies, procedures, and practices. Key principles include safety, trustworthiness, choice, collaboration, and empowerment.

Trust: Confidence in the reliability, honesty, and good intentions of another party. Trust is often damaged in conflicts and must be rebuilt through consistent actions, kept promises, transparency, and demonstrated good faith. Trust is essential for parties to share information openly and commit to agreements.

UNGP (United Nations Guiding Principles on Business and Human Rights): An international framework establishing standards for preventing and addressing business-related human rights impacts. The UNGP outlines state duties to protect human rights, corporate responsibility to respect human rights, and the need for access to remediation for those affected. They inform standards for company grievance mechanisms and mediation processes.

Vicarious Trauma: The cumulative psychological transformation that occurs in professionals who are repeatedly exposed to the traumatic material of their clients. Unlike secondary traumatic stress, which focuses on symptoms, vicarious trauma refers to deeper shifts in the mediator's worldview, trust, sense of safety, and beliefs about human nature.

Victim Mentality: A psychological state in which individuals or groups perceive themselves as powerless victims with no responsibility for or ability to change their situation. While acknowledging genuine victimization, mediators help parties move from victimhood to agency by focusing on what they can do to improve their circumstances.

Voluntariness: The principle that participation in mediation is entirely voluntary, with no party compelled to attend or to agree. Voluntariness ensures genuine engagement, respects autonomy, and produces more durable outcomes. Parties must be able to withdraw at any time without penalty.

WATNA (Worst Alternative to a Negotiated Agreement): The least favorable outcome a party might face if negotiations fail and they pursue alternatives. Understanding WATNAs alongside BATNAs provides a realistic assessment of the range of likely outcomes outside mediation, motivating parties to find agreement when alternatives are unattractive.

Win-Win Solution: An outcome that satisfies the core interests of all parties, creating value rather than simply dividing a fixed pie. Win-win solutions become possible when mediators help parties move beyond positions to interests, revealing opportunities for creative arrangements that address multiple needs simultaneously.

Zone of Possible Agreement (ZOPA): The range within which an agreement is possible because it would satisfy both parties' minimum requirements. ZOPA exists when party A's acceptable outcomes overlap with party B's acceptable outcomes. Understanding parties' BATNAs and reservation points helps identify whether a ZOPA exists.

APPENDIX C
COMPREHENSIVE INDEX

This index provides an alphabetical listing of key concepts, terms, and topics covered in this handbook. Chapter numbers refer to the chapter where each term is substantively discussed.

W

Y

Z

APPENDIX D
CURATED BIBLIOGRAPHY AND FURTHER READING

This bibliography provides a curated selection of essential texts for practitioners working in company-community mediation, with particular emphasis on the mining and extractive sectors. Entries are organized by topic to help readers deepen their knowledge in specific areas.

Mediation Theory and Practice

American Arbitration Association, American Bar Association, & Association for Conflict Resolution (2005). Model Standards of Conduct for Mediators. American Bar Association.

Bush, R. A. B., & Folger, J. P. (2005). The Promise of Mediation: The Transformative Approach to Conflict. Jossey-Bass.

Fisher, R., & Ury, W. (1981). Getting to Yes: Negotiating Agreement Without Giving In. Houghton Mifflin.

Kolb, D. M., & Associates (1994). When Talk Works: Profiles of Mediators. Jossey-Bass.

LeBaron, M. (2002). Bridging Troubled Waters: Conflict Resolution from the Heart. Jossey-Bass.

Lederach, J. P. (1997). Building Peace: Sustainable Reconciliation in Divided Societies. United States Institute of Peace Press.

Mayer, B. (2004). Beyond Neutrality: Confronting the Crisis in Conflict Resolution. Jossey-Bass.

Moore, C. W. (2014). The Mediation Process: Practical Strategies for Resolving Conflict (4th ed.). Jossey-Bass.

Riskin, L. L. (1996). Understanding Mediators' Orientations, Strategies, and Techniques: A Grid for the Perplexed. Harvard Negotiation Law Review, 1, 7-51.

Stone, D., Patton, B., & Heen, S. (1999). Difficult Conversations: How to Discuss What Matters Most. Viking.

Susskind, L., & Cruikshank, J. (2006). Breaking Robert's Rules: The New Way to Run Your Meeting, Build Consensus, and Get Results. Oxford University Press.

Ury, W. (2007). Getting Past No: Negotiating in Difficult Situations. Bantam Books.

Ury, W. L., Brett, J. M., & Goldberg, S. B. (1988). Getting Disputes Resolved: Designing Systems to Cut the Costs of Conflict. Jossey-Bass.

Zartman, I. W., & Rasmussen, J. L. (Eds.). (1997). Peacemaking in International Conflict: Methods and Techniques. United States Institute of Peace Press.

Mining, Extractives, and Community Relations

Ayres, R. U., & Ayres, L. W. (2010). A Handbook of Industrial Ecology. Edward Elgar Publishing.

Bebbington, A. (Ed.). (2012). Social Conflict, Economic Development and the Extractive Industry: Evidence from South America. Routledge.

Davis, R., & Franks, D. M. (2014). Costs of Company-Community Conflict in the Extractive Sector. Corporate Social Responsibility Initiative Report No. 66. Harvard Kennedy School.

Franks, D. M. (2015). Mountain Movers: Mining, Sustainability and the Agents of Change. Routledge.

Harvey, B., & Bice, S. (2014). Social Impact Assessment, Social Development Programmes and Social Licence to Operate: Tensions and Contradictions in Intent and Practice in the Extractive Sector. Impact Assessment and Project Appraisal, 32(4), 327-335.

ICMM (2015). Good Practice Guide: Indigenous Peoples and Mining (2nd ed.). International Council on Mining and Metals.

ICMM (2020). Mining Principles. International Council on Mining and Metals.

Kemp, D., & Owen, J. R. (2013). Community Relations and Mining: Core to Business but Not Core Business. Resources Policy, 38(4), 523-531.

Owen, J. R., & Kemp, D. (2017). Extractive Relations: Countervailing Power and the Global Mining Industry. Routledge.

Owen, J. R., & Kemp, D. (2023). Social Licence and Mining. In G. M. Mudd & S. A. Mohr (Eds.), Handbook of Mineral Resources. Springer.

Thomson, I., & Boutilier, R. G. (2011). Social Licence to Operate. In P. Darling (Ed.), SME Mining Engineering Handbook (pp. 1779-1796). Society for Mining, Metallurgy and Exploration.

World Bank (2004). Striking a Better Balance: The Extractive Industries Review. World Bank Group.

Conflict Resolution in Resource Disputes

Collier, P., & Hoeffler, A. (2005). Resource Rents, Governance, and Conflict. Journal of Conflict Resolution, 49(4), 625-633.

Daniels, S. E., & Walker, G. B. (2001). Working Through Environmental Conflict: The Collaborative Learning Approach. Praeger.

Haslam, P. A., & Tanimoune, N. A. (2016). The Determinants of Social Conflict in the Latin American Mining Sector: New Evidence with Quantitative Data. World Development, 78, 401-419.

IFC (2007). Stakeholder Engagement: A Good Practice Handbook for Companies Doing Business in Emerging Markets. International Finance Corporation.

IFC (2012). Performance Standards on Environmental and Social Sustainability. International Finance Corporation.

IFC (2012). Guidance Notes: Performance Standards on Environmental and Social Sustainability. International Finance Corporation.

Mnookin, R. H., & Susskind, L. E. (Eds.). (1999). Negotiating on Behalf of Others. Sage Publications.

Rees, C. (2011). Piloting Principles for Effective Company-Stakeholder Grievance Mechanisms: A Report of Lessons Learned. Corporate Social Responsibility Initiative, Harvard Kennedy School.

UN OHCHR (2011). Guiding Principles on Business and Human Rights: Implementing the United Nations 'Protect, Respect and Remedy' Framework. United Nations.

UN Working Group on Business and Human Rights (2021). UNGPs 10+: A Roadmap for the Next Decade of Business and Human Rights. United Nations.

Trauma, Psychology, and Mediator Wellbeing

Cloke, K. (2001). Mediating Dangerously: The Frontiers of Conflict Resolution. Jossey-Bass.

Ericsson, K. A., Krampe, R. T., & Tesch-Römer, C. (1993). The Role of Deliberate Practice in the Acquisition of Expert Performance. Psychological Review, 100(3), 363-406.

Herman, J. L. (2015). Trauma and Recovery: The Aftermath of Violence (Revised ed.). Basic Books.

Kahneman, D. (2011). Thinking, Fast and Slow. Farrar, Straus and Giroux.

Knowles, M. S. (1984). The Adult Learner: A Neglected Species (3rd ed.). Gulf Publishing.

McCann, I. L., & Pearlman, L. A. (1990). Vicarious Traumatization: A Framework for Understanding the Psychological Effects of Working with Victims. Journal of Traumatic Stress, 3(1), 131-149.

Pearlman, L. A., & Saakvitne, K. W. (1995). Trauma and the Therapist: Countertransference and Vicarious Traumatization in Psychotherapy with Incest Survivors. W. W. Norton.

Rothschild, B. (2006). Help for the Helper: The Psychophysiology of Compassion Fatigue and Vicarious Trauma. W. W. Norton.

Schön, D. A. (1983). The Reflective Practitioner: How Professionals Think in Action. Basic Books.

Stamm, B. H. (Ed.). (1999). Secondary Traumatic Stress: Self-Care Issues for Clinicians, Researchers, and Educators (2nd ed.). Sidran Press.

Van der Kolk, B. (2014). The Body Keeps the Score: Brain, Mind, and Body in the Healing of Trauma. Penguin Books.

Power, Gender, and Human Rights

Ackerly, B., & True, J. (2010). Doing Feminist Research in Political and Social Science. Palgrave Macmillan.

Amnesty International (2017). This is What We Die For: Human Rights Abuses in the Democratic Republic of the Congo Power the Global Trade in Cobalt. Amnesty International.

Hill, C., Madden, C., & Collins, N. (2017). A Guide to Gender Impact Assessment for the Extractive Industries. Oxfam Australia.

Lahiri-Dutt, K. (Ed.). (2011). Gendering the Field: Towards Sustainable Livelihoods for Mining Communities. ANU E Press.

Oxfam (2017). Position Paper on Gender Justice and the Extractive Industries. Oxfam International.

Ruggie, J. (2013). Just Business: Multinational Corporations and Human Rights. W. W. Norton.

UN Women (2018). Towards a Gender-Responsive Implementation of the Extractive Industries. UN Women Policy Brief.

Digital Mediation and Technology

Ebner, N., & Zeleznikow, J. (2015). No Sheriff in Town: Governance for Online Dispute Resolution. Negotiation Journal, 31(4), 297-323.

Katsh, E., & Rabinovich-Einy, O. (2017). Digital Justice: Technology and the Internet of Disputes. Oxford University Press.

Poblet, M. (2011). Mobile Technologies for Conflict Management: Online Dispute Resolution, Governance, Participation. Springer.

Rule, C. (2002). Online Dispute Resolution for Business. Jossey-Bass.

Schmitz, A. J., & Wing, L. (Eds.). (2021). Dispute Resolution and E-Discovery. Cambridge University Press.

Sourdin, T., Li, B., & McNamara, D. M. (2020). Court Innovation and Access to Justice in Times of Crisis. Monash University.

Wahab, M. S. A., Katsh, E., & Rainey, D. (Eds.). (2012). Online Dispute Resolution: Theory and Practice. Eleven International Publishing.

Social Performance, Impact Assessment, and Community Engagement

Esteves, A. M., Franks, D., & Vanclay, F. (2012). Social Impact Assessment: The State of the Art. Impact Assessment and Project Appraisal, 30(1), 35-44.

Franks, D. M. (2012). Social Impact Assessment of Resource Projects. In International Mining for Development Centre, Mining for Development: Guide to Australian Practice.

Hanna, P., & Vanclay, F. (2013). Human Rights, Indigenous Peoples and the Concept of Free, Prior and Informed Consent. Impact Assessment and Project Appraisal, 31(2), 146-157.

IFC (2014). A Strategic Approach to Early Stakeholder Engagement: A Good Practice Handbook for Junior Companies in the Extractive Industries. International Finance Corporation.

Kemp, D. (2010). Mining and Community Development: Problems and Possibilities of Local-Level Practice. Community Development Journal, 45(2), 198-218.

Moffat, K., & Zhang, A. (2014). The Paths to Social Licence to Operate: An Integrative Model Explaining Community Acceptance of Mining. Resources Policy, 39, 61-70.

Prno, J., & Slocombe, D. S. (2012). Exploring the Origins of 'Social License to Operate' in the Mining Sector: Perspectives from Governance and Sustainability Theories. Resources Policy, 37(3), 346-357.

UN Global Compact Network France (2023). Businesses and Affected Communities: Adopting a Human Rights-Based Approach for Meaningful Engagement and Effective Impact Management. UN Global Compact Network France.

Vanclay, F. (2003). International Principles for Social Impact Assessment. Impact Assessment and Project Appraisal, 21(1), 5-12.

Vanclay, F., & Esteves, A. M. (Eds.). (2011). New Directions in Social Impact Assessment: Conceptual and Methodological Advances. Edward Elgar Publishing.

Vanclay, F., & Esteves, A. M. (Eds.). (2024). Handbook of Social Impact Assessment and Management. Edward Elgar Publishing.

Kemp, D., & Owen, J. R. (2021). Corporate Readiness and the Human Rights Responsibilities of Extractive Companies. Business and Human Rights Journal, 6(1), 44-66.

Vanclay, F., Esteves, A. M., Aucamp, I., & Franks, D. (2015). Social Impact Assessment: Guidance for Assessing and Managing the Social Impacts of Projects. International Association for Impact Assessment.

Zandvliet, L., & Anderson, M. B. (2009). Getting It Right: Making Corporate-Community Relations Work. Greenleaf Publishing.

Essential Reports and Frameworks

CAO (2008). A Guide to Designing and Implementing Grievance Mechanisms for Development Projects. Compliance Advisor Ombudsman, IFC/MIGA.

Equator Principles Association (2020). The Equator Principles (EP4): A Financial Industry Benchmark for Determining, Assessing and Managing Environmental and Social Risk in Projects. Equator Principles Association.

European Parliament (2024). Corporate Sustainability Due Diligence Directive (CSDDD). Official Journal of the European Union.

ICMM & World Bank (2012). Community Development Toolkit: A Set of 20 Revised and Updated Tools Intended for Use Throughout the Mining Project Cycle. International Council on Mining and Metals.

ICMM (2019). Integrated Mine Closure: Good Practice Guide (2nd ed.). International Council on Mining and Metals.

ILO (1989). Convention 169 Concerning Indigenous and Tribal Peoples in Independent Countries. International Labour Organization.

IRMA (2018). IRMA Standard for Responsible Mining. Initiative for Responsible Mining Assurance.

Responsible Mining Foundation (2022). Responsible Mining Index 2022: Results. Responsible Mining Foundation.

OECD (2017). OECD Due Diligence Guidance for Meaningful Stakeholder Engagement in the Extractive Sector. OECD Publishing.

UN General Assembly (2007). United Nations Declaration on the Rights of Indigenous Peoples (UNDRIP). A/RES/61/295.

Voluntary Principles Initiative (2000). Voluntary Principles on Security and Human Rights. Voluntary Principles Initiative.

World Bank (2001). Operational Policy 4.12: Involuntary Resettlement. World Bank Group.

TABLE OF FIGURES

ABOUT THE AUTHOR

Thomas Gaultier is a mediator and international legal consultant who specializes in navigating high-stakes projects across global markets. With over 15 years of experience in dispute resolution throughout Sub-Saharan Africa, Europe, and Asia, he has resolved more than 2,000 historic and grievance claims within the extractive and energy sectors.

Thomas is a practitioner who bridges the gap between corporate operational imperatives and community needs. His expertise is grounded in significant field experience, including serving as a Community Relations Manager for a lithium mining operation in Portugal and mediating and advising on complex conflicts in countries such as Mozambique and Zambia. He applies rigorous, field-tested methodologies to foster successful stakeholder engagement and create shared value in industrial transitions.

An educator at heart, Thomas teaches mediation and negotiation at leading academic institutions, including the Universidade Católica Portuguesa, and is the co-founder and Vice-President of the ICFML (Instituto de Certificação e Formação de Mediadores Lusófonos).

Admitted to the New York Bar, Thomas holds an LL.M. in Alternative Dispute Resolution from the University of Texas at Austin and an MBA in Mining and Raw Materials from the Escuela de Organización Industrial in Seville, Spain. He is fluent in English, French, Portuguese, and Spanish, enabling him to operate seamlessly across diverse legal systems and cultural contexts.

www.ingramcontent.com/pod-product-compliance
Lightning Source LLC
LaVergne TN
LVHW060011210926
848481LV00013B/3686